Allusion to the Poets

Allusion to the Poets

CHRISTOPHER RICKS

OXFORD
UNIVERSITY PRESS

This book has been printed digitally and produced in a standard specification
in order to ensure its continuing availability

OXFORD
UNIVERSITY PRESS

Great Clarendon Street, Oxford OX2 6DP
Oxford University Press is a department of the University of Oxford.
It furthers the University's objective of excellence in research, scholarship,
and education by publishing worldwide in

Oxford New York

Auckland   Cape Town Dar es Salaam   Hong Kong   Karachi
Kuala Lumpur Madrid Melbourne Mexico City   Nairobi
New Delhi Shanghai Taipei Toronto
With offices in
Argentina Austria Brazil Chile Czech Republic France Greece
Guatemala Hungary Italy Japan South Korea Poland Portugal
Singapore Switzerland Thailand Turkey Ukraine Vietnam

Oxford is a registered trade mark of Oxford University Press
in the UK and in certain other countries

Published in the United States
by Oxford University Press Inc., New York

ISBN 978-0-19-926915-0

Contents

Prefatory Note

These essays attend to allusion, as the calling into play—by poets—of the words and phrases of previous writers. Largely, of earlier poets writing in English. There is an earlier essay of mine on the philosopher J. L. Austin and his allusive wit, collected in *Essays in Appreciation* (1996).

The first part of the book is chronological, and considers poets Augustan, Romantic, and Victorian: Dryden and Pope, Burns, Wordsworth, Byron, Keats, and Tennyson. All are seen under the aegis of the poet as heir. Allusion is one form that inheritance may take, even while inheritance takes diverse forms in different ages and for individual genius.

The second part consists of half a dozen pieces that have some relation to allusion. The one on plagiarism takes plagiarism to be allusion's contrary (the alluder hopes that the reader will recognize something, the plagiarist that the reader will not). That on metaphor is germane to allusion, in that allusion is one form that metaphor may take (as the illuminating perception of similitude in dissimilitude, and as a relation between two things that then creates a new imaginative entity). The essay on loneliness has its bearing on allusion in that one thing allusion provides and calls upon is company (the society of dead poets being a living resource in its company). The piece on A. E. Housman considers a particular cluster in one of his poems, alluding to a prejudicial prose tradition. The case of Yvor Winters is that of a poet-critic whose poems are unremittingly allusive but whose intransigent criticism can find no place for allusion. Finally, the poetic art of David Ferry may recall to us the ways in which translation constitutes one of the highest forms that allusion can take.

The undertaking is one that aims to contribute not to the theory of allusion[1] but to apprehending the allusive practice, principles, and tact

---

[1] For which, see, for instance, William Irwin, 'What Is an Allusion?', *Journal of Aesthetics and Art Criticism* 59 (2001); and Carmela Perri, 'On Alluding', *Poetics* 7 (1978).

of the poets. William Empson formulated a crucial principle when he commented on another kind of allusion, that to classical mythology. In 'The Nymph complaining for the death of her Faun', Andrew Marvell writes exquisitely:

> The brotherless *Heliades*
> Melt in such Amber Teares as these.

Empson's elucidation has its own beauty in acknowledging Marvell's:

It is tactful, when making an obscure reference, to arrange that the verse shall be intelligible even when the reference is not understood. Thus many conceits are prepared to be treated as subdued conceits, though in themselves they have been fully worked out. Consider as the simplest kind of example

> The brotherless Heliades
> Melt in such amber tears as these.
> (Marvell, *The Nymph complaining*)

If you have forgotten, as I had myself, who their brother was, and look it up, the poetry will scarcely seem more beautiful; such of the myth as is wanted is implied. It is for reasons of this sort that poetry has so much equilibrium, and is so much less dependent on notes than one would suppose. But something has happened after you have looked up the Heliades; the couplet has been justi-fied. Marvell has claimed to make a classical reference and it has turned out to be all right; this is of importance, because it was only because you had faith in Marvell's classical references that you felt as you did, that this mode of admir-ing nature seemed witty, sensitive, and cultured. If you had expected, or if you had discovered, that Marvell had made the myth up, the couplet might still be admired but the situation would be different; for instance, you would want the *brother* to be more relevant to the matter in hand.[2]

Empson imagines responsibly the responsibility of the poet who alludes, and he is at once speculative and precise when it comes to matters of learning. A poem, without being dependent on our knowing certain things, may yet benefit greatly from our doing so. For to say that poetry 'is so much less dependent on notes than one would suppose' is not at all to demean that which can be supplied by notes, those neces-sary evils.

Samuel Johnson issued advice, a warning that was not a disparage-ment:

---

[2] *Seven Types of Ambiguity* (1930, rev. 1947), pp. 167–8.

Notes are often necessary, but they are necessary evils. Let him, that is yet unacquainted with the powers of *Shakespeare*, and who desires to feel the highest pleasure that the drama can give, read every play from the first scene to the last, with utter negligence of all his commentators. When his fancy is once on the wing, let it not stoop at correction or explanation. When his attention is strongly engaged, let it disdain alike to turn aside to the name of *Theobald* and of *Pope*. Let him read on through brightness and obscurity, through integrity and corruption; let him preserve his comprehension of the dialogue and his interest in the fable. And when the pleasures of novelty have ceased, let him attempt exactness, and read the commentators.   (Preface to his edition of Shakespeare, 1765)

Caveat lector.

What the commentators offer might be thought of as the valuably over-and-above, or (in the best and true sense) *supererogation*: 'The performance of good works beyond what God commands or requires, which are held to constitute a store of merit which the Church may dispense to others to make up for their deficiencies'; 'Performance of more than duty or circumstances require; doing more than is needed'. The supererogatory should not be degradingly equated with the superfluous. There is no substitute for knowledge, even though the knowledge of who the Heliades were, and who their brother was,[3] is not a necessary, let alone a sufficient, condition of appreciating Marvell's lines. Tact will be called for, from all parties; sometimes a particular reader may stand in no need of the annotation, but then—as Empson said—'it does not require much fortitude to endure seeing what you already know in a note'.[4]

There are distinctions to be philosophized about: borrowings, parallels, sources, echoes, allusions. If you ask a philosopher whether there exists any indispensable account of allusion, he or she has a way of implicating you in implicatures, or of referring you to his or her work on referring—which is not the same as allusion. And although to speak of an allusion is always to predicate a source (and you cannot call into play something of which you have never heard), a source may not be an allusion, for it may not be called into play; it may be scaffolding such as went to the building but does not constitute any part of the building. Readers always have to decide—if they accept that such-and-such

---

[3] 'Disconsolate at the death of Phaethon, his sisters were turned into poplar trees and their tears into amber' (Elizabeth Story Donno's edition of Marvell's *Poems*, 1972).
[4] 1935; *Collected Poems* (1955), p. 93.

is indeed a *source* for certain lines—whether it is also more than a source, being part not only of the making of the poem but of its meaning. The question of intention bears upon allusion as it bears upon everything not only in literature but in every form of communication; suffice it (not) to say here that the present writer believes that it is not only proper but often obligatory to invoke authorial intention, while maintaining that there is (as Wittgenstein proposed) nothing self-contradictory or sly about positing the existence of unconscious or subconscious intentions—as in the case of the Freudian slip, where some part of you may wish to intimate something that another part of you would disavow. Coleridge sometimes despaired of writing 'on any subject without finding his poem, against his will and without his previous consciousness, a cento of lines that had pre-existed in other works'.[5] 'Previous consciousness' is telling.

In this, as in so much else, the unignorable clarifications are those of T. S. Eliot.[6] First, his famous comments in *Philip Massinger* (1920):

One of the surest of tests is the way in which a poet borrows. Immature poets imitate; mature poets steal; bad poets deface what they take, and good poets make it into something better, or at least something different. The good poet welds his theft into a whole of feeling which is unique, utterly different from that from which it was torn; the bad poet throws it into something which has no cohesion. A good poet will usually borrow from authors remote in time, or alien in language, or diverse in interest.[7]

Second, his address on *The Bible as Scripture and as Literature*, given in Boston, December 1932:

You cannot effectively 'borrow' an image, unless you borrow also, or have spontaneously, something like the feeling which prompted the original image. An 'image', in itself, is like dream symbolism, is only vigorous in relation to the feelings out of which it issues, in the relation of word to flesh. You are entitled to take it for your own purposes in so far as your fundamental purposes are akin to those of the one who is, for you, the author of the phrase, the inventor of the image; or if you take it for other purposes then your purposes must be consciously and *pointedly* diverse from those of the author, and the contrast is very much to the point; you may not take it merely because it is a good phrase or a lovely image. I confess that I never felt assured that

---

[5] *Collected Letters*, ed. E. L. Griggs (1956–71), iii 469–70.
[6] See the pages on annotation (sources and allusions) in the Introduction to T. S. Eliot, *Inventions of the March Hare: Poems 1909–1917*, ed. Christopher Ricks (1996).
[7] *Selected Essays* (1932, rev. 1951), p. 206.

Henry James was justified in naming a novel *The Golden Bowl*, though my scruples may only show that I have not understood the novel.[8]

Third, his issuing an acknowledgement, a distinction, and a reservation. He wrote to I. A. Richards, 11 November 1931, about *Ash-Wednesday*:

As for the allusions you mention, that is perfectly deliberate, and it was my intention that the reader should recognize them. As for the question why I made the allusions at all, that seems to me definitely a matter which should not concern the reader [*amended from* author]. That, as you know, is a theory of mine, that very often it is possible to increase the effect for the reader by letting him know [half *deleted*] a reference or a meaning; but if the reader knew more, the poetic effect would actually be diminished; that if the reader knows too much about the crude material in the author's mind, his own reaction may tend to become at best merely a kind of feeble image of the author's feelings, whereas a good poem should have a potentiality of evoking feelings and associations in the reader of which the author is wholly ignorant. I am rather inclined to believe, for myself, that my best poems are possibly those which evoke the greatest number and variety of interpretations surprising to myself. What do you think about this?[9]

One thing that I, for one, think about this is how fully it would—in a just world—preclude the misrepresentation by which recent literary politicians have insisted that in the bad old days there was held to be one authoritative authoritarian reading of a poem, constituted of a declaration by the writer himself.

Yet in one respect Eliot was, I believe, misleading, when he said of tradition that 'It cannot be inherited, and if you want it you must obtain it by great labour'.[10] For it is not true that inheritance does not have to be laboured for and at.

As to recent work on allusion in literature, four critics stand out. First, the pair (*père et fils*) who set allusion within a large history and romance: W. Jackson Bate, in *The Burden of the Past and the English Poet* (1970), and Harold Bloom, in *The Anxiety of Influence: A Theory of Poetry* (1973). Bate inaugurated a critical tradition in limning a poetic tradition, and of Bloom's energies we are all both beneficiaries and victims. Beneficiaries, granted his passion, his learning, and his so

---

[8] Houghton Library; b.MS.Am.1691 (26), pp. 11–12.
[9] The Library of Magdalene College, Cambridge.
[10] 'Tradition and the Individual Talent' (1919); *Selected Essays*, p. 14.

giving salience to the impulse or spirit of allusion. Victims, because of his melodramatic sub-Freudian parricidal scenario, his sentimental discrediting of gratitude, and his explicit repudiation of all interest in allusion as a matter of the very words. Second, there is the pair who have most elicited the resourcefulness of allusion in poetic practice: John Hollander, in *The Figure of Echo: A Mode of Allusion in Milton and After* (1981), and Eleanor Cook, in *Against Coercion: Games Poets Play* (1998). To these critics I am grateful, as I am to the poets' editors who supply so much knowledge for which there is no substitute.

C.R.

I

The Poet as Heir

Dryden and Pope

Augustan poetry is remarkable for its literary allusion; the poetry creates meanings, comprehends judgements, and animates experiences, by bringing into play other works of literature and their very words. This is 'the Poetry of Allusion', to cite the subtitle of Reuben Brower's *Alexander Pope*.[1] I should like to consider the implications of J. B. Broadbent's words: 'Literary allusion can be a lesson in the abuse of authority, as well as in the generous spending of an inheritance. We need an essay on "The poet as heir".'[2]

Literary allusion is a way of dealing with the predicaments and responsibilities of 'the poet as heir'; there are features of late seventeenth-century history and literary history, and of Dryden's biography (Dryden, the father of literary allusion for the Augustans), that parallel such predicaments and responsibilities; and many of the most telling instances of allusion in Augustan poetry have to do with the poet as heir. We should notice when the subject-matter of an allusion is at one with the impulse that underlies the making of allusions at all, because it is characteristic of art to find energy and delight in an enacting of that which it is saying, and to be rendered vigilant by a consciousness of metaphors and analogies which relate its literary practices to the great world.

There are many ways in which allusion can be self-delightingly about allusion, can catch fire from the rapidity of its own motion.

Pope:

> Back to the Devil the last echoes roll,
> And 'Coll!' each Butcher roars at Hockley-hole.
> (*The Dunciad* B, i 325–6)[3]

---

[1] *Alexander Pope: The Poetry of Allusion* (1959).
[2] *Paradise Lost: Introduction* (1972), pp. 100, 102.
[3] Quotations from Pope are from *The Poems of Alexander Pope*, ed. John Butt (1963), which I follow in citing as *The Dunciad* A the edition of 1728–9, and as *The Dunciad* B the edition of 1742–3.

Dryden:

> Echoes from *Pissing-Ally, Sh*— call.
> And *Sh*— they resound from *A*— Hall.
> (*Mac Flecknoe* 47–8)[4]

Pope's echoes reverberate, re-sound, because they depend on the allusion's echo; and the movement is not 'Back to the Devil' but gratefully back to Dryden. Again:

> But gentle *Simkin* just reception finds
> Amidst this Monument of vanisht minds.
> (*Mac Flecknoe* 81–2)

> Which some the *Monument of Bodies*, name;
> The Arke, which saves from Graves all dying kindes;
> This to a structure led, long knowne to Fame,
> And cald, The Monument of vanish'd Mindes.
> (Davenant, *Gondibert*, II v 36)

Dryden's geniality is a matter of his allusion's alluding to itself, its saying to Davenant that he spoke too soon and yet spoke more wisely than he knew. What survives from Davenant rather gives the lie to any grand claim of 'long knowne to Fame'; and yet it does survive, and it was a good phrase, and Dryden is suitably grateful. The allusion is charmingly aware of allusiveness; the scale of it is appropriate to the scale of Davenant.

When a poet the equal of Dryden alludes to a poet incomparably greater than Davenant, the scale is altogether grander, but the allusion still owes its fineness to its comprehending the nature of allusion.

> *The Dunciad* B, ii 9–12:
>
> His Peers shine round him with reflected grace,
> New edge their dulness, and new bronze their face.
> So from the Sun's broad beam, in shallow urns
> Heav'ns twinkling Sparks draw light, and point their horns.

> *Paradise Lost*, vii 364–6:
>
> Hither as to thir Fountain other Starrs
> Repairing, in thir gold'n Urns draw Light,
> And hence the Morning Planet guilds her horns.

---

[4] Quotations from Dryden's poems are from *The Poems of John Dryden*, ed. James Kinsley (1958).

Pope's allusion is doing truly what it contemplates in a travesty: it is gratefully drawing light from an even greater source of energy and illumination (Milton, the Sun); it is new-edging itself, and pointing itself, by means of a 'reflected grace'. To say this is not to smooth away the edged and pointed animosity in 'twinkling Sparks'; but the feeling is of Pope and Milton ('Peers' in a true sense) standing assuredly together against such mere sparks. The result is a genuine 'grace' in Pope's sense of Milton; Pope is both graceful and gracious in the respect which he evinces for Milton, a respect perfectly compatible with an affection which knows that it risks impudence in thus turning such great poetry to its purposes, an affection that twinkles filially and not vacantly. In short, not only do Pope's lines describe the nature of an allusion in the act of making one, they breathe the right spirit, 'the generous spending of an inheritance'.

Likewise, there is a special preposterousness of geniality at the moment in *Mac Flecknoe* when Fleckno's adjuration to Shadwell so amply refers to himself in the third person:

> Nor let false friends seduce thy mind to fame,
> By arrogating *Johnson*'s Hostile name.
> Let Father *Fleckno* fire thy mind with praise,
> And Uncle *Ogleby* thy envy raise.
>
> (171–4)

The breadth of Dryden's humour here is a matter of the allusion to Virgil:

> ecquid in antiquam virtutem animosque virilis
> et pater Aeneas et avunculus excitat Hector?
> (*Aeneid*, iii 342–3)

'Do his father Aeneas and his uncle Hector arouse him at all to ancestral valour and to manly spirit?' This is not the employment of Virgil as a wheel to break a butterfly; the risk of such an easily destructive comparison is what the poetry has to fend off, and it succeeds in doing so because Dryden's lines are themselves about the allusive habit and the poet as heir. For it is Father Virgil who here properly yet modestly fires Dryden's mind with praise, in lines splendidly free from that 'envy' to which they allude. Dryden, humane and unsaintly, speaks often about the possibility of envy in the poet, and about a generous recognition of succession:

> Auspicious Poet, wert thou not my Friend,
> How could I envy, what I must commend!
> But since 'tis Natures Law in Love and Wit
> That Youth shou'd Reign, and with'ring Age submit,
> With less regret, those Lawrels I resign,
> Which dying on my Brows, revive on thine.
>   ('To Mr Granville, on his Excellent Tragedy' 1–6)

Literary allusions to fathers (or to uncles) are liable to suggest a paternal–filial relationship between the alluded-to and the alluder, since the alluder has entered upon an inheritance; the great instances of allusion are often those where that to which allusion is liable ceases to be any kind of liability and becomes a source of energy and gratitude. As with the Virgilian allusion in one of Dryden's great poems, 'To the Memory of Mr. Oldham':

> Once more, hail and farewel; farewel thou young,
> But ah too short, *Marcellus* of our Tongue.
>   (22–3)

Dryden's translation of the *Aeneid* had discussed different interpretations of the lines at the end of Book vi:

'Tis plain, that *Virgil* cannot mean the same *Marcellus*; but one of his Descendants; whom I call a new *Marcellus*; who so much resembled his Ancestor, perhaps in his Features, and his Person, but certainly in his Military Vertues, that *Virgil* cries out, *quantum instar in ipso est*! which I have translated,

> *How like the former, and almost the same.*[5]—

> His Son, or one of his Illustrious Name,
> How like the former, and almost the same.
>   (*Aeneid*, vi 1194–5)

The beauty and the propriety of the Virgilian allusion in 'To the Memory of Mr. Oldham' derive from the gentle confidence that to Virgil, Dryden would be 'one of his Descendants'. If we had to sum up in one line both a true lineage and the true poetic lineage manifested in the art of allusion, it would be hard to better the similarity within difference of

> How like the former, and almost the same.

---

[5] *The Works of Virgil* (1697), p. 633.

Two influential books are particularly apt, though neither speaks of allusion: Walter Jackson Bate's *The Burden of the Past and the English Poet* and—a book which acknowledges its inheritance from Bate— Harold Bloom's *The Anxiety of Influence.*

'What is there left to do?': this cry animates Bate's book, in the belief that it has animated most poetry for the last three centuries.

The central interest of the eighteenth century is that it is the first period in modern history to face the problem of what it means to come immediately after a great creative achievement.

If Restoration England, through its delayed but now ready embrace of the neoclassic mode, at once secured standards that permitted it to avoid competition with the literature of the immediate past, this was especially because it could do so with that authority (in this case classical antiquity) which is always pleasing to have when you can invoke it from a distant (and therefore 'purer') source; pleasing because it is not an authority looming over you but, as something ancestral rather than parental, is remote enough to be more manageable in the quest for your own identity. . . . for that matter, the ancestral permitted one— by providing a 'purer', more time-hallowed, more conveniently malleable example—even to disparage the parent in the name of 'tradition'. And in the period from 1660 to about 1730 there were plenty of people ready to snatch this opportunity. If their ranks did not include the major minds and artists, there were enough of them to justify us in recognizing this as the first large-scale example, in the modern history of the arts, of the 'leapfrog' use of the past for authority or psychological comfort: the leap over the parental—the principal immediate predecessors—to what Northrop Frye calls the 'modal grandfather'.[6]

For Bate, the crisis of Augustanism (with its heroic self-renewal) in the mid eighteenth century is a parental and ancestral burden of the past:

In short, the poet was now becoming flanked, in his own effort, on both sides—the parental as well as the classical-ancestral. At the same time, in a deeply disturbing way the features of the dead parent (more removed now and therefore most susceptible to the reverential and idealizing imagination) seemed to be settling into a countenance more like that of the ancestor. Almost—to the mid-eighteenth-century poet—the parental and ancestral seemed to be linking arms as twin deities looming above him.[7]

---

[6] *The Burden of the Past and the English Poet* (1970). p. 12. To illustrate Bate's point: Charles Churchill, for example, tried to escape oppression from Pope by leaping back to Dryden. Ben Jonson, in *Discoveries*: '*Greatnesse* of name, in the Father, oft-times helpes not forth, but o'rewhelmes the Sonne: they stand too neere one another. The shadow kils the growth; so much, that wee see the Grand-child come more, and oftener, to be the heire of the *first*, then doth the *second*: He dies betweene; the Possession is the *thirds*.'   [7] Ibid., 43.

Harold Bloom's book, *The Anxiety of Influence*, seeks to further Bate's argument by making much more of the parental. 'I am afraid', says Bloom with the gloomy frisson that those words always promise, 'I am afraid that the anxiety of influence, from which we all suffer, whether we are poets or not, has to be located first in its origins, in the fateful morasses of what Freud, with grandly desperate wit, called "the family romance".'[8]

But Bloom's literary history too much plays at—and not just notices—leapfrog. He keeps saying 'post-Enlightenment English poetry', where 'post-' has the effect of a grand eliding; he says nothing about Dryden and Pope, but vaults from Milton to the Romantics, hovering only briefly over Gray. Yet a comprehension of Dryden and Pope, and of 'the family romance', could be greatly aided by such an observation as this by Bloom:

If one examines the dozen or so major poetic influencers before this century, one discovers quickly who among them ranks as the great Inhibitor, the Sphinx who strangles even strong imaginations in their cradles: Milton. The motto to English Poetry since Milton was stated by Keats: 'Life to him would be Death to me'.[9]

But English poetry since Milton was—first of all—Dryden and Pope, and it is unfortunate that the great Inhibitor has inhibited Bloom from attending to Dryden. Not that he can dismiss Dryden from his mind, as a repeated allusion attests:

Shakespeare belongs to the giant age before the flood, before the anxiety of influence became central to poetic consciousness.

Yet there was a great age before the Flood, when influence was generous (or poets in their inmost natures thought it so), an age that goes all the way from Homer to Shakespeare.[10]

Bloom is inheriting from his father, Bate, the lines by Dryden which provide the epigraph to the first chapter of *The Burden of the Past*, the lines from 'To my Dear Friend Mr. Congreve' which say of our poetic sires that 'Theirs was the Gyant Race, before the Flood'. Bate sees Dryden's greatness as intimately related to the shrewd generosity with which he recognized his predicament and its opportunity:

---

[8] *The Anxiety of Influence* (1973), pp. 56–7.
[9] Ibid., 32.   [10] Ibid., 11, 122.

In confronting a brilliantly creative achievement immediately before him in his own language, different from the mode he himself was to exploit, Dryden's situation as a seventeenth-century poet was almost unique. He is the first great European (not merely English) example of a major writer who is taking it for granted that the very existence of a past creates the necessity for difference—not for the audience, not *sub specie aeternitatis*, but for the writer or artist himself. It is typical of both his good sense and his courage as an artist—indeed one of the marks of his greatness—that he felt no defensive need to argue otherwise.[11]

When Johnson called Dryden 'the father of English criticism', his tribute (filial in its way) may have been partly to this very way of speaking. For Dryden is markedly the critic who conceives of poetic creation and influence as paternal. It is a natural way to speak; yet there are a great many important critics who have not found it a valuable way to speak, and there are some literary periods where it is particularly in demand. For Dryden, it is an essential figure of speech:

Shakespeare was the Homer, or father of our dramatic poets ... those two fathers of our English poetry [Waller and Denham].

Homer the common father of the stage [as well as of the epic].[12]

... as he [Chaucer] is the father of English poetry, so I hold him in the same degree of veneration as the Grecians held Homer, or the Romans Virgil.[13]

Dryden does not just adopt the figure of speech, he pursues it:

[11] *The Burden of the Past*, p. 31. On contemporary rivals as no less important than are predecessors, see Earl Miner, 'The Poetics of the Critical Act: Dryden's Dealings with Rivals and Predecessors', in *Evidence in Literary Scholarship* (ed. René Wellek and Alvaro Ribeiro, 1979). Eric Griffiths has warned against our sentimentalizing those giants: 'Dryden was less keen on giants than Professor Bate is. His giants are primarily those Greek equivalents of the builders of Babel, who were rightly put down by the Olympians, as can be seen from Dryden's earlier use of the same phrase in his translation of Ovid's Jove recalling the threat these bullies had posed: "our Universal State | Was put to hazard, and the Giant Race | Our Captive Skies, were ready to embrace" (II 806; 238–40). They are also the wicked giants from before the flood (Genesis 6 : 4), who, one legend had it, "on being warned of the Flood, had escaped to *Anglia*, then an extremity of the Continent and the most remote *angulus* of the world" and had become the first inhabitants of these islands. So that "our Syres" were not Angles, nor angels, but these monstrous angle-dwellers, on whom we look back with some awe, no doubt, but not with undiluted respect' ('Dryden's Past', *Proceedings of the British Academy 84: 1993 Lectures and Memoirs*, 1994, p. 141).
[12] Quotations from Dryden's criticism are from *Of Dramatic Poesy and Other Critical Essays*, ed. George Watson (1962), abbreviated hereafter to Watson. Here, 'Of Dramatic Poesy'; Watson, i 70. 'Discourse Concerning Satire'; Watson, ii 150. Dedication to the *Aeneis*; 'To John, Lord Marquess of Normanby'; Watson, ii 229.
[13] 'Preface to *Fables*'; Watson, ii 280.

Milton was the poetical son of Spenser, and Mr Waller of Fairfax; for we have our lineal descents and clans as well as other families: Spenser more than once insinuates that the soul of Chaucer was transfused into his body: and that he was begotten by him two hundred years after his decease.[14]

What may seem a passing thought—'This is that birthright which is derived to us from our great forefathers, even from Homer down to Ben'[15]—is crucial to the burden of the past, to the anxiety of influence, and to the son's need not to be oppressed by his father's greatness:

And this, Sir, calls to my remembrance the beginning of your discourse, where you told us we should never find the audience favourable to this kind of writing till we could produce as good plays in rhyme as Ben Jonson, Fletcher, and Shakespeare had writ out of it. But it is to raise envy to the living, to compare them with the dead. They are honoured, and almost adored by us, as they deserve; neither do I know any so presumptuous of themselves as to contend with them. Yet give me leave to say thus much, without injury to their ashes, that not only we shall never equal them, but they could never equal themselves, were they to rise and write again. We acknowledge them our fathers in wit; but they have ruined their estates themselves before they came to their children's hands. There is scarce an humour, a character, or any kind of plot, which they have not blown upon: all comes sullied or wasted to us: and were they to entertain this age, they could not make so plenteous treatments out of such decayed fortunes. This therefore will be a good argument to us either not to write at all, or to attempt some other way. There is no bays to be expected in their walks: *tentanda via est, qua me quoque possum* [for *possim*] *tollere humo.*[16]

But 'the sons of Ben'? The implication of the metaphor was that Jonson had many sons, sibling-poets. The one thing that there wasn't was a single son of Ben. But the preoccupation in Dryden's criticism, as in seventeenth-century life, is rather with succession, with primogeniture, with a burden that is a crown or a prophetic mantle which falls to you with or without a double portion of your father's art. The supremacy of Milton, and then of Dryden, and then of Pope, is not something to which there is an earlier counterpart; Shakespeare did not enjoy the same sort of supremacy as Pope, and nor did Jonson. Moreover, the striking thing about 'the sons of Ben' is not just the singularity of the instance (of whom else do we use the formula?), but

---

[14] 'Preface to *Fables*'; Watson, ii 270.
[15] 'The Author's Apology for Heroic Poetry'; Watson, i 206.
[16] 'Of Dramatic Poesy'; Watson, i 85.

also that this formula was so soon to be inapplicable and even unthinkable. Milton had a greater influence than Jonson, and yet no one invokes 'the sons of Milton'; something meanwhile had happened either to poetic influence or to the sense of what a family was or to both. Bloom is right:

We remember how for so many centuries, from the sons of Homer to the sons of Ben Jonson, poetic influence had been described as a filial relationship, and then we come to see that poetic *influence*, rather than *sonship*, is another product of the Enlightenment.[17]

By 1727, sonship is for boobies:

Who sees not that *De F—* was the Poetical Son of *Withers*, *T—te* of *Ogilby*, *E. W—rd* of *John Taylor*, and *E—n* of *Bl-k-re*?[18]

Dryden bantered the long-lived sons of Ben ('They can tell a story of Ben Jonson, and perhaps have had fancy enough to give a supper in Apollo that they might be called his sons')[19] but he took the idea of sonship seriously, in his sense of the antagonisms inseparable from emulation both as to one's contemporaries (siblings) and as to one's great fathers.

'Tis not with an ultimate intention to pay reverence to the *manes* of Shakespeare, Fletcher, and Ben Jonson that they commend their writings, but to throw dirt on the writers of this age: their declaration is one thing, and their practice is another. By a seeming veneration to our fathers they would thrust out us, their lawful issue, and govern us themselves, under a specious pretence of reformation. . . .

These attack the living by raking up the ashes of the dead; well knowing that if they can subvert their original title to the stage, we who claim under them must fall of course. Peace be to the venerable shades of Shakespeare and Ben Jonson! None of the living will presume to have any competition with them: as they were our predecessors so they were our masters. We trail our plays under them; but (as at the funerals of a Turkish emperor) our ensigns are furled or dragged upon the ground, in honour to the dead; so we may lawfully advance our own afterwards, to show that we succeed; if less in dignity, yet on the same foot and title.[20]

---

[17] *The Anxiety of Influence*, p. 26.
[18] *Of the Art of Sinking in Poetry* (1727), p. 38.
[19] 'Defence of the Epilogue'; Watson, i 181.
[20] 'To Lord Radcliffe'; Watson, ii 159–60.

This was best said when it was not his immediate predecessor but his great forefathers in whose steps—'on the same foot and title'—he was advancing. Of his translation of the *Aeneid* he remarked:

> I would say that Virgil is like the Fame which he describes:
>> mobilitate viget, viresque acquirit eundo.
>
> Such a sort of reputation is my aim, though in a far inferior degree, according to my motto in the title-page: *sequiturque patrem non passibus aequis.*[21]

The praise of Virgil is effected through an allusion to him as a father, Virgil himself speaking of a father. Likewise *Fables Ancient and Modern* (1700) offers this as its epigraph, in the year of Dryden's death:

> *Nunc ultro ad Cineres ipsius & ossa parentis*
> (*Haud equidem sine mente, reor, sine numine divum*)
> *Adsumus.*
>
>> Virg., Æn. lib. 5.

'But now, lo! by my sire's own dust and bones we stand—not, methinks, without the purpose and will of heaven'.

Pope said: 'To follow Poetry as one ought, one must forget father and mother, and cleave to it alone'; and again: 'To write well, lastingly well, Immortally well, must not one leave Father and Mother and cleave unto the Muse?'[22] But the father whom it is well-nigh impossible (or altogether impoverishing) to forget or to leave, is one's poetical father. Pope could not forget or leave his poetical father, Dryden; he dealt with this both by embracing it ('And win my way by yielding to the tyde')[23] and by a respectful good humour such as re-created Dryden not as his father but as his benign elder brother. Dryden may have felt some such strain from his relation to such different predecessors as Jonson, Shakespeare, and Milton.

> *Fame* then was cheap, and the first commer sped;
> And they have kept it since, by being dead.
> But were they now to write . . .
>> ('Epilogue to the Second Part of *Granada*',
>>> 11–13).

---

[21] Dedication to the *Aeneis*; 'To John, Lord Marquess of Normanby'; Watson, ii 244. 'Rumour grows with speed, and wins new strength as it goes'; 'He follows his father with unequal steps'.

[22] To Jervas, 16 August 1714; to Bolingbroke, 9 April 1724; quoted by Maynard Mack, *The Garden and the City* (1969), pp. 112–13. Alluding to Genesis 2: 24 ('Therefore shall a man leave his father and his mother, and shall cleave unto his wife'), but the application raises the matter of maternity and paternity in relation to the Muse.

[23] Pope, 'The First Epistle of the First Book of Horace Imitated' 34.

> Due Honours to those mighty Names we grant,
> But Shrubs may live beneath the lofty Plant:
> Sons may succeed their greater Parents gone;
> Such is thy Lott; and such I wish my own.
>   ('To Sir Godfrey Kneller' 120–3)

Harold Bloom quotes three apophthegms, each applicable to the predicament of poets since Dryden:

'He who is willing to work gives birth to his own father.'   (Kierkegaard)

'When one hasn't had a good father, it is necessary to invent one.' (Nietzsche)

'All the instincts, the loving, the grateful, the sensual, the defiant, the self-assertive and independent—all are gratified in the wish to be *the father of himself.*'   (Freud)[24]

This last calls to mind a profound jibe against Colley Cibber—profound because it sees Cibber as a travesty or parody of the poet-hero, not as quite unrelated:

And that he did not pass himself on the world for a Hero, as well by birth as education, was his own fault: For, his lineage he bringeth into his life as an Anecdote, and is sensible he had it in his power *to be thought no body's son at all*: And what is that but coming into the world a Hero?   (*The Dunciad* B, 'Aristarchus, of the Hero')

No poet-critic has found it as natural as Dryden to think in terms of succession—and this in an era when kingship was a pondering of succession.

Dryden was involved. His 'Heroique Stanza's, Consecrated to the Glorious Memory of his most Serene and Renowned Highnesse *Oliver late Lord Protector*' (1659); his *Astræa Redux. A Poem On the Happy Restoration and Return of His Sacred Majesty Charles the Second* (1660): from those early poems through to *Threnodia Augustalis: A Funeral-Pindarique Poem Sacred to the Happy Memory of King Charles II* (1685), and *Britannia Rediviva: a Poem on the Birth of the Prince* (1688), Dryden occupied himself with kingship and succession. And even thereafter, since (as William J. Cameron has most notably shown) Dryden's translation of the *Aeneid* is among other things a prudent remonstrance to William III:

²⁴   *The Anxiety of Influence*, pp. 56, 64.

William need only model himself on Dryden's hero, and he would automatically become a true monarch 'so as to gain the Affection of his Subjects, and deserve to be call'd the Father of his Country'.[25]

But then Dryden's greatest satire is about the succession to the throne. As George de F. Lord has said:

It is appropriate that *Absalom and Achitophel*, a poem dealing with threats to the Stuart dynasty and to the principle of succession, should embody in every way the principles that underlie succession.[26]

Yet the force of the poem lies in the congruity between such political principles and its literary principles and practice, since literary allusion (upon which *Absalom and Achitophel* so warrantedly relies) may itself be a matter of a principled literary succession, an inheritance neither grudgingly withheld (as by a literary Bill of Exclusion) nor irresponsibly squandered.

The felicity for which Dryden hopes is embodied in the word 'succeed' itself; so *The Medall*, in speaking of the politics of 'Our Temp'rate Isle', can assert that

> The wholesome Tempest purges what it breeds;
> To recommend the Calmness that succeeds.
>
> (254–5)

—where 'succeeds' is at once 'ensures', 'takes up the succession', and 'effects success'; the word recurs eighteen lines later ('Yet, shou'd thy Crimes succeed', line 273), and finally, sixteen lines later, Dryden plays 'Succession' beautifully against 'fail':

> If true Succession from our Isle shou'd fail . . .
>
> (289)

Once upon a time, fathers and kings were at one:

> When Empire first from families did spring,
> Then every Father govern'd as a King.
> (*To His Sacred Majesty* 93–4)

Yet the wished-for parallel between king and father survives for Dryden, and includes the realities of succession and inheritance. 'To my Dear Friend Mr. Congreve, on his Comedy, call'd The Double-Dealer' tightens

[25] 'John Dryden's Jacobitism', in *Restoration Literature: Critical Approaches*, ed. Harold Love (1972), p. 297.

[26] ' "Absalom and Achitophel" and Dryden's Politicial Cosmos', in *John Dryden*, ed. Earl Miner (1972), p. 171.

these relationships, with a freedom from repining that constitutes an image or an imagining of that true succession of which *Mac Flecknoe* is the grotesque travesty.

> Well then; the promis'd hour is come at last;
> The present Age of Wit obscures the past:
> Strong were our Syres; and as they Fought they Writ,
> Conqu'ring with force of Arms, and dint of Wit;
> Theirs was the Gyant Race, before the Flood;
> And thus, when *Charles* Return'd, our Empire stood . . .
>
> (1–6)

> All this in blooming Youth you have Atchiev'd;
> Nor are your foil'd Contemporaries griev'd;
> So much the sweetness of your manners move,
> We cannot envy you because we love . . .
>
> (31–4)

>   Oh that your Brows my Lawrel had sustain'd,
> Well had I been Depos'd, if You had reign'd!
> The Father had descended for the Son;
> For only You are lineal to the Throne.
> Thus when the State one *Edward* did depose;
> A Greater *Edward* in his room arose.
> But now, not I, but Poetry is curs'd;
> For *Tom* the Second reigns like *Tom* the first.
> But let 'em not mistake my Patron's part;
> Nor call his Charity their own desert.
> Yet this I Prophesy; Thou shalt be seen,
> (Tho' with some short Parenthesis between:)
> High on the Throne of Wit; and seated there,
> Not mine (that's little) but thy Lawrel wear . . .
>
> (41–54)

> Let not the Insulting Foe my Fame pursue;
> But shade those Lawrels which descend to You:
> And take for Tribute what these Lines express:
> You merit more; nor cou'd my Love do less.
>
> (74–7)

Inheritance binds together so much that mattered to Dryden and his time that it constitutes more than a manner of speaking. The affiliation is more than verbal between the lines of *Astræa Redux* which speak of political despair—

> We thought our Sires, not with their own content,
> Had ere we came to age our Portion spent.
>
>   (27–8)

—and those in *Of Dramatic Poesy* which speak of a literary predicament: 'We acknowledge them our fathers in wit; but they have ruined their estates themselves before they came to their children's hands'.[27]

Ian Watt has described the Augustan tradition:

The defensive postures of the landed interest and of Augustan literature can themselves be seen as having the same essential movement: to survey the broad acres of the human inheritance, to value them duly, and to unite for their preservation.[28]

Augustan poetry is an art of 'the human inheritance', an art therefore especially alert to that human inheritance which is literary allusion. What was metaphorically true for poets (genuinely but metaphorically true) was simply true, legally true, for the Augustan gentleman. For it is the late seventeenth century that witnesses the creation of the strict settlement, designed to see that fathers do not ruin their estates before they come into their children's hands. H. J. Habakkuk does not speak of literature, but much of what he says as an economic historian is pertinent to an age which was preoccupied with literary as well as legal inheritance—an age which in choosing the advantages of the strict settlement was also choosing to be burdened or pinioned by the past and by inheritance.

In the early eighteenth century, the arrangements by which the English aristocracy and gentry commonly provided for their families conformed to a standard pattern, the strict settlement, in which the essential questions were settled at the marriage of the eldest son. Not only was his immediate maintenance fixed and his wife's jointure, but the provision for the children of the marriage—how much they were to receive, in what form and when—was decided at the same time. In its essentials, the marriage settlement first secured that the family estate should in each generation descend to the eldest son. It did this by limiting the interest in the estate of the father of the husband, and, after him, of the husband himself, to that of a life-tenant, and entailing the estate on the eldest son to be born of the marriage.

About the middle of the seventeenth century the invention of a highly technical legal device, trustees to preserve contingent remainders, removed what had

---

[27] Watson, i 85.
[28] 'Two Historical Aspects of the Augustan Tradition', in *Studies in the Eighteenth Century*, ed. R. F. Brissenden (1968), pp. 83–4.

hitherto been the main deficiency in the more stringent forms of settlement, by protecting the interest of the unborn son of the marriage. By the use of this device it was possible for a landowner to settle an estate for life on his eldest son at marriage and prevent him enlarging his interest. A landowner could now ensure that the estate remained intact until the male issue of the marriage became twenty-one; the eldest son, being only a life-tenant, could not frustrate the provision for his sisters and younger brothers, and had himself to specify the provision which would, in fact, be made for his own younger children—for a life-tenant could mortgage his estate only for purposes and amounts laid down in the deed which created his life-tenancy.

Strict settlements employing this device were widely adopted in the late seventeenth century, and by the early eighteenth century they were the typical way of settling estates and providing for the children among landowning families. (Note: 'The earliest example I have found is dated 1647'.)[29]

That much of this may meet the subject-matter of Augustan literature (say, Dr Johnson's 'Short Song of Congratulation') is evident enough; and it is germane to the principles and proceedings of Augustan literature, preoccupied with literary inheritance.

One further aspect of the father–son pressures of which the Augustan poet was especially conscious asks mention: the patron. The patron, it is hoped at least, is a father; the King is the supreme patron—except that he himself has an even greater patron.

> Such were the pleasing triumphs of the sky
> For *James* his late nocturnal victory;
> The pledge of his Almighty patron's love . . .
> (*The Hind and the Panther*, ii 654–6)[30]

The Augustans were sensitive to the duties and the defections of the patron, and the finest Augustan poems ponder a crisis for patronage. The assurances and the dubieties of patronage were among the father–son parallels that pressed (sometimes benignly) upon the Augustan poet, making him alert to the implications of a central metaphor—the father—which was also variously an actuality (a king,

---

[29] From 'Marriage Settlements in the Eighteenth Century', *Transactions of the Royal Historical Society*, 4th ser., xxxii (1950), 15–30. I am grateful to Keith Thomas for drawing my attention to this.
[30] Geoffrey Hill has a fine poem on God and the patron, 'To the (Supposed) Patron' (*For the Unfallen*, 1959).

an actual father, a patron, a literary progenitor). Dryden links patron, parent, emperor, and literary father in his note to his *Aeneis v*:

Virgil seems to me, to have excell'd *Homer* in all those Sports, and to have labour'd them the more, in Honour of *Octavius*, his Patron; who instituted the like Games for perpetuating the Memory of his Uncle *Julius*. Piety, as *Virgil* calls it, or dutifulness to Parents, being a most popular Vertue among the Romans.[31]

Similarly the note to *Aeneis*, vi 1143–6:

> [Embrace again, my Sons, be Foes no more:
> Nor stain your Country with her Childrens Gore.
> And thou, the first, lay down thy lawless claim;
> Thou, of my Blood, who bear'st the *Julian* Name.]

Anchises here speaks to *Julius Cæsar*; And commands him first to lay down Arms; which is a plain condemnation of his Cause. Yet observe our Poet's incomparable Address: For though he shews himself sufficiently to be a Common-wealth's man; yet in respect to *Augustus*, who was his Patron, he uses the Authority of a Parent, in the Person of *Anchises*; who had more right to lay this Injunction on *Cæsar* than on *Pompey*; because the latter was not of his Blood. Thus our Author cautiously veils his own opinion, and takes Sanctuary under *Anchises*; as if that Ghost wou'd have laid the same Command on *Pompey* also, had he been lineally descended from him. What cou'd be more judiciously contrived, when this was the *Æneid* which he chose to read before his Master?[32]

But does this fatherhood of patronage connect with inheritance, the poet as heir? One of Dryden's most marked insistences is that patronage is itself a dual inheritance.

Yet I have no reason to complain of fortune, since in the midst of that abundance I could not possibly have chosen better than the worthy son of so illustrious a father. He was the patron of my manhood when I flourished in the opinion of the world; though with small advantage to my fortune, till he awakened the remembrance of my royal master. He was that Pollio, or that Varus, who introduced me to Augustus.

You are acquainted with the Roman history, and know without my information that patronage and clientship always descended from the fathers to the sons; and that the same plebeian houses had recourse to the same patrician line which had formerly protected them, and followed their principles and fortunes to the last. So that I am your Lordship's by descent, and part of your

[31] *The Works of Virgil*, pp. 630–1.   [32] Ibid., 633.

inheritance. And the natural inclination which I have to serve you adds to your paternal right, for I was wholly yours from the first moment when I had the happiness and honour of being known to you.[33]

My LORD

Some Estates are held in England, by paying a Fine at the change of every Lord: I have enjoy'd the Patronage of your Family, from the time of your excellent Grandfather to this present Day. I have dedicated the Lives of *Plutarch* to the first Duke; and have celebrated the Memory of your Heroick Father. Tho' I am very short of the Age of *Nestor*, yet I have liv'd to a third Generation of your House; and by your Grace's favour am admitted still to hold from you by the same Tenure. I am not vain enough to boast that I have deserv'd the value of so Illustrious a Line; but my Fortune is the greater, that for three Descents they have been pleas'd to distinguish my Poems from those of other Men; and have accordingly made me their peculiar Care. May it be permitted me to say, That as your Grandfather and Father were cherish'd and adorn'd with Honours by two successive Monarchs, so I have been esteem'd, and patronis'd by the Grandfather, the Father, and the Son, descended from one of the most Ancient, most Conspicuous, and most Deserving Families in *Europe*.[34]

'I have enjoyed the Patronage of your Family, from the time of your excellent Grandfather to this present Day.' And Dryden's sons: whose patronage did they enjoy? Dryden had three sons; one who bore the same name as his king (Charles, born 1666, died 1704), one named after himself (John, born 1668, died 1703), and one half-named after his father (Erasmus-Henry, born 1669, died 1710).[35] Dryden's sons enjoyed in the first place the patronage of the royal patron:

The King . . . seems to have been gracious enough to Dryden when his influence became a substitute for money. He had provided Dryden's eldest son a King's Scholarship at Westminster School; and we can be sure that upon the petition of the poet, he appointed, within a few months of this time, the second son, John, to a King's Scholarship, which he took up probably in the summer. The youngest son, Erasmus-Henry, was approaching his thirteenth year, and

---

[33] 'To Hugh, Lord Clifford'; Watson, ii 217, 221–2.   [34] 'Dedication of *Fables*'.
[35] Naming in this way was commonplace, yet it is true too that Dryden was interested in naming:

> Un-nam'd as yet; at least unknown to Fame:
> Is there a strife in Heav'n about his Name?
> Where every Famous Predecessour vies,
> And makes a Faction for it in the Skies?
>   ('Britannia Rediviva: a Poem on the Birth of the Prince' 192–5).

None of Dryden's sons married, an unusual circumstance at that date.

with two boys already at Westminster on scholarships it was perhaps too much to ask that the third be accorded the same honor. Consequently, Dryden petitioned the King to nominate the youngest boy to a place at the Charterhouse. On February 28 [1682], Charles recommended to the Governors of the foundation that 'Erasmus Henry Dryden' be elected and admitted one of the children of that foundation 'on the first Vacancy'. [He was admitted to the Charterhouse, 5 February 1683.][36]

But their later patron was a figure even more important to them: their father. Dryden was the father as patron as well as the patron as father. Is there any other English poet who has published his poetry within the same volume as poetry by two of his sons? That the poetry was translation (Charles Dryden translated Juvenal VII; and John Dryden Jr, Juvenal XIV) only intensifies the sense of a poetic inheritance—as does the wry coincidence that Juvenal XIV should have the subject it does: 'Since Domestick Examples easily corrupt our Youth, the Poet prudently exhorts all Parents, that they themselves should abstain from evil practices . . .'. Of the other contributors to his Juvenal, Dryden said: 'let their excellencies atone for my imperfections, and those of my sons'.[37] But not only was Dryden happy to figure alongside his sons as a translator,[38] he was happy to make a kindly assimilation; for the filial contribution was also to Persius. Of his Persius II, Dryden noted:

What I had forgotten before, in its due place, I must here tell the Reader; That the first half of this Satyr was translated by one of my Sons, now in *Italy*: But I thought so well of it, that I let it pass without any Alteration.[39]

Motteux, in his journal for February 1691/2, was impressed:

Poetry is it seems hereditary in his Family, for each of his Sons have done one Satyr of *Juvenal*, which, with so extraordinary a Tutor as their Father, cannot but be very acceptable to the world.[40]

> 'Twas well alluded by a son of mine,
> (I hope to quote him is not to purloin)
> (*The Hind and the Panther*, iii 366–7)

[36] Charles E. Ward, *The Life of John Dryden* (1961), pp. 178–9.

[37] 'Discourse Concerning Satire'; Watson, ii 152.

[38] See also 'Preface to *Sylvae*'; Watson, ii 33: 'Some of them [fellow-contributors to *Sylvae*] are too nearly related to me to be commended without suspicion of partiality'—said, apparently, of Latin verses by his son Charles.

[39] *The Satires of Decimus Junius Juvenalis. Together with the Satires of Aulus Persius Flaccus* (1693), p. 28 of the Persius pagination.

[40] Quoted by Ward, *The Life of John Dryden*, p. 255.

So there is a felicity in all the circumstances surrounding the publication of *The Husband His own Cuckold* by John Dryden Jr in 1696. First, there was the epigraph from the *Aeneid: Et pater Æneas et avunculus excitat Hector*, which Dryden himself had so deftly rotated in *Mac Flecknoe*:

> Let Father *Fleckno* fire thy mind with praise,
> And Uncle *Ogleby* thy envy raise.
>
> (173–4)[41]

The Virgilian line is reinstated, since for John Dryden Jr the true father is Father Dryden and the true uncle is—literally—the man to whom he dedicated the play, Sir Robert Howard (Dryden's brother-in-law). Second, the Dedication to Howard, by Dryden's son, whatever ironies may lurk in it, widens the family of a poet by descent:

I am confident I cou'd not chuse a more indulgent Foster-Father; and tho' my very Name bears an accusation against me, yet I have the honour also to be related to the Muses by the Mothers side; for you yourself have been guilty of Poetry, and a Family Vice is therefore the more excusable in me, who am unluckily a Poet by descent.

Third, there is 'the Preface of Mr. Dryden, to his Son's Play', which ends: 'Farewell, Reader, if you are a Father you will forgive me, if not, you will when you are a Father'. Fourth, there is Dryden's Epilogue to the play, an act of paternal patronage which incorporated a good-humoured pun on 'the Puny Poet'. Fifth, there is the Prologue, by Congreve, which ends:

> Hither an Offering his First-Born he sends,
> Whose good, or ill success, on you depends.
> Yet he has hope some kindness may be shown, ⎫
> As due to greater Merit than his own, ⎬
> And begs the Sire may for the Son attone. ⎭
> There's his last Refuge, if the PLAY don't take,
> Yet spare Young Dryden for his Father's sake.

How satisfying that it should have been Congreve who wrote this for Dryden's son (and for Dryden) in 1696; Congreve, to whom two years earlier Dryden had written as his true son by poetic inheritance:

---

[41] The link was observed by William Frost, *Dryden and the Art of Translation* (1955), pp. 63–4.

> Oh that your Brows my Lawrel had sustain'd,
> Well had I been Depos'd, if You had reign'd!
> The Father had descended for the Son;
> For only You are lineal to the Throne.
>   ('To my Dear Friend Mr. Congreve' 41–4)

Dryden honours fathers, and finds foolish the belief that they were fools:

> A Tempting Doctrine, plausible and new:
> What Fools our Fathers were, if this be true!
>   (*The Medall* 111–12)

His religion is likewise imbued with a disdain for

> Disdain of Fathers which the daunce began.
>   (*The Hind and the Panther*, iii 407)

> If not by Scriptures how can we be sure
> (Reply'd the *Panther*) what tradition's pure? . . .
> How but by following her, reply'd the Dame,
> To whom deriv'd from sire to son they came.
>   (ii 212–13, 216–17)

So his scorn is in wait for those who offer only a travesty of pious succession; the Hollanders and the Spanish for instance:

> They cheat, but still from cheating Sires they come;
> They drink, but they were christ'ned first in Mum.
> Their patrimonial Sloth the *Spaniards* keep,
> And *Philip* first taught *Philip* how to sleep.
>   ('Prologue to *The Spanish Fryar*' 25–8)

But the likeness of that last line to a later severity—

> For *Tom* the Second reigns like *Tom* the first.
>   ('To Mr. Congreve' 48)

—suggests again the affiliation of the patrimonial to the literary. The association had been strong for Dryden from the start; his first poem, 'Upon the death of the Lord Hastings' begins:

> Must Noble *Hastings* Immaturely die,
> (The Honour of his ancient Family?)

—passes, after his real sires, through his imaginary sires, whom he would have outdone (Seneca, Cato, Numa, Caesar):

> Must all these ag'd Sires in one Funeral
> Expire? All die in one so young, so small?
>   (73–4)

—and arrives naturally enough at a literary metaphor, in urging Hastings's widow:

> With greater than *Platonick* love, O wed
> His Soul, though not his Body, to thy Bed:
> Let that make thee a Mother; bring thou forth
> Th' *Idea's* of his Vertue, Knowledge, Worth;
> Transcribe th' Original in new Copies . . .
>   (97–101)

But my argument is not simply that Dryden was preoccupied with fathers and poetic lineage, but that the parallel with the nature of allu- sion—the poet as heir—lent particular life to this preoccupation, his most creative allusions being those of which the quick is paternity and inheritance. Let us juxtapose two passages which end poems by Dryden and which invoke the same ideas and images:

> But to write worthy things of worthy men
> Is the peculiar talent of your Pen:
> Yet let me take your Mantle up, and I
> Will venture in your right to prophesy.
>
> "This Work by merit first of Fame secure
> "Is likewise happy in its Geniture:
> "For since 'tis born when *Charls* ascends the Throne,
> "It shares at once his Fortune and its own."
>   ('To My Honored Friend, Sr Robert Howard'
>   99–106)
>
> Sinking he left his Drugget robe behind,
> Born upwards by a subterranean wind.
> The Mantle fell to the young Prophet's part,
> With double portion of his Father's Art.
>   (*Mac Flecknoe* 214–17)

The throne, mantle, fame, and prophecy in the world of Sir Robert Howard strike me as much less telling than those in Fleckno's. The explanation is not just that *Mac Flecknoe* calls upon allusion, but that the particular allusion upon which it calls is an evocation of a true lineage such as an allusion does well to embody:

> And it came to pass, when they were gone over, that Elijah said unto Elisha, Ask what I shall do for thee, before I be taken away from thee. And Elisha said, I pray thee, let a double portion of thy spirit be upon me.
>
> . . . and Elijah went up by a whirlwind into heaven. And Elisha saw it, and he cried, My father, my father . . . He took up also the mantle of Elijah that fell from him . . .   (2 Kings 2: 9–13)

Dryden's art of allusion derives its energy and acumen from the fact that allusion itself is something which falls to his part and which he has to employ with double art.

Which is why the best study of Dryden's allusions—that by Michael Wilding—finds itself drawing our attention so often to allusions of paternity, succession, and poetic inheritance. It is not simply that *Mac Flecknoe* is about these things, but that its allusions are at once given point and protected against too easy a pointedness by themselves continually being engaged—as a matter of principled literary procedure—with that paternity, succession, and poetic inheritance of which they speak. This is audible not only in the concluding lines of *Mac Flecknoe*, but—another of Wilding's illuminations[42]—in the way in which Milton is at work within Dryden's line, 'Sh— alone my perfect image bears' (15). For whereas the Son of God is 'the radiant image of his Glory' (*Paradise Lost*, iii 63), and Adam and Eve shine with 'The image of thir glorious Maker' (iv 292), the 'perfect image' is that which Satan narcissistically loved in his daughter Sin:

> Thy self in me thy perfect image viewing
> Becam'st enamourd.
>
> (ii 764–5)

Dryden here writes as a true son of a true poet, about a false son of a false poet, and the words 'perfect image' bear a perfect image of this filial allusion.

Likewise with Wilding's comment on:

> At his right hand our young *Ascanius* sate
> *Rome's* other hope, and pillar of the State.
>
> (108–9)

---

[42] 'Dryden and Satire', in *John Dryden* (ed. Miner), p. 199. (This essay is in part a revision of 'Allusion and Innuendo in *Mac Flecknoe*', *Essays in Criticism*, xix (1969), 355–70.)

Wilding writes:

The allusions to Aeneas have a force additional to the simple provision of a
heroic context for the enthronement, through a play on the word 'author', the
categorization of Aeneas in those lines of the *Aeneid* alluded to in lines 106–9
of *Mac Flecknoe*:

> *Then issu'd from the Camp, in Arms Divine,*
> Aeneas, *Author of the* Roman *Line*:
> *And by his side* Ascanius *took his Place,*
> *The second Hope of* Rome's *Immortal Race.*
>   (xii 251–4)

Yet the authentication of the allusion is that it does itself keep alive
Rome's immortal race in a second, other, way; Dryden himself is here
an 'Author of the *Roman* line'. The word 'line' is a fertile one for him,
since it compacts the actual and the literary geniture;

> And from whose Loyns recorded Psyche sprung
>   (125)

is a telling line because, as Earl Miner[43] has pointed out, 'loins' was then
pronounced as 'lines'.

   The same considerations underlie the unforgettable passage from
Absalom and Achitophel which Reuben Brower chose as his instance of
Dryden's allusive mode.

> Yet, *Corah*, thou shalt from Oblivion pass;
> Erect thy self thou Monumental Brass:
> High as the Serpent of thy mettall made . . .
>   (632–4)

Brower excellently relates Corah's brazen effrontery to its literary allusion (adding to the Biblical play the possibility of 'a preposterous
parody of Horace's *Exegi monumentum Aere perennius*') before gathering
in the other associations:

our hero is worthy of a 'monumental brass' in an English church, the rude
command implying that this monument, contrary to decent custom and the
laws of gravity, will rise of its own power.[44]

But what binds all this together is the relation of lineage to the poetic
inheritance: Horace's line is itself shown to be as lasting as it had hoped,
since it is present to be piously and reprovingly used; the church's

---

[43] *Dryden's Poetry* (1967), p. 92.   [44] *The Poetry of Allusion*, p. 6.

monumental brass would be a pious tribute to lineage; and yet Corah's erection is hideously uncreating. 'Erect thy self thou Monumental Brass': I think of the brazen Colley Cibber: 'he had it in his power *to be thought no body's son at all*: And what is that but coming into the world a Hero?'[45]

The allusion involving fatherhood can be a particularly potent allusion, because it can question, or corroborate, or qualify the nature of literature itself, so frequently conceived of, and especially by the Augustans, as a profound geniture. Dryden himself was much drawn to one Biblical allusion, Noah's cursing of Ham for seeing him naked in his drunkenness. Noah's curse is recalled in the Preface of 'Religio Laici'; in the 'Preface of Ovid's Epistles', where Ovid 'gives occasion to his translators, who dare not cover him, to blush at the nakedness of their father';[46] in 'The Character of St Evremond' ('As I am a religious admirer of Virgil, I could wish that he [St Evremond] had not discovered our father's nakedness')[47]; and in the 'Second Part of Absalom and Achitophel':

> But, tell me, did the Drunken Patriarch Bless
> The Son that shew'd his Father's Nakedness?
>
> (384–5)

Which is why the best use of an allusion turned against Dryden not only involves one of Dryden's favourite allusions but does itself depend upon the peculiar power of an allusion to discriminate the truly filial from the falsely so; I am thinking of the closing words of John Fowler's acute essay on 'Dryden and Literary Good Breeding', and of the severe equability with which the father of English criticism is rebuked for his condescension to the father of English poetry, Chaucer:

Only the dress was wanting, and Dryden out of disinterested veneration for that founder of English poetry who 'in the beginning of our language' laboured so well to write good things—Dryden, the restorer, is charitably willing to cover the nakedness of this Father.[48]

A son, especially a gifted son, needs to contain his father, and in more senses than one. A poet needs to do the same, and allusion is a way of containing one's predecessors. They could overshadow all one's potentialities.

---

[45] Pope, *Poems* (ed. Butt), p. 718.   [46] Watson, ii 266.
[47] Watson, ii 57.   [48] In *Restoration Literature* (ed. Love), p. 245.

> Due Honours to those mighty Names we grant,
> But Shrubs may live beneath the lofty Plant:
> Sons may succeed their greater Parents gone;
> Such is thy Lott; and such I wish my own.
> ('To Sir Godfrey Kneller' 120–3)

Dryden is the first major poet in English to allude extensively—not just infrequently or in passing, and as allusion, not as being a source only—to poetry in English; creating his own meanings by bringing into play the meanings of other English poets. He does so without malignity or belittling, and yet to do so is necessarily to do something about what might otherwise be the crippling burden of the past; for to allude to a predecessor is both to acknowledge, in piety, a previous achievement and also is a form of benign appropriation—what was so well said has now become part of my way of saying, and in advancing the claims of a predecessor (and rotating them so that they catch a new light) the poet is advancing his own claims, his own poetry, and even poetry. By an open recognition of the predicament of the poet as heir, and of the burden of the past, by embracing rather than merely failing to evade the predicament, the poet can be saved by allusion, by being an alert and independent dependant. One might again apply Pope's dexterity: 'And win my way by yielding to the tyde'.

Through allusion, Dryden and Pope were enabled to cope with their immediate predecessors; and of these the most giant-like, in all his power to enable or to disable, was Milton—the poet whom Harold Bloom has called the great Inhibitor. Yet he did not inhibit either Dryden or Pope. Pope had the advantage of a certain distance and of the mediation of Dryden, but Dryden had to face the full glare of Milton's immediate and gigantic genius. Dryden's gifts, far from being inhibited, were never more truly exhibited than when, with dignity and without presumption, he recognized Milton's genius by making it serve his purposes in allusion.

'*This Man* (says *Dryden*) *Cuts us All Out, and the Ancients too*':[49] Dryden's reported reaction to *Paradise Lost* is compounded of awe and dismay. His feelings about Milton sound as though they have many strains and strands: he could write with a sheerly unenvying generosity

---

[49] Recorded by Jonathan Richardson; see *The Early Lives of Milton*, ed. Helen Darbishire (1932), p. 296. *OED*, cut out, f.: 'To get in front of a rival so as to intervene between him and success, or take the first place from him . . . A driver or rider who "cuts in", cuts out some one else'. This of Dryden is the first citation.

about Milton's heroic achievement, but he could also manifest a resistance to Milton which was less than disinterested but was also forgivable in a poet fighting for survival, for breathing-space. 'Milton's *Paradise Lost* is admirable; but am I therefore bound to maintain that there are no flats among his elevations . . .?'[50]—where Dryden speaks the truth but does at the same time convey a sense that something personal was binding him to maintain it. 'As for Mr Milton, whom we all admire with so much justice, his subject is not that of an heroic poem, properly so called . . .';[51] this last is from the discussion of the possibilities for epic (in *A Discourse Concerning Satire*), where, as George Watson has pointed out, there is a strange blankness or wilfulness in Dryden's urgings as to the kind of epic of which we stand in need. 'The reference to *Paradise Lost* . . . seems long delayed: Dryden is reluctant to admit that his proposal for an epic combining classical and scriptural imagery has already been fulfilled'.[52] And is it a coincidence, or a jockeying, that when Dryden proffers a subject for such an epic, it should be one—King Arthur—which 'Milton had considered as a young man'?[53] Again: 'And Milton, if the Devil had not been his hero . . .; if . . .; and if . . .':[54] the reservations obdurately unroll. And then there is the bizarre endeavour that converted *Paradise Lost* into *The State of Innocence*; Milton, who had no cause to fear Dryden, could be laconically civil:

Jo: Dreyden Esq. Poet Laureate, who very much admires him, & went to him to have leave to putt his Paradise-lost into a Drama in Rhyme: Mr. Milton received him civilly, & told him he would give him leave to tagge his Verses.[55]

Marvell was aware of the shadow of the impure motive in Dryden:

> Jealous I was that some less skilful hand
> (Such as disquiet alwayes what is well,
> And by ill imitating would excell)
> Might hence presume the whole Creations day
> To change in Scenes, and show it in a Play . . .
>
> Thou hast not miss'd one thought that could be fit,
> And all that was improper dost omit.

---

[50] 'Preface to *Sylvae*'; Watson, ii 32.
[51] *Discourse Concerning Satire*; Watson, ii 84.   [52] Watson's note, ii 91.
[53] Watson's note, ii 92.
[54] 'To John, Lord Marquess of Normanby'; Watson, ii 233.
[55] Recorded by John Aubrey; see *The Early Lives of Milton* (ed. Darbishire), p. 7.

So that no room is here for Writers left,
But to detect their Ignorance or Theft.
                    ('On Mr. Milton's *Paradise Lost*',
                              1674, 18–22, 27–30)

'So that no room is here for Writers left': here, or anywhere, after
Milton and Shakespeare? Dryden's genius was to make room from this
very fact, with the help of allusion. It is not that he was grudging
towards Milton, but he needed room for himself; and it is to the point
that when in a subsequent edition of *Paradise Lost* (1688) Dryden
followed Marvell's example by providing commendatory verses, his
fervid 'Lines on Milton' appeared without attribution; they were not
printed as Dryden's until well after his death (in *Miscellany Poems*, 1716).

'So that no room is here for Writers left': Marvell meant only here
within this subject, but it is an ample thought. And if I had to pick a
single reason why Dryden was so importantly and so unusually a late-
developer as a poet (for all his precocity)—*Annus Mirabilis*, which is
immature and patchy, did not appear until he was 35, and he was 50
when he published *Absalom and Achitophel*—it would be the shadow of
Milton, a shadow which became a shelter, and a kind of shading, only
after the death of Milton in 1674. Within ten years of Milton's death
(the death of a poetic father sometimes being as enabling to a poet as
can be the death of his actual father), Dryden had magnificently come
into his inheritance, as the poet of *Absalom and Achitophel*, *The Medall*,
Mac Flecknoe, and 'To the Memory of Mr. Oldham'—and with further
masterpieces especially of translation, still to come.

That Milton continued to be a fatal as well as a fertile fascination,
and that the imitative and allusive mode converts into generous energies what can be mean-spirited or blundering impulses, is clear from *Of
the Art of Sinking in Poetry* in 1727:

As *Virgil* is said to have read *Ennius*, out of his Dunghil to draw Gold; so may
our Author read *Shakespear*, *Milton*, and *Dryden*, for the contrary End, to bury
their Gold in his own Dunghil. A true Genius, when he finds any thing lofty
or shining in them, will have the Skill to bring it down, take off the Gloss, or
quite discharge the Colour, by some ingenious Circumstance, or Periphrase,
some Addition, or Diminution, or by some of those Figures the use of which
we shall shew in our next Chapter.

The Book of *Job* is acknowledg'd to be infinitely sublime, and yet has not
our Father of the *Bathos* reduc'd it in every Page?

IMITATION is of two Sorts: the First is when we force to our own Purposes the Thoughts of others; The Second consists in copying the Imperfections, or Blemishes of celebrated Authors. I have seen a Play professedly writ in the Stile of *Shakespear*, wherein the greatest Resemblance lay in one single Line,

> And so good Morrow t'ye, good Master Lieutenant.

And sundry Poems in Imitation of Milton, where with the utmost Exactness, and not so much as one Exception, nevertheless was constantly *nathless*, embroider'd was *broider'd*, Hermits were *Eremites*, disdain'd was *'sdeign'd*, shady *umbrageous*, Enterprize *Emprise*, Pagan *Paynim*, Pinions *Pennons*, sweet *dulcet*, Orchards *Orchats*, Bridge-work *Pontifical*; nay, her was *hir*, and their was *thir* thro' the whole Poem. And in very Deed, there is no other Way by which the true modern Poet could read to any purpose the Works of such Men as *Milton* and *Shakespear*.[56]

But the force of irony here derives from the fact that by 1727—after *Mac Flecknoe* and *The Rape of the Lock*—there was manifestly another way by which the true modern poet could read to some purpose the works of Milton. Dryden and Pope wrote poetry 'in Imitation of Milton'; the imitation is not parasitic or servile, it is allusive, and the allusions derive their geniture from the very nature of allusion, its sense of the paternal and filial. The alternative was 'our Father of the *Bathos*'.

Dryden, of Shimei:

> During his Office, Treason was no Crime.
> The Sons of *Belial* had a glorious Time.
> (*Absalom and Achitophel* 597–8)

Milton:

> And when Night
> Darkens the Streets, then wander forth the Sons
> Of *Belial*, flown with insolence and wine.
> (*Paradise Lost*, i 500–2)

The flare, pungency, and propriety of the allusion are alive because in speaking of 'the Sons of *Belial*' Dryden is acknowledging Milton, without 'insolence', as his father; Dryden shares in the truly 'glorious', the glory of Milton.

Likewise, Pope:

> She saw old Pryn in restless Daniel shine,
> And Eusden eke out Blackmore's endless line.
> (*The Dunciad* A, i 101–2)

---

[56] *The Early Lives of Milton* (ed. Darbishire), pp. 39, 41–2.

Milton:

> Beyond compare the Son of God was seen
> Most glorious, in him all his Father shon
> Substantially express'd, and in his face
> Divine compassion visibly appeerd,
> Love without end, and without measure Grace,
> (*Paradise Lost*, iii 138–42)

The allusion itself shines, and—modestly—it ekes out, and thus it contributes to a truly 'endless line' (not the interminable maundering of Blackmore, but a true poetic succession); and the shining of the allusion is dependent upon Pope's establishing ('Substantially express'd', as it could not be in the Dunces' poetry) a filial and independent relationship with Milton such as is a counterpart of Milton's Son and Father—and such as blasts the travesty of divine progeny which is 'Blackmore's endless line' (not Milton's 'Love without end').

Less richly, but not less tellingly, there is in Pope the ghost of Dr Busby, headmaster of Westminster School:

> His beaver'd brow a birchen garland wears,
> Dropping with Infant's blood, and Mother's tears.
> (*The Dunciad* B, iv 141–2)

Milton:

> First Moloch, horrid King besmear'd with blood
> Of human sacrifice, and parents tears.
> (*Paradise Lost*, i 392–3)

Dr Busby is a travesty of a paternal–filial relationship; Pope's relation to Milton manifests the alternative, an affectionate and independent respect.

Dryden's respect for Milton was not less real, but it was necessarily more imperilled, its animation overlapping with animus. So his greatest allusion to Milton, *Absalom and Achitophel*, implies a repudiation of Milton's politics while gaining energy from Milton's poetic energy; the partial repudiation left room for Dryden to breathe. Here too there is a parallelism between heavenly fathers, royal fathers, political fathers, and poetic fathers; as Leonora Leet Brodwin says:

To turn Milton's poetry against the party of his political heirs while using it to dignify his style would have been a brilliant enough point of wit to justify Dryden's use. But fortunately, there were points at which *Paradise Lost* paralleled contemporary events. In *Paradise Lost*, Satan is first incited to rebellion because of his refusal to accept the decree of God exalting the Son to a position of sovereignty over all the angels next only to Himself. As soon as contemporary events are seen in this light, any questioning of the legal succession or hierarchy of power becomes Satanic. . . . But if allusion to *Paradise Lost* provides Dryden with his satiric norm, it also makes for his most devastating satire on Milton's political heirs. For is it not the highest point of satire to tell a faction that is opposing the legal succession on the religious grounds of opposition to James's Catholicism that it is Satanic, and to prove it to them by invoking a parallel to the greatest work of their greatest literary exponent?[57]

The mention of James—not son succeeding father, but brother succeeding brother—calls to mind a further, complicating, strain in Dryden's relationship with Milton. For while Milton stood in something of a paternal role to Dryden as a poet, the strain was exacerbated by the fact that Milton stood too in the role of an elder brother. He was, after all, not quite twenty-three years older than Dryden. Dryden, like his contemporaries, was very aware of the grievances of younger sons (just as he praises James for being so free from envy of Charles), and he naturally found the word brother coming to his pen when speaking— late and early, 1697 and 1669—of poetic emulation and of poetic lineage:

A native of Parnassus, and bred up in the studies of its fundamental laws, may receive new lights from his contemporaries; but 'tis a grudging kind of praise which he gives his benefactors. He is more obliged than he is willing to acknowledge; there is a tincture of malice in his commendations. For where I own I am taught, I confess my want of knowledge. A judge upon the bench may, out of good nature, or at least interest, encourage the pleadings of a puny counsellor; but he does not willingly commend his brother serjeant at the bar.[58]

> Nature is old, which Poets imitate,
> And for Wit, those that boast their own estate,
> Forget *Fletcher* and *Ben* before them went,
> Their Elder Brothers, and that vastly spent:
> So much 'twill hardly be repair'd again,
> Not, though supply'd with all the wealth of *Spain*.
> ('Prologue to *The Wild Gallant*' 43–8)

Two of Dryden's greatest poems, *Absalom and Achitophel* and *Mac*

---

[57] 'Milton Allusion in *Absalom and Achitophel*', *JEGP*, lxviii (1969), 28.
[58] Dedication to *Aeneis*; 'To John, Lord Marquess of Normanby'; Watson, ii 230–1.

Flecknoe, are witty humane explorations of the truths and falsities of paternal–filial relationships. Almost every line of *Mac Flecknoe* bears upon—and is borne upon by—the considerations of inheritance (literary and worldly) that especially compact themselves in the art of allusion. How fresh remains the opening of *Mac Flecknoe*.

> All humane things are subject to decay,
> And, when Fate summons, Monarchs must obey:
> This *Fleckno* found, who like *Augustus*, young
> Was call'd to Empire, and had govern'd long:
> In Prose and Verse, was own'd, without dispute
> Through all the Realms of *Non-sense*, absolute.
> This aged Prince now flourishing in Peace,
> And blest with issue of a large increase,
> Worn out with business, did at length debate
> To settle the succession of the State:
> And pond'ring which of all his Sons was fit
> To Reign, and wage immortal War with Wit;
> Cry'd, 'tis resolv'd; for Nature pleads that He
> Should onely rule, who most resembles me:
> *Sh*— alone my perfect image bears,
> Mature in dullness from his tender years.
> *Sh*— alone, of all my Sons, is he
> Who stands confirm'd in full stupidity.

The poet who subsequently matured the concept of dullness, and who was of all the sons of Dryden the true heir, with a generous adroitness created room for himself by establishing a fraternal relation with Dryden. Pope's notes to *The Dunciad*, and especially 'Appendix VI: A Parallel of the Characters of Mr. Dryden and Mr. Pope, as Drawn by Certain of their Contemporaries', establish a fraternity free from the usual parental–filial intimidations. Some such large-minded room for honourable manœuvre was essential to Pope; after all there has at no other point in English literature been a poetic succession where the features of a poet were, at first glance, so astonishingly like those of his distinguished predecessor. Fraternity was one way of dealing with the less welcome aspects of this similarity. Pope, again, was fortunate both in his confidence that he possessed a genius not less than Dryden's and in the fact that this confidence was justified. But a corroborative strength of his poetry is that it uses its allusions to Dryden to embody this sense of the succession, of Pope's being Dryden's heir and sharing

many of his lineaments. Take the conclusion of the introductory paragraph of *The Dunciad* A: what is it that the Muses must say?—

> Say from what cause, in vain decry'd and curst,
> Still Dunce the second reigns like Dunce the first?
>
> > Alluding to a verse of Mr. *Dryden's* not in *Mac Flecno* (as it is
> > said ignorantly in the Key to the *Dunciad*, *pag.* 1.) but in his
> > verses to Mr. *Congreve*.
> > *And* Tom *the Second reigns like* Tom *the First*.

It is a crucial allusion, the first to *Mac Flecknoe* in this poem which proffers itself as the son of *Mac Flecknoe* or *Mac 'Mac Flecknoe'*; and it is a
penetratingly proper allusion because it so simply enacts its own enterprise. It is because Pope, without belittling or patronizing Dryden's line,
can so deftly turn it to new purposes, both literary and public (George
II had recently succeeded George I), that we can have the equally
amused confidence that what we are witnessing is not a Dunce or a Tom
succeeding a Dunce or a Tom, but a true poetic majesty reigning as its
predecessor had done. Pope is a King the Second who reigns like a King
the First, and pays tribute in the act of saying so in those very words.
Dryden's previous couplet had said something that would prove true
about the reign of Dryden and of Pope:

> Thus when the State one *Edward* did depose;
> A Greater *Edward* in his room arose.
> > ('To Mr. Congreve' 45–6)

For Pope, it was subsequently a God-given providence that furnished
Colley Cibber with a son Theophilus, and so furnished Pope with a
Bentleian footnote:

this Poet being the only one who was universally known to have had a Son so
exactly like him, in his poetical, theatrical, political, and moral Capacities, that
it could justly be said of him
> *Still Dunce the second reign'd like Dunce the first.*
> BENTL.[59]

Likewise with many of Pope's best allusions, themselves demonstrating
their right to that true succession which indicts the Dunces' travesty of
succession.

Pope:

---

[59] Introductory note to *The Dunciad* B, Book I (*Poems*, ed. Butt, p. 720).

> Much she revolves their arts, their ancient praise,
> And sure succession down from Heywood's days.
>> (*The Dunciad* A, i 95–6)

Dryden:

> And setl'd sure Succession in his Line.
>> (*Aeneis*, i 8)

> Th'immortal Line in sure Succession reigns.
>> (*Georgics*, iv 303)

Pope's conclusive tribute to Dryden was the ending of his translation of the *Odyssey*, with its mandate from an earlier ending:

> So *Pallas* spoke: The mandate from above
> The King obey'd. The Virgin-seed of *Jove*
> In *Mentor's* form, confirm'd the full accord,
> "And willing nations knew their lawfull Lord".

Dryden:

> He said. Th' Almighty, nodding, gave Consent;
> And Peals of Thunder shook the Firmament.
> Henceforth a Series of new time began,
> The mighty Years in long Procession ran:
> Once more the Godlike *David* was Restor'd,
> And willing Nations knew their Lawfull Lord.
>> (*Absalom and Achitophel* 1026–31)

The beauty of Pope's assimilation is its openness, its recognition of a due gratitude. Once more Dryden is restored. A series of new time begins, and yet it does not break faith with the old series. Pope's concluding and conclusive allusion has 'confirm'd the full accord' of his relation to his predecessor; Pope, as willingly as the nations, knows the lawful lordship of Dryden—and this without any mock self-subordination. Dryden, the mentor, is acknowledged 'in *Mentor's* form'.

The vast enterprise of Dryden's later life was his translation of Virgil. In 'To the Memory of Mr. Oldham', Dryden had exemplified the nature of allusion, and of the poet as heir, in the act of making an allusion to the *Aeneis*:

> His Son, or one of his Illustrious Name,
> How like the former, and almost the same.
>> (*Aeneis*, vi 1194–5)

It is characteristic of Pope not just that he should allude to Dryden but that he should allude to a passage which had furnished Dryden with a memorable allusion. Pope:

> All as the vest, appear'd the wearer's frame,
> Old in new state, another yet the same.
> Bland and familiar as in life, begun
> Thus the great Father to the greater Son.
> (*The Dunciad* A, iii 31–4)

In alluding to Dryden, Pope speaks both as a brother and as a true descendant ('Sons may succeed their greater Parents gone'), and in modifying the line of verse that can epitomize one element within allusion ('How like the former, and almost the same'), that is, its likeness-in-difference for the poet as heir, Pope has again manifested that of which he speaks, since 'Old in new state, another yet the same' is itself old and new, sharing but modifying the illustrious lineaments of 'How like the former, and almost the same'.

'He who writes much', Samuel Johnson was to write in his life of Dryden, 'will not easily escape a manner, such a recurrence of particular modes as may be easily noted'. But Dryden is different, though paradoxically: 'Dryden is always *another and the same*, he does not exhibit a second time the same elegances in the same form'. Yet Johnson, with perfect propriety, is himself exhibiting something a second time, for he is alluding. Dryden's translation from Ovid's *Metamorphoses*, Book XV ('Of the Pythagorean Philosophy'), had imagined the self-begetting of the phoenix, a feat beyond human art:

> All these receive their Birth from other Things;
> But from himself the Phœnix only springs:
> Self-born, begotten by the Parent Flame
> In which he burn'd, another and the same.
> (578–81)

Burns

Robert Burns, who was highly and deeply educated in poetry, liked to suggest otherwise. He trusted that his poems would transcend considerations of education, of classes and of class. At the time when he was still thinking of himself as both Robert Burness and Robert Burns, he set about validating this claim. His First Commonplace Book (1783–5) announces:

Observations, Hints, Songs, Scraps of Poetry &c. by Robert Burness; a man who had little art in making money, and still less in keeping it; but was, however, a man of some sense, a great deal of honesty, and unbounded good-will to every creature rational or irrational.—As he was but little indebted to scholastic education, and bred at a plough-tail, his performances must be strongly tinctured with his unpolished, rustic way of life; but as I believe, they are really *his own*, it may be some entertainment to a curious Observer of human-nature to see how a ploughman thinks, and feels, under the pressure of Love, Ambition, Anxiety, Grief with the like cares and passions, which, however diversified by the Modes, and Manners of life, operate pretty much alike I believe, in all the Species—[1]

Cares and passions operate pretty much alike in all the species: this conviction (essentialism?) might in our day brand someone the gullible victim of the powers that be. But Burns understood his claim as the essence of democratic equality and equity: however diversified were the modes and manners of life, in cares and passions—as in dignity—'A Man's a Man for a' that'.[2] *For all that*, as meaning despite all that and because of all that. Of his poetical performances, he says: 'but as I believe, they are really *his own* . . .', where *I* and *he* are happily the same person and where the play of 'I believe' against 'his own' evokes Burns's characteristic combination of being himself and of trying to see himself as others see him.[3]

---

[1] *The Poems and Songs of Robert Burns*, ed. James Kinsley (1968), iii 968. The poems are quoted from this edition, indispensable for its findings.
[2] 'Song: For a' that and a' that' 12.
[3] Bob Dylan begins his song 'Highlands' with the words of Burns ('My heart's in the Highlands'); in 'Lay, Lady, Lay' he shows himself the heir of Burns in the loving comedy of

> O wad some Pow'r the giftie gie us
> *To see oursels as others see us!*
> ('To a Louse, On Seeing one on a
> Lady's Bonnet at Church' 43–4)

In one of his letters, there is simple comedy as well as complicated truth in his becoming so literarily allusive when he is insisting that the readers for whom he most wishes are those who in their simplicity are not likely to be takers of allusions:

my first ambition was, and still my strongest wish is, to please my Compeers, the rustic Inmates of the Hamlet, while everchanging language and manners will allow me to be relished and understood . . . and in a language where Pope and Churchill have raised the laugh, and Shenstone and Gray drawn the tear; where Thomson and Beattie have painted the landskip, and Littleton and Collins described the heart; I am not vain enough to hope for distinguished Poetic fame.[4]

This, before it speaks openly of Gray, divulges and diverts the famous line of Gray, 'The rude Forefathers of the hamlet',[5] with that 'rude' changed to 'rustic' and with 'Forefathers' brought into the company of Compeers.

Carol McGuirk has remarked that 'Burns's praise of other writers tends to focus on them as brothers in feeling rather than masters in style.'[6] One creative form that praise of other writers may take is adopting and adapting their words, and the word 'others', as part of a quoted phrase that exults in brotherhood, is the rhyme for 'brothers' when Burns characteristically pits against the mean-minded the open-hearted:

Awa ye selfish, warly race,	*worldly*
Wha think that havins, sense an' grace,	*good manners*
Ev'n love an' friendship should give place	
To *catch-the-plack*!	*money-grubbing*
I dinna like to see your face,	
Nor hear your crack.	*gossip*

But ye whom social pleasure charms,
Whose heart the *tide of kindness* warms,
Who hold your *being* on the terms,

a third person / first-person turn: 'Stay, lady, stay with your man awhile | Until the break of day, let me see you make him smile'. Robert Burns puts in an appearance in *Tarantula*.

[4] To John Moore, January 1787; *The Complete Letters of Robert Burns*, ed. James A. Mackay (1987), pp. 246–7. The letters are quoted from this edition.
[5] 'Elegy Written in a Country Church Yard' 16.
[6] *Robert Burns and the Sentimental Era* (1985), p. 54.

> 'Each aid the others,'
> Come to my bowl, come to my arms,
>   My friends, my brothers!
>   ('Epistle to J. L[aprai]k, An Old Scotch Bard' 115–26)

This ('come to my arms') is an embrace of a rhyme, *others / brothers*, incorporating a phrase happily cited: ' "Each aid the others" ', this phrase from others then doing just what it urges, that is, aiding another (a brother in the art). There is a variation on all this in another poem where 'love fraternal' contrasts the thrusting and the trusting.

> The warly race may drudge an' drive,
> Hog-strouther, jundie, stretch an' strive,   *justle, elbow*
> Let me fair NATURE's face descrive,
>   And I, wi' pleasure,
> Shall let the busy, grumbling hive
>   Bum owre their treasure.   *hum*
>
> Fareweel, 'my rhyme-composing brither!'
> We've been owre lang unkenn'd to ither:
> Now let us lay our heads thegither,
>   In love fraternal:
> May *Envy* wallop in a tether,   *thrash about in a noose*
>   Black fiend, infernal!
>   ('To W. S[imso]n, Ochiltree' 91–102)

'Love fraternal': it is Burns's contempt for sanctimony that makes him see how little of any true 'love fraternal' there was in Laertes' maximonious advice to Ophelia. Laertes is a chip off the old shoulder when he resentfully anticipates his father Polonius's sententiousness and takes it on himself to admonish his sister. Yet we can be grateful for, though not to, Laertes when we appreciate how much Burns could rightly learn from the self-righteous. His 'Epistle to a Young Friend' offers a prayer, not a presumption, at parting. For Burns understands that it is easier to give advice than to heed it oneself.

> Adieu, dear, amiable Youth!
>   Your *heart* can ne'er be wanting!
> May Prudence, Fortitude and Truth
>   Erect your brow undaunting!
> In *ploughman phrase* 'GOD send you speed,'
>   Still daily to grow wiser;
> And may ye better reck the *rede*,
>   Than ever did th' *Adviser*!
>   (81–8, conclusion)

Those last two lines do not turn on their heel; they turn away, with good will in their farewell. In bowing at parting, the rueful adviser is more of a brother than Laertes ever proved, because Burns as adviser is nothing of a prig. And because he acknowledges that it was his brother-poet Shakespeare, and through him Ophelia, who had originated this ruefulness of a retort. At the very end of her speech, Ophelia has the last word:

> I shall th'effect of this good Lesson keepe,
> As watchman to my heart: but good my Brother
> Doe not as some ungracious Pastors doe,
> Shew me the steepe and thorny way to Heaven;
> Whilst like a puft and recklesse Libertine
> Himselfe, the Primrose path of dalliance treads,
> And recks not his own reade.
>
> (*Hamlet*, I. iii)

Having hailed 'my rhyme-composing brither!', Burns spurns envy: 'May *Envy* wallop in a tether'. Acknowledging without envy the achievements of his predecessors, he wrote that he was not vain enough to hope for poetic fame. Yet when he transmutes into poetry this tribute to those same poets Thomson, Shenstone, and Gray, his lines deserve to win poetic fame, and not just because they catch discriminatingly the poets' particular talents. In 'The Vision', the poet is addressed by his native muse; she concedes much but then at once proceeds to 'Yet'.

> 'Thou canst not learn, nor I can show,
> 'To paint with *Thomson*'s landscape-glow;
> 'Or wake the bosom-melting throe,
>   'With *Shenstone*'s art;
> 'Or pour, with *Gray*, the moving flow,
>   'Warm on the heart.
>
> 'Yet all beneath th' unrivall'd Rose,
> 'The lowly Daisy sweetly blows;
> 'Tho' large the forest's Monarch throws
>   'His army shade,
> 'Yet green the juicy Hawthorn grows,
>   'Adown the glade.
>
> ('The Vision' 247–58)

There the second stanza achieves an exquisite evocation of the claims that can modestly and unenviously be made, made by the hawthorn in the presence of the oak, or by the daisy in the presence of the rose—this, by the author of a great poem that appeared in this same volume of 1786, 'To a Mountain-Daisy, On turning one down, with the Plough, in April—1786'. The cadence of the two lines that move on from what they have granted to what they will not disclaim—

> 'Yet all beneath th' unrivall'd Rose,
> 'The lowly Daisy sweetly blows;

—is itself unrivalled, with then the tender undulation of 'lowly Daisy sweetly' coming to rest in the full open rhyme of *Rose / blows / throws / grows* that yet tucks *lowly* up within it. This rhyme moves in modulation from that of the preceding stanza, which had been *show / glow / throe / flow*. And then there is the lilt that echoes on from 'lowly Daisy sweetly' to 'army' and 'juicy'. The peace here is at one with the glimpse of the great tree and its arms as 'His army shade'.[7] The epithet is an anti-pun: not-army-but-arm-y. No military monarch. A shelter and a kind of shading cool.

'It may be some entertainment to a curious Observer of human-nature to see how a ploughman thinks, and feels'. Thinks and feels, not just plods, though Gray's plodding ploughman—the most famous ploughman in our literature—is in the picture. Francis Jeffrey, for his part, was convinced that Burns 'will never be rightly estimated as a poet, till that vulgar wonder be entirely repressed which was raised on his having been a ploughman'.[8] But one good reason why readers have always been reluctant to let go of the ploughman is that Burns himself did such wonders with it ('In *ploughman phrase* "GOD send you speed" '). Another good reason is that ploughing lends itself—as this great erotic poet well knew—to erotic imagination. Take Cleopatra.

> Royal Wench:
> She made great *Cæsar* lay his Sword to bed,
> He ploughed her, and she cropt.
> (*Antony and Cleopatra*, II. ii)

This beats any other way of beating a sword into a plough-share. Max Beerbohm was moved to mischief in *The Poets' Corner*, where his light-

---

[7] The *OED* does not give 'army' in this sense (having arms as does, say, a tree).
[8] *Edinburgh Review*, January 1809; *Robert Burns: The Critical Heritage*, ed. Donald A. Low (1974), p. 178.

footed loving caricature brings together the words of Burns (his poem 'Highland Mary') and the word of God: *Robert Burns, having set his hand to the plough, looks back at Highland Mary.* The drawing 'was inspired by Luke ix. 62: "And Jesus said unto him, No man, having put his hand to the plough, and looking back, is fit for the kingdom of God" '.[9]

There are other kingdoms. One of the things that diversifies the modes and manners of life is nationality. Scotland is not England. When John Logan wrote, in of all places the *English Review*, that Burns 'is better acquainted with the English poets than most English authors that have come under our review',[10] he was delivering not an inadvertent insult to a Scottish poet but a double tribute. Jeffrey, too, saw that Burns, whatever his disavowals, was a learnèd poet, and that the learning was not lumber but limber. It is Jeffrey's adverb 'intimately' that brings this home:

before he had ever composed a single stanza, he was not only familiar with many prose writers, but far more intimately acquainted with Pope, Shakespeare and Thomson, than nine tenths of the youth that leave school for the university.[11]

The critics of Burns all tried to catch the paradox of his so combining literary feats with untutored simplicities. Allan Cunningham got hold of the right thing by the wrong end when he worded his tribute like this:

We can see to whom other bards have looked for inspiration—like fruit of the finest sort, they smack of the stock on which they were grafted. Burns read Young, Thomson, Shenstone, and Shakspeare; yet there is nothing of Young, Thomson, Shenstone, or Shakspeare about him; nor is there much of the old ballad. His light is of nature, like sunshine, and not reflected.[12]

True, there is about Burns nothing of Young, Thomson, Shenstone, or Shakespeare if by this we mean that no poem by Burns has quite the taste, the smack, of his predecessors; but there is much of these and other poets about him if we have in mind all that he can call up from them and bring to mind. For Cunningham averts his eyes from the

⁹ *Beerbohm's Literary Caricatures*, ed. J. G. Riewald (1977), p. 40.
¹⁰ February 1787; *Burns: The Critical Heritage*, p. 76.
¹¹ *Burns: The Critical Heritage*, p. 179.
¹² Cunningham's edition (1834); *Burns: The Critical Heritage*, p. 410.

sun's nightly counterpart when he says of Burns that 'His light is of nature, like sunshine, and not reflected'. Moonshine, you might retort. For moonshine is no less of nature than is sunshine. Reflect on how poets have enjoyed bringing their allusive illuminations into relation with the light of the moon, allusion itself being a reflection from and upon a borrowed light, something that may be a lesser light but is no less light for having been borrowed.[13] Thomas Carlyle wrote of Burns: 'he is ever clear, simple, true, and glitters with no lustre but his own'.[14] True, but only if we see that the light of the moon both is not and is her own.

Jeffrey knew that he needed to speak of a paradox when it came to the educability of poets. No one has written better about the influence of anxiety.

We ventured, on a former occasion, to say something of the effects of regular education, and of the general diffusion of literature, in repressing the vigour and originality of all kinds of mental exertion. That speculation was perhaps carried somewhat too far; but if the paradox have proof any where, it is in its application to poetry. Among well educated people, the standard writers of this description are at once so venerated and so familiar, that it is thought equally impossible to rival them, and to write verses without attempting it. If there be one degree of fame which excites emulation, there is another which leads to despair; nor can we conceive any one less likely to add one to the short list of original poets, than a young man of fine fancy and delicate taste, who has acquired a high relish for poetry, by perusing the most celebrated writers, and conversing with the most intelligent judges. The head of such a person is filled, of course, with all the splendid passages of antient and modern authors, and with the fine and fastidious remarks which have been made even on these passages. When he turns his eyes, therefore, on his own conceptions, they can scarcely fail to appear rude and contemptible. He is perpetually haunted and depressed by the ideal presence of those great masters and their exacting critics.[15]

Critics: on one occasion, Burns followed this word immediately with 'appalled', and yet he would not have been appalled by Jeffrey's criticism and its power to teach to him and to others, both writers and readers, something about the glories and perils of teaching.

> Critics—appalled, I venture on the name,
> Those cut-throat bandits in the paths of fame:

[13] See Pope's lines, p. 10 above.
[14] *Edinburgh Review*, December 1828; *Burns: The Critical Heritage*, p. 357.
[15] *Burns: The Critical Heritage*, p. 179.

> Bloody dissectors, worse than ten Monroes;
> He hacks to teach, they mangle to expose.
>   ('To R[obert] G[raham] of F[intry],
>   Esq.' 37–40)

Like Pope before him, Burns loved pure coincidence, especially one that turned upon, rounded upon, a name. For though there might not be ten Monroes, there were at least two of them.

Alexander Monro (1697–1767) was professor of anatomy at Edinburgh from 1726; his son Alexander (1733–1817) succeeded him in 1754, and was also the first occupant of the chair of surgery (1777); his grandson Alexander (1773–1859) was still in training in 1791 [the year of Burns's lines], but came to both chairs in 1798. The appointment of Monro *primus* marked the beginning of Edinburgh's medical fame. But Burns's phrase echoes Pope's reference to James Monro, the physician of Bedlam: 'Sure I should want the Care of ten *Monroes*' (*Imitations of Horace*, Ep. II ii, l.70).[16]

Burns's phrase 'worse than ten Monroes' does not suppose itself better than the previous 'ten Monroes', those of Pope. (That would be lunatic, would want the care of Bedlam's Monro.) Anyway, Burns is not in competition with Pope, and is happy to have been taught a thing or two by him, including the pleasures of exercising a name as a rhyme-word, given that a name both is and is not a word.

    Pope's lines move to a climax with this couplet on those Monroes, but *en route* they pay tribute to his father in the matter of teaching. In particular, moral teaching:

> Besides, my Father taught me from a Lad,
> The better Art to know the good from bad:
>   (*Imitations of Horace*, Ep. II ii 54–5)

Pope had learnt not only this art but a sister art: to know the good from bad in art, and to know how to create art from art. Pope's greatest calling into play (all work but much play) may be his translation of Homer, not least because its financial triumph freed him to undertake all those further realizations of his genius:

> But (thanks to *Homer*) since I live and thrive,
> Indebted to no Prince or Peer alive,

> Sure I should want the Care of ten *Monroes*,
> If I would scribble, rather than repose.
>   (*Imitations of Horace*, Ep. II ii 68–71)

Pope's couplet came to rest in his imagining rest and respite: 'repose'. But (thanks to *Pope*) Burns lives and thrives, his couplet keeps up his fight with dissector-critics, rhyming 'Monroes' with the wounding word 'expose'. We sell Burns short if we begrudge him his skill with allusion, or if we begrudge allusion itself, as did Josiah Walker when he spoke with concessive condescension: 'Instances of imitation may be discovered in the poems of Burns, but they are neither numerous nor unpleasant'.[17]

Burns's pleasing tribute to the poet Robert Fergusson is winged with the powers of song that derive from other poets, Pope and Gray again among them. The first quatrain constitutes the inscription itself.

> Epitaph. Here lies Robert Fergusson,
>   Poet
> Born, September 5th, 1751—Died 16th October, 1774
>
> No sculptur'd marble here, nor pompous lay,
>   'No story'd urn nor animated bust;'
> This simple stone directs pale SCOTIA's way
>   To pour her sorrows o'er her POET's dust.
>
> [She mourns, sweet, tuneful youth, thy hapless fate,
>   Tho' all the pow'rs of song thy fancy fir'd;
> Yet Luxury and Wealth lay by in state,
>   And thankless starv'd what they so much admir'd.
>
> This humble tribute with a tear he gives,
>   A brother Bard, he can no more bestow;
> But dear to fame thy Song immortal lives,
>   A nobler monument than Art can show.]

Fergusson's fate had been not only death but insanity. He had lost his mind before losing his breath, and there is poignancy in Burns's invocation of the line from Gray's *Elegy*. The very placing by Burns of his quotation marks plays its small part, for one might misguidedly wonder by what right he includes what is not Gray's word but his own word, 'No', within the quotation. Gray had asked

---

[17] *Account of the Life and Character of Robert Burns* (1811); *Burns: The Critical Heritage*, p. 237.

> Can storied urn or animated bust
> Back to its mansion call the fleeting breath?
> ('Elegy Written in a Country
> Church Yard' 41–2)

'No' is the answer, and it is this that validates Burns's quietly incorporating the word at the head of his line (and changing Gray's *or* to *nor*), for all the world as though it were Gray's. No . . . nor . . . No . . . nor:

> No sculptur'd marble here, nor pompous lay,
> 'No story'd urn nor animated bust;'

So though the stone itself may be 'This simple stone', the lines themselves are animated by the line of poets that they enshrine.

Animated, too, by the anger that is then, in the next quatrain, bent upon those who, despite their affluence, neglected the poet's plight:

> Yet Luxury and Wealth lay by in state,
> And thankless starv'd what they so much admir'd.

The rich, ignoring their patronly duty, are thankless not only as being ungrateful for Fergusson's poems but as deserving no thanks. But Burns's lines (thanks to Pope) are fired by a memory of a bitter mock-prostration before a patron in 'An Epistle to Dr. Arbuthnot' 247–8:

> But still the Great have kindness in reserve,
> He help'd to bury whom he help'd to starve.

Pope's couplet survived, in reserve; what saves Burns from being only parasitically helped by it is his reconstitution of the couplet's antithesis within the differently antithetical scheme of the abab quatrain. Furthermore, Burns appreciated that there was much more to Pope than such bitter truths; an essential sweetness is invoked by Burns in lines of a different spirit, written to be voiced by a woman.

> I could no more—askance the creature eyeing,
> D'ye think, said I, this face was made for crying?
> I'll laugh, that's pos—nay more, the world shall know it;
> And so your servant, gloomy Master Poet.
> ('Occasional Address, Spoken by Miss Fontenelle,
> on her Benefit-Night' 18–21)

This not only acknowledges Pope's generosity, it insists that all the world shall know it:

The gen'rous God, who Wit and Gold refines,
And ripens Spirits as he ripens Mines,
Kept Dross for Duchesses, the world shall know it,
To you gave Sense, Good-humour, and a Poet.
('Of the Characters of Women' 289–92,
conclusion)[18]

The Benefit-Night benefited from this old gold. Burns does not imagine that in devising lines for Miss Fontenelle he has ripened and refined Pope's tribute to Miss Blount, lines which were ripened and refined already. But he maintains the precedent that contrasts the good-humoured person and the ill-humoured ones. The allusion makes sense by virtue of being given sense, along with such good humour as goes to the making of a poet.

The making of an allusion will sometimes profit from its being compounded. Yet this further duality (not only an allusion as itself dual, but a particular one as calling two past moments into present play) may amount to nothing more than going through a couple of motions. Burns is stagnant when there is no crepitating discrepancy between what he takes and what he makes, or between the two things that he is taking. The meeting of Burns and Pope, and of Pope and Pope, can be too much the meeting of a willed likemindedness.

Then kneeling down to HEAVEN'S ETERNAL KING,
The *Saint*, the *Father*, and the *Husband* prays:
Hope 'springs exulting on triumphant wing,' *
That *thus* they all shall meet in future days:
('The Cotter's Saturday Night' 136–9)

* Pope's Windsor Forest.

Burns's note directs us to Pope: 'And mounts exulting on triumphant Wings' (*Windsor-Forest* 112). Presumably Burns hopes that we will not recall what immediately follows: the death of the pheasant, with the words 'triumphant Wings' followed at once by 'Short is his Joy!' Yet Burns's punctuation has its cunning, with Hope not as part of the quotation and yet with the much-quoted 'Hope springs . . .' making a claim upon us. For that other line springs to mind: 'Hope springs eternal in the human breast'.[19] But though the plaiting is adept, Burns is

---

[18] Not noted by Kinsley.
[19] *Essay on Man*, i 5. Burns has 'Eternal', and Pope two lines earlier speaks, as Burns does, of the 'future'. Not noted by Kinsley.

truer to himself when the effect is of sparks being struck, not of plaiting or of the pat.

> I like to have quotations ready for every occasion.—They give one's ideas so pat, and save one the trouble of finding expression adequate to one's feelings.[20]

That is less like it.

Two bodies of thought came together to conceive and foster Burns's deepest triumphs of allusion: his conviction about the human inheritance, and his feeling for those who were among his personal inheritors, his heirs. His conviction is that we inherit at birth original sinlessness. We are born with a goodness that is then wrested from us by distortion and contortion, by religious grimness. And the other thing that is natural, whatever the rigidly righteous (the unco guid)[21] may say, is sexual pleasure and what is so often its issue: natural children, bastard children. Burns's allusions need to be read between the lines of the wrong side of the sheets.

> What a poor, blighted, rickety breed are the Virtues & charities when they take their birth from geometrical hypothesis & mathematical demonstration? And what a vigorous Offspring are they when they owe their origin to, and are nursed with the vital blood of a heart glowing with the noble enthusiasm of Generosity, Benevolence and Greatness of Soul?[22]

He spoke against what stuck in his throat: that we are heirs to and of perdition, and that passion is from hell. When his muse speaks to him, she reprehends his misconduct without palliating it, but she is then moved to a 'But yet' that leaves room for humanity, his and hers:

> I saw thy pulse's maddening play,
> Wild-send thee Pleasure's devious way,
> 'Misled by Fancy's *meteor-ray*,
>   By Passion driven;
> 'But yet the *light* that led astray,
>   Was *light* from Heaven.
>   ('The Vision' 235–40)

---

[20] To Agnes McLehose, 14 January 1788; *Letters*, p. 383.

[21] See 'Address to the Unco Guid, or the Rigidly Righteous', which opens: 'O ye who are sae guid yoursel, | Sae pious and sae holy, | Ye've nought to do but mark and tell | Your Neebours' fauts and folly!'

[22] To Frances Dunlop, 22 June 1789; *Letters*, p. 174.

Dangerous, this, clearly; though it does not exactly lend itself to excuse and exculpation, it can be borrowed on their behalf since it is presented as a mitigation. But one of the things that protects Burns's lines against being deviously self-serving is that this light from Heaven is also light from the poet Young. Burns is calling a witness, not relying on his own testimony alone. Young urges: 'Think not our Passions from *Corruption* sprung':

> I feel a Grandeur in the *Passions* too,
> Which speaks their high Descent, and glorious End;
> Which speaks them Rays of an Eternal Fire.
> In Paradise itself they burnt as strong,
> Ere *Adam* fell.
> (*Night Thoughts*, Night vii, 524, 528–32)[23]

Burns was of one mind, and he spoke it.

I am in perpetual warfare with that doctrine of our Reverend Priesthood, that 'we are born into this world bond slaves of iniquity & heirs of perdition, wholly inclined' to that which is evil and wholly disinclined to that which is good until by a kind of Spiritual Filtration or rectifying process Called effectual Calling &c.—The whole business is reversed, and our connections above & below completely change place.—I believe in my conscience that the case is just quite contrary—We come into this world with a heart & disposition to do good for it, untill by dashing a large mixture of base alloy called Prudence alias Selfishness, the too precious Metal of the Soul is brought down to the black-guard Sterling of ordinary currency.[24]

Women, he found (he was writing this to Rachel Dunlop), are less often blackguards.

I had not been fifteen minutes in Miss Cathcart's company till I set her down in the dearest records of my observation as one of those 'Ministering Spirits' who delight in doing kind offices to 'The Heirs of Salvation'[25]

Blessed are those who believe that we are heirs of salvation. To hell with those whose self-fulfilling prophecy—for themselves no less than for others—is that we are heirs of perdition. Being an heir to previous poets may be one's salvation.

Many of Burns's heirs in life were bastards of his. By Elizabeth Paton

---

[23] *Night Thoughts*, ed. Stephen Cornford (1989), p. 192.
[24] To Rachel Dunlop, 2 August 1788; *Letters*, p. 475.
[25] To Josiah Walker, 29 September 1787; *Letters*, p. 355.

(1785). By Jean Armour (1786, twins, and twins again in 1788; she was acknowledged as Burns's wife, April 1788). By Anne Park, and by Jenny Clow (both 1791). Sometimes he sounds too burly, saying 'solid' twice:

We talk of air & manner, of beauty & wit, and lord knows what unmeaning nonsense; but—there—is solid charms for you—Who would not be in raptures with a woman that will make him 300£ richer?—And then to have a woman to lye with when one pleases without running any risk of the cursed expence of bastards and all the other concomitants of that species of Smuggling—These are solid views of Matrimony.[26]

At other times, the cursed expense is of spirit and of shame, as when he writes with simple dignity of his wish to emigrate:

I will go for Jamaica. Should I stay, in an unsettled state, at home, I would only dissipate my little fortune, and ruin what I intend shall compensate my little ones, for the stigma I have brought on their names.[27]

Whose name does a bastard, a love-child, bear?

Hatred, unlike love, did not come easily to Burns. But he hated murder, especially when masked as military glory, and in his Song, 'I murder hate by field or flood', he called to mind and in question the violence of the Old Testament in the face of fornication and miscegenation.

Song

I murder hate by field or flood,
   Tho' glory's name may screen us;
In wars at home I'll spend my blood,
   Life-giving wars of Venus:
The deities that I adore
   Are social Peace and Plenty;
I'm better pleas'd *to make one more*,
   Than be the death of twenty.—

I would not die like Socrates,
   For all the fuss of Plato;
Nor yet would I with Leonidas,
   Nor yet would I with Cato:
The Zealots of the Church, or State,
   Shall ne'er my mortal foes be,

---

[26]   To John Tennant, 13 September 1784; *Letters*, p. 72.
[27]   To James Smith, 11 June 1787; *Letters*, p. 119.

> But let me have bold *ZIMRI's fate,
> Within the arms of COSBI!

> * Vide. Numbers Chap. 25th
> Verse 8th–15th

In her edition of the poems, Carol McGuirk has deftly annotated the teeming names:

Socrates drank hemlock, Leonidas died attempting to hold the pass at Thermopylae for Sparta, and Cato committed suicide to protest Caesar's destruction of the Roman republic: all were martyrs of the classical world. The alternative heroic martyrdom Burns proposes is Scriptural: the Lord approved Phineas's slaying (and genital mutilation) of Zimri, a prince of the tribe of Simeon, and Cosbi, a Midianite princess, during the act of fornication.[28]

Not that Burns approved of the Lord's approving of this, and not that the Lord approved of Zimri's death as a heroic martyrdom. For Burns, though, Zimri is a martyr to sexual love, as against God's love. And his killer is no hero, he who 'rose up from among the congregation, and took a javelin in his hand; and he went after the man of Israel into the tent, and thrust both of them through, the man of Israel, and the woman through her belly' (Numbers, 25: 8). The javelin's thrust is appallingly at one with the erotic thrust. And why the killing?—because she was 'a Midianitish woman'. The religious hatred is hated by Burns, for all the exultant extravagant comedy of the poem's climax (what a way to go!). And the old time Old Testament hatred is seen by him as continuous with the genital mutilation and with the hatred bent upon bastards in the good book, the book that so encourages the stiff-necked, the unco guid.

He that is wounded in the stones, or hath his privy member cut off, shall not enter into the congregation of the LORD. A bastard shall not enter into the congregation of the LORD; even to his tenth generation shall he not enter into the congregation of the LORD.   (Deuteronomy 23: 1–2)

'Even to his tenth generation'. Burns: 'To endless generations!'[29]
  Not that the New Testament is more welcoming.

For whom the Lord loveth he chasteneth, and scourgeth every son whom he receiveth. If ye endure chastening, God dealeth with you as with sons; for what

---

[28] *Robert Burns: Selected Poems* (1993), p. 287, where McGuirk clarifies Burns's attitudes to war.
[29] See 'Nature's Law', p. 75 below.

son is he whom his father chasteneth not? But if ye be without chastisement, whereof all are partakers, then are ye bastards, and not sons.   (Epistle to the Hebrews, 12: 6–8)

Bastards, and not sons? But bastard sons are sons.

Love, not hate, came first, companioned with desire, when Burns entered upon poetry. He wrote to a friend in 1787:

This kind of life, the chearless gloom of a hermit with the unceasing moil of a galley-slave, brought me to my sixteenth year; a little before which period I first committed the sin of RHYME.—You know our country custom of coupling a man and woman together as Partners in the labors of Harvest.—In my fifteenth autumn, my Partner was a bewitching creature who just counted an autumn less.—My scarcity of English denies me the power of doing her justice in that language; but you know the Scotch idiom, She was a bonie, sweet, sonsie lass.—In short, she altogether unwittingly to herself, initiated me in a certain delicious Passion, which in spite of acid Disappointment, gin-horse Prudence and bookworm Philosophy, I hold to be the first of human joys, our dearest pleasure here below.—How she caught the contagion I can't say; you medical folks talk much of infection by breathing the same air, the touch, &c. but I never expressly told her that I loved her.—Indeed I did not well know myself, why I liked so much to loiter behind with her, when returning in the evening from our labors; why the tones of her voice made my heart-strings thrill like an Eolian harp; and particularly, why my pulse beat such a furious ratann when I looked and fingered over her hand, to pick out the nettle-stings and thistles.—Among her other love-inspiring qualifications, she sung sweetly; and 'twas her favorite reel to which I attempted giving an embodied vehicle in rhyme.—I was not so presumtive as to imagine that I could make verses like printed ones, composed by men who had Greek and Latin; but my girl sung a song which was said to be composed by a small coun-try laird's son, on one of his father's maids, with whom he was in love; and I saw no reason why I might not rhyme as well as he, for excepting smearing sheep and casting peats, his father living in the moors, he had no more Scholarcraft than I had.—

Thus with me began Love and Poesy; which at times have been my only, and will within this last twelvemonth have been my highest enjoyment.[30]

Lovely, this coming together of Love and Poesy in the singular noun, enjoyment. Equally lovely, the memory of Goldsmith and his hermit, a memory respectfully dissented from: Burns's 'our dearest pleasure here

---

[30] To John Moore, 2 August 1787; *Letters*, p. 250.

below', Goldsmith's 'Man wants but little here below, | Nor wants that little long' ('Edwin and Angelina' 31–2).

The intertwining of love and poetry, in Burns's experience (though not in his alone), is caught in the comedy of 'first committed the sin of RHYME.—', followed as it is by mention of 'our country custom of coupling a man and woman together as Partners in the labors of Harvest'. The filaments of desire are there in the move from 'breathing the same air' to the airs that are music when she sings (airs as in Milton's Paradise); in the assonantal interplay of 'heartstrings . . . like an Eolian harp', followed by 'fingered' and 'the nettle-stings'; and in the corporeality given to 'embodied'. Once this conjunction of love and poetry had created actual poems, Burns was to be moved to thoughts of a double posterity, not airy at all, his issue in both senses:

My presents, so far as I am a Poet, are the presents of Genius; & as the gifts of R. BURNS, they are the gifts of respectful gratitude to the WORTHY.—I assure you, I am not a little flattered with the idea, when I anticipate children pointing out in future Publications the tribute of respect I have bestowed on their Mothers.—[31]

Gratitude became him and it becomes us.

However, life is chequered, joy & sorrow, for on Saturday morning last Mrs. Burns made me a present of a fine boy, rather stouter but not so handsome as your God-son at his time of life was.—Indeed I look on your little Namesake to be my chef d'oeuvre in that species of manufacture, as I look on 'Tam o' Shanter' to be my standard performance in the Poetical line.—'Tis true, both the one & the other discover a spice of roguish waggery that might perhaps be as well spared; but then they also shew in my opinion a force of genius & a finishing polish that I despair of ever excelling.[32]

Sometimes, though, the note is not of roguish waggery but of a rogue's swaggery. He is often uneasy with the conjunction of these species of manufacture, as well he should be, given that his misconduct, though forgiveable, was not forgettable.

Making a poem is like begetting a son: you cannot know whether you have a wise man or a fool, untill you produce him to the world & try him.—For that reason I send you the offspring of my brain, *abortions* & all; & as such, pray look over them, & forgive them, & burn them.[33]

---

[31] To John McMurdo, July 1793; *Letters*, p. 495.
[32] To Frances Dunlop, 11 April 1791; *Letters*, p. 194.
[33] To George Thomson, September 1794; *Letters*, p. 655.

The inclosed is one which, like some other misbegotten brats, 'too tedious to mention,' claims a parental pang from my Bardship.[34]

The brio there risks heartlessness, in its play with *Pericles*: 'Twould be too tedious to repeat, but the mayne griefe springs from the losse of a beloved daughter & a wife' (V. i). But then Pericles' love for his daughter Marina was not to come entirely to grief.

'Misbegotten brats': other poets' words are not of Burns's begetting, and he particularly likes to call upon such words when they treat of misbegotten brats and when he can tousle them with affectionate disrespect. There is a touch of bastardizing in this, as when he mocks at once the fashionable epigraph and the age-old text for a sermon. As in this opening of a letter:

Edinburgh, 23rd August 1787

'As I gaed up to Dunse
          'To warp a pickle yarn,
'Robin, silly body,
          'He gat me wi' bairn.'—

From henceforth, my dear Sir, I am determined to set off with my letters like the periodical Writers, viz. prefix a kind of text quoted from some Classic of undoubted authority, such as the Author of the immortal piece of which my text is a part.—[35]

The coupling of Love and Poesy is at one with the coupling of Burns's genius with the genius of his predecessors (this being always a distinctive mark of his greatness). Some of the predecessors were famous, others are the anonymous folk. 'There be of them, that have left a name behind them, that their praises might be reported. And some there be, which have no memorial'[36]—or rather, have no memorial that bears their name.

Allusion plays into this, in that it can bring together different intercourses. Burns speaks of

holding an intrigue with the muses, the only gipseys with whom I have now any intercourse. As I am entered into the holy state of matrimony, I trust my

[34] To James Hoy, 27 October 1787; *Letters*, p. 361. The figure of speech is everywhere in Burns; a plan to marry is 'a legitimate child of Wisdom and Goodsense' (22 February 1788; *Letters*, p. 399); and a poem is 'a flagrant instance of the Poetica Licentia', 'this Byblow' (24 April 1795; *Letters*, p. 716).
[35] To Robert Ainslie; *Letters*, p. 330.
[36] Ecclesiasticus, 44: 8–9.

face is turned completely Zion-ward; and as it is a rule with all honest fellows to repeat no grievances, I hope that the little poetic licences of former days will of course fall under the oblivious influence of some good-natured statute of celestial proscription. In my family devotion; which, like a good presbyterian, I occasionally give to my household folks, I am extremely fond of the psalm, 'Let not the errors of my youth,' &c. and that other, 'Lo, children are God's heritage,' &c. in which last Mrs. Burns, who, by the by, has a glorious 'wood-note wild' at either old song or psalmody, joins me with the pathos of Handel's Messiah . . .[37]

His wife's voice is aligned with the notes of a composer and with the words (Milton's) of a poet about a poet:

> Or sweetest *Shakespear* fancies childe,
> Warble his native Wood-notes wilde,
> ('L'Allegro' 132–3)

Fancy's child is related to a natural child, as though there were about Shakespeare something endearingly illegitimate (neo-classical criticism found the illegitimacy of his art unendearing). Though Milton's tone has a curled condescension, Burns's way with Milton's phrase does not; it has nothing of the *de haut en bas*, for Burns is aware of the paradoxical comedy which derives from making even a half-learnèd use of an allusion that turns upon a particular poet's being held not to be learnèd. Trust Burns, in his very tomfoolery about his being no more than a shepherd (a cut above a ploughman?), to have recourse to Latin and to educated artistry:

I am a bit of a Herald; & shall give you, Secundum artem, my ARMS.—On a field, azure, a holly-bush, seeded, proper, in base; a Shepherd's pipe & crook, Saltier-wise, also proper, in chief.—On a wreath of the colors, a woodlark perching on a sprig of bay-tree, proper, for Crest.—Two Mottoes: Round the top of the Crest—'Wood-notes wild'—At the bottom of the Shield, in the usual place—
    'Better a wee bush than nae bield.'—[38]

Misbegotten brats are not to be confused with the love-begotten, though it suited the punitively envious to insist that there be no euphemisms for bastards. The self-righteous might have enjoyed taking issue with the title of one of Burns's most generous poems: 'A Poet's

---

[37] To John McAuley, 4 June 1789; *Letters*, p. 531.
[38] To Alexander Cunningham, 3 March 1794; *Letters*, p. 471.

Welcome to his love-begotten Daughter'. Not that Burns would have spat out the word 'bastard'; he would have understood the natural and surprising way in which it is the contemptuous terms that most lend themselves to affectionate rescue (Good to see you, you old bastard). But he would have been aware of the different enterings upon the poem that would have issued from different titles.

Glenriddell MS: 'A Poet's Welcome to his love-begotten
    Daughter'
Alloway MS: 'A Welcome to a bastart wean'.
Rosenbach MS: 'The Poet's Welcome to His Bastart Wean'.
Stewart's edition (1801): 'Address to an Illegitimate Child'.

It was left to a man of God, Richard Chenevix Trench, a man to whom we owe a great deal (though not for this, rather for his part in the *OED*), to remonstrate with monstrous relish:

But worst perhaps of all are names which throw a flimsy veil of sentiment over some sin. What a source, for example, of mischief without end in our country parishes is the one practice of calling a child born out of wedlock a 'love-child', instead of a bastard. It would be hard to estimate how much it has lowered the tone and standard of morality among us; or for how many young women it may have helped to make the downward way more sloping still. How vigorously ought we to oppose ourselves to all such immoralities of language; for many that will endure to commit a sin, will profoundly resent having that sin called by its right name.[39]

But there are more ways than one of being a bastard, and there are other routes to Hell than the primrose path of dalliance. 'He gat me wi' bairn'. Laertes: I warn you, Ophelia. Country parishes, country matters.

---

[39] *On the Study of Words* (1851), Lecture III. William Empson was obliged to make clear that his ideas about complex words have 'nothing to do with etymology, because otherwise I might find myself in rather bad company. For example the father of the great N.E.D. [now *OED*], Archbishop Trench, may be found saying:

"But there is a deeper feeling in the heart of man, bearing witness to something very different from this shallow explanation of the existence of pain in the present economy of the world—namely, that it is the correlative of sin, that it is *punishment*; and to this the word 'pain', which there can be no reasonable doubt is derived from 'poena', bears continual witness. Pain *is* punishment; so does the word itself, no less than the conscience of everyone that is suffering it, continually declare."

If you came fresh from the factory conditions of the time and heard the good archbishop on this point you might perhaps have tried kicking that important figure. He might then have found himself claiming that though in pain he did not deserve to suffer' (*The Structure of Complex Words*, 1951, pp. 81–2).

Burns's love begets his poem.

A Poet's Welcome to his love-begotten Daughter;
the first instance that entitled him to the venerable
appellation of Father—

Thou's welcome, Wean! Mischanter fa' me,	*mishap*
If thoughts o' thee, or yet thy Mamie,	
Shall ever daunton me or awe me,	*discourage*
My bonie lady;	
Or if I blush when thou shalt ca' me	
Tyta, or Daddie.—	[*pet name for father*]

Tho' now they cal' me, Fornicator,	
And tease my name in kintra clatter,	*country gossip*
The mair they talk, I'm kend the better;	
E'en let them clash!	
An auld wife's tongue's a feckless matter	*worthless*
To gie ane fash.—	*bother*

Welcome! My bonie, sweet, wee Dochter!
Tho' ye come here a wee unsought for;
And tho' your comin I hae fought for,
Baith Kirk and Queir;
Yet by my faith, ye're no unwrought for,
That I shall swear!

Wee image o' my bonie Betty,	
As fatherly I kiss and daut thee,	*pet*
As dear and near my heart I set thee,	
Wi' as gude will,	
As a' the Priests had seen me get thee	
That's out o' h——.—	

Sweet fruit o' monie a merry dint,	
My funny toil is no a' tint;	*sportive*
Tho' ye come to the wearld asklent,	*on the side*
Which fools may scoff at,	
In my last plack your part's be in't,	*farthing*
The better half o't.—	

Tho' I should be the waur bestead,	*worse circumstanced*
Thou's be as braw and bienly clad,	*fine and warmly*
And thy young years as nicely bred	
Wi' education,	
As ony brat o' Wedlock's bed,	
In a' thy station.—	

> Lord grant that thou may ay inherit
> Thy Mither's looks an' gracefu' merit;
> An' thy poor, worthless Daddie's spirit,
>   Without his failins!
> 'Twad please me mair to see thee heir it
>   Than stocked mailins!   *pieces of land*
>
> For if thou be, what I wad hae thee,
> And tak the counsel I shall gie thee,
> I'll never rue my trouble wi' thee,
>   The cost nor shame o't,
> But be a loving Father to thee,
>   And brag the name o't.—[40]

This is love-begotten, and it is a merry-begotten (glossed by Grose in his dictionary as 'a bastard'). The baby is 'Sweet fruit o' monie a merry dint'. Many, merry: they marry, even if the parents don't.

The poem welcomes and honours the baby Elizabeth, born of Elizabeth Paton: 'Wee image o' my bonie Betty'. The name is handed down, itself an inheritance, as though a happy counterpart to the unhappiness that moved Ben Jonson to honour his child, not newly born but newly dead: 'On My First Sonne'. 'BEN. IONSON his best piece of *poetrie*'. Jonson had to pen, not a welcome, but a farewell: 'Farewell, thou child of my right hand, and ioy'. Joy departed. For Burns, joy arrived.

The art has its merry-making, and its allusions range wildly. No studied propriety here. There is splicing, perhaps, but not the formal getting spliced that is matrimony; rather, affairs that are not without effrontery. Burns embraces *King Lear*. His pair of lines, 'Tho' ye come here a wee unsought for' and 'Tho' ye come to the warld asklent', is itself paired with the opening scene of *King Lear*: 'though this Knave came somthing sawcily to the world before he was sent for . . .'. Edmund, a bastard child who is no longer a child, is being uglily boasted about, to his face, by his father. The Earl of Gloucester's wife (like Elizabeth Paton) had 'a Sonne for her Cradle, ere she had a husband for her bed':

though this Knave came somthing sawcily to the world before he was sent for:

---

[40] Kinsley notes that the Glenriddell MS omits the penultimate stanza, perhaps accidentally, and he prints it within square brackets. In her edition, Carol McGuirk offers a different text and an appreciation of the poem.

yet was his Mother fayre, there was good sport at his making, and the horson must be acknowledged.[41]

Burns, in no way heartlessly, does have his own sport with this, and makes something of it, and would be happy to acknowledge it. The world of tragedy is there in Burns but as reminder and contrast. The destructive division of the kingdom is brought within the constructive spirit of the poem in lines that promise an inheritance in due course, an inheritance all the better for not being on the scale of a kingdom but of a last farthing:

> In my last plack your part's be in't,
> The better half o't.—

But then the more enduring inheritance that Burns wishes to grant his daughter is unworldly though not otherworldly:

> Lord grant that thou may ay inherit
> Thy Mither's looks an' gracefu' merit;
> An' thy poor, worthless Daddie's spirit,
>   Without his failins!
> 'Twad please me mair to see thee heir it
>   Than stocked mailins!

A blithely offhand rhyme, 'inherit' with 'heir it'. And this is at one with the manner, offhand and open-handed, with which Burns calls upon allusion. The bastard Edmund evinces an exacerbated superiority to the 'dull stale tyred bed' of matrimony; Burns can imagine how Edmund feels but can take a different tone in telling his as-yet-uncomprehending infant that she is treated as well 'As ony brat o' Wedlock's bed'.

But Burns's literary (as against hands-on) knowledge of bastards will not have been limited to *King Lear*. There is only one famous poem in English called *The Bastard*, and its author—Richard Savage—was put alongside Burns (and the marvellous boy) in Scott's stocks:

From the lives of some poets a most important moral lesson may doubtless be derived, and few sermons can be read with so much profit as the Memoirs of Burns, of Chatterton, or of Savage.[42]

Sermons: but what Burns sees is the propensity of preachers to be prurient.

---

[41] Kinsley does not adduce *King Lear*.
[42] 1812; *Burns: The Critical Heritage*, p. 42.

> Wee image o' my bonie Betty,
> As fatherly I kiss and daut thee,
> As dear and near my heart I set thee,
> > Wi' as gude will,
> As a' the Priests had seen me get thee
> > That's out o' h——.——

Even Kinsley, for all his love of Burns and of this poem, was a touch defensive when he characterized as 'defensive' some lines that are staunch:

This generous and affectionate poem (despite the defensive swagger in ll. 7–12, 43–48 [the second and the last stanzas]) is one of Burns's most endearing personal statements; contrast the attitude of the 'unco guid' fornicator [in 'Holy Willie's Prayer'].

Which brings us to Wordsworth, the unco guid fornicator who was a great poet—though not in his poem 'To the Sons of Burns, after Visiting the Grave of Their Father'.

> Through twilight shades of good and ill
> Ye now are panting up life's hill,

—no primrose path of dalliance for them. But the sons stand in need, it seems, of a warning about their father.

> For honest men delight will take
> To spare your failings for his sake,
> Will flatter you,—and fool and rake
> > Your steps pursue;
> And of your Father's name will make
> > A snare for you.

Whereupon the father who had abandoned his bastard child in France (Caroline, by Wordsworth, out of Annette Vallon) takes the high moral ground.

> His judgement, with benignant ray
> Shall guide, his fancy cheer, your way;
> But ne'er to a seductive lay
> > Let faith be given;
> Nor deem that 'light which leads astray,
> > Is light from Heaven.'
>
> Let no mean hope your souls enslave;
> Be independent, generous, brave;

> Your Father such example gave,
> And such revere;
> But be admonished by his grave,
> And think, and fear!

Dorothy Wordsworth wrote: 'The grave of Burns's son, which we had just seen by the side of his father, and some stories heard at Dumfries respecting the dangers his surviving children were exposed to, filled us with melancholy concern, which had a kind of connexion with ourselves'.[43] What kind of connexion exactly? Manifestly not of a kind that would move Wordsworth to contemplate himself and his past conduct. The climax of sanctimony is reached when Wordsworth makes out that it is Burns's grave that is doing the admonishing. Never does one feel more sympathy with Burns than when one sets him beside Wordsworth on Burns. Or when one sets Wordsworth's pinched invoking of Burns's lines ('Nor deem that "light which leads astray, | Is light from Heaven" ') alongside the magnanimity of Burns's lines themselves, and of their openly owing some of their light to the poet Young.

The terms 'legitimate' and 'illegitimate', then, when they are used of Burns's poems or their wording, touch something central to his life and his art.[44] John Logan said of Burns in 1787 that 'he has a genuine title to the attention and approbation of the public, as a *natural*, though not a *legitimate*, son of the muses'.[45] Jeffrey, in 1809, wrote of 'faults for which the defects of his education afford an obvious cause, if not a legitimate apology.'[46] Josiah Walker, in 1811, of out-of-the-way words: 'He afterwards employs them to express the meaning which they had conveyed to himself, and they come by his authority and adoption to be legitimated.'[47] Lockhart, in 1819, on 'The Jolly Beggars': 'half of the best ballads Campbell has written, are the legitimate progeny of some of these lines'.[48] The nineteenth-century editions of *The Merry Muses*

---

[43] *Recollections* (18 August 1803).

[44] As is clear from one of Burns's best critics and historians, Carol McGuirk, in *Robert Burns and the Sentimental Era*: for instance, 'when he attacks the legitimacy of marriage' (p. 19); 'attacking the whole idea that rituals can (and must) confer legitimacy on actions' (p. 25); 'Not only the legitimacy of being poor, but the ultimate salvation of "none but" the "social, friendly, honest man" is emphasized' (p. 29); 'This Muse which appears out of nowhere [in "The Vision"] to legitimize Burns has all the characteristics he has been promoting' (p. 39).

[45] *Burns: The Critical Heritage*, p. 76.

[46] Ibid., 181.   [47] Ibid., 35.   [48] Ibid., 308.

are 'illegitimate children' of the 1799 edition.[49] Kinsley: 'If any part of the song is a legitimate twin to the air, it is the second stanza, which has the appearance of a traditional fragment.'[50]

Again, if legitimacy or illegitimacy is critically to the point, so—repeatedly—is marriage. Here too is a commonplace figure of speech that is yet addressed to something uncommon in its nature and success. Scott speaks of one form of marriage for which Burns is famous:

> When his soul was intent on suiting a favourite air with words humorous or tender, as the subject demanded, no poet of our tongue ever displayed higher skill in marrying melody to immortal verse.[51]

Thomas Moore in 1841 likewise praised Burns's exercise of 'the rare art of adapting words successfully to notes, of wedding verse in congenial union with melody', as against 'the divorce between song and sense' in Moore's early days: 'That Burns, however untaught, was yet, in ear and feeling, a musician, is clear from the skill with which he adapts his verse to the structure and character of each different strain'.[52] But what Moore further valued in Burns was something more than this congruity, it was a new congruity, a fitness now first seen and heard:

> Still more strikingly did he prove his fitness for this peculiar task, by the sort of instinct with which, in more than one instance, he discerned the real and innate sentiment which an air was calculated to convey, though always before associated with words expressing a totally different feeling.

Yet there is another stage too. For the associations of an air are often set by Burns *against* the words. It is a good thing that Burns dissented from his publisher George Thomson, who was 'clearly and invariably for retaining the cheerful tunes joined to their own humorous verses, wherever the verses are passable'. To have concurred with Thomson would, as Kinsley remarks, 'have prevented the conception of some of Burns' best songs'.[53]

Burns knew, in playing the one element against the other, that he was playing along with a good old tradition:

> Do you know a droll Scots song, more famous for its humour than delicacy, called The grey goose & the gled?—Mr Clarke took down the notes, such as they are, at my request, which I shall give with some decenter verses to

---

[49] Kinsley, iii 993, quoting Egerer.   [50] Ibid. iii 1263, of 'Jumpin John'.
[51] *Burns: The Critical Heritage*, pp. 32–3.   [52] Ibid., 174–5.
[53] Kinsley, iii 1444, of 'Thou hast left me ever'.

Johnson.—Mr Clarke says that the tune is positively an old Chant of the ROMISH CHURCH; which corroborates the old tradition, that at the Reformation, the Reformers burlesqued much of the old Church Music with setting them to bawdy verses.[54]

It will often constitute the challenge to a critic of Burns, this need to discriminate between artistic failure (a bad fit of the words to the tune), and a particular kind of artistic success: the very good odd fit that is created when one of the media of a song, its tune, is set at right angles— or at any one of many pertinent angles—to the words. 'Moral indignation has caused Burns to slip unconsciously into the intonation of the Scottish Metrical Psalms' (Crawford).[55] Unconsciously? Perhaps. 'Some lyrics that work beautifully on the page are ill-matched to their tunes' (McGuirk).[56] Perhaps. But ill-matched may be well-judged. On occasion.

The other marriage within Burns's art is manifestly more troubled, less congenial—or rather is one of which the deeply congenial achievement is based upon an appreciated friction. This, in Crawford's compound words, is 'the task of wedding Celtic or semi-Celtic music to Scots-English words'.[57] For 'task', read 'challenge'. And let this be more than a wedding, let it be a marriage. (On the other hand, shouldn't *The Marriage of Figaro* be called *The Wedding of Figaro*?) And then let it be a marriage that, for all its true minds and its true relations of minds to bodies, does something benign with marriage's inevitable antagonisms and tensions.

Jeffrey needed to 'apprise our Southern readers, that all his best pieces are written in Scotch.'[58] By contrast, Crawford argues vividly that 'Burns's best work was produced by the coming together of two traditions, rather than by the victory of the Scottish one over the English.'[59] But what needs to be maintained is a sense that such a coming together is never easy. The art of union, like the Act of Union, is not simply either legitimate or illegitimate. The tension between one tongue and another, or between one form of a tongue and another, may itself offer possibilities for the making of a love that is unsentimentally alert to the clashes of life. Such art may well register the clash of one linguistic register against another.

[54] To George Thomson, September 1794; *Letters*, pp. 656–7; Burns then transcribed the poem.
[55] *Burns: A Study of the Poems and Songs* (1960), p. 88n.
[56] *Robert Burns and the Sentimental Era*, p. 120.   [57] *Burns: A Study*, p. 327.
[58] *Burns: The Critical Heritage*, p. 186.   [59] *Burns: A Study*, p. 133n.

'As always with Burns at his best, the motive for intermingling Scots and Scots-English is primarily an artistic one'.[60] But *intermingling* will not always be the best way to put it—too waterily at one, not relishing those discrepant colours and textures that are precipitated by oil's and water's refusal to intermingle. Unlike Burns's less smooth word ('intermixture'), intermingling is hostile to roughage.

This sense of valuable antagonism is in danger when David Murison, in his ranging essay on 'The Language of Burns',[61] mentions with entire equability 'Burns's skill in wedding the two linguistic traditions' (pronounced man and wife), and praises the poet's ability to 'marry the language of feeling with that of thought by conceiving both in their most concrete terms'. The word 'concrete' is blankly abstract there, and the move from 'marry' to 'conceiving' had better remain disembodied, given Burns's way of conceiving first and marrying afterwards if at all. But then in the vicinity of Burns's bawdy, sexual suggestions are unavoidable; Burns might have smiled at the description of 'the verses moving into and out of the vernacular idiom of the chorus'. Kinsley, who speaks so,[62] goodhumouredly distanced himself from what he called 'Burns's lurid (and fictitious) comparison'—involving three bastards at one apocryphal birth—when it came to 'Dainty Davie':

Dainty Davie,—I have heard sung, nineteen thousand, nine hundred & ninety nine times, & always with the chorus to the low part of the tune; & nothing, since a Highland wench in the Cowgate once bore me three bastards at a birth, has surprised me so much, as your opinion on this Subject.[63]

The hostile critics were right to feel that discrepancies and even hostilities, musical or linguistic, were at issue. Are we faced with a jumble of dialects? Was Southey right when he indicted the irresponsibilities of Scottishry?

The language is no more *spoken* there than here. It is a sort of Rowleyism, composed of all the Scotch words they can collect—as Chatterton raked in glossaries ... which allows him [an author] to introduce all the beastliest phrases and images in cant language, for which, if they had been in plain English or plain Scotch the book would have been deservedly thrown behind the fire.[64]

---

[60]   *Burns: A Study*, p. 233.
[61]   *Critical Essays on Robert Burns*, ed. Donald Low (1975), pp. 68–9.   [62] iii 1438.
[63]   To George Thomson, September 1793; *Letters*, p. 644.
[64]   Letter, 6 April 1805; *Burns: The Critical Heritage*, p. 169.

The appeal was to propriety, as it later was (though the propriety is different) when Iain Crichton Smith remarked: 'I do not think that "Mary Morison" is a typical Burns lyric. It seems to me to be too vitiated by a foreign poetic diction'.[65] But then Burns knew that he would be frisked in the Customs House of Language.

He was quick to bring together mischievously the linguistic and the sexual in his flyting, 'Literary Scolding—Hints'. It begins: 'Thou Eunuch of language—Thou Englishman who never was south the Tweed—Thou servile echo of fashionable barbarisms'. It proceeds to 'Thou Marriage-maker between vowels and consonants on the Gretna-green of Caprice', 'Thou Pimp of Gender', and 'Thou brood of the speech-distracting builders of the tower of Babel—Thou lingual confusion worse confounded'. And it indicts 'Thou murderous Accoucheur of Infant-learning'.[66] The bastard baby is not to live, for the accoucheur is the infanticidal midwife in league with the shamed unmarried mother.

Is *heteroglossia* then the unlovely word that we have been waiting for? David B. Morris needs it for 'Burns and Heteroglossia', an essay that condescends to and misrepresents Augustan poetry[67] but manages to move on from its straw men to the poet who is a brick. Morris posits persuasively that, 'as a Scottish poet who lived in the eighteenth-century, Burns might be considered a native speaker of heteroglossia'. It is misleading to follow the words 'Burns's writing' with the parenthetical 'however silent about its literary sources' (there are specific acknowledgements to poets and to poems), but it is true that 'There is no richer subject for illustrating the multiplicity of Burns's styles than love'. And Morris's evocation of heteroglossia would be applicable to the comedy, linguistic and social, of Burns's rhymes and of their relation of rhyme to such mischief as does not reason exactly. Say, *Pater / Fornicator*.

And my roguish boy his Mother's joy,
And the darling of his Pater,

[65] *The Art of Robert Burns*, ed. R. D. S. Jack and Andrew Noble (1982), p. 31.
[66] *Letters*, p. 726 (1787–8? 1791?); this flyting is acknowledged by the editor not to be a letter.
[67] *The Eighteenth Century*, xxviii (1987) 8–9: 'Burns moves his verse away from the homogeneous and stratified language of Augustan poetry and brings it much closer to the social discourses of everyday life. For example, his poetic epistles sound nothing like Pope's'. True, but for nothing like the reason given, and not with the implied adverse judgement on Pope's art.

> For him I boast my pains and cost,
>   Although a Fornicator.
>   ('The Fornicator' 29–32)

Or the rhymes in 'O leave novels, ye Mauchline belles', off to a good start with that very first rhyme (novéls?), and liking to set one voice against another: 'Your fine Tom Jones and Grandisons' (Fielding versus Richardson, there's heteroglossia for you, especially when Richardson is he of Sir Charles Grandison, what with the throbbing drawl that has to be put into the last syllable of Grandison if it is ever to rhyme with Jones). Or playing one tongue off another:

> The frank address, the soft caress,
>   Are worse than poisoned darts of steel,
> The frank address, and politesse,
>   Are all finesse in Rob Mossgiel.
>   ('O leave novels' 13–16, conclusion)

Tipped with high-gloss French, this, with its finesse. There is a touch of steel, as though in a duel between those whom the poem styles 'rakish rooks'. It is not that the languages marry in such heteroglossia. They circle one another warily, sparks who strike sparks.

There are more such linguistic duels, affairs of honour that have their links to the affairs of dishonour that bring bastards into the world. Take the bizarre couplings, of words with words and of tongues with tongues, in the 'Epistle to Captn. Willm. Logan at Park':

Ochon! for poor CASTALIAN DRINKERS,	*Alas*
When they fa' foul o' earthly Jinkers!	*sprightly girls*
The witching, curst, delicious blinkers	*oglers*
Hae put me hyte;	*crazed*
An' gart me weet my waukrife winkers,	*made . . . wet . . . wakeful eyes*
Wi' girnan spite.	*snarling*
	(55–60)

It is then itself 'cantraip' (witching) to rhyme the phrase 'Some cantraip hour' with 'Then, VIVE L' AMOUR!', an alliance between the Scots and the French that strikes or boxes the English ear. Burns had just spoken of taking off for the Indies; this makes him wax more than usually polyglottal, so that the very next lines follow 'Then, VIVE L' AMOUR!' with a further Frenchish polish, brightly running rhymes like this:

Faites mes BAISEMAINS respectueuse,	
To sentimental Sister Susie,	
An' honest LUCKY; no to roose ye,	*flatter*

> Ye may be proud,
> That sic a couple Fate allows ye
> To grace your blood.

Such a couple, or a triple: these are not *legitimate* rhymes; rather, they
are linguistic feats that judge legitimacy a narrow notion. One of
Burns's most generous bawdy poems, 'Libel Summons', proffers AMEN
at the end not of its last line but of its first (slily aware of the occasions
on which this, though surprising, is formally appropriate):

> In Truth and Honour's name, AMEN—
> Know all men by these Presents plain:—
>
> This fourth o' June, at Mauchline given,
> The year 'tween eighty five and seven,
> WE, Fornicators by profession,
> As per extractum from each Session,
> In way and manner here narrated,
> Pro bono Amor congregated;
> And by our brethren constituted,
> A COURT OF EQUITY deputed.—
> WITH special authoris'd direction
> To take beneath our strict protection,
> The stays-out-bursting, quondam maiden,
> With GROWING LIFE and anguish laden;
> Who by the rascal is deny'd,
> That led her thoughtless steps aside.—
>
> ('Libel Summons' 1–16)

'The stays-out-bursting, quondam maiden': this bastardized inspired
line owes its inspiration to Shakespeare, the taunt of Hector to
Agamemnon: 'Your *quondam* wife sweares still by *Venus* glove'.[68] But
Burns fills his line to bursting, with a compound epithet that is very like
and very unlike Hopkins: 'stays-out-bursting', a sequence that enacts
what it envisages. 'Libel Summons' is all for heterogeneity, and it
summons as witnesses both 'The coof that stands on clishmaclavers' and
(four lines later) 'We take cognisance thereanent'.

For we are to take cognisance of the ways in which the bastardy is
realized in a bastardized linguistic congress, Pro bono Amor, the poem
itself a by-job ('subsidiary employment, fornication'[69]):

---

[68] *Troilus and Cressida*, IV. v.
[69] A by-job, by extension, was a bastard, along with by-chop, by-blow, by-leap, by-slip,
and by-start.

He who when at a lass's by-job,
Defrauds her wi' a fr-g or dry-b-b;
The coof that stands on clishmaclavers   *fool . . . wordy talk*
When women haflins offer favors:—   *in half measure, nearly*
All who in any way or manner
Distain the Fornicator's honor,
We take cognisance thereanent,
The proper Judges competent.

(21–8)

'Clishmaclavers' clashes in its register with 'Defrauds' (here is no marriage register), as does 'fr-g' with 'honor', itself clashing with, though not annulled by, 'Fornicator': 'Distain the Fornicator's honor'. Yet all this is 'In truth and Honour's name', for the opening line does command this poem for all its comedy (or because of its comic apprehension of the serious virtues).

YOUR CRIME, a manly deed we view it,
As MAN ALONE, can only do it;
But, in denial persevering,
Is to a SCOUNDREL'S NAME adhering.

(109–12)

Women's honour is not as shamefully lost as is a man's honour when he settles for masturbation or never comes ('Defrauds her wi' a frig or dry-bob'), or when he denies that he got her with child, or when—ugliest of all—he presses her to abort her bastard child:

That ye hae made repeated trials
Wi' drugs and draps in doctor's phials,
Mixt, as ye thought, wi' fell infusion,
Your ain begotten wean to poosion.—

(69–72)[70]

No, the better part is that played by Burns, who loved his love-begotten weans, and who enjoys a duplicate pretension. Doubly so in that he had bastards by both Elizabeth Paton and Jean Armour—and twins, duplicates, by the latter: 'amorous mortgages double'.[71]

---

[70] Burns shuddered at the 'mildews of abortion'; see 'Nature's Law', p. 75 below.
[71] To Robert Muir, 8 Sept. 1786; *Letters*, p. 87: 'You will have heard that poor Armour has repaid my amorous mortgages double.—A very fine boy and girl have awakened a thousand feelings that thrill, some with tender pleasure and some with foreboding anguish, thro' my soul.—' To James Johnson, 25 May 1788; *Letters*, p. 293: 'I am so enamoured with a certain

FIRST, POET B—s he takes the chair;
Allow'd by a', his title's fair;
And pass'd nem. con. without dissension,
He has a DUPLICATE pretension.—
(29–32)

Nem. con. derives some of its comedy from its Latinate combination of the formal and the familiar (*nemine contradicente*? rather the reverse, linguistically), and the rest from the way in which nem. con. gazes straightfacedly across at crim. con. (criminal conversation, adultery). Byron, who learned a good deal from Burns, was later to spell out the pun in *Don Juan*:

And then he had good looks;—that point was carried
Nem. con. amongst the women, which I grieve
To say leads oft to *crim. con.* with the married—
(canto XV, stanza 84)

'Let me fair NATURE'S face descrive':[72] Burns was granted his wish. Nature recognizes natural children; but we must recognize, for our part, that nature offers not lawlessness but Nature's Law:

Keeping a proper regulation
Within the lists of FORNICATION.
('Libel Summons' 51–2)

Nowhere is Burns's art more properly regulated than in the play of registers in 'Nature's Law', a poem which, fecundated by a deep gratitude to Dryden and Pope, is one of Burns's greatest.

Nature's Law
Humbly inscribed to Gavin Hamilton, Esq.
'Great Nature spoke; observant man obey'd'—POPE

Let other heroes boast their scars,	
The marks of sturt and strife;	*violence*
And other poets sing of wars,	
The plagues of human life;	
Shame fa' the fun; wi' sword and gun	*boisterous sport*
To slap mankind like lumber!	
I sing his name, and nobler fame,	
Wha multiplies our number.	

girl's prolific twin-bearing merit, that I have given her a *legal* title to the best blood in my body; and so farewell Rakery!'
[72] 'To W. S[imso]n' 93.

Great Nature spoke, with air benign,
'Go on, ye human race;
This lower world I you resign;
Be fruitful and increase.
The liquid fire of strong desire
I've poured it in each bosom;
Here, on this hand, does Mankind stand,
And there, is Beauty's blossom.'

The Hero of these artless strains,
A lowly bard was he,
Who sung his rhymes in Coila's plains,
With meikle mirth an' glee;
Kind Nature's care had given his share
Large, of the flaming current;
And, all devout, he never sought
To stem the sacred torrent.

He felt the powerful high behest
Thrill, vital, thro' and thro';
And sought a correspondent breast,
To give obedience due:
Propitious Powers screen'd the young flow'rs,
From mildews of abortion;
And lo! the Bard—a great reward—
Has got a double portion!

Auld cantie Coil may count the day,
As annual it returns,
The third of Libra's equal sway,
That gave another Burns,
With future rhymes, an' other times,
To emulate his sire,
To sing auld Coil in nobler style,
With more poetic fire.

Ye Powers of peace, and peaceful song,
Look down with gracious eyes;
And bless auld Coila, large and long,
With multiplying joys;
Lang may she stand to prop the land,
The flow'r of ancient nations;
And Burnses spring, her fame to sing,
To endless generations!

'Make love, not war'—just as the tongues that are English and Scots make love in this song itself. Let others laud their military heroes; for my part,

> I sing his name, and nobler fame,
> Wha multiplies our number.

—where 'his name' is mine. Burns rings the changes on his own name (his own, yet not his alone), a father celebrating a day of birth, the day 'That gave another Burns', the day that anticipates the days of the future:

> And Burnses spring, her fame to sing,
> To endless generations!

Generations, as not only the offspring in descent but as the acts of generation to which the later generations will owe their existence. 'And Burnses spring': this is happily fluid, since the mountain streams— burns, overflowing into Burnses—all flow from springs. The exultant conclusion succeeds in turning into true singing what is usually a mere form of words, and this, not because other Burnses are intrinsically more important than 'other Blairs', but because the wilfully comic can be so much more serious than the willedly funereal:

> 'And I will join a Mother's tender cares,
> 'Thro' future times to make his virtues last,
> 'That distant years may boast of other BLAIRS—'
> She said, and vanish'd with the sweeping blast.
> ('On the Death of Sir J. Hunter Blair'
> 41–4, conclusion)

'Nature's Law' has at its head an epigraph from Pope. It has, throughout the body of the poem, words and phrases that would be appropriate to allusiveness, to the nature of allusion: 'multiplies', 'with air benign', 'Be fruitful and increase', 'share', 'a correspondent breast', 'equal sway', 'future rhymes', 'To emulate his sire', 'With more poetic fire', 'multiplying joys', and 'endless generations'. Of course all of these words are first and foremost evocations of sexual love, but all are happy to add to their happiness a sense of what it is to sing rhymes that are both yours and others', the poet grateful no less to the past than to the present and the future.

Burns's title, 'Nature's Law', combines with the epigraph to evince a

double gratitude to Pope. But then Pope had doubled here. For the
moment in *Eloisa to Abelard* recurs (is alluded to?) in the *Essay on Man*.

> O happy state! when souls each other draw,
> When love is liberty, and nature, law:
> > (*Eloisa to Abelard* 91–2)
> Converse and Love mankind might strongly draw,
> When Love was Liberty, and Nature Law.
> > (*Essay on Man*, iii 207–8)

This last couplet is to be found half a dozen lines after the line that
furnished Burns's epigraph (with Pope's 'men' changed to 'man'): 'Great
Nature spoke; observant Men obey'd'. Observant, as observing the
injunction, and as exercising powers of observation. Burns, too, is
observant.[73] He has Pope's lines play through many of his poems, 'Love
and Liberty' for one. And through his letters, where he speaks of a loved
one in the third person and addresses her in the second:

> I will regard my E. with the tenderest affection, and for this plain reason,
> because she is still possessed of these noble qualities, improved to a much
> higher degree, which first inspired my affection for her.

> > 'O happy state! when souls each other draw,
> > 'When love is liberty, and nature law.'

> I know, were I to speak in such a style of many a girl, who thinks herself
> possessed of no small share of sense, she would think it ridiculous—but the
> language of the heart is, my dear E., the only courtship I shall ever use to you.[74]

This is alive to, and with, Pope, 'this plain reason' being a wry memory
of the *Essay on Man*, i 193–4:

> Why has not Man a microscopic eye?
> For this plain reason, Man is not a Fly

—and 'the language of the heart' learned from 'An Epistle to Dr.
Arbuthnot' 398–9:

---

[73] See p. 55 above: 'till I set her down in the dearest records of my observation as . . .'.

[74] To Ellison Begbie, 1781?; *Letters*, pp. 45–6. Also to George Thomson, November 1794;
Letters, p. 662: 'Conjugal-love is a Passion which I deeply feel, & highly venerate; but somehow it does not make such a figure in Poesy as that other species of the Passion—"Where Love
is liberty & Nature law.—" Musically speaking, the first is an instrument of which the gamut
is scanty & confined, but the tones inexpressibly sweet; while the last, has powers equal to all
the intellectual Modulation of the Human Soul.—Still, I am a very Poet in my enthusiasm of
the Passion'.

Un-learn'd, he knew no Schoolman's subtle Art,
No Language, but the Language of the Heart.[75]

There is in Burns a characteristic rueful comedy that derives from speaking of the language of the heart in another's words, in the language of the poet.

'Nature's Law' honours his country ('auld Coila') in the act of rejoicing in the birth of (bastard) twins, 'a double portion!' The thought of inheriting this markedly Augustan term for inheritance, 'portion', pleases Burns: 'how do you like the following Apostrophe to Dulness, which I intend to interweave in "The Poet's Progress."—"O Dulness, portion of the truly blest!" '[76] The Poet's Progress is from Pope (and his goddess Dulness) to Burns. But there would have been no such progress had it not been for the progress from Dryden to Pope. It was Dryden who brought it about that there fell to Burns a double portion of his fathers' art.

> Or if thou would'st thy diff'rent talents suit,
> Set thy own Songs, and sing them to thy lute.
> He said, but his last words were scarcely heard,
> For *Bruce* and *Longvil* had a *Trap* prepar'd,
> And down they sent the yet declaiming Bard.
> Sinking he left his Drugget robe behind,
> Born upwards by a subterranean wind.
> The Mantle fell to the young Prophet's part,
> With double portion of his Father's art.
>   (*Mac Flecknoe* 209–17, conclusion)

'Set thy own Songs'? But Dryden's different talents are set within 'Nature's Law'.

Dryden: Songs, sing / Burns: sing (four times), song
Dryden: the . . . bard / Burns: the Bard
Dryden and Burns: the young
Dryden and Burns: double portion

<hr>

[75] The phrase is also in a letter to Margaret Chalmers, 21 October 1787?; *Letters*, p. 231: 'I hate dissimulation in the language of the heart'.

[76] To Frances Dunlop, 1 January 1789; *Letters*, p. 164. Also to James Smith, *c.*1 August 1786; *Letters*, p. 117: 'For me, I am witless wild, and wicked; and have scarcely any vestige of the image of God left me, except a pretty large portion of honour and an enthusiastic, incoherent Benevolence'. And to William Nicol, 20 February 1793; *Letters*, p. 349: 'May one feeble ray of that light of wisdom which darts from thy sensorium, straight as the arrow of Heaven against the head of the Unrighteous, & bright as the meteor of inspiration descending on the holy & undefiled Priesthood—may it be my portion'.

> Dryden: his father / Burns: his sire
> Dryden: art / Burns: artless

The thought of a double portion included a literary colouring for Burns: 'For my own part, a thing that I have just composed, always appears through a double portion of that partial medium in which an Author will ever view his own works'.[77] But he knew that the words 'double portion' were not simply his own work, since they were Biblical and moreover were Dryden's.

By a double portion of scholarship, Dryden's Oxford editor was also Burns's Oxford editor. James Kinsley cites for 'double portion' in *Absalom and Achitophel* 2 Kings 2: 9–13:

And it came to pass, when they were gone over, that Elijah said unto Elisha, Ask what I shall do for thee, before I be taken away from thee. And Elisha said, I pray thee, let a double portion of thy spirit be upon me. And he said, Thou hast asked a hard thing: nevertheless, if thou see me when I am taken from thee, it shall be so unto thee; but if not, it shall not be so. And it came to pass, as they still went on, and talked, that, behold, there appeared a chariot of fire, and horses of fire, and parted them both asunder; and Elijah went up by a whirl-wind into heaven. And Elisha saw it, and he cried, My father, my father, the chariot of Israel, and the horsemen thereof. And he saw him no more: and he took hold of his own clothes, and rent them in two pieces. He took up also the mantle of Elijah that fell from him, and went back.

Yet when it came to 'Nature's Law', Kinsley chose not to annotate 'double portion', either from the Bible or from Dryden.

True, there is 'Burns's own statement to Mrs Dunlop, 28 April 1788 that he had not read Dryden until early in 1788'.[78] Or is this a misreading? 'Your books have delighted me: Virgil, Dryden & Tasso were all equally strangers to me; but of this more in my next'.[79] But probably 'Virgil, Dryden' is one thing, not two. For a week later, Burns writes to Frances Dunlop: 'Dryden's Virgil has delighted me', and goes on to say: 'for, from every thing I have seen of Dryden, I think him, in genius and fluency of language, Pope's master'.[80] The accents of this are not those of a man who has just read Dryden for the first time.

---

[77] To Alexander Cunningham, 11 March 1791; *Letters*, p. 462.

[78] Crawford, *Burns: A Study*, p. 21n.

[79] To Frances Dunlop, 28 April 1788; *Letters*, p. 144. The word 'all' (not *both*) makes against my interpretation, but Burns did see Dryden's translation as multiple, and he was to contrast Dryden's Aeneid (by which he was 'disappointed') with the Georgics ('by far the best of Virgil').   [80] p. 145, 4 May 1788.

The bard got the loved bastard-twins because of his love for Jean Armour:

> And lo! the Bard—a great reward—
> Has got a double portion!

He got his verses because of his love for John Dryden. Allusion is itself not only a portion but a double portion. It is, moreover, a generation. This is the stronger in Burns because of his feeling for the erotic energy of the word 'double' itself.

> He stell'd his foot against a stane,   *fixed*
> And doubl'd ilka stroke in.
> ('The Trogger' 13–14)
>
> It's no the length that makes me loup,   *leap*
> But it's the double drivin.—
> ('Come rede me, dame' 19–20)[81]

To which may be added that poem that Burns loved, and quoted in his letters, about 'a grey goose & a gled': 'Double your dunts, the dame replied'. 'And a hey ding it in, it's lang to day'.[82]

So that when Burns hymns his native land with a prayer for fecundity:

> And bless auld Coila, large and long,
> With multiplying joys;

the words 'large and long' are to swell not only with the expanse of space and time but with the erotic energies of, say, a haggis:

> Fair fa' your honest, sonsie face,
> Great Chieftan o' the Puddin-race!
> Aboon them a' ye tak your place,
> Painch, tripe, or thaim:
> Weel are ye wordy of a grace
> As lang's my arm.
> ('To a Haggis' 1–6)[83]

In Thomas Crawford's eyes, Burns is not seen as practising allusion:

The reader is not at all conscious of these echoes [in 'The Twa Dogs'], because

---

[81] 7–8: 'I learnt a sang in Annandale, | Nine inch will please a lady'.
[82] To George Thomson, September 1794; *Letters*, p. 657. See p. 68 above.
[83] *OED* pudding, 5 b. the penis; since 1719.

in this poem, as in all his best works, Burns is no passive copyist but a creative artist fusing every scrap of tradition into a poetic whole that is qualitatively different from any extraneous elements which it may happen to have ingested.[84]

Read, mark, learn, and inwardly digest. For on occasion the creative fusion consists in what this contention (*because?*) rules out. A poet who alludes creatively is not a passive copyist, and a poetic whole may take up within itself a consciousness of echoes.

[84] *Burns: A Study*, p. 169.

Wordsworth

What, for Wordsworth, is the central or essential inheritance? And how might this validate the inheritance that is allusion?

That there are, for him as for all of us, irresponsible forms of inheriting is clear from how this figure of speech itself, inheritance, is at work within his evocation of lazy figures of speech. Deprecating such poetical diction as is slackness, which is content to rest upon others' laurels (and wilted ones at that), he writes in the Preface to *Lyrical Ballads* (1800):

> I hope it will be found that there is in these Poems little falsehood of description, and that my ideas are expressed in language fitted to their respective importance. Something I must have gained by this practice, as it is friendly to one property of all good poetry, namely good sense; but it has necessarily cut me off from a large portion of phrases and figures of speech which from father to son have long been regarded as the common inheritance of Poets.[1]

'The common inheritance of Poets' is sardonic in disowning an idle misapprehension, and this is registered in Wordsworth's language of indolent inheritance, his knowing but not minding that he has been *cut off from a large portion*. *From father to son*: Wordsworth, though his tone is not Dryden's, is no less sceptical when it comes to the thought of any easy and conclusive transference:

> The Mantle fell to the young Prophet's part,
> With double portion of his Father's Art.
> (*Mac Flecknoe* 216–17, conclusion)

But then Wordsworth's disrespect for any casually presumptuous inheriting is at one, naturally enough, with his deep respect for all true feelings of inheritance, those that respond to central responsibilities. For, as he says of 'Michael',

---

[1] Preface to *Lyrical Ballads* (1800); *The Prose Works of William Wordsworth*, ed. W. J. B. Owen and Jane Worthington Smyser (1974), i 132.

I have attempted to give a picture of a man, of strong mind and lively sensibility, agitated by two of the most powerful affections of the human heart; the parental affection, and the love of property, *landed* property, including the feelings of inheritance, home, and personal and family independence.[2]

Wordsworth's emphasis on *landed* underlines and underlies the word, giving the grounds for it. His manifest continuity with Augustan values is heard in these calm insistences, in the way in which these same words about affection, property, and independence might be used to call up so much in that very different poet, Pope.

Something as to a poet's sense of influence, and the particular forms that influence may take within allusion, may be seen in how he or she uses the word 'influence' itself. The invocations of influence in Wordsworth that follow here are all either allusions, or in the immediate vicinity of allusions, or both; moreover, all are either given or retain benignant adjectives, such as 'benignant' itself. This practice—to pick up Wordsworth's word as to the decisions that come to constitute a style—both ministers to reflection upon the nature of allusion itself (the word 'influence' itself enacting a relation that is a witness to influence) and at the same time braces this inward turn against a turn outward, towards the due acknowledgement of other creators from whom good things continue to flow.

Yet the equivocal aspect of influence or of being influenceable, influence as both inevitable and fraught (a feather for each wind that blows? plagiarism? are you your own man, or woman?), is manifest in the presence of those epithets of benignity upon which Wordsworth so calls. For they raise the question that adjectives always raise. Do they *introduce* a valuation, a distinction, acknowledging, say, that not all influence is of its nature benignant? (Or why would one be calling upon the adjective?) Or does the adjective *maintain* a valuation, confirming and corroborating what is already present within the noun, emphasizing an inherent benignity? This perennial possibility of doubt as to just how an adjective asks to be taken must make both for and against Harold Bloom's anxiety of influence. In so far as to call influence benign may be to concede that it is not always such, this introduces influence as a threat. In so far as to call influence benign may perfectly well be to maintain that this (*pace* Bloom and his insistence on the war-like) is exactly what influence is: this would be to find the relished anxiety a melodramatic luxuriation. Which leaves the possibility that in any relation of influence, it is not the inevitability of but the potentiality for envy and antagonism and malignity that is an encompassing element. Competitiveness may be the thing that should be competed with.

In any case, such is Wordsworth's way with the word and one familiar pairing with it: 'that shed | Mild influence'; 'Shed kindly influence'; 'Shedding benignant influence'; 'Shedding sweet influence'³—all of these acknowledging, without repining, the influence of Milton (mild, kindly, benignant, sweet) and his words, 'Shedding sweet influence', all seen by 'the sacred influence | Of light' (influence flowing over the line-ending).⁴

Since allusion depends upon apprehending a newly true combination of similitude and dissimilitude, allusion may be seen under the aspect of metaphor, may be seen as one form that metaphor may take, since just such a combination is what constitutes metaphor—and is what justifies the very high regard in which metaphor is held by Aristotle and by Wordsworth. Of 'the various causes upon which the pleasure derived from metrical language depends', Wordsworth says in one of his noblest rangings and gatherings:

Among the chief of these causes is to be reckoned a principle which must be well known to those who have made any of the Arts the object of accurate reflection; I mean the pleasure which the mind derives from the perception of similitude in dissimilitude. This principle is the great spring of the activity of our minds and their chief feeder. From this principle the direction of the sexual appetite, and all the passions connected with it take their origin: It is the life of our ordinary conversation; and upon the accuracy with which similitude in dissimilitude, and dissimilitude in similitude are perceived, depend our taste and our moral feelings.⁵

The prose is no less fine than is the invocation in the poetry:

---

³ *The Prelude* (1850), i 102–3; 'On Man, on Nature' 90; 'The Wishing-Gate' 20; *The Excursion*, vi 187.

⁴ *Paradise Lost*, vii 375; ii 1034–5. Wordsworth's epithets for *influence* further include: benign, blissful, breathing, congenial, diviner, 'fairest, softest, happiest', gladsome, heavenly, 'highest, holiest', kind, kindly, meek, reanimating, soft, touching, and wondrous. On one occasion a poem speaks of 'bad influence' but immediately transmutes it to the good: faced by pain, fear, and bloodshed, the Happy Warrior 'Controls them and subdues, transmutes, bereaves | Of their bad influence, and their good receives' ('Character of the Happy Warrior' 17–18). Such a redemption is sought everywhere by Wordsworth. For Wordsworth's 'A happy, genial influence', see p. 160 below, on Keats.

⁵ Preface to *Lyrical Ballads* (1800); *Prose Works*, i 148.

> Nature had framed them both, and both were marked
> By circumstance, with intermixture fine
> Of contrast and resemblance.
>
> (*The Excursion*, v 453–5)[6]

'Contrast and resemblance': not *or*. This or such was T. S. Eliot's way:

Readers of my *Waste Land* will perhaps remember that the vision of my city clerks trooping over London Bridge from the railway station to their offices evoked the reflection 'I had not thought death had undone so many'; and that in another place I deliberately modified a line of Dante by altering it—'sighs, short and infrequent, were exhaled.' And I gave the references in my notes, in order to make the reader who recognized the allusion, know that I meant him to recognize it, and know that he would have missed the point if he did not recognize it.[7]

Eliot's poem takes place here by courtesy of Dante's, and it courteously asks recognition of Dante and of this fact. Eliot would not have phrased things as Wordsworth did, would not have spoken so ringingly of 'The Poet, singing a song in which all human beings join with him', but he would have known what Wordsworth meant and would have granted that other poets are human beings too.

   Allusion takes a cue, especially when it calls drama into play, so let me take the cue of one of Wordsworth's emphatic allusions to *Hamlet* in his criticism: 'Emphatically may it be said of the Poet, as Shakspeare hath said of man, "that he looks before and after" '.[8]

> Sure he that made us with such large discourse,
> Looking before and after, gave us not
> That capabilitie and god-like reason
> To fust in us unusd.
>
> (IV. iv)

Allusion is itself a way of looking before and after, a retrospect that opens up a new prospect. To have been and to be, as against *to be or not to be*. Those words of Hamlet's (III. i) are among the most alluded-to in English literature. There is Eliot, or rather there is J. Alfred Prufrock, with his 'No! I am not Prince Hamlet, nor was meant to be'. There is Blake:

---

[6] The poems are quoted from John O. Hayden, *William Wordsworth: The Poems* (1977), to which is added *The Prelude: The Four Texts*, ed. Jonathan Wordsworth (1995).

[7] 'What Dante Means to Me' (1950); *To Criticize the Critic* (1965), p. 128.

[8] Preface to *Lyrical Ballads* (1850); *Prose Works*, i 141.

> To be or not to be
> Of great capacity
> Like Sir Isaac Newton
> ('An Island in the
> Moon')

And there is Wordsworth, who in a late poem, a Victorian poem (written 1846, published 1850), alludes to Hamlet's words with a hushed momentous equanimity:

> The unremitting voice of nightly streams
> That wastes so oft, we think, its tuneful powers,
> If neither soothing to the worm that gleams
> Through dewy grass, nor small birds hushed in bowers,
> Nor unto silent leaves and drowsy flowers,—
> That voice of unpretending harmony
> (For who what is shall measure by what seems
> To be, or not to be,
> Or tax high Heaven with prodigality?)
> Wants not a healing influence that can creep
> Into the human breast, and mix with sleep
> To regulate the motion of our dreams
> For kindly issues—as though every clime
> Was felt near murmuring brooks in earliest time;
> As, at this day, the rudest swains who dwell
> Where torrents roar, or hear the tinkling knell
> Of water-breaks, with grateful heart could tell.

The unremitting voice of this poem is heard winding its way, exercising its own tuneful powers, through a single sentence, seventeen lines of verse, 128 words. It not only speaks of, it realizes, an unpretending harmony, a flow, an unfacile fluency.

The poem has amplitude and leisure, wonder and ease—'Yet ease is cause of wonder', in the words of *Little Gidding*. It comes to rest with the words 'could tell' (both speak of, and count up), which is itself—within this pastoral poem—a healing of the pastoral split, for pastoral usually puts before us an encounter between those who can live truths and those who can tell of them, a leech-gatherer and a poet, say. 'If youth knew, if age could': this is a classic pastoral evocation of a meeting where each of the parties is to be both envied and pitied, and this without malignity or condescension. But the heart of the poem is in its allusion—

> To be, or not to be,

—the line that is at once a full line and a half line, half the length (the only such) of the other lines, while being half of a line in *Hamlet* (III. i):

> To be, or not to be, that is the Question.

Since 'To be, or not to be' is in Wordsworth both a complete line and a half line, it consorts happily with allusion, which is itself alert to the way in which there may be created a complete and even completely new thing that yet owes half its being to another.

'To be, or not to be, that is the Question': as soon as Wordsworth omits the second half of the measure, he cannot but invite the thought 'What is the question?', especially since he has lodged his words 'To be, or not to be' within a question, concluding with a question mark:

> (For who what is shall measure by what seems
> To be, or not to be,
> Or tax high Heaven with prodigality?)

In other words, less good words but perhaps a help: 'For who would be so presumptuous as to equate what is the case with what seems to be, or seems not to be, the case? And who would then be so presumptuous as to accuse Heaven of being wasteful, just because the music of the nightly streams may have no listeners?'

The words 'To be, or not to be' are old but are newly called into play, and with a new syntactical setting ('. . . measure by what seems | To be, or not to be'), while at the same time—or rather two and three lines later, ensuing even as they ensue in *Hamlet*—there arrive those other words of Hamlet's that likewise have become Wordsworth's, 'sleep' and 'dreams':

> to sleepe,
> To sleepe, perchance to Dreame; ay, there's the rub,
> For in that sleepe of death, what dreames may come,
> When we have shuffel'd off this mortall coile,
> Must give us pawse.

Wordsworth gives us pause. What he does in this poem is what he loves to do: to transmute nightmares into dreams for kindly issues. Such redemptions, such feats of rescue and renovation, are characteristic of how his mind works with allusions, and not his mind only but his heart.

What of his poem's form? It ends, as sonnets do not, with a rhyming triplet, and yet it might suggest a sonnet, being fourteen lines but with these lines encompassing within themselves a (parenthetical) three lines. It is within these three lines that Hamlet's six words live. Many a parenthesis is, by a traditional paradox of the parenthesis, at once central and an aside; Wordsworth's here calls to my mind the finely judged—and finely judging—'September Song' of Geoffrey Hill, which has as both centre and circumference a parenthesis:[9]

> (I have made
> an elegy for myself it
> is true)

What saves Wordsworth's poem from being too indebted, in its sober wit, to Shakespeare is its being happy to be scarcely less indebted to Milton.

> The unremitting voice of nightly streams
> That wastes so oft, we think, its tuneful powers,

—that's what *we* think. Or what we are tempted to think, presumptuously. Is it a waste of the streams' music that no one is awake to hear it? In *Paradise Lost* Adam, not yet fallen, entertains such misguided thoughts:

> How Nature wise and frugal could commit
> Such disproportions, with superfluous hand
> So many nobler Bodies to create,
> Greater so manifold to this one use,
> For aught appears,
>
> (viii 26–30)[10]

—whereupon Adam is benignly but stringently put right by Raphael.

'That wastes so oft . . .': there is no waste in Wordsworth's poem, no 'superfluous hand' (any more than there is with an imaginative allusion), and there is so much to receive 'with grateful heart'. Itself a richly Miltonic word, 'grateful' plays its part in the evocation of something paradisal, for in the best old days the word grateful meant pleasing as well as thankful, within a world in which if you were pleased you could not but be thankful. The sad split which prompts ingratitude is healed, even if only for the good while of Wordsworth's lovely poem. Paradise

---

[9] I have written about this in an essay on Hill, *The Force of Poetry* (1984), pp. 300–1.
[10] Wordsworth's 'by what seems | To be' owes something to Milton's 'For aught appears'.

is neither lost nor regained, but something of it is preserved, and is audible not only in the nightly streams but in the memory of the affable archangel who speaks to Adam with kindness and evenness: Raphael 'Benevolent and facil thus repli'd'.

The parenthesis that holds Hamlet's words is of three lines, and there is the final triplet, and there are three shaping spirits of imagination that foster the poem: Shakespeare, Milton, and Wordsworth. These are the three whom Keats honoured in an imaginative triangulation that understands the nature not only of a compliment but of complementarity too.[11] In this poem, the triangle is realized by Wordsworth himself. Neither Shakespeare nor Milton is an alluder to poetry within their own tongue, or—to put it more circumspectly—is much of an alluder hereabouts. There may be particular gains in this for a poet who duly alludes, uncompetitively then, to their art.

More ruefully, there is the reminder given by T. S. Eliot:

A poet cannot help being influenced, therefore he should subject himself to as many influences as possible, in order to escape from any one influence. He may have original talent: but originality has also to be cultivated; it takes time to mature, and maturing consists largely of the taking in and digesting various influences.[12]

Various influences: Wordsworth's poem (with the help of others' voices) speaks in its own voice of how 'The unremitting voice of nightly streams', 'That voice of unpretending harmony', 'Wants not a healing influence'. The poem is exquisitely and calmly alive to the nature of influence and of allusion, while not narrowing into the wrong kind of self-attention. For one unremitting voice is that of allusion itself, that does not waste its tuneful powers, and that is a voice of unpretending harmony (not pretending and not pretentious, and harmonizing its voice with another's), such as exercises a healing influence, that mixes with, and regulates, and moves to kindly issues—coming together in an art of (among other things) allusion, telling all this 'with grateful heart', the gratitude of one poet to another as issuing in a creation which leaves readers grateful to them both, to them all.

[11] Letter to J. H. Reynolds, 3 May 1818; *The Letters of John Keats*, ed. Hyder Edward Rollins (1958), i 275–83.
[12] A lecture in Dublin, 1936, published in *Southern Review* (Autumn 1985), and then in *T. S. Eliot: Essays from the Southern Review* (ed. James Olney, 1988), as 'Tradition and the Practice of Poetry', p. 13.

All this, then, as the flowing of influence, the streams and brooks coming together in the single sentence that is the river and the rhythm of this poem. One might apply John Beer's words from his essay on 'Coleridge and Wordsworth: Influence and Confluence': 'One could not grow up in the Lake District without being aware of water flowing and pouring on all sides—often from seemingly inexhaustible sources'.[13]

The nature of Wordsworth's success in 'The unremitting voice of nightly streams' may be seen the more clearly if it is contrasted with a quirk of his making that is offered as a cento. Putting together a poem that is nothing but lines from other poems is a parlour game such as on occasions may achieve a felicitous levity or wit. But Wordsworth was not cut out for parlour games or wit. The 'poem' (which he published in 1835 but wisely did not reprint) had an uneasy note:

For printing the following Piece, some reason should be given, as not a word of it is original: it is simply a fine stanza of Akenside, connected with a still finer from Beattie, by a couplet of Thomson. This practise, in which the author sometimes indulges, of linking together, in his own mind, favourite passages from different authors, seems in itself unobjectionable; but, as the *publishing* such compilations might lead to confusion in literature, he should deem himself inexcusable in giving this specimen, were it not from a hope that it might open to others a harmless source of *private* gratification.

The word 'source' ushered in a ninety word poem, all of it sources. The note was a hundred words.

> Throned in the Sun's descending car
> What Power unseen diffuses far
> This tenderness of mind?
> What Genius smiles on yonder flood?
> What God in whispers from the wood
> Bids every thought be kind?
>
> O ever-pleasing Solitude,
> Companion of the wise and good,
> Thy shades, thy silence, now be mine,
>   Thy charms my only theme;
> My haunt the hollow cliff whose Pine
>   Waves o'er the gloomy stream;
> Whence the sacred Owl on pinions grey

---

[13] *New Approaches to Coleridge*, ed. Donald Sultana (1981), p. 197.

> Breaks from the rustling boughs,
> And down the lone vale sails away
> To more profound repose!

Far from being more than the sum of its parts, this is less. But why? If broaching the nature of allusion while alluding (and what could be more allusive than a cento?) is such a good thing, why is this cento a bad thing? After all, or rather before all, it teems with phrases that are applicable to what allusion is. The opening six lines from Mark Akenside speak of an unseen power that diffuses far a tenderness of mind, and of a genius that smiles, that whispers, and that conduces to kind thoughts; what happier invocations of allusion could there be? More, the Akenside poem is called 'Against Suspicion', and this too is apt to allusion (suspicious readers or critics will call it plagiarism or appropriation). Yet again, the Akenside lines are themselves indebted to, and allude to, Milton's 'Il Penseroso' 153–4:

> Sent by som spirit to mortals good,
> Or th'unseen Genius of the Wood.

The seventh and eighth lines of the cento are from Thomson's 'Hymn on Solitude' (allusion being a way of escaping solitude, since allusion is companionship of a kind), and they speak of a companion and of properties of another that may 'now be mine', so again the allusion is related to allusiveness. And the rest of the cento is from Beattie's 'Retirement'—retirement with company, though, no longer 'lone'. So why does the cento amount to nothing (as Wordsworth himself came to realize)? Because the allusions to allusiveness are played against nothing; because Akenside, Thomson, and Beattie cannot bring to Wordsworth any resources to match not only Shakespeare's or Milton's but his, Wordsworth's own; and because nothing new is brought forth since there is no perception of similitude in dissimilitude—worse, there are not even similitude and dissimilitude, there is only the same, the lines from those three poets remaining obstinately the self-same self. These nullities vitiate the poem, these and the fact that playfulness (of the kind that would rescue a cento from flippancy or frivolity) is never Wordsworth's forte. Homo alludens he is, but not ludens.

That he misjudges his disposition (not just his character) in such matters is clear in the famous or notorious mock-heroic moments of his. Allusion often likes to play at or with a game ('A Game of Chess').

But Wordsworth solemnizes, and is never more unbending than when he tries to unbend. Take this memory of childhood:

> Eager and never weary we pursued
> Our home amusements by the warm peat-fire
> At evening, when with pencil and with slate
> (In square divisions parcelled out, and all
> With crosses and with cyphers scribbled o'er)
> We schemed and puzzled, head opposed to head
> In strife too humble to be named in verse;
>
>   (*The Prelude*, 1805, i 534–40)

This is an uneasy combination of quasi-epic ('too humble to be named in verse') and mock-epic, since this game of noughts and crosses toys with Milton's cosmic vastness as well as the archangel Raphael's warning within that reply to Adam's inquiry of which Wordsworth makes such imaginative use in 'The unremitting voice of nightly streams'. Raphael joins his God in mocking the future technicalities of vain astronomers:

>   how they will weild
> The mightie frame, how build, unbuild, contrive
> To save appeerances, how gird the Sphear
> With Centric and Eccentric scribl'd o're,
> Cycle and Epicycle, Orb in Orb:
>
>   (*Paradise Lost*, viii 80–4)

Milton's sardonic note, though harsh, carries weight. John Aubrey:

Extremely pleasant in his conversation, and at dinner, supper, etc, but Satyricall. He pronounced the letter "R"* [* Littera canina] very hard: a certain Signe of a Satyricall Witt. From John Dreyden.

In which case there could hardly be a better line for a satirical wit than 'With Centric and Eccentric scribl'd o're'. But Wordsworth's mock-heroic diminution is as nothing compared to Raphael's—and God's—mockery; 'With crosses and with cyphers scribbled o'er' is a weak attempt at what had been a strength in Pope: his bantering Milton.

    No, Wordsworth is at his best not when he toys with the mock-heroic but when he reverses such an impulse. He restores. Often it is dignity that he restores. The word is one that has its own power restored in his verse. Sometimes the restoration is of a unity at once personal, bodily, and political, since the body politic had in the seventeenth century taken pride in a tranquil Restoration:

> sensations sweet,
> Felt in the blood, and felt along the heart;
> And passing even into my purer mind,
> With tranquil restoration:—
> ('Lines Composed a Few Miles above
> Tintern Abbey, on Revisiting the
> Banks of the Wye . . .' 27–30)

Sometimes what is revisited and restored is a religious gratitude, as in the lines 'Composed upon an Evening of Extraordinary Splendour and Beauty':

> Oh, let Thy grace remind me of the light
> Full early lost, and fruitlessly deplored;
> Which, at this moment, on my waking sight
> Appears to shine, by miracle restored;
>
> (73–6)

'Appears to shine', not (it insists) as merely seeming to do so but as making its appearance now in order to shine. In this very poem he seeks to restore to his art the early art that had contemplated all that finds itself lost, adding in a note at the end: 'Allusions to the Ode entitled "Intimations of Immortality" pervade the last Stanza of the foregoing Poem'. (Yet in another sense 'Intimations of Immortality' *is* the foregoing Poem.)

Wordsworth regrets what was lost, but he regrets even more what was thrown away, wasted, demeaned. He is the great poet of restoration, of the restorative. Subversion has been overrated recently, or has at least been complacently promoted. Wordsworth is the opposite of subversive, since he is subversive of misguided subversion. The very early poem 'An Evening Walk' already shows him engaged in a progression that is a principled regression. For one of its lines alludes not only to a lovely one from Abraham Cowley ('And undisturb'd by *Moons* in silence sleep') but also to Dryden's parodic ways with Cowley's line in *Mac Flecknoe*, in mockery of it. Wordsworth restores the original, not only the line but the original spirit of the line, its positive standing as against the demeaning that it had suffered.

> Where peace to Grasmere's lonely island leads,
> To willowy hedge-rows, and to emerald meads;
> Leads to her bridge, rude church, and cottaged grounds,
> Her rocky sheepwalks, and her woodland bounds;

Where, undisturbed by winds, Winander sleeps
'Mid clustering isles, and holly-sprinkled steeps;
Where twilight glens endear my Esthwaite's shore,
And memory of departed pleasures, more.

Fair scenes, erewhile, I taught, a happy child,
The echoes of your rocks my carols wild:

('An Evening Walk' 5–14)

The allusiveness—the pertinence to allusion itself—of such a line as 'And memory of departed pleasures, more', like the mention of 'echoes', might alert us to a presence here.[14] 'Where, undisturbed by winds, Winander sleeps': this does not disturb the rhythm of the original line from Cowley ('And undisturb'd by *Moons* in silence sleep'), for Wordsworth chooses instead to introduce the undisturbing undulation of 'winds, Winander'. The placing of 'undisturbed' is not disturbed either (Cowley: 'And undisturb'd . . . .'; Wordsworth 'Where, undisturbed . . .').[15] Nor is the sound of the rhyme disturbed though it is modified: Cowley, *keep / sleep*; Wordsworth, *sleeps / steeps*.

Wordsworth is restoring something of Cowley's gravity, after Dryden's levity, a levity that had its own seriousness but of a kind that Wordsworth deprecated. The tables that had been turned are now turned again by the poet who would later write 'The Tables Turned'. Here is Cowley's remarkable passage, remarked and re-made by Wordsworth, sensitive to its understanding of Influence.

Beneath the silent chambers of the earth,
Where the *Suns* fruitful beams give *metals* birth,
Where he the growth of *fatal Gold* does see,
Gold which above more *Influence* has than *He*.
Beneath the dens where *unfletcht Tempests* lye,
And infant *Winds* their tender *Voyces* try,
Beneath the mighty *Oceans* wealthy Caves,
Beneath th'eternal *Fountain* of all Waves,
Where their vast *Court* the *Mother-waters* keep,

---

[14] On allusion and echo, see John Hollander, *The Figure of Echo: A Mode of Allusion in Milton and After* (1981).

[15] There is the same place within the line for the word, despite its being preceded by 'Not', in 'A Night-Piece', which ends:

At length the Vision closes; and the mind,
Not undisturbed by the delight it feels,
Which slowly settles into peaceful calm,
Is left to muse upon the solemn scene.

> And undisturb'd by *Moons* in silence sleep,
> There is a place deep, wondrous deep below,
> Which genuine *Night* and *Horrour* does o'reflow;
> No bound controls th'unwearied space, but *Hell*
> *Endless* as those dire *pains* than in it dwell.
>
> (*Davideis* i)

Dryden notoriously taunted this:

> Close to the Walls which fair *Augusta* bind,
> (The fair *Augusta* much to fears inclin'd)
> An ancient fabrick, rais'd t'inform the sight,
> There stood of yore, and *Barbican* it hight:
> A watch Tower once; but now, so Fate ordains,
> Of all the Pile an empty name remains.
> From its old Ruins Brothel-houses rise,
> Scenes of lewd loves, and of polluted joys.
> Where their vast Courts the Mother-Strumpets keep,
> And, undisturb'd by Watch, in silence sleep.
> Near these a Nursery erects its head,
> Where Queens are form'd, and future Hero's bred;
> Where unfledg'd Actors learn to laugh and cry, ⎫
> Where infant Punks their tender Voices try, ⎬
> And little *Maximins* the Gods defy. ⎭
> Great *Fletcher* never treads in Buskins here,
> Nor greater *Johnson* dares in Socks appear.
> But gentle *Simkin* just reception finds
> Amidst this Monument of vanisht minds:
>
> (*Mac Flecknoe* 64–78)[16]

Dryden's dealings with Cowley precipitated one of T. S. Eliot's most vivid demonstrations, responsibly speculative and finely focused:

Dryden continually enhances: he makes his object great, in a way contrary to expectation; and the total effect is due to the transformation of the ridiculous into poetry. As an example may be taken a fine passage plagiarized from Cowley, from lines which Dryden must have marked well, for he quotes them directly in one of his prefaces. Here is Cowley:

> *Where their vast courts*[17] *the mother-waters keep,*
> *And undisturbed by moons in silence sleep.* . . .
> *Beneath the dens where unfledged tempests lie,*
> *And infant winds their tender voices try.*

---

[16] On these lines as themselves alluding, see above, p. 10.   [17] Cowley has '*Court*'.

In *Mac Flecknoe* this becomes:

> *Where their vast courts the mother-strumpets keep,*
> *And undisturbed by watch, in silence sleep.*
> *Near these, a nursery erects its head,*
> *Where queens are formed, and future heroes bred;*
> *Where unfledged actors learn to laugh and cry,*
> *Where infant punks their tender voices try,*
> *And little Maximins the gods defy.*

The passage from Cowley is by no means despicable verse. But it is a common-place description of commonly poetic objects; it has not the element of *surprise* so essential to poetry, and this Dryden provides. A clever versifier might have written Cowley's lines; only a poet could have made what Dryden made of them. It is impossible to dismiss his verses as 'prosaic'; turn them into prose and they are transmuted, the fragrance is gone.[18]

As with so much true criticism by true poets, this tells us a great deal about the writer himself even while it does not reduce the objects of his attention to a mere excuse for self-attention. One is moved to think, for instance, of the contrast of Dryden's practice, which involves no disruption by Dryden of Cowley's rhythm, and Eliot's practice with a disturbed cadence and counterpoint, his ways not being the original's ways. (Not Goldsmith, 'When lovely woman stoops to folly', but 'When lovely woman stoops to folly and | Paces about her room again, alone'.) Again, Eliot not only cuts Cowley's lines but reverses the sequence of the couplets, without saying so; this, to bring the lines into line with Dryden's sequence—but necessarily changing the change that Dryden has made, his liberties—and making Dryden a touch more like Eliot himself when it comes to poetic licence or liberty.

Eliot takes some critical liberties, too. He doesn't say that Cowley is ridiculous, but the phrase 'the transformation of the ridiculous into poetry' sounds for a moment as if it might intimate such a judgement. There is some equivocation: Cowley's is 'a fine passage', which is more than what it is later granted ('by no means despicable verse'), with an insinuating slide in 'A clever versifier might have written Cowley's lines; only a poet could have made what Dryden made of them' (which puts Cowley in with the clever versifiers, not the poets . . .). In other words, there is a lot more going on in Eliot's criticism than an impartial reck-oning with Cowley and Dryden, and in some ways this is to the good.

---

[18] 'John Dryden' (1921), *Selected Essays* (1932, 1951), p. 308. The ellipsis is Eliot's.

What is distinctly odd, though, is Eliot's phrase 'a fine passage plagiarized from Cowley'. Plagiarized? And this even though Dryden quotes the lines 'directly in one of his prefaces'? Dryden is not plagiarizing but alluding.[19] And that he is doing so might be supported, yet once more, by the moments that are apt to allusiveness itself: Cowley's speaking of the fruitful, of giving birth, and of Mother-waters, and Dryden not only taking up and polluting those Mother-waters into Mother-Strumpets but speaking of a 'Monument of vanisht minds', itself alluding to yet another poet, Davenant. When Cowley imagines the exercising of 'more *Influence*', we might think again of influence in relation to confluence, and of the amniotic waters that minister to birth, 'the *Mother-waters*'.

In Dryden's sardonic setting, the 'ancient fabrick' is staged as 'Brothel-houses' and theatre-houses. He picked up Cowley's line 'And undisturb'd by *Moons* in silence sleep' while it slept, and carried it bodily from the silent chambers of the earth to the theatre-district, the red-light district, the combat zone, the world not only of the watch but of the watch-committee: 'And, undisturb'd by Watch, in silence sleep'. Wordsworth, in his turn, took the line from the dust and din and steam of town, out into the country: 'Where, undisturbed by winds, Winander sleeps'.

Wordsworth is not a poet who goes in for descending wittily from the sublime or the pseudo-sublime to the ridiculous (Eliot's word: 'the transformation of the ridiculous into poetry') or the ridiculed. True, 'the wordsworthian or egotistical sublime' (Keats's paradoxical paean-cum-caveat for Wordsworth)[20] does sometimes have its ridiculous side, but the Wordsworthian hope and feat are restorative, not demeaningful. See what he does with the tiny sketch of the passing of time, the chronographia, and in particular the one that speaks of night descending. Pope, having learned a trick or two from Dryden, had turned this chronographia upon his enemies, by contrasting this transitory passing with the vista of art's immortality—and next with the ephemerality of a poetaster's verses:

---

[19] See the essay on plagiarism, below, p. 219, with its insistence by Eliot himself in an interview in August 1961: 'In one of my early poems [*Cousin Nancy*] I used, without quotation marks, the line "the army of unalterable law . . ." from a poem by George Meredith, and this critic accused me of having shamelessly plagiarised, pinched, pilfered that line. Whereas, of course, the whole point was that the reader should recognise where it came from and contrast it with the spirit and meaning of my own poem'. (*Yorkshire Post*; *The Bed Post*, 1962, ed. Kenneth Young, pp. 43–4.)

[20] To R. Woodhouse, 27 October 1818; *Letters*, i 387.

> Now Night descending, the proud scene was o'er,
> But liv'd, in Settle's numbers, one day more.
> (*The Dunciad* A, i 87–8)

Wordsworth restores to its old dignity this turn, in a passage which has so many filaments to Pope's lines as to make this more plausible than it would be if everything turned upon two or three words, even when placed identically as they are.[21] Wordsworth bids the cuckoo God-speed:

> Thee gentle breezes waft—or airs that meet
> Thy course and sport around thee softly fan—
> Till Night, descending upon hill and vale,
> Grants to thy mission a brief term of silence,
> And folds thy pinions up in blest repose.
> ('The Cuckoo at Laverna' 108–12, conclusion)

Again, as with Wordsworth's rescuing Cowley's words from Dryden's clutches, there is a move from the fetid air of a cityscape ('Where City-Swans once sung within the walls', Pope's line 94) to the fresh air and 'airs' of the country. Again, there is the move from the wittily malign to the 'gentle' and benign, so that what in Pope had been the conversion of a traditional voicing of respect into the curled lip of contempt, to 'But liv'd, in Settle's numbers, one day more', has been restored by Wordsworth to the happy granting of 'a brief term of silence'.

Wordsworth comes to the end of his poem, comes to rest, with the word 'repose'. Pope, half a dozen lines after the settling of Settle's hash, arrives at his own kind of repose:

> Much she revolves their arts, their ancient praise,
> And sure succession down from Heywood's days.

Settle's one day is back again, in the sure succession of Dullness and dullards down from Heywood's days. For Pope, the sure succession, the one thing that can be counted on, is that of one bad poet after another. For Wordsworth, in his lines to the cuckoo and its voice ('Voice of the Desert, fare-thee-well; sweet Bird!'), there is such a thing as a positively sure succession, threatened though it always is by sarcasm, satire, and cynicism: the voices of nature, and the human voices that wake us so

---

[21] Pope, *The Dunciad* A, i 73–90, includes 'glads', 'flow'rs', 'green', 'snow', 'Glad', and 'Now Night descending'. Wordsworth, 'The Cuckoo at Laverna' 103, includes 'Now', 'snows', 'flowers', as well as later in the passage 'glad', 'green', and 'Till Night, descending'.

that we do not drown. Wordsworth's mission is to second their mission, as he can do by invoking, with perfect simplicity, the passing of time in 'Till Night, descending', where the sequence is that of Pope but the syntax is not, for in Pope the clause was absolute—the comma after 'descending', not before it: 'Now Night descending, the proud scene was o'er'. Wordsworth's night, unlike Pope's, is active in its syntax; it does something; it grants, and folds up.

Pope used a note in *The Dunciad* to mock not only Settle but the dead use of the 'But-lived-in-X's-art' compliment:

A beautiful manner of speaking, usual with the Poets in praise of Poetry, in which kind nothing is finer than those lines of Mr. Addison. [*A Letter from Italy* 31–6]

But it was Wordsworth's, not Pope's, ways with this turn that were to move Longfellow within two stanzas from one of his lasting poems, 'The Fire of Drift-Wood':

> We sat and talked until the night,
>   Descending, filled the little room;
> Our faces faded from the sight,
>   Our voices only broke the gloom.
>
> We spake of many a vanished scene,
>   Of what we once had thought and said,
> Of what had been, and might have been,
>   And who was changed, and who was dead;

Longfellow's turn—'until the night, | Descending'—shows its own new facet in what it does with time and with the line-ending. The voices that break the gloom are not 'ours', theirs, alone; scenes may have vanished but not entirely or how could they be spoken of?; what we once had thought and said finds itself corroborated by what others had thought and said; and the dead are not dead but alive, since their words are restored, changed. In these moving sobrieties, Longfellow, who recalls 'The long-lost ventures of the heart', is the heir of Wordsworth, warming himself at Wordsworth's heart and hearth. Allusion is, among other things, driftwood that supplies the fire.

Elsewhere in Wordsworth, Dryden and Pope play their part or parts, in ways that would have surprised them, within a poem that is remarkable, though not unfortunately unusual, in being so uneven: the sonnet, 'Roman Antiquities Discovered at Bishopstone, Herefordshire'.

While poring Antiquaries search the ground
Upturned with curious pains, the Bard, a Seer,
Takes fire:—The men that have been reappear;
Romans for travel girt, for business gowned;
And some recline on couches, myrtle-crowned,
In festal glee: why not? For fresh and clear,
As if its hues were of the passing year,
Dawns this time-buried pavement. From that mound
Hoards may come forth of Trajans, Maximins,
Shrunk into coins with all their warlike toil:
Or a fierce impress issues with its foil
Of tenderness—the Wolf, whose suckling Twins
The unlettered ploughboy pities when he wins
The casual treasure from the furrowed soil.

The inert complacency of Wordsworth's opening culminates in the absurd 'why not?' It is not until 'fresh and clear' that the poem becomes fresh and clear. And this is because it then discovers or uncovers the time-buried riches of Augustan poetry, Britain's Augustan age, not Rome's although the coins are Roman. From the self-same 'ancient fabrick' of Dryden's *Mac Flecknoe*, there surfaces the line 'And little *Maximins* the Gods defy'. Wordsworth shrewdly does not try to compete with Dryden's wit, the alternating expansion and contraction from 'little' into 'Maxi' and from 'Maxi' into 'mins' and hence into the preposterousness of 'the Gods defy'.[22] Instead, Wordsworth comes simply upon this: 'Hoards may come forth of Trajans, Maximins', a line that is followed by 'Shrunk into coins', with the plural 'Maximins' not a coinage of Wordsworth's. But then nor is this following line Wordsworth's coinage exactly or entirely: 'Shrunk into coins with all their warlike toil'. For this too is at once a borrowing and an allusion. Pope contemplated Ambition:

> Convinc'd, she now contracts her vast design,
> And all her Triumphs shrink into a Coin:[23]
> ('To Mr. Addison, Occasioned by his
> Dialogues on Medals' 23–4)

---

[22] In due course 'the gods' were to become 'the occupants of the gallery' in the theatre; not till 1752, though, if the *OED* is to be believed; 'the gods' would then be just the crowd for Dryden's 'unfledg'd Actors' to defy. The 'unfledg'd Actors' return, benignly playing their part in creating Wordsworth's 'unlettered ploughboy', and Dryden's sardonic 'tender' was restored as Wordsworth's 'tenderness'.

[23] Emrys Jones gave me this; I am grateful.

Dialogues: Pope engages in dialogue with Addison here, and then Wordsworth engages Pope in dialogue, not only thanks to 'shrink into a Coin' ('Shrunk into coins') but because behind Wordsworth's 'poring Antiquaries' there can be glimpsed not only the earlier antiquaries but the earlier poet: 'With sharpen'd sight pale Antiquaries pore' (Pope, line 35). Again there are the moments that might be seen as allusions to allusiveness: the 'search' that is conducted by poets as well as 'antiquaries'; the way in which something 'takes fire', and 'The men that have been reappear'; the sense of something 'fresh and clear' that 'dawns' from 'this time-buried pavement', all this rising to that which is so unexpected and so valuable though one always knew that such treasures lurk under the ground, 'when he wins | The casual treasure from the furrowed soil'. The unlettered ploughboy may not be able to read or write, but he is moved to pity, to a pity that moves the poet who can write of all this but who cannot live it as simply as does the ploughboy, who is no antiquary. The pastoral meeting is once again touchingly re-enacted by Wordsworth, and this with the help of allusions such as only the lettered can in certain ways understand. Dryden's fierce dislike of the squeaking youngsters ('Where infant Punks their tender Voices try') is hushed by Wordsworth into tenderness itself:

> Or a fierce impress issues with its foil
> Of tenderness—the Wolf, whose suckling Twins
> The unlettered ploughboy pities . . .

What in *Mac Flecknoe* had been at the expense of the Maximins is in Wordsworth credited, not debited. Pope, in his epistle to Addison, had not been engaged in his favourite art of shrinking in poetry when he visualized coins as at once contracted and vast:

> Convinc'd, she now contracts her vast design,
> And all her Triumphs shrink into a Coin.

So Wordsworth's allusion ('Shrunk into coins') is here happy to align itself with Pope's spirit, as against reversing the impulse.

But it remains crucial to Wordsworth's powers of affirmation that he should repeatedly, though not repetitively, give a further turn to what had previously been turned in a direction that he judges to be damaging; damaging, at any rate, whenever it implies that its direction leads not only to a truth but to the truth, the whole truth, and nothing but the truth.

Of his respect for Milton there can be no doubt, and this incorporates his respecting Milton for not respecting, not being taken in by, his own amazing feat of engineering, the building of Pandæmonium. It would have been sad but not surprising if Milton, devising and erecting this palace, had yielded for a moment to thinking better of it than it deserved, had taken pride in his own creation. But the evocation of Pandæmonium is unremittingly alive not only to the place's amazingness but to how far short it falls of the cosmic achievements of the true creator (Pandæmonium's fittings 'yeilded light | As from a sky').

> Anon out of the earth a Fabrick huge
> Rose like an Exhalation, with the sound
> Of Dulcet Symphonies and voices sweet,
> Built like a Temple, where *Pilasters* round
> Were set, and Doric pillars overlaid
> With Golden Architrave;
> (*Paradise Lost*, i 710–15)

The fallen angels were misguided in thinking they could compete with the supreme architect, superb though their creation is in its superbia. But Milton had forewarned mankind against feeling superior to the fallen angels' inferiority of creation.

> And here let those
> Who boast in mortal things, and wondring tell
> Of *Babel*, and the works of *Memphian* Kings,
> Learn how thir greatest Monuments of Fame,
> And Strength and Art are easily outdone
> By Spirits reprobate, and in an hour
> What in an age they with incessant toyle
> And hands innumerable scarce perform.
> (*Paradise Lost*, i 692–9)

It is characteristic of Milton to issue such a warning. What is characteristic of Wordsworth is the courage, effrontery even, with which he invokes Milton's Pandæmonium in order to help erect, or rather, to help complete, the cathedral at Cologne, and to help complete his sonnet. As so often, Wordsworth is audacious beyond belief.

> O for the help of Angels to complete
> This Temple—Angels governed by a plan
> Thus far pursued (how gloriously!) by Man
> ('In the Cathedral at Cologne')

Angels, not fallen angels. Gloriously, not vaingloriously. It is to the angels that Wordsworth appeals:

> 'twere an office meet
> For you, on these unfinished shafts to try
> The midnight virtues of your harmony:—

Yet how strange that Wordsworth wishes to invoke not Milton's Heaven but his Hell and its hellish simulacrum. For Wordsworth's sonnet ends:

> This vast design might tempt you to repeat
> Strains that call forth upon empyreal ground
> Immortal Fabrics, rising to the sound
> Of penetrating harps and voices sweet!

What we cannot close our ears to is the sound of Milton's lines and of his 'Fabrick' that 'rose' 'with the sound of' 'voices sweet'. Moreover, Wordsworth's 'tempt' and 'repeat' acknowledge the diabolical pastiche and how it was once rendered by Milton, while at the same time Wordsworth is convinced that the true cathedral will purify the false one, not the false one stain the true one. Again there is a reversal of the parodic. Milton realized, with immense art, the travesty or parody that is Pandæmonium; Wordsworth does not seek to compete with this (it is for fallen angels to enter into such competition), but he reverses the impulse, confident that he can purify the dialect of even this tribe. What Milton has legitimately parodied, Wordsworth will restore. What the devils have put asunder, Milton will join, rejoin.

Such a reversal from evil and its directions is central to Wordsworth's understanding of allusion. In his sonnet on godparents, 'Sponsors', Wordsworth sees no reason not to avail himself of certain wordings just because they might seem to have been irreparably soiled by their earlier utterance. (Take those words out of your mouth, you don't know where they've been. Or rather you do.) Sponsors underwrite allusions.

The sonnet ends without misgivings:

> Benign and pure
> This Ordinance, whether loss it would supply,
> Prevent omission, help deficiency,
> Or seek to make assurance doubly sure.
> Shame if the consecrated Vow be found
> An idle form, the Word an empty sound!

It is extraordinary (thrilling, perilous) that Wordsworth supposes that he can make his own assurance doubly sure by invoking 'the Word' only after he has invoked the words of Macbeth:

> SECOND APPARITION.   For none of woman borne
>   Shall harme Macbeth.
> MACBETH.   Then live Macduffe: what need I feare of thee?
>   But yet Ile make assurance double sure,
>   And take a Bond of Fate: thou shalt not live.
> (*Macbeth*, IV. i)

Allusion is itself a doubling (plagiarism is a duplicity), and allusion can constitute an assurance. Yet even Wordsworth cannot succeed here in cleansing Macbeth's ugly threat so that it can become the beautiful promise of a godparent. The point is not that it is out of the question for Wordsworth to possess the power to turn Macbeth's words through 180 degrees so that they will run in the opposite direction. 'My mind did at this spectacle turn round | As with the might of waters' (*The Prelude*, 1805, vii 615–16). But in the cathedral Wordsworth makes a spectacle of himself. It would take more than a little water, even from the godparents' font, to clear the words of Macbeth's deed. Wordsworth has not imagined what would effect what he honourably and responsibly seeks. This ordinance of allusion does not here supply enough, does not help deficiency, does not make doubly sure; rather, though itself 'conjoined' (Wordsworth's word for the formation *godfather*) allusion is found an idle form, the words an empty sound.

The contrast might be with what he does when, for instance, he directly challenges and reverses the impulse of the line in *Measure for Measure* (I. v), 'The wanton stings, and motions of the sence', so that it is purified into 'Those hallowed and pure motions of the sense' (*The Prelude*, 1805, i 578).[24] But a more telling contrast might be of another allusion to *Macbeth*, except only that whether there is an allusion is in dispute. It will sometimes be a characteristic of a successful allusion that its very existence is in question, for a successful allusion, like a successful pun of certain kinds, might be one that did not rely upon the allusion's being recognized but rather offered plenty to the reader who did not take the allusion—rather it may be harder to establish that there *is* a pun on occasions when each meaning makes perfect sense. (The one sense being quite sufficient.) One of Wordsworth's most touching

[24] William Empson has a superb essay on 'Sense in *Measure for Measure*', in *The Structure of Complex Words* (1951), contrasted with 'Sense in the *Prelude*'.

poems, 'The Two April Mornings', comes to its close after telling of a walk with Matthew, of how Matthew speaks of the death of his daughter, and of his visit to her grave, full thirty years ago:

> 'Nine summers had she scarcely seen,
> The pride of all the vale;
> And then she sang:—she would have been
> A very nightingale.
>
> 'Six feet in earth my Emma lay;
> And yet I loved her more,
> For so it seemed, than till that day
> I e'er had loved before.
>
> 'And, turning from her grave, I met,
> Beside the churchyard yew,
> A blooming Girl, whose hair was wet
> With points of morning dew.
>
> 'A basket on her head she bare;
> Her brow was smooth and white:
> To see a child so very fair,
> It was a pure delight!
>
> 'No fountain from its rocky cave
> E'er tripped with foot so free;
> She seemed as happy as a wave
> That dances on the sea.
>
> 'There came from me a sigh of pain
> Which I could ill confine;
> I looked at her, and looked again:
> And did not wish her mine!'
>
> Matthew is in his grave, yet now,
> Methinks, I see him stand,
> As at that moment, with a bough
> Of wilding in his hand.

The poem, one of Wordsworth's most heartfelt, asks the most tactful touch upon the word 'his' in that concluding stanza: '*his* grave', though lighter than those italics of mine suggest, itself 'turning from her grave' that was visited earlier in the poem. 'Matthew is in his grave, yet now': am I imagining a memory of *Macbeth*, or was Wordsworth doing the imagining? '*Duncane* is in his Grave'.

It is one resource of Wordsworth's genius that he restore to peace and peacefulness what is torn and rent. 'The Two April Mornings' touches upon the possibility of envy only to waive it ('I looked at her, and looked again: | And did not wish her mine!'); this, partly because of wishing never again to be put through the anguish visited upon a parent whose young child dies. The poem seems to me alive with, and alive to, the ways in which it differs, profoundly, from the world of *Macbeth*. These differences may be read as meaning that *Macbeth* has nothing to do with the poem, but they may no less be read as meaning more than one would ever have imagined for oneself. A pastoral relief, and elegiac release, from blood-boltered tragedy's brutal world of the killing of old men and of young children: this move from grand guignol to an ordinary sorrow of man's life is not nothing, yet it knows that it can never do enough to ameliorate these daily sorrows, here where young children die even when they are not killed, and when old men die too in their fullness of time. *Macbeth* is a parricidal play; it confronts the killing of a father, beyond even a father-figure ('Had he not resembled | My Father as he slept, I had done't', II. ii). 'The Two April Mornings' contemplates a father's mourning his child. Macbeth and Lady Macbeth have no children, or rather they no longer have any children. True, nothing could be more remote from the spirit of 'The Two April Mornings' than the aggrieved aggression of Macbeth's speech, but this remoteness may be to the point, may bring something home. 'Both the Worlds suffer'.

> But let the frame of things dis-joynt,
> Both the Worlds suffer,
> Ere we will eate our Meale in feare, and sleepe
> In the affliction of these terrible Dreames,
> That shake us Nightly: Better be with the dead,
> Whom we, to gayne our peace, have sent to peace,
> Than on the torture of the Minde to lye
> In restless extasie. *Duncane* is in his Grave:
> After Lifes fitfull Fever, he sleepes well,
> Treason ha's done his worst: nor Steele, nor Poyson,
> Mallice domestique, forraine Levie, nothing,
> Can touch him further.
>
> (III. ii)

This speech of perverse envy had previously shown Macbeth moving into self-protection, averting his eyes—and not only his eyes—from the aversion that he has from and for what he has done. Such murders as that of Duncan are—he would have it seem—brought about not by people but by abstractions (treason, steel, poison, malice domestic, foreign levy), all of them disowning Macbeth's own agency. Against this desperate sense of the world might be set Wordsworth's move—sad, yet not without gladness—to the specific, the authentic, the particular:

> Matthew is in his grave, yet now,
> Methinks, I see him stand,
> As at that moment, with a bough
> Of wilding in his hand.

Yet one might glimpse—with a sense of dissimilitude's outdoing similitude—in that bough of wilding in his hand a memory of an oracular particularity in *Macbeth*, Birnam Wood.

Norman Fruman has taken this suggestion by editors of Wordsworth as exemplarily ridiculous:

One might also wish that the editors were less accommodating in citing 'parallels' and 'influences' that have been claimed down the years. Why dignify the absurdity of quoting *Macbeth*'s 'Duncan is in his grave' as a possible source for Wordsworth's 'Matthew is in his grave'?[25]

Yet my position is closer to Fruman's than it might seem, for if I believed that what mattered about 'Duncan is in his grave' were its being a *source*, I'd hardly think it worth quoting. I believe that it is more vitally an allusion, and an allusion that is at one, first, with his particular gift for reversing an ugly or unlovely impulse into a dignified chastening one; and second with his general sense of a supreme principle: 'upon the accuracy with which similitude in dissimilitude, and dissimilitude in similitude are perceived, depend our taste and our moral feelings.'[26]

---

[25] *TLS* 27 August 1993, a review of the Cornell edition of *Lyrical Ballads*.

[26] I should distinguish from mine the position of Edwin Stein in *Wordsworth's Art of Allusion* (1988). His Conclusion says of 'comparative borrowings' (which he distinguishes from 'assimilative echoes'): 'the reader pursues the confrontation of texts demanded by such an allusion in expectation of an enriched understanding. But with assimilative echoes, the value of recognizing and of pursuing the relevance of the markers is less certain. Is there any value in knowing that "The Sparrow's Nest" appropriates some no longer well-known phrases from a poem by Charles Churchill that is thematically quite unrelated to Wordsworth's poem?' In a note, Stein adduces both Wordsworth, 'The Sparrow's Nest': 'She gave me eyes, she gave me ears' etc., and Churchill, 'Independence': 'she gave them eyes, | And they could see; she gave them ears—they heard' etc. Stein then comments: 'I feel confident that this echo is either coincidental or unconscious (the urtext for both poets is Acts 28: 27). Awareness of Churchill's context is counterproductive for the reader, and it would have proved counterproductive for Wordsworth in the act of composing had he brought it into focus. It is not simply that Churchill's satirical tone is so opposite to the homely mystique of Wordsworth's lines, but that the reversal of satire can have no functional meaning in the borrowing poet's piece. The

I arrive, at last, at what is probably the most important and the most famous allusion in Wordsworth, though one that is only half acknowledged by the poet. Namely, the presence of Young's *Night Thoughts* in some of the greatest lines of 'Lines Composed a Few Miles above Tintern Abbey':

> And I have felt
> A presence that disturbs me with the joy
> Of elevated thoughts; a sense sublime
> Of something far more deeply interfused,
> Whose dwelling is the light of setting suns,
> And the round ocean and the living air,
> And the blue sky, and in the mind of man:
> A motion and a spirit, that impels
> All thinking things, all objects of all thought,
> And rolls through all things. Therefore am I still
> A lover of the meadows and the woods,
> And mountains; and of all that we behold
> From this green earth; of all the mighty world
> Of eye, and ear,—both what they half create,
> And what perceive; well pleased to recognize
> In nature and the language of the sense,
> The anchor of my purest thoughts, the nurse,
> The guide, the guardian of my heart, and soul
> Of all my moral being.
>
> ('Lines Composed a Few Miles above
> Tintern Abbey' 93–111)

As to Young, the Wordsworth scholars have a way of not holding Wordsworth strictly to account here, preferring genial approximation. Wordsworth:

---

same is true of the implied ideation: for Churchill, nature's original gift of eyes, ears, and heart is primal and automatic; for Wordsworth it is won through increase of consciousness and must be mediated'.

But in my judgement 'assimilative echoes', Stein's main occupation, should not be considered allusions at all (rather, analogues or sources *not* called into play); at the same time the fact that the tone of an earlier poet's lines is 'so opposite to the homely mystique of Wordsworth's lines' can be the condition of unparalleled feats of allusion that run not parallel but at pertinent cross-purposes. At least, such is my argument about 'To be, or not to be' in 'The unremitting voice of nightly streams', and about 'Matthew is in his grave' in 'The Two April Mornings'. Unlike *Macbeth*, which is itself unremittingly imaginative about cross-purposes, Charles Churchill does not incite Wordsworth's purposes and cross-purposes; Churchill does not interest Wordsworth enough to constitute a hiding place of his power, as against a phrase-kitty.

> of all the mighty world
> Of eye, and ear,—both what they half create,
> And what perceive.

In his Oxford Authors *Wordsworth*, Stephen Gill has a note: 'W. notes the borrowing from Edward Young's *Night Thoughts* (1742–5), vi. 426: "And half create the wondrous World they see" '. But the words of Wordsworth's note are not given by Gill with the poem or in the notes. Similarly, Jonathan Bate reports that 'the allusion to Young is marked by a footnote'.[27] But Wordsworth's published footnote to line 106 (ending 'half create') doesn't say that he is alluding. Not that it musters a full acknowledgement either: 'This line has a close resemblance to an admirable line of Young's, the exact expression of which I do not recollect'. This is not admirable, this failure of recollection in too much tranquillity. (Could you not have looked up this admirable line, Mr Wordsworth?) The William Wordsworth who disingenuously penned the note is not my Wordsworth, not truly Wordsworth, I should like to think. He has the grudgingness of an envious critic, not the gratitude and generosity of a poet. The poet is, I judge, 'well pleased to recognize' not only 'In nature and the language of the sense' but in the language of Edward Young something to be grateful for, to acknowledge with thanks.

But it is only with the full passage from Young before us that we can see just how much Wordsworth had to be grateful for (and furthermore we too, given Wordsworth's unmatched poem).

> Where thy *true* Treasure? Gold says, 'not in me,'
> And, 'not in me,' the Diamond. Gold is poor;
> *India*'s insolvent; Seek it in Thyself;
> Seek in thy naked Self, and find it There.
> In *Being* so Descended, Form'd, Endow'd;
> Sky-born, sky-guided, sky-returning Race!
> Erect, Immortal, Rational, Divine!
> In *Senses*, which inherit Earth, and Heavens;
> Enjoy the various riches *Nature* yields;
> Far nobler! *give* the riches they enjoy;
> Give tast to Fruits; and harmony to Groves;
> Their radiant beams to Gold, and Gold's bright Sire;
> Take in, at once, the Landscape of the world,

---

[27] Jonathan Bate, *Shakespeare and the English Romantic Imagination* (1986), p. 99.

At a small Inlet, which a Grain might close,
And half create the wonderous World, they see.
Our *Senses*, as our *Reason*, are Divine.

(*Night Thoughts*, Night VI, 413–28)

Young's lines themselves allude, most powerfully to Milton; they don't just acknowledge a source. And the lines themselves, in alluding, point to allusiveness, in their understanding of what a 'true treasure' is; of what it is nevertheless to 'seek it in thyself'; of how, thanks to allusion (among other resources), poets can

Take in, at once, the Landscape of the world,
At a small Inlet, which a Grain might close,
And half create the wonderous World, they see.

Young anticipates Wordsworth in the imaginative insistence that it is 'In *Senses*, which inherit Earth, and Heavens' that we possess the most astonishing and indubitable human inheritance. 'Our *Senses*, as our *Reason*, are Divine'.

'And half create the wonderous world, they see': Young's passage is itself half-created from *Paradise Lost*. (Eight lines later in Young: 'Like *Milton's Eve* when gazing on the Lake'.) For Young's 'Erect' and 'Far nobler' not only derive from but are meant to set before our eyes 'Two of far nobler shape erect and tall, | Godlike erect' (*Paradise Lost*, iv 288–9), even while Young is well aware that his art and his vision are not 'Far nobler' than Milton's. No less germane is the allusion within the line that Wordsworth came to allude to: 'And half create the wonderous World, they see'. For this itself, though created by Young, is only half created by him, since it too comes by courtesy of Milton:

who overcomes
By force, hath overcome but half his foe.
Space may produce new Worlds; whereof so rife
There went a fame in Heav'n that he ere long
Intended to create,

(*Paradise Lost*, i 648–52)

When Wordsworth finds himself drawn to a line of Young's, then, it is one that is not entirely of Young's making, any more than Wordsworth's line or lines will be. Yet there remains a vast difference in the scale of the accomplishment that these allusions that reflect upon allusiveness can effect. Young makes something of Milton, but Wordsworth creates

immensely from Young. How? Through his deep sense of all that can
become animated in the scrupulously surprising details of what might
seem to be a simple succession, a sure succession, of words:

> of all the mighty world
> Of eye, and ear,—both what they half create,
> And what perceive;

It was to the word 'create' that Wordsworth appended his notorious
note about 'This line'. But it is not this line alone that resembles the
'admirable line of Young's'; rather, this and the previous line of
Wordsworth, since he owes not only 'half create' to Young but 'world'
too. Moreover, what follows in Wordsworth, 'And what perceive', must
owe something to Young ('they see'). Young is diffused through several
lines, just as his repeated tribute to 'the senses' plays some part in what
immediately follows in Wordsworth:

> And what perceive; well pleased to recognize
> In nature and the language of the sense,

To speak in the singular, of 'This line', is along the wrong lines, for it is
in the 'exact expression' of Wordsworth that the genius is realized. What
is so fine about the sequence

> —both what they half create,
> And what perceive

is that these clauses themselves constitute two half lines, and the more
so in that they could perfectly well, or rather much less perfectly, have
constituted a single line: 'Both what they half create, and what
perceive', an unimpeachable line of Wordsworthian blank verse but
much less of an enactment than are the two half lines. Wordsworth's
genius was in his seeing that Young's line, 'And half create the wonderous World, they see', would be the more wondrous for dramatizing the
word *half*. A swell of complacency, of inordinate pleasure in the
cadence, is resisted by the need to move across the line-ending, just as
it is in Shakespeare's lineation in *King Lear* (III. ii): not 'I am a man,
more sinn'd against than sinning', but

> 'I am a man,
> More sinn'd against, than sinning.'
> 'Alacke, bare-headed?'

There is a similar resistance to the complaisancy of the single-line cadence in the original lineation of the ending to Robert Lowell's poem 'Water', in *For the Union Dead* (1965):

> We wished our two souls
> might return like gulls
> to the rock. In the end,
> the water was too cold for us.

In the unrhymed-sonnet return to the poem in *History*, Lowell relented, relaxed, and slackened this into the very different and less compelling story that is told by the words when they are straightforwardly marshalled, too plainly pointed, doubly, by periods and line-endings:

> We wish our two souls might return like gulls to the rock.
> In the end, the water was too cold for us.
>   ('For Elizabeth Bishop 1. Water')

Young's line, then, falls short of Wordsworth's because Young does not halve, he only speaks of half. But then nor had Wordsworth created this particular halving in a fragment ('Yet once again . . .', written a year or two before 'Tintern Abbey') that proffers what might have seemed to be the same thought:

>   that peculiar voice
> Heard in the stillness of the evening air,
> Half-heard and half-created.
>   (4–6, conclusion)

This little fragment leaves itself half-created, and ends with a half line, but Wordsworth has not yet arrived at the inspired lineation of 'Tintern Abbey'. Inspired not only in the lineation, though, for one of the best touches is the way in which Wordsworth, unlike in the fragment ('Half-heard and half-created'), does not offer an unequivocal half-and-half; rather,

>   —both what they half create,
> And what perceive;

Did Wordsworth consciously appreciate the art of that *semi*-colon of his?

I remember the pleasure with which in 1978 I read an advertisement:

Sixth Annual Conference on Twentieth-Century Literature
23–24 February 1978
University of Louisville, Louisville, Kentucky
An interdisciplinary conference
on all national literatures

For I liked the idea of an interdisciplinary conference on all national literatures that could effect its ends in a mere two days (fast food for thought). But it was not with pleasure that I saw the title of the conference:

NATURE: HALF-CREATED /
HALF-PERCEIVED.

This is a travesty as well as a misquotation. Wordsworth, for all his egotistical sublimity, did not judge himself to be in a position to assure his readers that it was six of one and half a dozen of the other: 'what they half create' is balanced against 'And what perceive' without claiming to know that the latter amounts to half exactly.

Since allusion involves availing yourself of another's game without just being a poacher, it likes to make play with the word 'half'. Any successful allusion is comprised of what is half created and what is perceived, and Wordsworth enjoys bringing the word 'half' into the immediate vicinity of a source or an allusion,[28] rather as he effected a great deal by positioning the words 'To be, or not to be' so that they were a whole line but looked like a half line.

> —As homeward through the lane I went with lazy feet,
> This song to myself did I oftentimes repeat;
> And it seemed, as I retraced the ballad line by line,
> That but half of it was hers, and one half of it was *mine*.
> ('The Pet Lamb: a Pastoral' 61–4)

In its capacity for love, 'half' may be understood as restorative, a making whole or holy (the words are at root one). And this may undertake the redemption of evil. So the poet who gives us the vision of the senses—the most important inheritance of all, with pre-eminent among

---

[28] For instance, 'An Evening Walk', with 'antique roots' (67) from *As You Like It*, followed two lines later by 'Half grey, half shagged', and with 'Gives one bright glance' (191) from Thomson who has 'half-immers'd' in the previous line. 'Louisa', with 'beneath the moon' (19, in quotation marks) from *King Lear* followed in the next line by 'half a noon'. 'The sun has long been set', with 'parading' / 'masquerading' (10–11, in quotation marks) from Burns followed two lines later by 'half-moon'.

them the eye and the ear—might try on occasion to redeem a very different half-creation, the unformed or malformed. This is what underlies another of Wordsworth's allusive decisions (one from which he later retreated), his wishing to call to mind—in a wholly holy setting—the unholy body and being of Richard, Duke of Gloucester:

> I, that am curtail'd of this faire Proportion,
> Cheated of Feature by dissembling Nature,
> Deform'd, un-finish'd, sent before my time
> Into this breathing World, scarse halfe made up,
> And that so lamely and unfashionable,
> That dogges barke at me, as I halt by them.
>
> (*Richard III*, I. i)

'Into this breathing World, scarse halfe made up': what was Wordsworth thinking of when he thought that he could simply disinfect those words of Richard's? (Well, I think that I know, but still.)

> When I began at first, in early youth
> To yield myself to nature, when that strong
> And holy passion overcame me first,
> Neither the day nor night, evening or morn,
> Were free from the oppression. But, great God,
> Who sendest thyself into this breathing world
> Through nature and through every kind of life,
> And makest man what he is, creature divine,
>
> (*The Prelude*, 1805, x 381–8)

This evokes not only 'into this breathing world', but the hideous harshness of Richard's line, 'Cheated of Feature by dissembling Nature', to be converted from gall to manna, to the serenity of 'Through nature and through every kind of life'. But then Richard, for all his faults, is one form that life does take. Whatever he may lack, it is not life.

J. C. Maxwell said flatly of Wordsworth's 'into this breathing world': 'A rather unfortunate echo, which Wordsworth perhaps removed for that reason'.[29] The last few lines of Wordsworth's passage, in relinquishing the obnoxious, were to become in 1850 innocuous:

> But, O Power Supreme!
> Without Whose call this world would cease to breathe,
> Who from the fountain of Thy grace dost fill

---

[29] *The Prelude: A Parallel Text* (1971).

> The veins that branch through every frame of life,
> Making man what he is, creature divine,
>> (*The Prelude*, 1850, x 420–4)

Wordsworth did not stand by his original act of courage; perhaps he judged that its insisting on the converse of the original was perverse. Or perhaps he found it ultimately ineffective as I find 'assurance doubly sure' singularly ineffective. But he never ceased to be haunted by those dark words of Richard's:

> Too late—or, should the providence of God
> Lead, through dark ways by sin and sorrow trod,
> Justice and peace to a secure abode,
> Too soon—thou com'st into this breathing world;
>> ('The Warning' 82–5)

> Memorial Pillar 'mid the wrecks of Time
> Preserve thy charge with confidence sublime—
> The exultations, pomps, and cares of Rome,
> Whence half the breathing world received its doom;
> Things that recoil from language;
>> ('The Pillar of Trajan' 35–9)

Sometimes Wordsworth recoiled from language, from others' language that he had thought to make his own, the words 'breathing world' for instance, fascinated by them though or because he was.

But what is lasting is that from which Wordsworth did not recoil,

> all the mighty world
> Of eye, and ear,—both what they half create,
> And what perceive.

In due course, Wallace Stevens was to do some half-creating along Wordsworth's lines.

> The Planet on the Table

> Ariel was glad he had written his poems.
> They were of a remembered time
> Or of something seen that he liked.

> Other makings of the sun
> Were waste and welter
> And the ripe shrub writhed.

> His self and the sun were one
> And his poems, although makings of his self,
> Were no less makings of the sun.

It was not important that they survive.
What mattered was that they should bear
Some lineament or character,

Some affluence, if only half-perceived,
In the poverty of their words,
Of the planet of which they were part.

Stevens was glad Wordsworth had written his poem, 'Whose dwelling is the light of setting suns'. This we can at least half-perceive, here where affluence meets influence, enriching with allusion what might otherwise be a poverty of the words.

The inheritance of the senses, though, ceases to be centrally animating in late Wordsworth. Instead of the vibrant, there comes the throbbing, a need for more voicing of the words than the great Wordsworth asks. Grandiloquence comes, even on true occasions, to take the place of simple eloquence. Allusion continues to play a part, but the part is less challenging, less challenged, in its relation both to the great predecessors and to the poet himself. The 'After-Thought' may be heard to dwindle into an afterthought.

The River Duddon: After-Thought

I thought of Thee, my partner and my guide,
As being past away.—Vain sympathies!
For, backward, Duddon! as I cast my eyes,
I see what was, and is, and will abide;
Still glides the Stream, and shall for ever glide;
The Form remains, the Function never dies;
While we, the brave, the mighty, and the wise,
We Men, who in our morn of youth defied
The elements, must vanish;—be it so!
Enough, if something from our hands have power
To live, and act, and serve the future hour;
And if, as toward the silent tomb we go,
Through love, through hope, and faith's transcendent dower,
We feel that we are greater than we know.

This has its own dignity, but it is not a dignity newly won, provocatively wrested from indignity. 'The Form remains, the Function never dies': this looks for a moment as though it might be sensitive to a cross-current, but no, 'The Form' and 'the Function' are equably at one, just as are 'remains' and 'never dies'. There is nothing inherently slack or slackened about gliding, and yet 'Still glides the Stream, and shall for ever glide' invests all its liquid assets in equanimity. One misses the crisp choppiness of Wordsworth's earlier waters, even when they might at first seem to be placidly level: 'Where, undisturbed by winds, Winander sleeps'. Not without knowledge of disturbance, for 'undisturbed' cannot but put us in mind of what disturbance is.

The whole of this fluence poem to the River Duddon bears upon and is borne upon by allusion; but Wordsworth no longer finds—or finds of deep interest—that which stands in need of redemption or which meets resistance. Unless, that is, the presence of *Paradise Lost* is more disturbing than it might seem. Wordsworth's note acknowledges viii 282:

> Tell, if ye saw, how came I thus, how here?
> Not of my self; by some great Maker then,
> In goodness and in power præeminent;
> Tell me, how may I know him, how adore,
> From whom I have that thus I move and live,
> And feel that I am happier than I know.
>
> (viii 277–82)

The allusion here acknowledges 'some great Maker', with the artist (Milton, Wordsworth. . .) exercising the præeminent power, the primary power. In the words of Coleridge:

The primary IMAGINATION I hold to be the living Power and prime Agent of all human Perception, and as a repetition in the finite mind of the eternal act of creation in the infinite I AM. (*Biographia Literaria*, chapter 13)

Allusion is, in the most straightforward sense, a secondary imagination, though it can achieve a primary power. If Wordsworth's allusion in the River Duddon sonnet falls short of his supreme re-creations, this may be because it does not altogether apprehend the greatness of which it avails itself. 'And feel that I am happier than I know': this in Milton is at once paradoxical and lucid, a contemplative strangeness that is the counterpart to the Irish charm of that oddly Wordsworthian writer, Samuel Beckett:

> Do you feel like singing? said Camier.
> Not to my knowledge, said Mercier.
> (*Mercier and Camier*)[30]

---

[30] (1974), chapter II, p. 25.

The paradox at the moment in *Paradise Lost* is authenticated by the double sense of 'happy', its invoking in addition to a feeling of felicity a state of felicity. Wordsworth's 'greater' cannot effect any such amplitude; it is the grander word but the narrower thought. And Wordsworth's 'We' (the perilous 'We' of 'While we, the brave, the mighty, and the wise') comes to lack appeal: 'We feel that we are greater than we know'.

A happier place to end, then, will be at a truer river-poem, and a truer allusion, on a smaller scale admittedly than the sonnet to the River Duddon, but returning to the intimate intermixture of streams and of gratitudes heard in 'The unremitting voice of nightly streams'.

Wordsworth's 'Remembrance of Collins Composed upon the Thames near Richmond' derives much of its beauty from its unrepining love of succession, its lines succeeding those of Milton that speak candidly of a turn that serves us all and is not just a matter of serving one's own turn:

> So may som gentle Muse
> With lucky words favour my destin'd Urn,
> And as he passes turn,
> And bid fair peace be to my sable shrowd.
>
> ('Lycidas' 19–22)

Gratitude is a nub of much art, and may be judged the nub of allusion, however mixed with other feelings may be 'The sweet creative voice of gratitude'.[31] A critic ought to participate in such gratitude, not only to poets but to critics. For instance, to John Hollander for his fine pages in *The Figure of Echo* on just how James Thomson, and Denham ('Cooper's Hill', on the Thames), live on in Wordsworth's poem, a ghost of remembrance. William Collins, least serene of men, gained serenity in his 'Ode Occasioned by the Death of Mr Thomson':

> REMEMBRANCE oft shall haunt the Shore
> When THAMES in Summer-wreaths is drest,
> And oft suspend the dashing Oar
> To bid his gentle Spirit rest!
>
> (13–16)

---

[31] 'Fragment: For let the impediment be what it may', where it is asked, of the poor man, 'Whence is he to hear | The sweet creative voice of gratitude?'

From Thomson to Collins, and then from Collins to Wordsworth, 'Bound each to each by natural piety'. In this poem the reiterated gliding can be felt to be less of a surrender than it is in the sonnet to the River Duddon, for now serenity is glimpsed as a perpetual victory over the despondency and madness that may imperil every poet.

Remembrance of Collins Composed upon the Thames near Richmond

Glide gently, thus for ever glide,
O Thames! that other bards may see
As lovely visions by thy side
As now, fair river, come to me.
O glide, fair stream! for ever so,
Thy quiet soul on all bestowing,
Till all our minds for ever flow
As thy deep waters now are flowing.

Vain thought!—Yet be as now thou art,
That in thy waters may be seen
The image of a poet's heart,
How bright, how solemn, how serene!
Such as did once the Poet bless,
Who murmuring here a later ditty,
Could find no refuge from distress
But in the milder grief of pity.

Now let us, as we float along,
For *him* suspend the dashing oar;
And pray that never child of song
May know that Poet's sorrows more.
How calm! how still! the only sound
The dripping of the oar suspended!
—The evening darkness gathers round
By virtue's holiest Powers attended.

One of the holiest of virtue's powers is gratitude, heartfelt in Wordsworth's feeling for the sweet creative voices of allusion.

Byron

There is no longer a word for what used to be called cant, or in Victorian times humbug. (Bullshit, for which a poem in 1915 by T. S. Eliot furnishes the earliest *OED* citation, is something else, since it doesn't have to imply a mouthful of piety.) We still have plenty of opprobrious terms for ways of speaking of which we disapprove, but none of them catches *cant*, with its insinuation of hypocrisy tinged with self-deception: 'a stock phrase that is much affected at the time, or is repeated as a matter of habit or form', 'phraseology taken up and used for fashion's sake, without being a genuine expression of sentiment' (*OED*). There 'genuine' is good, because it waives any need to enter upon the distinction between sincerity and authenticity.

Dr Johnson's urgings to Boswell have become famous for their genuine expression of sentiment.

'My dear friend, clear your *mind* of cant. You may *talk* as other people do: you may say to a man, "Sir, I am your most humble servant." You are *not* his most humble servant. You may say, "These are sad times; it is a melancholy thing to be reserved to such times." You don't mind the times. You tell a man, "I am sorry you had such bad weather the last day of your journey, and were so much wet." You don't care six-pence whether he was wet or dry. You may *talk* in this manner; it is a mode of talking in Society: but don't *think* foolishly.'[1]

'Come off it' calls cant's bluff. ('Come now' and 'Come come' are more admonitorily appealing.) This injunction puts it to you, not that you should stop talking, but that you should stop pretending—not only to your interlocutor but to yourself. For this 'come off', the *OED*'s citations include the *Century Dictionary* of 1899: 'to cease (fooling, flattering, chaffing or humbugging); desist; chiefly in the imperative'.

Byron, who honoured Johnson, is likewise and differently the puncturer of cant. He comes up with countless ways to intimate 'Come off it', while being aware that the phrase lends itself to a burliness that is

---

[1] 15 May 1783; Boswell, *Life of Johnson*, ed. George Birkbeck Hill, rev. L. F. Powell (1934–50), iv 221.

not his way. If we were to put it to him that for Dryden and Pope the most important human inheritance is the throne, or the succession from poet to poet, and for Wordsworth the eye and the ear as the paramount senses, Byron would suspect us of cant. Come now: the crucial or essential inheritance is money.

Byron's ways with allusion live within the familiar triangle of, first, literary reference; second, of reference to the nature of allusion itself (with the allusion's not only speaking of but being an inheritance of a sort); and, third, of historical reference (life and times). The life reference may be a death reference, as when in 1822 Byron imagines George III, who had died in 1820 and has been admitted to Heaven. Southey had mourned the royal passing in *A Vision of Judgment* (1821). The next year, Byron showed how much can be effected by a change of article (for *A*, read *The*), so that Southey might find himself snuffed out by an article.

> A general bustle spread throughout the throng,
> Which seem'd to hold all verse in detestation;
> The angels had of course enough of song
> When upon service; and the generation
> Of ghosts had heard too much in life, not long
> Before, to profit by a new occasion;
> The Monarch, mute till then, exclaim'd, 'What! what!
> *Pye* come again? No more—no more of that!'[2]
> (*The Vision of Judgment*, stanza 92)

Allusion had better not hold *all* verse in detestation, though it may be a way of holding verse. But the shades of the dead were not going 'to profit by a new occasion'. In this, the otherworldly ghosts differ from worldly Southey, who knew which side the royal slice of bread was buttered.

The publisher of Byron's poem was not to profit; he was prosecuted, convicted, and fined. But Byron profited from a ready and free and easy way with the common wealth that is allusion.

What is so telling about 'No more—no more of that!' is its casualness, its having no airs, its having the air of a perfunctory formula. And yet it is unobtrusively an allusion. The words say 'No more—no more' but they bring something more with them: a memory of another king

---

[2] The poems are quoted from Jerome J. McGann, *Lord Byron: The Complete Poetical Works* (1980–93).

who had gone mad. Or rather, two memories of him, since the simple words come from his lips twice, very differently and yet with excruciating coherence. The Knight speaks to Lear of Cordelia's exile:

> 'Since my young Ladies going into *France* Sir, the Foole
> hath much pined away.'
> 'No more of that, I have noted it well.'
> (*King Lear*, I. iv)
> 'Your old kind Father, whose franke heart gave all,
> O that way madnesse lies, let me shun that:
> No more of that.'
> (III. iv)

In its defiance of the thought 'No more of that' (by contrariously insisting on there being more of it, a repeated attempt to push something aside), this in *King Lear* is at once aligned with the nature of allusion itself and athwart.[3] Byron, in alluding to the moment of royal imperiousness that yet acknowledges madness, braces the doubly allusive (outwards and inwards) against the straightforwardly referential. For behind George III's exclamation ('What! what! | *Pye* come again? No more—no more of that!'), there lurks not only the fact that the execrable Poet Laureate Pye has been succeeded by the execrated Poet Laureate Southey (*Mac Flecknoe* to be succeeded by *Mac Pye*?); and not only the implication that the true succession, thanks to the allusion, is from Shakespeare and his King to Byron and his; but the further grounding in historical fact. For George III was a 'What! what!' man, and he vented this impatience upon those who honoured Shakespeare's memory not on this but on that side idolatry. Byron may have had a grudging admiration for George III's freedom from cant here; at least he was no Bardolater.

'Was there ever,' cried he, 'such stuff as great part of Shakespeare? only one must not say so! But what think you?—What?—Is there not sad stuff?—what?—what?'[4]

Shakespeare's art was often, for George III, sad stuff. The death of the King is, for Byron, not sad, though unfortunately it lent itself to the sad stuff that is Southey's funeral elegy. 'Only one must not say so!' Byron was born to say the things that people say one must not say.

---

[3] McGann's commentary does not adduce *King Lear*.
[4] Fanny Burney's journal, 19 December 1785.

'To profit by a new occasion': the fiscal figure of speech may have worn thin but is still legal and artistic tender. Not that Byron has to rely upon figures of speech when it comes to money. His burgeoning cata-logue of all that is sweet in life pauses here:

> Sweet is a legacy, and passing sweet
>   The unexpected death of some old lady
> Or gentleman of seventy years complete,
>   Who've made 'us youth' wait too—too long already
> For an estate, or cash, or country-seat,
>   Still breaking, but with stamina so steady,
> That all the Israelites are fit to mob its
> Next owner for their double-damn'd post-obits.
>
> (*Don Juan*, canto I, stanza 125)

Following the word 'legacy', as though a legacy of it, the surpassing epithet 'passing'—'and passing sweet | The unexpected death . . .'—is en route to death, with the passing bell softly sounded. Then the word 'complete' completes the first rhyme of the stanza (though happy then to run to a further rhyme). What saves 'complete' from being callous is its measured respect for the Book of Common Prayer and its human span: 'The days of our age are threescore years and ten'. 'Seventy years complete': nobody's life has been cut short, even though somebody's has been cut off. The fullness of time: nothing is here for tears . . . 'Still break-ing but with stamina so steady': for a moment this sounds as though it might be the person, not the estate and country-seat. But in due course it has to be the bankrupt country-seat, given the words 'its | Next owner'.

The heart of the stanza is the legacy that comes to it, the allusion that Byron then holds up for our attention as though conducting an auction: 'us youth'. Any dictionary-based supposition that allusion is characterized by being covert or indirect will have some explaining to do when it comes to Byron's practices. He often relishes the overt allu-sion, proffering it as possessing the indisputability, the clarity of outline, that money has.

'Bacon-fed Knaves, they hate us youth; downe with them, fleece them' (*1 Henry IV*, II. ii). Falstaff is robbing the travellers, only to be later robbed himself by Hal and Poins. Is allusion an act of fleecing? Not necessarily, but Byron does well to acknowledge ruefully that allusion must expect to be suspected of robbery. The alluder belongs to a later generation than the alluded-to; in this, and not only in this, Byron sides with 'us youth'. That it should be preposterous old Falstaff who speaks so:

this adds to the comedy. Does it add a personally Byronic note? Jonathan Bate thinks so: 'Occasionally he also reveals some of Falstaff's vulnerability, for example when he refers self-consciously to "us youth" '.[5] Byron, in arming himself with those two words of Falstaff's, may be judged to acknowledge vulnerability (for why else would he arm himself?), but 'self-consciously referring'?

Relatedly, one might both agree and disagree with Peter Manning when he says, with this instance in mind, that 'minor allusions in these stanzas typify the problems of discrimination that study of the texture of Byron's verse encounters'.[6] Yes, discriminations need to be made, but isn't 'minor' a major prejudgement?

Is the phrase 'us youth' in I, 125, one of Byron's favorite epithets, *calculated* to remind the reader of the desperate, aging Falstaff of *2 Henry IV*? And, whether deliberate or automatic, how much does it add to the reader's sense of the sordid world depicted in the stanza?

The phrase 'us youth' comes in the First Part of *Henry IV*; this would not rule out an extension to take in the 'desperate, aging Falstaff', but the moment in *1 Henry IV* is not of desperation but of aggressive effrontery. Manning's terms for Byron's allusive practice (*'calculated'*, italicized, and 'deliberate or automatic') too starkly limit the possibilities when it comes to things coming to a writer's mind and finding themselves called into play. Moreover, the tone of Byron's lines may be heard as less indignant, less censorious, than Manning posits. He values the stanza for its indictment of a sordid world, a money-hungry, unfeeling society. But the wish for money, and the need for it, are not limited to the avaricious; Byron was one of the least avaricious of men, true, but this doesn't mean that he didn't have a healthy respect for those who had a healthy respect for money. The love of money cannot be the root of *all* evil since the hatred of money can lend itself to self-righteous evil.

Granted, Jonathan Bate does well to contrast Byron's ways and Keats's, when it comes to another allusion to Shakespeare:

> This is the literary *lower* Empire,
>   Where the Praetorian bands take up the matter;—
> A 'dreadful trade,' like his who 'gathers samphire,'
>   (*Don Juan*, canto XI, stanza 62)

---

[5] *Shakespeare and the English Romantic Imagination*, p. 241.
[6] *Byron and His Fictions* (1978), p. 203.

This gathers something, at some risk (including the risky Empire/ samphire rhyme), from Dover Cliff in *King Lear*, IV. v:

> Halfe way downe
> Hangs one that gathers Samphire: dreadful Trade:[7]

But should Byron's means be reduced to Bate's account of what we are to gather from the samphire-gatherer?:

For Keats, he is an image of the poet precipitately at work on the 'Cliff of Poesy'; for Byron, 'dreadful trade' acts as an image of the reduction of literature to commerce (the tyranny of the cash-nexus is a theme that recurs throughout *Don Juan*).[8]

But the literary *lower* empire is not the entire empire of literature, and anyway Byron's attitudes to money, inside or outside the poetry, are not those of Carlyle or Marx. Byron might take the credit and let the cash-nexus go. Clenching money was something that Byron deplored, yes, as he deplored all meanmindedness, but 'the reduction of literature to commerce'?

There can hang around these ways of putting it a whiff of priggishness or of cant. Byron's genius was for comedy, not satire, and he has uncommon common sense. Dr Johnson was not cynical but realistic when he put it to the world that 'No man but a blockhead ever wrote, except for money',[9] and that 'There are few ways in which a man can be more innocently employed than in getting money'. 'If you suppose I don't mind the money—': Byron's sequence of thought characteristically passes on but it never repudiates the worldly wisdom, for he goes on to make clear that although there are things that trump money, they can't afford to be sanctimonious:

If you suppose I don't mind the money—you are mistaken—I do mind it most damnably—it is the only thing I ever saw worth minding—for as *Dervish* told me it comprehends all the rest;—but Honour must be considered before it & friendship also—[10]

It is his word 'post-obits' that holds together the daily world of finan-

---

[7] *Sampire* in the Folio.
[8] *Shakespeare and the English Romantic Imagination*, p. 241. *The Letters of John Keats*, ed. Rollins, i 141; May 1817; see p. 174 below.
[9] Boswell, 5 April 1776; 27 March 1775.
[10] To J. C. Hobhouse, 25 January 1819. *Byron's Letters and Journals*, ed. Leslie A. Marchand (1973–1982, 1994), vi 96.

cial transactions and the larger air that will value those things such as art, the laying up of treasures where neither rust nor moth doth corrupt and where thieves do not break through and steal. 'I do mind it most damnably'. 'Their double-damn'd post-obits'. Allusions are, with luck or felicity, double-*blest* post-obits. 'Bonds, payable after someone's death, made to secure payment of a loan with interest': Byron appreciates the term not only for its fiscal hardheadedness but for its casting a cold eye on art and its high hopes. Here, too, he urged realism—and grateful approbation before it was too late. He translated Martial, Book I, epigram i:

> He unto whom thou art so partial,
> Oh, reader! is the well-known Martial,
> The Epigrammatist: while living,
> Give him the fame thou wouldst be giving;
> So shall he hear, and feel, and know it:
> Post-obits rarely reach a poet.[11]

There is a happy dryness in 'rarely' (I'm not saying never), with something of the judiciousness as to pronouncements about the afterlife that is evinced by the two simple words 'I think' in Marvell's 'To His Coy Mistress':

> The Grave's a fine and private place,
> But none I think do there embrace.

What was *Don Juan* going to be taken to be? Byron could not help wondering, and he put forward more than one possibility:

> or it may be supposed the work of a rival poet obscured, if not by the present ready popularity of Mr. Southey, yet by the post-obits he has granted upon posterity and usurious self-applause in which he has anticipated with some profusion perhaps the opinion of future ages, who are always more enlightened than contemporaries—[12]

Byron despises such gullibilities. He has no time for the other-worldly, for 'the post-obits of theology' or for 'a firm Post Obit on posterity'[13]. Post Obit / posterity: preposterous.

---

[11] Martial: 'cui, lector studiose, quod dedisti | viventi decus atque sentienti, | rari post cineres habent poetae' (Loeb: 'Devoted reader, the glory you have given him while he lives and feels comes to few poets in their graves'). This comes in at a different angle from Byron.

[12] Unincorporated preface to *Don Juan*, canto I, about the Dedication to Southey.

[13] *Don Juan*, canto I, stanza 103; canto XVII, stanza 9. The word 'post-obits' was valued too by Thomas Moore and was of the day.

> He that reserves his laurels for posterity
> (Who does not often claim the bright reversion?)
> Has generally no great crop to spare it, he
> Being only injured by his own assertion;
> (*Don Juan*, Dedication, stanza 9)

But we are Pope's posterity, and his laurels and lines are a reserve upon which we may call, a crop that was garnered, a bright reversion themselves—and this with the pleasure that comes from Byron's reversing the consonants so that 'reserves' enjoys a conversion as 'reversion'.

> Is there no bright reversion in the sky,
> For those who greatly think, or bravely die?
> ('Elegy to the Memory of an
> Unfortunate Lady' 9–10)

Reversion: 'the return of an estate to the donor or grantor, or his heirs, after the expiry of the grant'; 'a sum which falls to be paid upon the death of a person, esp. as a result of life-insurance'.

Byron is our best poet of reversions, of money, often by largesse with the change that is allusion. 'Minor allusions'? Small change? But Byron's allusions, like his rhymes, enjoy the music that is made possible by coins, not large notes. Other denominations: this is one way of thinking about allusions. Byron is the rhymester who breaks the rhyme-word 'posterity' down into the jingling change of 'spare it, he'; or 'forty' down into 'in short, I' / 'to retort; I'; or 'economy' down into 'not one am I' / 'alone am I'.[14] And Byron is the poet who has the coinage 'us youth' chinking in his pocket or in his purse.

> Then Money came, and chinking still,
> What tune is this, poore man? said he:
> I heard in Musick you had skill.
> *But thou shalt answer, Lord, for me.*
> (George Herbert, 'The Quip' 9–12)

You would think that so important, contentious, and everyday a thing as money would have figured variously and vigorously in English poetry.[15] Pouncings in Pope ('Of the Use of Riches'), grotesquerie in Hood ('Miss Kilmansegg and Her Precious Leg'), a parable from Larkin

---

[14] *Don Juan*, canto I, stanza 213; *The Vision of Judgment*, stanza 13.
[15] I draw here upon a review of Doris Langley Moore's *Lord Byron: Accounts Rendered* (1974) that I wrote for the *Sunday Times*.

('Money'): these are much in credit. But Byron is the poet who has shown the multiplicity and oddity of our attitudes to money, all of them human and some of them humane. In the most direct, most properly novelistic way, Byron is warmly adept—Dickensian in his casual quick-sightedness—at catching what it feels like to see somebody buying something. Or even buying someone, as at the slave-market:

> At last they settled into simple grumbling,
>   And pulling out reluctant purses, and
> Turning each piece of silver o'er, and tumbling
>   Some down, and weighing others in their hand,
> And by mistake sequins with paras jumbling,
>   Until the sum was accurately scann'd,
> And then the merchant giving change, and signing
> Receipts in full, began to think of dining.
>
> (*Don Juan*, canto V, stanza 29)

How differently the rhythm and rhyme of 'signing' and 'dining' work upon us, in comparison with what they are meant to call to mind, the famous 'declining' moment in Pope when 'sign' meets 'dine':

> Mean while declining from the Noon of Day,
> The Sun obliquely shoots his burning Ray;
> The hungry Judges soon the Sentence sign,
> And Wretches hang that Jury-men may Dine;
> The Merchant from th' *Exchange* returns in Peace,
> And the long Labours of the *Toilette* cease—
> (*The Rape of the Lock*, iii 19–24)[16]

The merchant in Byron is glimpsed 'giving change', which makes play with Pope's glance towards 'The Merchant from th' *Exchange*'. Giving change, engaging in exchange: this is what an alluder does, and Byron is one who likes to wave small calculations aside—'Keep the change'. Moral probity meets financial responsibility in a turn of phrase that Byron enjoyed: 'good upon Change'.

I have written to our friend Douglas Kinnaird on my own matters—desiring him to send me out all the further credits I can command—(and I have a year's

---

[16] For Byron's admiration for Pope, see, for instance, his superb letter to John Murray, 15 September 1817: 'I was really astonished (I ought not to have been so) and mortified—at the ineffable distance in point of sense—harmony—effect—and even *Imagination* Passion—& *Invention*—between the little Queen Anne's Man—& us of the lower Empire' (*Letters and Journals*, v 265).

Income—and the sale of a Manor besides (he tells me) before me) for till the Greeks get *their* Loan—it is probable that I shall have to stand partly Paymaster—as far as I am "good upon *Change*"—that is to say.[17]

Pope is only one of the Paymasters, for another poet is current in Byron's couplet:

> And then the merchant giving change, and signing
> Receipts in full, began to think of dining.

For whereas the rhyme *signing / dining* acknowledges Pope's signature ('Receipts in full', this being a responsible allusion), the sequence 'think of dining' is meant to make us think of Goldsmith and the banter bent upon Burke,

> Who, too deep for his hearers, still went on refining,
> And thought of convincing, while they thought of dining.
> ('Retaliation' 35–6)

Who, we may ask, rule? The judges, of Pope's lines?

> The hungry Judges soon the Sentence sign,
> And Wretches hang that Jury-men may Dine.

The legislators, statesmen, of Goldsmith's? No, the merchants. And yet not every merchant is a slave merchant.

Pope is the more mordant. Yet Byron's milder manner is not a toothless mumbling. For the train of thought which had started by describing the haggling for slaves as like buying 'a lamb' moves on from dining to a dyspeptic costive brooding:

> I wonder if his appetite was good?
>   Or, if it were, if also his digestion?
> Methinks at meals some odd thoughts might intrude,
>   And conscience ask a curious sort of question,
> About the right divine how far we should
>   Sell flesh and blood. When dinner has opprest one,
> I think it is perhaps the gloomiest hour
> Which turns up out of the sad twenty-four.
>   (*Don Juan*, canto V, stanza 30)

---

[17] To John Bowring, October 1823; *Letters and Journals*, xi 77. Leslie Marchand has a note: 'Unidentified'. But the phrase needs a gloss, not necessarily an identification. The *OED* includes Fuller's Worthies: 'He is called a Good Man upon the exchange, who hath a responsible estate'.

F. R. Leavis saw the central vein of Byron's art as a giving vein, its
appeal to 'a generous common humanity',[18] and it is the word generous
that unites the critic's considerations with those biographical financial
ones that Doris Langley Moore counts and recounts in *Lord Byron:
Accounts Rendered*. The generosity is there in such a line as 'Her dowry
was as nothing to her smiles' (*Don Juan*, canto II, stanza 128). It is there
in Byron's refusal to be bamboozled by lavishness. He grants a stanza's
climactic couplet to a heaping-up:

> A dazzling mass of gems, and gold, and glitter,
> Magnificently mingled in a litter.
>
> (canto V, stanza 93)

But he follows this with the laconicism of 'Wealth had done wonders—
taste not much'. The unmisgiving giving is there too in the gruff good
humour of this:

> But now at thirty years my hair is gray—
> (I wonder what it will be like at forty?
> I thought of a peruke the other day)
> My heart is not much greener; and, in short, I
> Have squander'd my whole summer while 'twas May,
> And feel no more the spirit to retort; I
> Have spent my life, both interest and principal,
> And deem not, what I deem'd, my soul invincible.
>
> (*Don Juan*, canto I, stanza 213)[19]

And what did Byron himself inherit? His father, who was to die six
weeks later, dictated his will, 'charging his penniless son of three to pay
his debts and funeral expenses'.[20]

Byron came of age on January 22nd 1809, and it was by no means the escape
from bondage that he had longed for. He could contract debts, it is true, without roundabout procedures, but he was also personally liable for what he owed,
and that was something in the region of £12,000.[21]

Byron is not fooling when he says roundly 'I love money', or when he
goes on to say: '& money like "motley is the only wear".—I name no

---

[18] *Revaluation* (1936), p. 150.
[19] For Tennyson's allusion to Shakespeare's interest and principal, see p. 197.
[20] *Lord Byron: Accounts Rendered* (1974), p. 42; 'charging' is sharp; Mrs Langley Moore
always puts these things very well.
[21] *Lord Byron: Accounts Rendered*, pp. 99–100.

sum from Murray—but you may suppose that I shall greatly admire the largest possible.'[22] For the jingling of *money* into *motley* into *Murray* (Byron's publisher) rings true. As does the allusion to *As You Like It*, II. vii: 'A worthie foole: Motley's the onely weare'. You want a Touchstone to tell the fool from the wise man? Try money.

As my notions upon the score of monies coincide with yours and all men's who have lived to see that every guinea is a philosopher's stone—or at least his *touch-stone*—you will doubt me the less when I pronounce my firm belief that Cash is Virtue.—[23]

Cynic or realist? The poet who asks 'Why call the miser miserable?', and who avers 'He is your only poet'[24], is not (it is true) asking that these words simply be credited; but this is not because money is valued only by lucre-lovers but because the miser hoards. The good man, like the good poet, spends, responsibly but uncalculatingly.

Byron's letters spend to the point of spilling, with postscripts as insistent as post-obits.

P.S.—Whatever Brain-money—you get on my account from Murray—pray remit me—I will never consent to pay away what I *earn*—that is *mine*—& what I get by my brains—I will spend on my b——ks—as long as I have a tester or a testicle remaining.—I shall not live long—& for that Reason—I must live while I can—so—let him disburse—& me receive—"for the Night cometh."—If I had but had twenty thousand a year I should not have been living now—but all men are not born with a silver or Gold Spoon in their mouths.—My balance—also my balance—& a Copyright—I have another Canto—too—ready—& then there will be my half year in June—recollect—*I care for nothing but "monies".*[25]

The great letter-writer was born with a silver tongue in his mouth.

The allusion to John 9: 4, 'for the Night cometh' ['when no man can work'], is at once disturbing and discreetly obscene. 'A tester or a testicle' plays with sexpence, but it is 'monies', with its allusion-marks (more than quotation marks), that lays its bet. For here is a single-word allusion, with

[22] To Douglas Kinnaird, 6 March 1819; *Letters and Journals*, vi 101.
[23] To Kinnaird, 23 February 1822; *Letters and Journals*, ix 113. Again to Kinnaird, 12 September 1822, *Letters and Journals*, ix 207: 'The longer I live—the more I perceive that Money (honestly come by) is the Philosopher's Stone . . . my avarice—or cupidity—is *not* selfish'.
[24] *Don Juan*, canto XII, stanzas 7–8. Suggesting 'Motley's the onely weare'.
[25] To Hobhouse and Kinnaird, 19 January 1819 (the postscript, 20 January); *Letters and Journals*, vi 92.

all its risk of asking too much of us (can one word bring that much with it?), or of calling in doubt whether there really is an allusion at all (just one word? well, if it were Eliot's 'juvescence' . . .). It is the single-word allusion that most suggests allusion as ready money, a single coin with its clarity of outline, its daily uncontested currency. Yet 'monies' is the miser's word. Still, although Byron is no miser, he grants that the miser is in a position to say to others 'Come off it'—or to try to hold others to their word. As Shylock does, he who says 'my monies', and '*Shylocke, we would have moneyes*', and 'moneyes is your suite', and 'Ile lend you thus much moneyes' (all these in the one speech, *The Merchant of Venice*, I. iii). Byron does not sound like or behave like Shylock, but he jingles Shylock's word: 'though I have a very decent sum of monies in hand—yet I love Monies—& like to have more always'.[26] The difference is that Byron likes having monies in hand so that he may be open-handed. As he is with allusions, which he will often encourage to pair and to breed as money does. Or as 'monies' does, accompanied as it often is by the bond that Shylock invokes and that Byron is lent by Shylock, it having been drawn up by Shakespeare.

An allusion is a bond. But Byron's allusions are not the (organic) flesh, the pound of flesh, but pounds sterling. He is not organic, not holistic (unlike Wordsworth), and he values money as releasingly, liberatingly, *not* holistic, as not insisting that the alternative to all is nothing. What a relief to be dealing—in money—with something that is content to be subdivided, something that is then agreed to amount to the same thing.[27]

Wordsworth and the high poets may wish to see things under the aspect of eternity, *sub specie aeternitatis*. Byron, who (like eternity, Blake says) is in love with the productions of time, would prefer people to see things *sub specie temporis*; and there could hardly be a more daily form of this production than specie, the word for actual coin, money, that was still current in Byron's day.

[26] To Kinnaird, 16 November 1821; *Letters and Journals*, ix 62.
[27] This is to agree with Peter Manning and with Jonathan Bate about the nature of Byron's allusions, while trying to elucidate the good light in which the allusions should be seen. Manning, *Byron and His Fictions*, pp. 200–1: 'a mode of incessant but curiously casual, apparently inconsistent allusion', practising fragmentation and the disintegrative; Byron 'breaks up' the works of classical authors. (But to break a five-pound note is not 'fragmentation', does not disintegrate it.) Bate, *Shakespeare and the English Romantic Imagination*, p. 240: '*Don Juan* as a whole is an accumulative, disparate, unorganic work, so its quotations are not integrated. Byron makes a virtue of the incidental, the momentary, the superficial'. (But the virtue is not only momentary, it is monetary, and the handling of money is far from a superficial matter.)

Marriage palls.

> Yet what can people do, except despair?
>   The same things change their names at such a rate;
> For instance—passion in a lover's glorious,
>   But in a husband is pronounced uxorious.
>
> Men grow ashamed of being so very fond;
>   They sometimes also get a little tired
> (But that, of course, is rare), and then despond:
>   The same things cannot always be admired,
> Yet 'tis 'so nominated in the bond,'
>   That both are tied till one shall have expired.
> Sad thought! to lose the spouse that was adorning
> Our days, and put one's servants into mourning.
>
>   (*Don Juan*, canto III, stanzas 6–7)

'Men grow ashamed of being so very fond': the rhyme that will arrive in due course is 'bond' (rhyme, like allusion again, being itself a bond). 'Expired': the marriage licence expiring? No, marriage remaining valid till death us do part. The recurrence in the successive stanzas of the same words ('The same things . . .' | 'The same things . . .') is wittily weary; and allusion puts before us something that both is and is not the same thing. 'Yet 'tis so nominated in the bond': in *The Merchant of Venice* the bond is a promissory note not of dying but of killing:

PORTIA.   Have by some Surgeon *Shylock* on your charge
           To stop his wounds, least he should bleede to death.
SHYLOCK.   Is it so nominated in the bond?
PORTIA.   It is not so exprest: but what of that?
           'Twere good you do so much for charitie.
SHYLOCK.   I cannot finde it, 'tis not in the bond.

                                                     (IV. i)

This is a travesty of legal responsibilities. Yet it cannot but extort some sympathy not only for Antonio but for Shylock. Byron was exasperated by the irresponsibility of those to whom he had been responsibly generous:

Ten years ago I lent him a thousand pounds on bond, on condition that he would not go to the *Jews*.—He took the money and went to the Jews.— Hanson has this bond—and there is ten years interest due upon it.——I have never dunned him—but I think that he might at least have paid some of the interest.—The Bond (though a good bond) is—I presume—valuable according to the possibility or probability of recovering said monies.[28]

[28] To Kinnaird, 1 December 1822; *Letters and Journals*, x 48.

Jews, bond, monies: this is Shylock's world, though Byron is well aware
that it is the world of 'Jew Rothschild, and his fellow Christian Baring'
(*Don Juan*, canto XII, stanza 5). Several of Byron's letters are bonded
together by their feeling for what a bond is. As when he leaned over
backwards to be a lenient lender, trusting that people would trust him:

> I have before told you & now repeat very sincerely—that when the time of
> your bond [£1000] is up—I shall not enforce it . . . and you know me well
> enough not to doubt me on such *wordly* matters.[29]

'*Wordly*' (the emphasis is Byron's) is a good word, because it means that
Byron is giving his word, and is repudiating not only the worldly but
the hollow sense of wordly: *OED*, *rare*, 'Dealing in, or consisting in,
mere words; verbal'.

Again linked by such a bond, Byron makes an entry in his book-
keeping. Enter Shakespeare and Shallow, with Shylock soon to arrive,
invoking his 'bond'.

> Mem. I must write to-morrow to "Master Shallow, * *, who owes me a thou-
> sand pounds," and seems, in his letter, afraid I should ask him for it; as if I
> would!—I don't want it (just now, at least,) to begin with; and though I have
> often wanted that sum, I never asked for the repayment of £10 in my life—
> from a friend. His bond is not due this year, and I told him when it was, I
> should not enforce it. How often must he make me say the same thing?
>   I am wrong—I did once ask * * * [Hobhouse] to repay me. But it was under
> circumstances that excused me *to him*, and would to any one. I took no inter-
> est, nor required security. He paid me soon,—[30]

This acknowledges that it owes much to Shakespeare: 'Master *Shallow*,
I owe you a thousand pound' (*2 Henry IV*, V. v), while deftly turning
the whole matter around: 'Master Shallow, who owes me a thousand
pounds'. Byron gives and takes *interest*, with the widest range of the
word often called upon by him. He appeals to and for others, as when
writing to John Murray on behalf of Madame A. de Yosy:

> Can the "Literary fund" do nothing for her? by your interest—which is great
> among the pious—I dare say that something might be collected—can you get
> any of her books published? suppose—you take her as *author* in my place now
> vacant amongst your ragamuffins.[31]

[29] To J. W. Webster, 22 November 1813; *Letters and Journals*, iii 172.
[30] Journal, 17 November 1813; *Letters and Journals*, iii 212.
[31] 31 October 1822; *Letters and Journals*, x 23.

The resources of allusion constitute a form of Literary Fund, the responsible sibling of the disreputable 'myth-kitty' that Larkin saw as a slush-fund.

Does responsibility demand accuracy? When in polemical mode, Byron was prepared to insist that it did. He castigated Thomas Campbell:

In the life of Burns, Mr. C. quotes Shakespeare thus,—

> To gild refined gold, to paint *the rose*,
> Or *add fresh* perfume *to* the violet, etc.

This version by no means improves the original, which is as follows:

> To gild refined gold, to paint the *lily*,
> To *throw a perfume on* the violet, etc.
>
> King John

A great poet quoting another should be correct; he should also be accurate, when he accuses a Parnassian brother of that dangerous charge 'borrowing': a poet had better borrow any thing (excepting money) than the thoughts of another—they are always sure to be reclaimed.[32]

So does responsibility demand accuracy? Not if the point—in the poetical mode—is equable looseness, anything other than the uptight.

> She was so like a vision; I might err,
> But Shakespeare also says 'tis very silly
> 'To gild refined gold, or paint the lily.'
> (*Don Juan*, canto III, stanza 76)

It is not merely that whatever Shakespeare said, he didn't say it was very *silly* to do this. (The rhyme *silly* / *lily* is charmingly lackadaisical.) Nor did Shakespeare say 'or', or rather he didn't say it in this line, although (picking up 'Therefore' and 'before') he did say it twice in the succeeding lines:

> Therefore, to be possess'd with double pompe,
> To guard a Title, that was rich before;
> To gilde refined Gold, to paint the Lilly;
> To throw a perfume on the Violet,
> To smooth the yce, or adde another hew
> Unto the Raine-bow; or with Taper-light

---

[32] Note to *Don Juan*, canto V, stanza 147.

To seeke the beauteous eye of heaven to garnish,
Is wastefull, and ridiculous excesse.

(*King John*, IV. ii)

Pretty well everything in this lavish speech could be seen as applying in its way to allusion: double pomp, a title that was rich before, gilding gold and painting the lily, adding another hue, garnishing sunlight . . .: what can save allusion from being wasteful and ridiculous excess? Only such felicity as may surprisingly effect these very things: add something new to the old title, achieve a new pomp that is entirely without pomposity. And although the whole passage from *King John* may be seen as applicable to allusion, it is characteristic of Byron that it is the gilding line that he takes, first because it has become a proverb or a cliché (Byron's verse is no occasion for snobbery), and second because it deals in gold.

Don Juan puts it to us that in middle life, love lingers:

And money, that most pure imagination,
Gleams only through the dawn of its creation.

(canto XII, stanza 2)

Money is that most pure imagination not because it cannot be smutched by impurity but because its value is purely imaginary, depending upon an extraordinary sequence of social creditings. Its value is a feat of social imagination, a shared delusion even, unlike the value of (say) water; and yet money possesses such indisputable solidity. Is it abstract or concrete or both? Byron has the small round coin of the word *or* roll through the opening stanzas of this canto,[33] and he chimes it against its tangible homonym, the gold itself, what he calls in these stanzas 'the ore', 'the very ore', 'the thin ore' (stanzas 8, 10, 12). Veined with *or*.

Love or lust makes man sick, and wine much sicker;
Ambition rends, and gaming gains a loss;
But making money, slowly first, then quicker,
And adding still a little through each cross

[33] For instance, over and above stanza 4 that is quoted: 'royalist or liberal', 'pain | Or pleasure', 'seats a nation or upsets a throne', 'saint or cynic', 'Inde, or far Cathay', 'To build a college, or to found a race', 'Or revel in the joys of calculation', 'all, or each, or none of these', 'Or do they benefit mankind' (stanzas 5–11) . . . One of the limitations of even the best concordances is that they don't include mighty little words like *or*. True, an electronic search now makes this possible, had we but world enough and time.

> (Which *will* come over things) beats love or liquor,
>   The gamester's counter, or the statesman's *dross*.
> Oh Gold! I still prefer thee unto paper,
>   Which makes bank credit like a bark of vapour.
>   (*Don Juan*, canto XII, stanza 4)

'Love *or* lust' is succeeded (compound interest) by 'love *or* liqu*or*', culminating in the full line of perfect balance (the scales weigh the money) that gives us the syntactical pairing, three words apiece, pivoting upon the word *or*: 'The gamester's counter, or the statesman's dross.'

Dross? Byron loved bodies, especially bodies that felt love, no less than had Donne.

> But O alas, so long, so farre
>   Our bodies why do wee forbeare?
> They are ours, though they are not wee, Wee are
>   The intelligences, they the spheare.
> We owe them thankes, because they thus,
>   Did us, to us, at first convay,
> Yeelded their forces, sense, to us,
>   Nor are drosse to us, but allay.
>   ('The Extasie' 49–56)

Allusion is not dross to us, but allay. We owe it thanks for what it conveys to us. Byron offers it as an invaluable alloy, not as pure gold.

He deprecates sentimentality about romantic love; granted, 'there may be something' in its hopes, but less than the verse-proud have a way of claiming. Scott may soar:

> Love rules the court, the camp, the grove,
> And men below, and saints above;
> For love is heaven, and heaven is love.
>   (*Lay of the Last Minstrel*, canto III,
>   stanza ii)

Will Byron have none of it? No, but he will not have all that much of it. As a later minstrel, he has the right to say *but*:

> 'Love rules the camp, the court, the grove,'—'for Love
>   'Is Heaven, and Heaven is Love;'—so sings the bard;
> Which it were rather difficult to prove,
>   (A thing with poetry in general hard.)

Byron 139

Perhaps there may be something in 'the grove,'
    At least it rhymes to 'Love;' but I'm prepared
To doubt (no less than Landlords of their rental)
    If 'courts' and 'camps' be quite so sentimental.
                    (*Don Juan*, canto XII, stanza 13)

'Perhaps there may be something in "the grove," | At least it rhymes to "Love" ': oh no it doesn't (not even with a Scottish accent), except in the insufficiently hard world of poetry in general, of bards, of their idle eye-rhymes. And then come those words that might have emblazoned Byron's scutcheon: 'but I'm prepared | To doubt'—succeeded at the head of the next stanza by a yet more emphatic *But*:

But if Love don't, *Cash* does, and Cash alone:
    Cash rules the grove, and fells it too besides;
Without cash, camps were thin, and courts were none;
    Without cash, Malthus tells you, 'take no brides.'
So Cash rules Love the ruler, on his own
    High ground, as Virgin Cynthia sways the tides;
And as for 'Heaven being Love,' why not say honey
Is wax? Heaven is not Love, 'tis Matrimony.
                    (canto XII, stanza 14)

Byron looks down on those who claim the high ground; he'll take the low road—as long as he doesn't have to travel in the company of the hard-faced hard-nosed Malthus. 'Cash' clashes like cymbals half a dozen times in as many lines. Oddly, his art is in its low-falutin' way as much an art of redemption as was Wordsworth's high thinking.

But where Wordsworth takes the blackened moments within Shakespearean anguish and cleanses them, Byron is on his guard against any whitewashing.

Macbeth sells his soul—worse, gives it for all but nothing:

                mine eternall Jewell
Given to the common Enemie of Man,
To make them Kings, the Seedes of *Banquo* Kings.
Rather than so, come Fate into the Lyst,
And champion me to th'utterance.
                    (III. i)

Byron trades in these words for a different model. For the words of his Lord Henry call up another king than Duncan, and another butcher than Macbeth ('this dead Butcher', V. viii). Macbeth's cosmic challenge is reduced to our comic gauntlet. Here is no longer damnation but the slangily damnable, entailing the thought of being damnably hard-up.

> But could he quit his king in times of strife
>   Which threatened the whole country with perdition?
> When demagogues would with a butcher's knife
>   Cut through and through (oh! damnable incision!)
> The Gordian or the Ge*o*rdi-an knot, whose strings
> Have tied together Commons, Lords, and Kings.
>
> Sooner 'come place into the civil list
>   And champion him to the utmost'—he would keep it,
> Till duly disappointed or dismissed:
>   Profit he cared not for, let others reap it;
> But should the day come when place ceased to exist,
>   The country would have far more cause to weep it;
>   (*Don Juan*, canto XVI, stanzas 74–5)

'Disappointed' is glumly the right opposite of 'appointed'. And, as with the earlier invoking of 'profit' in the vicinity of an allusion, the lines profit from Shakespeare. *For* 'come Fate into the list', *read*—and you can read it in the public prints—'come place into the civil list'. (The assonance Fate / place reminds us that we are placed by Fate.) The Civil List was of moneys granted by Parliament, to the Royal Family among others. And is not allusion itself a form of civil list, with appropriations and grantings some of which are sure to be an abuse? Editors have pointed out that 'Byron's substitution of "utmost" for "utterance" conveys the meaning of the Shakespearean word: to the last extremity'.[34] To which might be added that Byron's utterance thereby becomes something other than simply Shakespeare's; this, even apart from Byron's civilly adding the word 'civil'.

Byron himself earned good money from his poems, and never pretended that this was unimportant to him; at the same time there were cuts other than financial ones that he roundly resisted, as when he defended Canto II of *Don Juan*: 'you shan't decimate nor mutilate—no—"rather than that come Critics into the list—and champion me to the uttermost" '.[35] The replacing of the word 'Fate' with the differently grim challenge 'Critics' brings home that a writer's fate is the critics.

---

[34] From the edition of *Don Juan* by T. G. Steffan, E. Steffan, and W. W. Pratt (1973, 1996).
[35] To Kinnaird, 24 April 1819; *Letters and Journals*, vi 114.

There then happens to be some comedy in the fact that the scholar-critic Leslie Marchand has a note to the words within quotation-marks in the letter: 'Unidentified'.

Fate is fortune, and over time fortune changes its meaning. It comes to mean money. It means business. And business, like poetry, must venture.

> There is a Tide in the affayres of men,
> Which taken at the Flood, leades on to Fortune:
> Omitted, all the voyage of their life,
> Is bound in Shallowes, and in Miseries.
> On such a full Sea are we now a-float,
> And we must take the current when it serves,
> Or loose our Ventures.
>
> (*Julius Caesar*, IV. iii)

It was left to Byron to catch the tide of those lines, to follow their current, and to win his venture, he being the merchant of Venus.

> 'There is a tide in the affairs of men
>   Which taken at the flood'—you know the rest,
> And most of us have found it, now and then;
>   At least we think so, though but few have guess'd
> The moment, till too late to come again.
>   But no doubt every thing is for the best—
> Of which the surest sign is in the end:
> When things are at the worst they sometimes mend.
>
> There is a tide in the affairs of women
>   'Which taken at the flood leads'—God knows where:
> Those navigators must be able seamen
>   Whose charts lay down its current to a hair;
> Not all the reveries of Jacob Behmen
>   With its strange whirls and eddies can compare:—
> Men with their heads reflect on this and that—
> But women with their hearts or heaven knows what!
>
> (*Don Juan*, canto VI, stanzas 1–2)

Exquisitely suggestive yet decorous, those seamen and that hair, reinforced as they are by the wave of the hand in 'heaven knows what'. (Earth knows better, and is contented that 'heaven knows what!' does no more than to intimate—through its sly rhyme with one unspoken or unspeakable word—the part of a woman's body that is not a heart.)[36]

---

[36] McGann remarks on the puns here, and he records alternative readings:

'There is a tide in the affairs of men': the allusion itself invites comparison (of which the lines speak), and it combines many different kinds of affair—amatory, literary, commercial. The young Alexander Pope wrote in a letter to William Walsh (2 July 1706):

I wou'd beg your opinion too as to another point: It is how far the liberty of *Borrowing* may extend. I have defended it sometimes by saying, that it seems not so much the Perfection of Sense, to say things that have *never* been said before, as to express those *best* that have been said *oftenest*; and that Writers in the case of borrowing from others, are like Trees which of themselves wou'd produce only one sort of Fruit, but by being grafted upon others, may yield variety. A mutual commerce makes Poetry flourish; but then Poets like Merchants, shou'd repay with something of their own what they take from others; not like Pyrates, make prize of all they meet.[37]

Pope values the concession ('but then Poets . . .'). Byron, too, loves the word 'but' and he loves such borrowing as amounts to allusion, and the two loves go together. The first half-dozen stanzas of Canto VI include: 'But no doubt'; 'But women'; 'But Actium'; 'But whether such things'; '— but Chronology best knows'. With *but* joined by its brother *yet*: 'And yet'; 'Yet', 'yet still . . .'. As he wrote in his journal: 'I am now six-and-twenty; my passions have had enough to cool them; my affections more than enough to wither them,—and yet—and yet—always *yet* and *but*—'.[38]

    One happy compounding of these energies, then, may occur when the very word *but* has a part to play within what is alluded to.

> 'Tis not in mortals to command success,
> But we'll do more, Sempronius; we'll deserve it.
>   (Addison, *Cato*, I. ii)

Addison's high-toned sentiment is just the sort of thing that Byron was sent to the planet to bring down to earth. But this is unjust to Addison, who was conscious of the envious snarl that the *sententia* invited. Exit; then Sempronius, *solus*:

 (i) Man with his head reflects—(as Spurzheim tells)
       But Woman with the heart—or something else.
 (ii) Man's pensive part is <mostly in> / (now and then) the head
       <But> Woman's <in> the heart—or anything instead.

[37] *Alexander Pope: Selected Letters*, ed. Howard Erskine-Hill (2000), p. 13. The letter supplies the title and the 'vectors' for Wolfgang E. H. Rudat's book, *The Mutual Commerce* (1985).
[38] Journal, 18 February 1814; *Letters and Journals*, iii 243.

Curse on the stripling! How he apes his sire!
Ambitiously sententious!

Still, Byron was within his rights when he too came to ape his sire,
ambitiously unsententious:

> 'Tis not in mortals to command success;
>   But *do you more*, Sempronius—*don't* deserve it;'
> And take my word, you won't have any less:
>   Be wary, watch the time, and always serve it;
>   (*Don Juan*, canto XIII, stanza 18)

Allusion is a form of succession that nurses the hope of success. Saki has
some of Byron's raffish marksmanship in *The Unbearable Bassington*:
''Tis not in mortals to insure succession, and Egbert was admittedly
mortal' (chapter XI).

'But we'll do more': Byron's allusion proceeds to do more with these
words, as an allusion is wont to do (*not* 'No more—no more of that!').
The word *but* duly proves indispensable for Byron. 'In short, I deny
nothing, but doubt everything':[39] what makes this an embodiment of
Byron and Byronism is not only the sentiment but the form: it all
hinges on *but*.[40] Byron's greatness is his various insistence upon the
word and upon the thousand ways in which it is urgent. His limitation,
by the same token, is that he is unjust to those things in life that find
'but' to be paltering; at such moments, Byron's 'but' manifests itself as
obsessive, mechanical, or cheap. But me no buts?

> SENATOR.   I mean not
>   To oppose them, *but*—
> MEMMO.   In Venice '*But's*' a traitor.
>   But me no '*buts*,' unless you would pass o'er
>   The Bridge which few repass.
>   (*The Two Foscari*, IV. i)

In Venice, *but* might be a traitor, but in Byron, it is usually his faithful
servant. Byron seeks to but himself no end of buts:

it is said I am "much out of spirits." I wonder if I really am or not? I have
certainly enough of "that perilous stuff which weighs upon the heart," and it is

---

[39] To Francis Hodgson, 4 December 1811; *Letters and Journals*, ii 136.
[40] I draw here on a review of the first two volumes of Byron's *Letters and Journals* that I
wrote for *The Listener* (27 September 1973).

better they should believe it to be result of these attacks than of the real cause; but—ay, ay, always *but*, to the end of the chapter.[41]

Some day or other, when we are *veterans*, I may tell you a tale of present and past times; and it is not from want of confidence that I do not now,—but—but—always a *but* to the end of the chapter.[42]

Else why do we live at all? because Hope recurs to Memory—both false—but—but—but—but—and—this *but* drags on till—What? I do not know, & who does? "He that died o' Wednesday"[43]

One of the fascinations of the early letters is their showing that from the start Byron's world hinged upon 'but'. He writes to his mother at 16:

I am informed From creditable authority that Dr. Drury, Mr. Evans and Mark Drury said I was a *Blackguard*, that Mark Drury said so I *know*, but I am inclined to doubt the authenticity of the report as to the rest, perhaps it is true perhaps not, but thank God they may call me a Blackguard, but they can never make me one, if Dr. Drury can bring one boy or any one else to say that I have committed a dishonourable action, and to prove it, I am content, but otherwise I am stigmatized without a cause, and I disdain and despise the malicious efforts of him and his Brother.[44]

Four *buts* swirl within this sequence.

In the letters, this is perplexity most of the time; in the poetry, it is vigilant, disciplined, and witty. Melville famously praised Hawthorne: 'He says NO! in thunder; but the Devil himself cannot make him say *yes*. For all men who say *yes*, lie'.[45] But what about saying 'Yes, but . . .'? What Byron says is not No! in thunder, but But! in all weathers. Or, on occasion, *Yes, but . . .*, allusion itself being a *Yes, but . . .* As with the *But* that turns upon, though it does not round upon, an allusion to *Hamlet*:[46]

> But I am apt to grow too metaphysical:
> 'The time is out of joint,' and so am I;
> I quite forget this poem's merely quizzical,

---

[41] Journal, 18 February 1814; *Letters and Journals*, iii 243. *Macbeth*, V. iii, for 'that perilous stuff which weighs upon the heart'.

[42] To Thomas Moore, 3 March 1814; *Letters and Journals*, iv 77.

[43] Detached Thoughts, 15 October 1821–18 May 1822; *Letters and Journals*, ix 33. Quoting *1 Henry IV*, V. i.

[44] 1–10 May 1804 (?); *Letters and Journals*, i 49.

[45] Letter, April (?) 1851; *Hawthorne: The Critical Heritage*, ed. J. Donald Crowley (1970), p. 190.

[46] I. v: 'The time is out of joynt: Oh cursed spight, | That ever I was borne to set it right'.

And deviate into matters rather dry.
I ne'er decide what I shall say, and this I call
Much too poetical. Men should know why
They write, and for what end; but, note or text,
I never know the word which will come next.
(*Don Juan*, canto IX, stanza 41)

Revolve how often the great turns in Byron depend upon and from this
hinge, the word *but*, the word most crucial to him and yet one that does
not make it into the concordances to his poems (too small a word, too
frequent, though now retrievable by an electronic search at no greater
cost than one's sanity):

But—Oh! ye lords of ladies intellectual,
Inform us truly, have they not hen-peck'd you all?
(canto I, stanza 22)

For my part I say nothing—nothing—but
This I will say—my reasons are my own—
(canto I, stanza 52)

But it was all a mystery. Here we are,
And there we go:—but *where*? five bits of lead,
Or three, or two, or one, send very far!
And is this blood, then, form'd but to be shed?
(canto V, stanza 39)

But let it go:—it will one day be found
With other relics of 'a former world,'
When this world shall be *former*, underground—
Thrown topsy-turvy, twisted, crisped, and curled,
(canto IX, stanza 37)

But now I'm going to be immoral; now
I mean to show things really as they are,
Not as they ought to be: for I avow
That till we see what's what in fact, we're far
From much improvement with that virtuous plough
Which skims the surface, leaving scarce a scar
Upon the black loam long manured by Vice,
Only to keep its corn at the old price.
But [. . .]
(canto XII, stanzas 40–1)

So it is not surprising that Byron's great praise of his great poem should
turn and lunge with the same word: '—it may be bawdy—but is it not

good English?—it may be profligate—but is it not *life*, is it not *the thing?*[47]

Beckett was to voice the conjunction in *Mercier and Camier*:

One does what one can, but one can nothing. Only squirm and wriggle, to end up in the evening where you were in the morning. But! There's a vocable for you if you like! All is vox inanis save, certain days, certain conjunctions, such is Mercier's contribution to the squabble of the universals.[48]

'But' is the vocable for a profound and generous sceptic, a sceptic who fears that scepticism may have notice taken of it only if it has the air of cynicism. Yet there is more to it than this, since 'but' is also a word that recognizes conflicting impulses, and conflicting impulses are at the heart of Byron's feat—as a man and as poet—of unembarrassability.[49]

'The affairs of men' are sometimes 'the affairs of women'. At which, adultery rears its head. The jealous husband Don Alfonso has just left his wife Antonia's bedroom where his search had come to nothing. 'The door was fasten'd in his legal face'. Whereupon the hidden Don Juan surfaces. As does a money matter.

> No sooner was it bolted, than—Oh shame!
>   Oh sin! Oh sorrow! and Oh womankind!
> How can you do such things and keep your fame,
>   Unless this world, and t'other too, be blind?
> Nothing so dear as an unfilch'd good name!
>   But to proceed—for there is more behind:
> With much heart-felt reluctance be it said,
> Young Juan slipp'd, half-smother'd, from the bed.
>
>   (*Don Juan*, canto I, stanza 165)

This filches, inspiredly, from the tragedy of uncommitted adultery, *Othello*. Iago, like so many of Shakespeare's evil men, is given truths to tell, though to tell them ill-becomes him. But then ill does become him.

> Good name in Man, & woman (deere my Lord)
> Is the immediate Jewell of their Soules;
> Who steales my purse, steales trash:
> 'Tis something, nothing;
> 'Twas mine, 'tis his, and has bin slave to thousands:
> But he that filches from me my good Name,

---

[47] To Kinnaird, 26 October; *Letters and Journals*, vi 232.

[48] *Mercier and Camier* (1974), chapter VI, p. 84.

[49] I have written about this in a chapter of *Keats and Embarrassment* (1974), 'Keats, Byron, and "Slippery Blisses" '.

Robs me of that, which not enriches him,
And makes me poore indeed.

(III. iii)

Lucky young Juan was only 'half-smothered', unlike poor Desdemona ('half' again in the company of an allusion, half and half the imaginative creation). Shakespeare is robbed of nothing by Byron, for Shakespeare's words remain his; tribute is paid. And that which Byron filches does not make Shakespeare poor indeed, but on the contrary bears witness yet once more to the treasury that is Shakespeare; this, even while the filching, stealing, or robbery (Iago scatters them all, in perverse largesse) does enrich Byron's art. And again, as often with allusion, there is the protection against inert dependency that comes from acknowledging not one but more than one enrichment. For Byron owes something to his admired Pope. 'Nothing so dear as an unfilch'd good name!': after 'Oh womankind!', this must call up the name not only of Shakespeare but of Pope.

> Nothing so true as what you once let fall,
> 'Most Women have no Characters at all'.
> ('To a Lady: Of the Characters of
> Women', opening)

Trust Pope to start with a prudent acknowledged filching—this remark about women, let me make perfectly clear immediately, was made by a woman who is moreover a lady. And trust Byron to borrow this brightness, along with Iago's darkness, with heartfelt unreluctance.

Both a borrower and a lender be. The spirit of the allusion is at the furthest remove from envious malignity, though the possibility of envy and malignity must always hang around any allusion. (The emulous or enemy?) Which is why some of Byron's most magnanimous allusions arise from moments of envy—not envy of the rich and famous, but of the greatly gifted. Byron knows full well that the word 'genius', when Macbeth is in envious awe of Banquo, has the meaning 'spirit', not transcendent powers; but an allusion to these lines acknowledges that Shakespeare is a genius in the face of whose art one's own may feel rebuked:

> There is none but he,
> Whose being I doe feare: and under him,
> My *Genius* is rebuk'd, as it is said
> *Mark Anthonies* was by *Cæsar*.
> (III. i)

> For there are few things by mankind less brook'd,
> And womankind too, if we so may say,
>   Than finding thus their genius stand rebuked,
> Like 'Anthony's by Caesar,' by the few
> Who look upon them as they ought to do.
>
> (*Don Juan*, canto XV, stanza 53)

The restless envy within Macbeth is transmuted by Byron into something that rues the days, a tone that is truly sad (though the phrase 'the sad truth' has its idiomatic equanimity) but far from desolation. He takes Macbeth's desolate vision of an empty old age—

> I have liv'd long enough: my way of life
> Is falne into the Seare, the yellow Leafe
>
> (V. iii)

—and colours it with a mellow fellowship (allusion may be a form of fellowship):

> As boy, I thought myself a clever fellow,
>   And wish'd that others held the same opinion;
> They took it up when my days grew more mellow,
>   And other minds acknowledged my dominion:
> Now my sere fancy 'falls into the yellow
>   Leaf,' and imagination droops her pinion,
> And the sad truth which hovers o'er my desk
> Turns what was once romantic to burlesque.
>
> (*Don Juan*, canto IV, stanza 3)

This goodnaturedly concedes Shakespeare's dominion, and is relaxedly uncompetitive. For *Macbeth* was something other than romantic. But then *Don Juan* is something more than burlesque. At the line-ending the single leaf falls:

> Now my sere fancy 'falls into the yellow
> Leaf,'

The unfussy approximation to the lines from *Macbeth*, and then the replacing of Macbeth's bone-deep life-weariness, his hideous envy of Duncan ('Whom we, to gayne our peace, have sent to peace'), by the blasé, the world-weary, this is the gist. And the acute listlessness of the allusion can be the more sharply seen if it is contrasted with what Byron made, or failed to make, of this elsewhere.

> My days are in the yellow leaf
> The flowers and fruits of love are gone—
> The worm, the canker and the grief
> Are mine alone.
> ('January 22nd 1824. Messalonghi. On
> this day I complete my thirty sixth
> year' 5–8)

Ill worded, for he does not mean 'Are mine alone' (as though he were the only sufferer in the world—does self-pity know no limits?), he means 'Alone are mine'. (Only these are mine, not these are mine only.) So again I find myself both agreeing and disagreeing with Jonathan Bate. Agreeing when he gazes down the vistas to and from *Macbeth*:

The narrator's quotation from *Macbeth* early in the canto during which Haidée dies, 'Now my sere fancy "falls into the yellow / Leaf", and imagination droops her pinion' (*DJ* iv.3), not only prepares for the sadness to come, but also suggests the coming of his own old age—something that obsessed Byron, who seemed to live so fast that he treated his middle age as old age.[50]

But disagreeing when Bate makes a further claim:

This feeling reaches its most intense pitch when he alludes to *Macbeth* for the last time in his lyric, 'On this day I complete my thirty-sixth year'.

Intense, perhaps, but intensely unconvincing to my ear; for it is one of the many paradoxes of Byron and of his art that he so often achieves true intensity at the moments when he might most seem to be relaxed to the point of perfunctoriness. When he pitches himself intensely, he relaxes his intelligence—something very different from the relaxed intelligence that eases him into catching so much and so much.

Byron dissipates. The case for his art will have to explain why this can be a virtue. With allusion, he breaks lines or phrases down, and his poetry is then shard-borne. With rhyme, he breaks bread and scatters it like crumbs from the rich man's table: 'intellectual' into 'hen-peck'd you all'; 'you or me hopes' into 'Cheops'. And there remains another divisive device of which he is a master: the anagram. This, in its combination of similitude and dissimilitude, is—as is a rhyme—one form that metaphor may take. Byron brings anagram and allusion into a generative relation. But first I need to show that anagram in itself—or in its selves—is sometimes one of his resources.

[50] *Shakespeare and the English Romantic Imagination*, p. 241.

Queen Gulbeyaz had wanted to keep to herself handsome young Don Juan (who is disguised as a woman and ensconced in the harem); now the eunuch Baba is being quizzed by her about his dereliction of duty:

> Baba, with some embarrassment, replied
> To this long catechism of questions asked
> More easily than answered,—that he had tried
> His best to obey in what he had been tasked;
> But there seemed something that he wished to hide,
> *Which* hesitation more betrayed than masqued;—
> He scratched his ear, the infallible resource
> To which embarrassed people have recourse.
>
> (*Don Juan*, canto VI, stanza 100)

Resource / recourse: this is itself both a resource and a recourse, an anagram as well as a rhyme. There is something that the lines wish both to hide and to betray (but then 'masqued' is exactly right for this duplicity). 'Resource' pulls itself together, albeit differently, as 'recourse'. Baba is recourseful and resourceful. And this has its affinity to the way in which Baba's *ear* plays its body-part within the ensuing word 'embarrassed' (directly related to this body-language of his) that has in sequence *e*, *a*, and *r*: 'embarrassed'—a word that then has the three letters again, this time in reverse order, *r*, *a*, *e*, as though in a palindrome (*two* ears!). Far-fetched, this last, but perhaps it is worth the carriage, not least in making clear how different is the entire simple re-shuffling that gives us the rhyme *resource / recourse*.

In their felicitous rearrangements and movements, anagrams are well adapted to show how things can move in concert. As in love:

> Such kisses as belong to early days,
> Where heart, and soul, and sense, in concert move,
> And the blood's lava, and the pulse a blaze,
> Each kiss a heart-quake,—for a kiss's strength,
> I think, it must be reckon'd by its length.
>
> (*Don Juan*, canto II, stanza 186)

This, too, does what it speaks of, since 'heart-quake' is shaken into being by passion's earthquake.[51]

---

[51] Compare *Don Juan*, canto XIII, stanza 26: 'there is scarce a single season | Which does not shake some very splendid house | With some slight heart-quake of domestic treason—'.

Resource / recourse, and *heart-quake / earthquake*: these are full anagrams, but Byron (again murmuring, Keep the change) also liked partial ones, a cluster or clutter of some letters.

> Love bears within its breast the very germ
> Of change; and how should this be otherwise?
>
> (*Don Juan*, canto XIV, stanza 94)

The very germ of change is *bears* into *breast*, becoming otherwise.

> She was not violently lively, but
> Stole on your spirit like a May-day breaking;
>
> (*Don Juan*, canto VI, stanza 43)

Within 'violently' there does lurk (as so often in life) something 'lively', something that can steal on your spirit with its own kind of breaking: word breaking, and Word Making and Taking, as in that party game itself, scrabbling at the sharers' feast.

In an anagrammatic turn, where one word alludes to another, there is exchange or repayment, valuing fluidity as against fixity. Which is where money comes in. Sometimes sordidly, as when an expansion of one word into another can be seen to accuse the mercenary poets, with the insinuation that their *conversion* had as its beginning and end the round word *coin*:

> I would not imitate the petty thought,
>   Nor coin my self-love to so base a vice,
> For all the glory your conversion brought,
>   Since gold alone should not have been its price.
> You have your salary—was't for that you wrought?
> And Wordsworth has his place in the Excise.
>
> (*Don Juan*, Dedication, stanza 6)

Jerome McGann elucidates 'conversion': 'of gold into coinage and of the Lake Poets into Tories (which Byron ascribes here to venal motives)'. It is the unobtrusive yet gross growth of *coin* into *conversion* that effects the imputation.

Not that it is the money that is at fault. Byron was not embarrassed to love money: 'I have imbibed such a love for money that I keep some Sequins in a drawer to count, & cry over them once a week—'.[52] He

---

[52] To Kinnaird, 27 January 1819; *Letters and Journals*, vi 98.

later recorded that 'The "Sequin Box" never came into requisition'.[53] But *sequin* comes into *requisition*, thrown in.

Byron throws in an allusion and then guides it with something of an anagrammatic turn. As when Donna Inez is eager to berate her husband.

> This was an easy matter with a man
>   Oft in the wrong, and never on his guard;
> And even the wisest, do the best they can,
>   Have moments, hours, and days, so unprepared,
> That you might 'brain them with their lady's fan;'
>   And sometimes ladies hit exceeding hard,
> And fans turn into falchions in fair hands,
> And why and wherefore no one understands.
>
> (Don Juan, canto I, stanza 21)

The allusion is to Hotspur's contempt for 'a shallow cowardly Hinde': 'By this hand, if I were now by this Rascall, I could braine him with his Ladies Fan' (*1 Henry IV*, II. iii). Such was Byron's inspiration for the lines, but what then inspires them is his extravagantly witty play with the little letters. A fan can be expanded into a flutter or a flirt of feeling, so Byron expands the word, with a flick and a shake, into 'falchions' (swords): *fans / fa*lchio*ns*; and then manages to trump even this hand with the expansion into two words, again preserving the sequence of the letters: '*fa*ir ha*nds*'.

And fans turn into falchions in fair hands—you can say that again, and Byron does, twice more. Or rather, he does better than say, he sets it flutteringly before our eyes. 'And why and wherefore no one understands'? But the *how* at any rate we can understand.

There is a decorum to the line 'And fans turn into falchions in fair hands'. But it would be wrong, might even verge on cant, to give the impression that Byron is unremittingly decorous. He quite likes the thought of clearing not only our minds but our tongues of cant. And this may entail his intimating the odd obscenity to us—oh, not shriekingly, perhaps no more than tacitly and yet in such as way as is likely to go unregistered only by the pharisaical.

As to "Don Juan"—confess—confess—you dog—and be candid—that it is the sublime of *that there* sort of writing—it may be bawdy—but is it not good

---

English?—it may be profligate—but is it not *life*, is it not *the thing*?—Could any man have written it—who has not lived in the world?—and tooled in a post-chaise? in a hackney coach? in a Gondola? against a wall? in a court carriage? in a vis a vis?—on a table?—and under it?—I have written about a hundred stanzas of a third Canto—but it is damned modest—the outcry has frightened me.—I had such projects for the Don—but the *Cant* is so much stronger than *Cunt*—now a days,—that the benefit of experience in a man who had well weighed the worth of both monosyllables—must be lost to despairing posterity.[54]

Posterity, again. His Canto finds itself up against Cant. And how does Byron's bawdy get to be such good English? Partly by its sense of languages other than English. 'My English text is chaste', wrote Edward Gibbon, notoriously, 'and all licentious passages are left in the decent obscurity of a learned language'. Byron, who would have enjoyed the suggestiveness of 'licentious passages', takes advantage of the learned language when he nears the insatiable Catherine the Great and therefore hears those two monosyllables: 'Oh, thou "teterrima Causa" of all "belli"—' (*Don Juan*, canto IX, stanzas 55–6).

Jerome McGann as editor is a model of propriety: 'The Horace allusion (*Satires*, I iii 107–8) initiates some complex and ribald word-play. The two stanzas are a kind of riddle glancing at the one (key) word from the Horace text which Byron does *not* quote ("cunnus teterrima belli causa") as the "worst cause of war" '.[55]

> Oh, thou 'teterrima Causa' of all 'belli'—
>   Thou gate of Life and Death—thou nondescript!
> Whence is our exit and our entrance,—well I
>   May pause in pondering how all Souls are dipt
> In thy perennial fountain:—how man *fell*, I
>   Know not, since Knowledge saw her branches stript
> Of her first fruit, but how he falls and rises
> *Since, thou* hast settled beyond all surmises.
>
> Some call thee 'the worst Cause of war,' but I
>   Maintain thou art the *best*: for after all
> From thee we come, to thee we go, and why
>   To get at thee not batter down a wall,

---

[54] To Kinnaird, 26 October 1819; *Letters and Journals*, vi 232. Marchand's is the first edition to print an unbowdlerized text. Even Peter Quennell, in his excellent *Byron: A Self-Portrait* (1950) had, for 'tooled', '[f]ooled', and did not risk more than an asterisk for the four-letter word.
[55] McGann, v 740.

> Or waste a world? Since no one can deny
>   Thou dost replenish worlds both great and small:
> With, or without thee, all things at a stand
> Are, or would be, thou Sea of Life's dry Land!

This has a refreshing lack of pudor when it comes to pudenda. The paean is without envy. But the consummation of the refusal to go in for cant is in the fecund play of letters in the ensuing stanzas, the play of consonance and assonance that never crystallizes out as a pure anagram (as it later would in Lawrence Durrell's novel *Tunc*) but remains fluid.

> Catherine, who was the grand Epitome
>   Of that great Cause of war, or peace, or what
> You please (it causes all the things which be,
>   So you may take your choice of this or that)—
> Catherine, I say, was very glad to see
>   The handsome herald, on whose plumage sat
> Victory; and, pausing as she saw him kneel
> With his dispatch, forgot to break the seal.
>   (*Don Juan*, canto IX, stanza 57)

But what we readers may be glad to see, taking our choice of this or that, even if we may sometimes wonder whether we are imagining things, is the way in which Catherine the Great has this 'grand Epitome' about her person, tucked inside the words that contain her.

> Though somewhat large, exuberant, and truculent,
>   When *wroth*; while *pleased*, she was as fine a figure
> As those who like things rosy, ripe, and succulent,
>   Would wish to look on, while they are in vigour.
> She could repay each amatory look you lent
>   With interest, and in turn was wont with rigour
> To exact of Cupid's bills the full amount
> At sight, nor would permit you to discount.
>
> With her the latter, though at times convenient,
>   Was not so necessary; for they tell
> That she was handsome and though fierce *looked* lenient,
>   And always used her favourites too well.
> If once beyond her boudoir's precincts in ye went,
>   Your 'Fortune' was in a fair way 'to swell
> A Man,' as Giles says; for though she would widow all
> Nations, she liked Man as an individual.
>   (*Don Juan*, canto IX, stanzas 62–3)

Several words of stanza 62 offer a grand epitome: 'truculent', 'succulent', 'discount', plus the full phrases 'could repay each amatory look you lent' (or, phonetically k/c, 'look you lent'), and 'Cupid's bills the full amount'. They all rhyme, yes.

> But there seemed something that he wished to hide,
> *Which* hesitation more betrayed than masqued.
>
> (*Don Juan*, canto VI, stanza 100)

Moreover, there are two languages in play, or three if the French concurrence with the Latin is allowed to enter. This is cunningly 'convenient', the first rhyme-word in stanza 63. And Catherine's openness will be stressed a few stanzas later with the ample word 'condescension'— rhyming with 'pension' but also with what ensues: 'With other *extras*, which we need not mention'.

> Her sweet smile, and her then majestic figure,
>   Her plumpness, her imperial condescension,
> Her preference of a boy to men much bigger,
>   (Fellows whom Messalina's self would pension)
> Her prime of life, just now in juicy vigour,
>   With other *extras*, which we need not mention,—
> All these, or any one of these, explain
> Enough to make a stripling very vain.
>
> (stanza 72)

Given these charms and powers, it is not surprising that

> If once beyond her boudoir's precincts in ye went,
>   Your 'Fortune' was in a fair way 'to swell
> A Man,' as Giles says.

For at this point in the stanza Byron's teasing with letters is seconded by the expansive spirit of an allusion. Byron supplies a note:

'His fortune swells him, it is rank, he is married.'—Sir Giles Overreach; Massinger. See 'A New Way to Pay Old Debts'.

The allusion swells the lines, though Byron does not overreach himself since he is aware that an imaginative allusion is itself a new way to pay old debts. Cant has many fields in which to sport, and the opportunities offered by, say, patriotism, or the church, or politics, are ample; but the two paramount sources of cant in English life, as in much life elsewhere, were (and are?) sex and money. How deftly the allusion marries them.

WELLBORN.   'Tis all I owe you.
OVERREACH.   Have your redeem'd rags
Made you thus insolent?
WELLBORN.   Insolent to you!
Why, what are you, sir, unless in your years,
At the best, more than myself?
OVERREACH.   His fortune swells him:
'Tis rank, he's married.

(*A New Way to Pay Old Debts*, V. i)

And poor Overreach exclaims: 'I lent a thousand pound!'[56]

McGann is missing something when he says that 'The allusion slightly obscures Byron's ribald joke'. On the contrary. The allusive amplification, at once fiscal and physical, is just what Byron desires, as it is again later in the poem when he glimpses the prostitutes of London,

several score
Of those pedestrian Paphians, who abound
In decent London when the daylight's o'er.

(*Don Juan*, canto XI, stanza 30)

How very delicately 'In' steps towards 'decent', taking care not to be indecent. And a moment later we glimpse our hero:

But Juan now is stepping from his carriage

—with the verse stepping from one stanza to the next, a very rare thing in *Don Juan*:

But Juan now is stepping from his carriage

Into one of the sweetest of hotels,
Especially for foreigners—and mostly
For those whom favour or whom fortune swells [. . .]

(stanzas 30–1)

Byron rightly sees no reason to be embarrassed, financially or otherwise, by the acknowledgement that his own fortune as an artist, an artist for love and money, is swelled by the earnings and yearnings of others.

---

[56] For Master Shallow and his thousand pounds, see p. 135.

Keats

Allusion need not be covert or indirect. Like other poets, Keats sometimes announces his allusion as direct quotation:

> —Of bad lines a Centaine dose
> Is sure enough—and so 'here follows prose.'
> ('Dear Reynolds' 112–13)[1]

Keats follows *Twelfth Night. Or, What You Will*. With any allusion the play's the thing (wherein I'll catch the conscience and the consciousness). The concept of allusion and its application ask to be flexible, as with the due amount of play in any steering wheel.

Keats alludes to mythology, history, topical circumstance, and so on, but the present focus is on the calling into play of the words or phrases of a previous writer. An allusion predicates a source (no coincidence), but identifying a source is not the same as postulating an allusion, for a source is not necessarily called into play by its beneficiary. What goes to the making of a poem does not necessarily go to its meaning. Sometimes readers will disagree as to whether a line of Keats had its source in, say, *Hamlet*; sometimes, readers may agree that such was a source but disagree as to whether he was alluding; and often readers will disagree as to just what they should make of what Keats made of that which he alluded to. This, not because in criticism anything goes, but because much goes. Poems have a way of being undulating and diverse.

Allusions respect inheritance, but a sense of the central inheritance must change within history, the change both creating and created by changes within literature and its shaping spirit of imagination. For Keats, the paramount inheritance is that of English poetry itself. This simultaneously simplifies and complicates his art of allusion. Simplifies, because there is no longer the imaginative enterprise of reconciling two things (literary inheritance and something importantly other); complicates, because if there be no tension between the literary and the non-literary, where will this leave literature? Nowhere because everywhere?

[1] The poems are quoted from Jack Stillinger's edition, *The Poems of John Keats* (1978).

Keats's singular art might be seen as fulfilling allusion or as nullifying it. Interplay between art and all that is not art: this pinpoints the crux. Is Keats the great poet of aestheticism, of art for art's sake? Or does he put aestheticism in its place, a place of honour that does not enjoy a monopoly of honour? Not the be-all ye need to know, leave alone the end-all.

What (in the good old mot) is art, that it should have a sake? Keats made much of his poetic inheritance. Those who knew him thought of him as an heir who would have heirs. 'Though born to be a poet,' his friend Charles Brown averred, 'he was ignorant of his birthright until he had completed his eighteenth year'.[2] This is to respect Keats along his own lines: 'The Genius of Milton, more particularly in respect to its span in immensity, calculated him, by a sort of birthright, for such an "argument" as the paradise lost'.[3] In praising Milton, Keats wields words in a way that both is and is not Milton's: 'its span in immensity' is a paradox of the kind with which Milton illuminated the world (the immense is the immeasurable, how then can it have a *span*?); yet the wording does not mimic Milton, whose own paradoxes are differently jointed, compressed into oxymorons: 'darkness visible', 'precious bane'.

Reviewing *Endymion*, Francis Jeffrey had recourse to the figure of inheritance. Praising Keats's evocation of the richly strewn ocean-floor (iii 119–36), Jeffrey was sure that, though 'abundantly extravagant', it 'comes of no ignoble lineage, nor shames its high descent.'[4] Keats's seascape acknowledges its lineage, its unrepressed memory of Clarence's dream in *Richard III* (I. iv). How deftly, in the words *high descent*, Jeffrey catches the paradox of a creativity that owes much to another's creativity: *high*, noble, even royal of blood, like Clarence; *descent*, to the ocean-bed. It is true of Keats's deepest imaginings that they enjoy a seachange, for *Endymion* gathers strength of life not only from Shakespeare's imagining but, within that, from Shakespeare's dreamer's imaginings. Imagination within imagination.

Even when down to earth, Keats relishes Shakespeare's flights. Return to those lines that bring his letter to Reynolds to a close, or

---

[2] *The Keats Circle*, ed. Hyder Edward Rollins (2nd edn., 1965), ii 55.
[3] Keats's notes or marginalia (*c.* 1818) in his copy of *Paradise Lost*. These constitute Appendix 4 of *John Keats: The Complete Poems*, ed. John Barnard (2nd edn., 1977).
[4] *Edinburgh Review*, August 1820. *Keats: The Critical Heritage*, ed. G. M. Matthews (1971), p. 207.

rather bring to a close the verse part so as to open the prose part: 'Of bad lines a Centaine dose | Is sure enough—and so "here follows prose" '.[5]
Enough? Not until we comprehend that Keats has Malvolio in play, as had those pranksters in *Twelfth Night* who gulled him with the spoof love-letter from the great lady of the house:

Soft, here followes prose.—*If this fall into thy hand, revolve. In my stars I am above thee; but be not afraid of greatness: Some are born great, some achieve greatness, and some have greatness thrust upon them.* (II. v)

Keats was born great, whatever his social class; he achieved greatness; and he did so because greatness was thrust upon him, by courtesy of his predecessors, their greatness. Keats wished well. Benvolio, not Malvolio. The poetry of the past was very seldom social oppression and was very often the means of escape not only from class but from something else that may oppress, a grievance as to class.

What Keats most valued in the English poets, irrespective of anything with which they could furnish his art, was a sense of brotherhood with his peers. He declines the invitation to figure in the dark melodrama of *The Anxiety of Influence*. How unmisgivingly he speaks of influence, especially while happily under it.

> And many a verse from so strange influence
> That we must ever wonder how, and whence
> It came. Also imaginings will hover
> Round my fire-side . . .
>   ('Sleep and Poetry' 69–72)

This verse knows what it owes to Wordsworth, and playfully is pleased if we know too. Keats finds in 'To the Daisy' the gift of which Wordsworth speaks, 'A happy genial influence, | Coming one knows not how, or whence'. With this proviso only, that this time we do know how and whence the happy genial influence came, and need not ever wonder. The 'imaginings' within Keats's lines embody the kindly hovering of which they speak. A mystery remains, but it is mitigated by the simply unmisgiving. For Keats, allusions are debts of honour. He is indebted to Wordsworth's lines about a debt, about what is owing:

> And all day long I number yet,
> All seasons through, another debt,

[5] *The Letters of John Keats*, ed. Hyder Edward Rollins (1958), i 263.

> Which I, wherever thou art met,
>   To thee am owing;
> An instinct call it, a blind sense;
> A happy genial influence,
> Coming one knows not how, or whence,
>   Nor whither going.
>
> ('To the Daisy' 65–72)

Thither, to Keats, this is one place where these lines—unbeknownst to their creator—were going.

Keats spoke with inspiration of inspiration, its astonishment. His friend Richard Woodhouse set this down vividly in the summer of 1820:

He has said, that he has often not been aware of the beauty of some thought or expression until after he has composed & written it down—It has then struck him with astonishment—& seemed rather the production of another person than his own—He has wondered how he came to hit upon it [. . .]—Perhaps every one in the habit of writing verse or prose, may have had a somewhat similar feeling, that of the extreme appositeness & happiness (the *curiosa felicitas*) of an idea, of the excellence of which he was unaware until he [. . .] came to read it over. It seems scarcely his own; & he feels that he could never imitate it or hit upon it again: & he cannot conceive how it came to him—Such Keats said was his Sensation of astonishment & pleasure when he had produced the lines 'His white melodious &c—It seemed to come by chance or magic—to be as it were something given to him.—[6]

This is itself inspired and astonishing. Much of what Keats says is germane to the local wonders of allusion. Paradoxically it is often by courtesy of another, with the aid of allusion, that a poet becomes himself. Allusion calls into play 'the production of another person', 'something given to him', something 'scarcely his own'. 'He cannot conceive how it came to him': and this is partly because the conceiving is not his alone, any more than is the conceiving of a baby, a new lease of life.

And, as Woodhouse remarked, Keats's insight is 'expressed in these lines so happily that they are an illustration of the very thing itself':

> Apollo then,
> With sudden scrutiny and gloomless eyes,
> Thus answer'd, while his white melodious throat

---

[6] *The Keats Circle*, i 129, expanding contractions and eliding cancelled readings.

Throbb'd with the syllables.—"Mnemosyne!
Thy name is on my tongue, I know not how".

(Hyperion, iii 79–83)

The cry itself is on Keats's tongue, he knows not how. Yet perhaps one
aspect of the how is the grace of Wordsworth, 'Coming one knows not
how'.

Keats's play with allusion animates his great letters. In a letter-jour-
nal to his brother George and his sister-in-law far away in America (12
March 1819), he described not only what but how, physically how, he
had been reading, exactly how he stood and sat the while:

—the fire is at its last click—I am sitting with my back to it with one foot
rather askew upon the rug and the other with the heel a little elevated from the
carpet—I am writing this on the Maid's tragedy which I have read since tea
with Great pleasure—Besides this volume of Beaumont & Fletcher—there are
on the tabl[e] two volumes of chaucer and a new work of Tom Moores call'd
'Tom Cribb's memorial to Congress—nothing in it—These are trifles—but I
require nothing so much of you as that you will give me a like description of
yourselves, however it may be when you are writing to me—could I see the
same thing done of any great Man long since dead it would be a great delight:
as to know in what position Shakspeare sat when he began 'To be or not to
be"—such thing[s] become interesting from distance of time or place. I hope
you are both now in that sweet sleep which no two beings deserve more that
[than] you do—I must fancy you so—and please myself in the fancy of speaking a prayer and a blessing over you and your lives—God bless you—I whisper
good night in your ears and you will dream of me—[7]

This takes its origin, as so often in Keats, from the imagining of someone
imagining (Shakespeare writing *Hamlet*). Although 'To be or not to be' is
simply referred to, it hangs in a web of allusion. A happy web withal.

'There's magick in the web of it'. To the curse upon Hamlet and
death's troubled sleep ('To sleep! perchance to dream; ay, there's the
rub', III. i) is added the curse upon Othello. Iago's imaginings are
malign as he exults over Othello:

Look, where he comes! Not poppy, nor mandragora,
Nor all the drowsy syrups of the world,
Shall ever medicine thee to that sweet sleep
Which thou ow'dst yesterday.

(III. iii)

[7] *Letters*, ii 73–4.

But what in Iago was sickly sweet is turned by Keats, by magic, into sheer love, not a gloating curse but 'a prayer and a blessing':

I hope you are both now in that sweet sleep which no two beings deserve more that [than] you do—I must fancy you so—and please myself in the fancy of speaking a prayer and a blessing over you and your lives—God bless you—I whisper good night in your ears and you will dream of me—[8]

The words 'that sweet sleep' are rinsed, restored; their having been so is part of love's point.

True, it is a simple run of words, but Keats deepens its simplicity, gracing Iago's disgrace. Iago had assured himself, a few lines earlier: 'Trifles, light as air, | Are, to the jealous, confirmations strong | As proofs of holy writ' (III. iii). Keats had doffed his thoughts on posture: 'These are trifles'.

Keats's imagination can transubstantiate, can convert gall to manna. Not imagining only, but imagining into. He speculated on this furtherance in Milton:

One of the most mysterious of semi-speculations is, one would suppose, that of one Mind's imagining into another. Things may be described by a Man's self in parts so as to make a grand whole which that Man himself would scarcely inform to its excess. A Poet can seldom have justice done to his imagination— for men are as distinct in their conceptions of material shadowings as they are in matters of spiritual understanding: it can scarcely be conceived how Milton's Blindness might here ade [aid] the magnitude of his conceptions as a bat in a large gothic vault.   (His note in his *Paradise Lost*, i 53–75)

But is this a semi-speculation or a double one? There is imagining, and there is imagining *into*. And there is imagining *after*. Keats needed this further prepositional extension to express his awe at Pandemonium:

What creates the intense pleasure of not knowing? A sense of independence, of power, from the fancy's creating a world of its own by the sense of probabilities. We have read the Arabian Nights and hear there are thousands of those sort of Romances lost—we imagine after them—but not their realities if we had them nor our fancies in their strength can go further than this Pandemonium.[9]

A world of its own, and yet one open to us all. A palace of art, or rather—in this grim case of Milton's Pandemonium—of devilish aestheticism.

---

[8] *Letters*, ii 74.   [9] His note in his *Paradise Lost*, i 710–30.

Elsewhere in *Paradise Lost*, Keats catches Milton's imagination on the wing:

> but featherd soon and fledge
> They summ'd thir Penns, and soaring th' air sublime
> With clang despis'd the ground, under a cloud
> In prospect;
>
> (vii 420–3)

What Keats sees is that such soarings are a case not of Milton's imagination pursuing something, but of Milton pursuing his imagination:

Milton in every instance pursues his imagination to the utmost—he is 'sagacious of his Quarry,' he sees Beauty on the wing, pounces upon it and gorges it to the producing his essential verse. 'So from the root springs lighter the green stalk', etc. But in no instance is this sort of perseverance more exemplified than in what may be called his *stationing or statu[a]ry*. He is not content with simple description, he must station,—thus here, we not only see how the Birds '*with clang despised the ground,*' but we see them '*under a cloud in prospect.*' So we see Adam '*Fair indeed and tall—under a plantane*'—and so we see Satan '*disfigured—on the Assyrian Mount.*' This last with all its accompaniments, and keeping in mind the Theory of Spirits' eyes and the simile of Gallilio, has a dramatic vastness and solemnity fit and worthy to hold one amazed in the midst of this *Paradise Lost*—

In their own stationing and statuary, Keats's marginalia in his copies of Milton and Shakespeare offer no less vivid evidence than do his letters of how his poetic imagination worked and played. It is in this spirit that he evokes Edmund Kean's acting. Here Keats's prepositional extension of *imagine* is *to*, with Kean acting to perfection a thoroughgoing character from Massinger:

In the hypocritical self-possession, in the caution, and afterwards the pride, cruelty, and avarice, Luke appears to us a man incapable of imagining to the extreme heinousness of crimes.

Kean's Shakespearean acting as continuous with Shakespeare's own imaginative powers: 'There is an indescribable gusto in his voice, by which we feel that the utterer is thinking of the past and the future, while speaking of the instant'.[10] Gliding from 'the past' to 'the future', this then swoops, not as you expect, upon 'the present' but upon 'the

---

[10] 'Mr. Kean', *The Champion*, 21 December 1817; Appendix 5 in Barnard's edition of the poems.

instant'. He is imagining not only the consummate actor, but the character and the playwright. His insight commands the vistas, at once exhilarating and dizzying, of the imagining of imagining.

It is characteristic of Keats's sense of how past and future meet that he should have entered upon this praise of Kean with the words 'In our unimaginative days'—well aware that he owes those very words to an imaginative genius of those days, Wordsworth:

'In our unimaginative days'—*Habeas Corpus'd* as we are, out of all wonder, uncertainty and fear;—in these fireside, delicate, gilded days,—these days of sickly safety and comfort, we feel very grateful to Mr Kean for giving us some excitement by his old passion in one of the old plays.

This is grateful to Wordsworth: *The Excursion*, ii 23–4: 'ranging through the tamer ground | Of these our unimaginative days'.

Ever-alert on allusion's traces, Keats is drawn to such moments, moments when an imagination creates imaginers, actors for instance. Or imaginings that are dreams; Mercutio's imagining of dreams' imaginings in *Romeo and Juliet* is midwife to Keats's lines:

> Look not so wilder'd; for these things are true,
> And never can be born of atomies
> That buzz about our slumbers, like brain-flies
> (*Endymion*, i 850–2)

These atomies were born of Shakespeare and of Mercutio, a team now joined by Keats in team-work, dream-work:

> Drawn with a team of little atomies
> Athwart men's noses as they lie asleep.
> (*Romeo and Juliet*, I. iv)

Dreams are real but do not present realities exactly; the same is true of actors.

Dreams and actors, engaging in feats of imagination, meet in the post-masque moment of *The Tempest* (IV. i)

> These our actors,
> As I foretold you, were all spirits, and
> Are melted into air, into thin air:
> And, like the baseless fabrick of this vision,
> The clowd-capp'd towers, the gorgeous palaces,
> The solemn temples, the great globe itself,
> Yea, all which it inherit, shall dissolve;

And, like this insubstantial pageant faded,
Leave not a rack behind: we are such stuff
As dreams are made of, and our little life
Is rounded with a sleep.—

The actor playing Prospero speaks of the actors of the masque within
the play. He intimates to the audience that each of us is an actor. A line-
ending ('spirits, and | Are melted') pauses and poises upon *and* for a
minuscule moment, to intimate such vistas.

This supreme speech was for Keats a source and a resource, inviting
his art of allusion:

> The Morphean fount
> Of that fine element that visions, dreams,
> And fitful whims of sleep are made of, streams
> Into its airy channels with so subtle,
> So thin a breathing, not the spider's shuttle,
> Circled a million times within the space
> Of a swallow's nest-door, could delay a trace,
> A tinting of its quality: how light
> Must dreams themselves be; seeing they're more slight
> Than the mere nothing that engenders them!
>
> (*Endymion*, i 747–56)

The traces are there for all to see and feel, light but not slight, engen-
dered not by a mere nothing but by a great something, Shakespeare's
vision (itself of another's vision). 'A tinting of its quality' is there, a
Shakespearean quality. 'That fine element that visions, dreams, | And
fitful whims of sleep are made of': Keats is finely in his element, which
is Shakespeare's element, for such is what it breathes, what it is made
of—*made of*, the reading in Keats's volume of Shakespeare, subsequently established as *made on*.

Prospero prophesies. 'The great globe itself, | Yea, all which it
inherit, shall dissolve' (IV. i). Keats inherits this, this thought, these very
words. Not until all dissolves will Shakespeare's words (he trusts)
dissolve.

Two points of principle underlie all this. First, that Keats's way with
Shakespeare does not insist that a reader know Prospero's lines.
Irrespective of Shakespeare, Keats's lines are a thing of beauty and a joy
for ever. A poet does well to have the courtesy and the prudence not to
make the taking of an allusion a precondition of a reader's appreciation.
The allusion is a bonus, not an entrance-fee.

Some impulse that underlies allusion (inheriting, playing, borrowing) may fit happily with the preoccupations and subject-matter of the
work itself. Keats inherits Shakespeare's evocation, 'all which it inherit';
Shakespeare's spirit and spirits inspire him and his breathing; his art is
tinted with its quality. Recall Woodhouse on Keats and inspiration, an
insight 'expressed in these lines so happily that they are an illustration
of the very thing itself'.

Keats's respect for Milton and Shakespeare is inseparable from,
though not indistinguishable from, the allusive achievements that are
thanks to them. He is truly grateful, as the allusive poet had better be.
Take his excitement at a great speech in *A Midsummer Night's Dream* (II.
i) in which ill will arrives at good will. Titania's speech begins in an
evocation of jealousy, but how poor is jealousy in comparison with
goodnesses, with the gracious, with love and gratitude:

> These are the forgeries of jealousie,
> And never since the middle Summers spring
> Met we on hil, in dale, forrest, or mead,
> By paved fountaine, or by rushie brooke,
> Or in the beached margent of the sea,
> To dance our ringlets to the whistling Winde,
> But with thy braules thou hast disturb'd our sport.

Keats marvels lucidly:

There is something exquisitely rich and luxurious in Titania's saying "since the
middle summer's spring" as if bowers were not exuberant and covert enough
for fairy sports until their second sprouting—which is surely the most boun-
teous overwhelming of all Nature's goodnesses. She steps forth benignly in the
spring and her conduct is so gracious that by degrees all things are becoming
happy under her wings and nestle against her bosom: she feels this love and
gratitude too much to remain selfsame, and unable to contain herself buds
forth the overflowings of her heart about the middle summer. O Shakespeare
thy ways are but just searchable! The thing is a piece of profound verdure.[11]

Keats, like Nature (as Shakespeare has passionately imagined her), steps
forth benignly. Nature is grateful for our gratitude, is at one with all
imaginative energies, and Shakespeare is a force of nature. In crying 'O
Shakespeare thy ways are but just searchable', Keats stops 'but just' on
this side idolatry. Wycliffe's translation of Romans 11: 33 had praised

---

[11] Marginalia in his facsimile copy of the First Folio of Shakespeare. Caroline F. E.
Spurgeon, *Keats's Shakespeare* (1928), p. 52.

God 'and his ways unsearchable', and Boswell had exclaimed in his life
of Johnson (aetat.20): 'How wonderful, how unsearchable are the ways
of GOD!'

The filament between Keats's gratitude to Shakespeare and his
allusions can be glimpsed in the phrases within his commentary that
call allusion into play. For allusion too is a 'second sprouting', may
be gracious, does not 'remain selfsame'—yet this because of an extension, not a repudiation, of the self and the same. Like a due allusion,
'The middle Summers spring' is a renovation, generously two seasons
at once, its own and not its own. T. S. Eliot evoked another loveli-
ness of seasonable surprise that may owe something to Shakespeare
and to Keats (though probably as no more than source, not as allusion), there in the first line of *Little Gidding*: 'Midwinter spring is its
own season'.

'A piece of profound verdure': such was Keats's tribute to
Shakespeare's words, to Titania's words, to the nature of Nature. From
a speech later in the same scene there grew a piece of profound verdure
in Keats:

> I cannot see what flowers are at my feet,
>   Nor what soft incense hangs upon the boughs,
> But, in embalmed darkness, guess each sweet
>   Wherewith the seasonable month endows
> The grass, the thicket, and the fruit-tree wild;
>   White hawthorn, and the pastoral eglantine;
>   Fast fading violets cover'd up in leaves;
>   And mid-May's eldest child,
>   The coming musk-rose, full of dewy wine,
>   The murmurous haunt of flies on summer eves.
>   ('Ode to a Nightingale' 41–50)

> I know a banke where the wilde thyme blowes,
> Where Oxslips and the nodding Violet growes,
> Quite over-cannoped with luscious woodbine,
> With sweet muske roses, and with Eglantine;
> There sleeps *Tytania*, sometime of the night,
> Lull'd in these flowers, with dances and delight:
>   (*A Midsummer Night's Dream*, II. i)[12]

---

[12] Text of the First Folio (facsimile); the other edition he owned (text of Johnson and
Steevens, 1814) has 'whereon' and 'lush' for 'where' and 'luscious'.

The flowers, violets, musk roses, and eglantine; the darkness of the night; the sweet that is not sickly, and the wild that is not dangerous: all these are transplanted from Shakespeare's garden to Keats's. The violets re-double still and multiply.

Yet Keats has made the verdure his own. How much is effected by the imaginative simplicity that changes Oberon's couplets to diverse couplings of rhyme that incorporate, mid-way, the shortening, the compacting, of a line ('And mid-May's eldest child'). And how characteristic of Keats's good-will that what in Oberon's scene-setting is to issue only three lines later in ill-will ('And make her full of hateful fantasies') is in the Ode an imagining of love and ruth.

This too is then a 'second sprouting'. Though not the kind of allusion that crystallizes overtly (as does 'here follows prose'), this is allusion nevertheless, a diffusion of atmosphere that calls tenderly into play (for 'tender is the night') the air of an earlier play.

Shakespeare has soaked Keats's heart through. The heart of the passage in the Ode is Shakespearean. Or rather, one of the heart's chambers is. It was a needless either/or that led Helen Vendler to insist that here Keats draws upon poetry alone:

To deck his bower, Keats turns not to nature but to art: the violets and musk-roses and eglantine are borrowed from Titania's bower [. . .] described by Oberon (as this bower is described by Keats) from memory not sight.*

* Robert Pinsky, in *The Situation of Poetry* (1976), cites this passage as an example of the poetry of realist description. It is, in fact, just the opposite (since Keats is 'blind'); it is an example of pure imaginative conceiving and literary allusion.[13]

For Vendler, not nature but art. Why not both? Keats's husbandry sees to it that the second sprouting, rooted in poetry, is equally rooted in roots, in nature, in common or garden sproutings. Art's relations to art are the stronger when art acknowledges the power of what is not art: nature, say. This independent power is happy with interdependency.

> 'This is an art
> Which does mend nature, change it rather, but
> The art itself is nature'.
>   'So it is'.
>   (*The Winter's Tale*, IV. iv)

---

[13] *The Odes of John Keats* (1983), pp. 84, 306.

Keats is deeply touched by Shakespeare, because Shakespeare's words realize the true voice of feeling. His friend Charles Cowden Clarke never forgot this in the young Keats:

Once, when reading the 'Cymbeline' aloud, I saw his eyes fill with tears, and his voice faltered when he came to the departure of Posthumus, and Imogen saying she would have watched him—

> 'Till the diminution
> Of space had pointed him sharp as my needle;
> Nay followed him till he had *melted from*
> *The smallness of a gnat to air;* and then
> Have turn'd mine eye and wept.
> (I. iii) [14]

Keats's eyes fill with tears as he reads aloud of Imogen's tears, or rather, her imagining of tears. In her dear resilience she is not in tears, but is imagining how she would have ended in tears had she suffered (as had the man who tells her of it) the sight of her departing loved one.

The speech is among Shakespeare's greatest, with the art in the precision. There is 'from' at the line-brink, at a parting, the delicatest lattice. There is the movement from the open sound to the closed conclusion in the sequence 'mine eye and wept'. There is 'my needle', not *a* needle since the speaker is a woman. And how pointed *needle* is, for it pricks, and a needle has an eye, so Imogen's heart and mind move with rueful effortlessness from 'my needle' to 'mine eye', with a faint touch upon *mine* as against the needle's. Not only the mind's eye, but the heart's eye.[15]

'Nay followed him': and as with 'Here follows prose', Keats is happy to follow Shakespeare in imagining a sadness of departure. Shakespeare's passage is a point of departure for Keats:

> "Here must we leave thee."—At these words up flew
> The impatient doves, up rose the floating car,
> Up went the hum celestial. High afar
> The Latmian saw them minish into nought;
> And, when all were clear vanish'd, still he caught
> A vivid lightning from that dreadful bow.
> (*Endymion*, ii 579–84)

---

[14] Charles and Mary Cowden Clarke, *Recollections of Writers* (1878), p. 126; their italics.

[15] 'To Hope' 1–3: 'When by my solitary hearth I sit, | And hateful thoughts enwrap my soul in gloom; | When no fair dreams before my "mind's eye" flit'; *Hamlet* (I. ii).

Keats's lines are buoyed not only by a memory of Shakespeare's Imogen but by Shakespearean powers. There is the elision (urged by the metre) that catches impatience in '*The im*patient doves', in the Augustan manner, 'Th'impatient'. There is the play of one linguistic world against another in the mildly oxymoronic phrase 'the hum celestial', as though the humdrum hum might always sit happily next to the celestial. Then the open endings 'afar' and 'bow' against the closed 'caught' and 'nought' (owing something to such an effect in Shakespeare's ear and Imogen's mouth). And the philosophical paradox 'minish into nought' (is this possible?), along with 'minish' as itself a 'minished form of *diminish*, not a diminishing of Shakespeare's 'diminution' but an extension of its imagination. With the sound effect of 'minish' into 'vanish'd', where minish does not vanish; it is still echoed, and so has not, at least, vanished from memory, from our hearing.

That Keats owes a debt to Shakespeare, and pays it, is not to be doubted. But are we contemplating a source or an allusion? We might learn from Keats, who never relaxes his intelligence but always has a relaxed intelligence. We might let memory play, let Mnemosyne be our muse, without insisting either/or:

several things dovetailed in my mind, & at once it struck me, what quality went to form a Man of Achievement especially in Literature & which Shakespeare possessed so enormously—I mean *Negative Capability*, that is when man is capable of being in uncertainties, Mysteries, doubts, without any irritable reaching after fact & reason—[16]

Dovetailing, Keats both does and does not depart from Shakespeare.

It is characteristic of his genius that what informs his art informs his life no less. He wrote to his loved one Fanny Brawne, two years after *Endymion*:

Yesterday and this morning I have been haunted with a sweet vision—I have seen you the whole time in your shepherdess dress. How my senses have ached at it! How my eyes have been full of tears at it! [. . .]—say what you think—confess if your heart is too much fasten'd on the world. Perhaps then I may see you at a greater distance, I may not be able to appropriate you so closely to myself. Were you to loose a favorite bird from the cage, how would your eyes ache after it as long as it was in sight; when out of sight you would recover a little.[17]

[16] *Letters*, i 193.   [17] ? May 1820; *Letters*, ii 290–1.

This, which owes as much to ordinary life as to Shakespeare's art and Keats's own, is not 'too consolatory to console' (to apply to Keats a fine formulation by Frank Kermode), and is itself art, as Keats's letters so often are. Keats has us exercise our imagination upon a poet's imaginings. This always has the danger that we may imagine something that is not there. Keats himself was aware that a poet's intentions cannot be limited to conscious intentions: 'One of the three Books I have with me is Shakespear's Poems,' he wrote to Reynolds, a brother poet: 'I neer found so many beauties in the sonnets—they seem to be full of fine things said unintentionally—in the intensity of working out conceits'.[18] Said in the sonnets, for sure, but said so as to surprise the sayer, as we have heard Keats himself say of inspiration:

He has said, that he has often not been aware of the beauty of some thought or expression until after he has composed & written it down—It has then struck him with astonishment—

'Said unintentionally—in the intensity of working out conceits': this immediately conveys that the intensity of poetry may be continuous with its being issued unintentionally, inspired as unpremeditated verse.

In this letter, Keats had to correct himself—not as to Shakespeare's greatness, but as to just where the instance that he loved was to be found:

He has left nothing to say about nothing or any thing: for look at Snails, you know what he says about Snails, you know where he talks about "cockled snails"—well, in one of these sonnets, he says—the chap slips into—no! I lie! this is in the Venus and Adonis: the Simile brought it to my Mind.

Audi—As the snail whose tender horns being hit,
  Shrinks back into his shelly cave with pain,
  And there all smothered up in shade doth sit,
  Long after fearing to put forth again:
  So at his bloody view her eyes are fled,
  Into the deep dark Cabins of her head.[19]

Yet far from having left nothing to say, Shakespeare helps others—Keats among them—to find what they have to say.

---

[18] 22 November 1817; *Letters*, i 188.
[19] *Letters*, i 189. Rollins notes that 'the tender horns of cockled snails' is from *Love's Labour's Lost* (IV. iii); Keats misquotes *Venus and Adonis* 1033–8: back into] backward in. put] creep.

'As the snail . . . So . . .': 'The Simile brought it to my Mind'. When Keats breathes open a sonnet with the line 'To one who has been long in city pent', there can be no doubt of an allusion to *Paradise Lost*: 'As one who long in populous City pent . . .'.[20] In Milton this had been something imagined within an imagining, in a simile, 'As one who . . . Such . . .'. In Keats, it has become the fresh air itself, a larger air than the psychic fresh air, the inner weather, that refreshed Satan for a while: 'Such Pleasure took the Serpent'.

The whole of Keats's sonnet is alive with diverse moments from Milton (the singular 'angel's tear' flows from the 'tears such as angels weep' that Milton had conceived, *Paradise Lost*, i 620). But Keats is not pent in Milton, nor Milton in him. Both breathe. The breathing-room comes in part from Keats's having been prompted by a simile, already an imagining upon imagining. Milton:

> As one who long in populous City pent,
> Where Houses thick and Sewers annoy the Aire,
> Forth issuing on a Summers Morn to breathe
> Among the pleasant Villages and Farmes
> Adjoynd, from each thing met conceaves delight,
> The smell of Grain, or tedded Grass, or Kine,
> Or Dairie, each rural sight, each rural sound;
> If chance with Nymphlike step fair Virgin pass,
> What pleasing seemd, for her now pleases more,
> She most, and in her looks summs all Delight.
> Such Pleasure took the Serpent to behold
> This Flourie Plat, the sweet recess of *Eve*
> Thus earlie, thus alone; her Heav'nly forme
> Angelic, but more soft, and Feminine,
> Her graceful Innocence, her every Aire
> Of gesture or lest action overawd
> His Malice, and with rapine sweet bereav'd
> His fierceness of the fierce intent it brought:
> That space the Evil one abstracted stood
> From his own evil, and for the time remaind
> Stupidly good, of enmitie disarm'd,
> Of guile, of hate, of envy, of revenge.
>   (*Paradise Lost*, ix 445–66)

---

[20] There is a further vista whenever an allusion may play with the fact that others have alluded hereabouts. Coleridge, for instance, calls up Milton's line in his 'How many bards in city garret pent' ('The Nightingale' 2), a line which Keats knew and which moreover went to

Keats:

> To one who has been long in city pent,
> 'Tis very sweet to look into the fair
> And open face of heaven—to breathe a prayer
> Full in the smile of the blue firmament.
> Who is more happy, when, with heart's content,
> Fatigued he sinks into some pleasant lair
> Of wavy grass, and reads a debonair
> And gentle tale of love and languishment?
> Returning home at evening, with an ear
> Catching the notes of Philomel,—an eye
> Watching the sailing cloudlet's bright career,
> He mourns that day so soon has glided by:
> E'en like the passage of an angel's tear
> That falls through the clear ether silently.

Milton's 'sweet recess' becomes the pleasant lair where was bred the 'very sweet' of Keats's sonnet. Milton's 'Heav'nly' becomes 'heaven'; what was 'pleasing' and 'pleases more', 'Such Pleasure', all turn in Keats to the relaxedly 'pleasant', rather as the 'tedded Grass', cut and drying, reverts to the relaxedly uncut, the 'wavy grass'. But 'to breathe' remains exactly, entirely, happily, the same. With a nimble leap, Milton's name 'Eve' returns home as 'evening'. With a dear new creation from Milton's creation, what in *Paradise Lost* had been 'the Aire', and of Eve 'her every Aire', becomes in Keats the 'debonair'. But then what is debonair but *de bon air*? Satan's disposition, though not his nature, is changed for a moment by the good air:

> That space the Evil one abstracted stood
> From his own evil, and for the time remaind
> Stupidly good, of enmitie disarm'd,
> Of guile, of hate, of envie, of revenge.

Again and again there is an *As* or a *So* or a *Like* in the passages to which Keats is drawn and upon which he draws, whether as source or as allusion. There is present not only the imagined but the imaginary. It is this act of imagining *within* a work of imagination that from one point of view compounds the store set upon imagination, imagination

the making of his 'How many bards gild the lapses of time!' On such incremental allusion, see Michael Whitworth, ' "Sweet Thames" and *The Waste Land*'s Allusions', *Essays in Criticism*, xlviii (1998), 35–58.

upon imagination after all. But from another point of view, to distinguish the imaginary from the imagined must be to introduce a crucial distinction that is in its turn germane to the distinction between imagination and all else. 'Imaginings will hover | Round my fire-side' ('Sleep and Poetry' 71–2). But in the words of Samuel Beckett—who alludes consummately to 'Ode to a Nightingale' in his story 'Dante and the Lobster': 'Take into the air my quiet breath'—there are, after all, 'Things and imaginings'.²¹ So there are, although things too have to be imagined, and although imagination is at work in all our seeing and our remembering. There remains a distinction between the imagined and the imaginary. Leave alone the imaginative.

The imaginary within the imagined, this most draws Keats. It may be a simile within description's imagination ('As the snail . . .'), or an imaginary landscape within an imagined world. Dover Cliff in *King Lear* (IV. iv) exists differently from all that is in its vicinity in the play, in that no such cliff is there for Gloucester to throw himself from. And if it should be retorted that, this being a play, no Earl of Gloucester and no therapeutic Edgar really exist either, it would still be the case that Dover Cliff has a different order of existlessness. It is fully imagined, yes, but known to be something other than imagined, to be imaginary on this occasion, while existing as a real cliff outside the play in geological time.

Dover Cliff (Shakespeare's, Edgar's) fascinated Keats. It dominates one of his greatest letters, that to the painter Haydon in May 1817, where Keats ponders what it is that might, in the words he quotes from *Love's Labour's Lost* (I. i), 'make us heirs of all eternity':

—truth is I have been in such a state of Mind as to read over my Lines and hate them. I am "one that gathers Samphire dreadful trade" the Cliff of Poesy Towers above me—yet when, Tom who meets with some of Pope's Homer in Plutarch's Lives reads some of those to me they seem like Mice to mine.²²

This gazes up the sheer cliff, not down it as Edgar had done with his here-imaginary cliff, but Keats still remembers the fishermen who in Edgar's vertiginous fancy 'appear like mice'. One kind of awe ('the Cliff of Poesy Towers above me') is blessedly countered by the opposite kind, the heartening, with *yet*: I hate my lines and yet Pope's lines 'seem like Mice to mine'.

---

²¹ *More Pricks than Kicks* (1934), p. 20. 'Things and imaginings': *Ill Seen Ill Said* (1981), p. 20.
²² *Letters*, i 141.

Keats makes new while not making free. Even his misquotations can catch a truth. The exchange in this scene when Edgar's false intimation, 'Hark, do you hear the sea?', is met by Gloucester's reply 'No, truly', is truly mis-remembered by Keats, as incorporating the pressure of *not*: 'the passage in Lear—"Do you not hear the Sea?"—has haunted me intensely'.[23] No *not* in Edgar, and yet Gloucester does not hear the sea, truly does not, there being no sea just there except in Edgar's words. Which is not quite the same, given the imaginary within the imagined, as saying Shakespeare's words, since different kinds of imagining are called for, called upon.

The currency that Keats's predecessors enjoy within his work is never small change (as Byron's allusive largesse ringingly is). The characteristic Keatsian wealth of allusiveness is more diffused than a coin of allusion. The distinction between a source and an allusion becomes more than usually elusive once what is in play is a more impalpable allusiveness. Here is saturation, and not crystallization:

> Fade far away, dissolve, and quite forget
>   What thou among the leaves hast never known,
> The weariness, the fever, and the fret
>   Here, where men sit and hear each other groan;
> Where palsy shakes a few, sad, last gray hairs,
>   Where youth grows pale, and spectre-thin, and dies;
>   Where but to think is to be full of sorrow
>   And leaden-eyed despairs,
>   Where Beauty cannot keep her lustrous eyes,
>   Or new Love pine at them beyond to-morrow.
>   ('Ode to a Nightingale' 21–30)

This never forgets Shakespeare's Sonnet 73 ('That time of yeeare thou maist in me behold'), a tissue of metaphors throughout, imaginings within an imagined state of mind, with what is beheld being beholden entirely to elaborated metaphors, one after the other: 'In me thou seest . . .', 'In me thou seest . . .', 'This thou percevst'. It is the poem that most dissolves into a poem of Keats.[24]

[23] *Letters*, ii 132.

[24] Shakespeare, though, is joined (David Ferry observes to me) by Wordsworth, whose 'Lines Composed a Few Miles above Tintern Abbey' speak of 'weariness', of the 'fretful', and of 'fever' (27, 52–3). See Keats's profound letter on Shakespeare, Milton, and Wordsworth: 'However among the effects this breathing is father of is that tremendous one of sharpening one's vision into the heart and nature of Man—of convincing ones nerves that the World is full of Misery and Heartbreak, Pain, Sickness and oppression—whereby This Chamber of

A tabulation may tell the story even though it conveys none of the feeling, the shared mood that is but one of Keats's moods in his poem. Keats's stanza is a second sprouting from Shakespeare's sonnet: *fade, away, thou, leaves, where, shakes, few, sad, youth, dies* (death), and *love*. More, Keats's entire poem, 'a piece of profound verdure', is alive with the verdurous glooms of this sonnet. Shakespeare's 'hange | Upon those boughes' becomes, with a different suspension, Keats's 'hangs upon the boughs'. Although no single shared word is unusual, the density achieves a cumulative plausibility: in the order of the sonnet, *time, sweet, birds / Bird, sang / sing, seest / see, twilight / light, such, day / days, fadeth / fading, night, take, death, self, whereon / wherewith, thy, more, well, long*.

F. R. Leavis, not usually a critic who went in for the tentativeness of 'It is as if . . .', was duly teased by Keats and aestheticism. 'It is as if Keats were making major poetry out of minor—as if, that is, the genius of a major poet were working in the material of minor poetry'.[25] Aestheticism may be judged both to overvalue art and to undervalue it, as valuing only art and as misrepresenting art's relation to all else. Alluding sardonically to the closing lines of 'Ode on a Grecian Urn', Philip Larkin spoke of

the two kinds of poem I sometimes think I write: the beautiful and the true. I have always believed that beauty is beauty, truth truth, that is not all ye know on earth nor all ye need to know, and I think a poem usually starts off either from the feeling How beautiful that is or from the feeling How true that is. One of the jobs of the poem is to make the beautiful seem true and the true beautiful, but in fact the disguise can usually be penetrated.[26]

T. S. Eliot, no aesthete, clarified what is at issue when he looked back upon the first year of *The Criterion*:

It is the function of a literary review to maintain the autonomy and disinterestedness of literature, and at the same time to exhibit the relations of litera-

---

Maiden Thought becomes gradually darken'd and at the same time on all sides of it many doors are set open—but all dark—all leading to dark passages—We see not the ballance of good and evil. We are in a mist—*We* are now in that state—We feel the "burden of the Mystery," To this point was Wordsworth come, as far as I can conceive when he wrote "Tintern Abbey" and it seems to me that his Genius is explorative of those dark Passages' (to J. H. Reynolds, 3 May 1818; *Letters*, i 281).

[25] *Revaluation* (1936), p. 251.
[26] James Gibson (ed.), *Let the Poet Choose* (1973), p. 102. Reprinted in Larkin's *Further Requirements*, ed. Anthony Thwaite (2001), p. 39.

ture—not to 'life', as something contrasted to literature, but to all the other activities, which, together with literature, are the components of life.[27]

Keats's greatest poems, and letters, realize the extremity both of heroic submission to art and of resistance to art's inordinacy or hubris. At the level of explicit asseveration (as against realization in art), this putting of art in its true place is not particularly difficult, whether in prose or in verse. Saying it is one thing, showing is another. So there is something unfelt about the amiable acrostic to Georgiana Keats, with its unimaginative invoking of the imagination, its orotund didacticism:

> Imagine not that greatest mastery
> And kingdom over all the realms of verse
> Nears more to heaven in aught than when we nurse
> And surety give to love and brotherhood.
>
> ('Give me your patience, sister' 6–9)

True love and brotherhood, or rather these qualities truly realized within art, issue from Keats's sense of the brotherhood of poets, calling sometimes upon allusion, a mastery and a surety.

'On First Looking into Chapman's Homer' achieves its own genius in acknowledging with gratitude the genius of George Chapman. For this, Keats had cause to be grateful to his friend and mentor Clarke:

One scene I could not fail to introduce to him—the shipwreck of Ulysses, in the fifth book of the "Odysseis," and I had the reward of one of his delighted stares, upon reading the following lines:—

> Then forth he came, his both knees falt'ring, both
> His strong hands hanging down, and all with froth
> His cheeks and nostrils flowing, voice and breath
> Spent to all use, and down he sank to death.
> *The sea had soak'd his heart through . . .*[28]

We share Clarke's delight at this delighted stare, with yet one more great writer to soak Keats's heart through. Keats was among the most magnanimous, great-hearted, of men and of poets. Of the politics of reviewing and of letters in his defence, he wrote to his brother and his sister-in-law: 'This is a mere matter of the moment—I think that I shall

---

[27] *The Criterion* (July 1923), i 421.
[28] Charles and Mary Cowden Clarke, *Recollections of the Poets*, p. 130; their italics.

be among the English Poets after my death.'[29] *I think* is pure Keats, in its confident freedom from arrogance, as is *among the English poets*, since his poems had always been among theirs, enjoying their company and having them live again in the life of his allusive art.

[29] To George and Georgiana Keats, 14 October 1818; *Letters*, i 394.

Tennyson

Tennyson was angered by those who told him that what he had so well expressed had oft been thought and indeed oft expressed. Their tone implied that he had been detected.

As is always the case with great writers, resemblances to something he had written were often found in books which he had never read, and in languages which he did not know, and he complained with much reason that there were critics who imagined that the same idea could never occur independently to two men looking on the same aspects of Nature. 'Tennyson suspected of plagiarism!' I once heard Browning say, when this subject was mentioned: 'Why, you might as well suspect the Rothschilds of picking pockets'.[1]

So, even to well-wishers, Tennyson was gruff.

> To the Rev. Arthur E. Moule
> Jan 6, 1880
> Dear Sir
> I thank you for your book and
> your quotation from the Chinese
> Poet.
> No man can write a single passage
> to which a parallel one may not be
> found somewhere in the literature
> of the world.
> Yours very faithfully
> A. Tennyson[2]

He was galled by this two-sided foolishness: a foolishness about his poetry (poetry which it was preposterous to yoke locally, in sentiment and wording, to all these *outré* analogues), and a foolishness about the nature of poetry (a glory of which is its unreflecting apprehension of the community and commonalty of man). When, at the end of his life, he

---

[1] W. E. H. Lecky in Hallam Tennyson, *Alfred Lord Tennyson: A Memoir* (1897), ii 204.
[2] *The Letters of Alfred Lord Tennyson*, ed. Cecil Y. Lang and Edgar F. Shannon, junior, iii (1990), 183.

agreed to furnish for his poems some notes, he prefaced them with a note:

My paraphrases of certain Latin and Greek lines seem too obvious to be mentioned. Many of the parallelisms here given are accidental. The same idea must often occur independently to two men looking on the same aspects of Nature. There is a wholesome page in Eckermann's 'Conversations with Goethe', where one or the other (I have not the book by me) remarks that the prosaic mind finds plagiarism in passages that only prove 'the common brotherhood of man'.[3]

'I have not the book by me . . .'. Yet, though he was exasperated by any suggestion that his poems were ubiquitously, deeply, and minutely in debt to foreign writers (whether from languages he knew, or with another fatuity, from those he did not know), such exasperation was necessarily different in kind from that which he felt when it was English poets whom he was told he was awash with. For to have translated must at least mitigate any tattle of plagiarism. If Tennyson did in fact call John Churton Collins a 'louse on the locks of literature' (I say 'if' because there is reason to believe that Edmund Gosse was prone to invention, and that what Tennyson really called Churton Collins was a jackass), this may have been because Churton Collins's nit-picking made it seem that literature, Tennyson's and others', always had in its locks many a louse from the locks of its forebears. My note in *Notes and Queries* (March 1963) gave the grounds for this suspicion. Tennyson spattered with exclamation-marks and with growls the margins of Churton Collins's *Cornhill* articles about parallel passages, articles which became a deferentially hurtful book *Illustrations of Tennyson* (1891).

Since Tennyson was often under attack here, most notoriously from the absurd Bulwer-Lytton, who in *The New Timon* (1846) had disdained Tennyson's 'borrowed notes' and his 'purloined conceits', it would not be wise to ask why he was so defensive. (*Cet animal est très méchant; quand on l'attaque, il . . . devient défensif.*) Yet for someone who had become so securely in possession of genius, talent, fame, respect, and reward, the mature Tennyson does manifest—in the intensity with which he responded to what he saw as the insinuation that he had unlocked other men's word-hoards—one aspect of that insecurity which is so evident in spite of his no-less-evident strength and staunchness of

---

[3] Eversley edition (1907–8).

character. Early in his life the hideous anguish of his father, and then his hopes deferred and his heart made sick; these, with the black blood of the Tennysons, may be alive in Tennyson's morbid (he knew it was morbid) propensity to feel as if he were tattooed with every dispraise of his work while brushing off the outnumbering praises. Not that a reader of Tennyson, the man and the poet, should feel secure of biographical-critical affiliation even in this case; and Tennyson's passion about parallel passages is even less amenable to biographical interposing.

Such a passion, though, is likely to be related to an intensive privacy in Tennyson's poetic practice. It was a privacy which took many forms because it guarded many different things from many different threats; a privacy, both personal and generalizable, which Tennyson publicly defended both inside and outside his poetry; a privacy which animated Tennyson's principles and practice as a poet, among other places in the tacit assurance which he finds within his own way of using the words of previous English poets. Tennyson, though the very words of previous English poets are of interest, value, and support to him, does not most characteristically *allude*. Or rather, the world of those readers who are to take Tennyson's allusions is in one respect (again most characteristically, not invariably) a smaller circle than what might be called the usual world of educated common readers such as one associates with Augustan allusion (or than the equally large world that T. S. Eliot assists—something between a hindrance and a help—with the notes to *The Waste Land*).

Tennyson addressed a huge audience in *In Memoriam*, and it is a poem which often avails itself of the words of previous poets, but some of its strongest and deepest poetical reminiscences (Verlaine on Tennyson: 'When he should have been broken-hearted, he had many reminiscences') are of words which only a tiny circle within the large circle of its original readers could ever have recognized and participated in. There is here one kind of privacy, the privacy of intimates. *In Memoriam* is and was magnificently accessible, because it has such anonymous amplitude of sense and of experience, open to such readers as know nothing of any particular words which had been uttered by that unnamed 'A.H.H.' whom it commemorates. But Tennyson was freed to achieve such width of accessibility by his incorporating within it, as a solid and substantial privacy, an intimate world of private allusion.

The most important of these confidential allusions are, naturally, those to the words of Arthur Hallam, whether in prose or in verse. Here

it may be enough to recall how delicately, with what freedom of gratitude and with what freedom from self-congratulation, Tennyson turned
one of Hallam's compliments.

> 'Tis well; 'tis something; we may stand
> Where he in English earth is laid,
> And from his ashes may be made
> The violet of his native land.
>
> (XVIII 1–4)

With quiet grace and with a deeper timbre (this is no affectionate
hyperbole), Tennyson is returning the compliment which Hallam had
paid him: in his essay on Tennyson's poems, Hallam had quoted Persius,
Nunc non e tumulo fortunataque favilla | nascentur violae, remarking:
'When this Poet dies, will not the Graces and the Loves mourn over
him?' 'And from his ashes may be made . . .': Tennyson truly makes
something, his allusion to Hallam's allusion murmuring something
special for some few special readers and for the poet himself.[4] For all
readers, there is a public allusion which is to mingle with the confidential one; Tennyson acknowledged the presence of *Hamlet*:

> Lay her i' th' earth,
> And from her faire and unpolluted flesh,
> May Violets spring.

And from Hallam's ashes, from his words (as Hallam had from Persius's)
may be made this violet of his native land—'native land' being words
not in Latin but in Hallam's and Tennyson's and Shakespeare's native
tongue, words which return to, yet change, the words 'English earth'.

Tennyson's love of Hallam was itself part of a community of feeling.
Section I of *In Memoriam* solemnly declares 'That men may rise on
stepping-stones | Of their dead selves to higher things'. The phrase
'their dead selves' recalls Tennyson's earlier self, and those of his other
Cambridge friends, which may yet live as part of a moral evolution: the
phrase had formed part of a poem by one of Tennyson's Cambridge
friends in 1829 about another.

One strange thing about *In Memoriam*'s relation to time is that the
modern reader is better able to appreciate the existence of these private
allusions than almost all of the poem's original readers. The words of

---

[4] Detailed references for parallel passages from other writers are given here only when
these do not appear in my edition of *The Poems of Tennyson* (1969, revised 1987).

Arthur Hallam, and of smaller men, are known to us, and can be marshalled for us, just because Tennyson's words have given these other men's words a lasting importance. So that though no modern reader can feel the poignancy of personal reminiscence (unavailable even then except to intimates of Hallam), a modern reader may at least be able to imagine the existence of such feelings—within the poem of 1850—as very few readers then could have done.

One last instance of these intimate allusions may act as a stepping-stone to the other crucial way in which Tennyson's words call up the words of other poems—poems rather than poets, since there is Tennyson's lifelong habit (remarked upon by Sir Charles Tennyson) of self-borrowing, of using again what he had originally created within quite another poem or passage. Tennyson rises on the stepping-stones of his past self, a self that is not dead. Tennyson combines these two aspects of allusive privacy—of sharing an intimate reference with a few special readers, and of sharing (with one's own earlier self alone, perhaps) a reference to the earlier origins of his own words—in the poem with which he chose to end his *Poems* (1832), 'To J.S.' (Edward, the brother of Tennyson's friend James Spedding, had died in August 1832.) For the opening of 'To J.S.', Tennyson adapted the opening (all he had written) of part two of a poem which he had already sent to James Spedding. Spedding had quoted this in a letter to Edward, and so the adaptation acts as a kindly private allusion.

> The wind, that beats the mountain, blows
> More softly round the open wold,
> And gently comes the world to those
> That are cast in gentle mould.

The lines themselves have now been gently cast in another mould. Is Tennyson alluding here? The word allusion is inappropriate in so far as we think of an availability which is that of education or culture; and yet the word is appropriate if we think of an intimate, well-nigh private availability. For James Spedding had already seen, cast in their original mould, all these lines about the 'open wold' which now open 'To J.S.', and the only respectful and touching way in which the poet could acknowledge this (this fact which, malignly construed, would suggest that Tennyson was not moved by Edward's death to a new grief, to first-hand first-felt art) was by making this very fact alive within the meaning of the lines; that is, by incorporating within them an allusion—for

J.S., at least (a person who is made public yet left private by being invoked by initials only, as 'A.H.H.' was later to be)—to their own changed movement and mould. Perhaps an allusion is like a congregation—it needs only one other than the priest. Perhaps even a single celebrant can allude, if he calls up that past self who first formed the lines which are now reformed in an inspiration of self-borrowing, the borrowing not only *from* a past self but *of* a past self.

I have written elsewhere about Tennyson's self-borrowing,[5] but I need now to do one further act of self-borrowing of my own: to reassert, first, that it was on the subject of time that Tennyson wrote those lines of his which are most likely to stand against time; second, that again and again Tennyson's self-borrowings explicitly concern time, so that the practice of self-borrowing manifests both an awareness of, and a means of countering, time; and, third, that Tennyson—often torn and tormented—stabilized his mind and found some rallying point in this particular evidence of the continuity of his own creativity.

Moreover, Tennyson quarried his past self and his past poems even when he was too young to have had much of a past. But then this self-borrower is the poet who said 'The first poetry that moved me was my own at five years old'[6]; who heard his own young voice call up an ancient voice: 'Before I could read, I was in the habit on a stormy day of spreading my arms to the wind, and crying out "I hear a voice that's speaking in the wind" '; and who, in a youthful poem, 'Ode to Memory' (92–4), characterized memory in just this spirit:

> Artist-like,
> Ever retiring thou dost gaze
> On the prime labour of thine early days.

Tennyson's earliest surviving letter, written at the age of 12, not only alludes but then alludes to another's alluding:

> This passage,

> > Restless thoughts, like a deadly swarm
> > Of hornets arm'd, no sooner found alone,
> > But rush upon me thronging, and present
> > Times past, what once I was, and what am now,

> puts me in mind of that in Dante, which Lord Byron has prefixed to his

---

[5] *Tennyson* (1972, 2nd edn. 1989), pp. 281–94.
[6] *Memoir*, ii 93, i 11.

'Corsair'. 'Nessun maggior dolore, Che ricordarsi del tempo felice, nella miseria.'[7]

Tennyson was later to recollect this sentiment of Dante's, in 'Locksley Hall' (75–6): 'this is truth the poet sings, | That a sorrow's crown of sorrow is remembering happier things'. But what matters to my present purposes is the self-referential nature of Tennyson's instance or rather instances, the way in which the lines from Milton's *Samson Agonistes* now themselves 'present | Times past'; the way in which 'thronging' then describes a restless activity of mind ('puts me in mind of . . .'), as not only Milton but in quick succession Dante and Byron throng in (rather as, in 'Timbuctoo', Tennyson's glimpse 'with ghastly faces thronged' is thronged with Milton: 'With dreadful Faces throng'd'); the way in which Byron's epigraph-allusion to Dante is itself an act of remembering, of being put in mind of times past. A restless hungry feeling for the life of past literature is in this young letter, and makes it a much more striking earnest of Tennyson's genius than is his poetical collocation elsewhere of three poets (two of them Milton and Dante again) in 'The Palace of Art':

> For there was Milton like a seraph strong,
>   Beside him Shakespeare bland and mild;
> And there the world-worn Dante grasped his song,
>   And somewhat grimly smiled.
>
> (133–6)

There is a truer sense of tragedy in that early letter, and there is a counterbalancing sense of comedy in an early poem which Tennyson never published. 'I dare not write an Ode', a poem which runs through all the reasons why the Muse or the reviewers will scorn him if he attempts an ode, a sonnet, an essay, an epic, or a sketchbook of sentiments, finally comes to rest:

> But ah! my hopes are all as dead as mutton,
>   As vain as Cath[oli]ck Em[anci]p[atio]n,
> E'en now my conscience pulls me by the button
>   And bids me cease to prate of imitation.
> What countless ills a minor bard environ—
> '*You're imitating Whistlecraft and Byron*'.

For even while writhing under the accusation of imitating, Tennyson is at it.

7 *The Letters of Alfred Lord Tennyson*, i (1982), 1.

> Ah! what is man? what perils still environ
> The happiest mortals even after dinner!
> A day of gold from out an age of iron . . .
>   (*Don Juan*)

But then why should Tennyson not avail himself of Byron, since Byron had availed himself of Butler? 'Ay me! what perils do environ | The Man that meddles with cold Iron!' (*Hudibras*). For if it was Butler, not Byron, who first brought out how charmingly the word *environ* may environ the word *iron*, it is Tennyson who then brings out that Byron's own name is in the environs.

But back to self-borrowing, which can act as a private or even secret act of allusion. It therefore has something in common with any allusion which calls upon secrecy itself, as when Tennyson created his line 'The secret bridal-chambers of the heart' ('The Gardener's Daughter', i 244) from memories among which was a phrase from Arthur Hallam, 'my heart's chambers'. The privacy or secrecy here is the opposite of Milton's open audacity with the word 'secret' within the opening of *Paradise Lost*:

> Sing Heav'nly Muse, that on the secret top
> Of *Oreb*, or of *Sinai*, didst inspire
> That Shepherd, who first taught the chosen Seed
>   (i 6–8)

—an audacity which made Bentley wish to change 'secret' to 'sacred'. Or, to stay more strictly with allusion, Tennyson's line from Hallam is the opposite (since Hallam's poems were a private possession, unlike Milton's) of Wordsworth's allusion, when, having unmistakably woven together his verbal reminiscences of *Paradise Lost*, 'On the Morning of Christ's Nativity', and *Comus*, Wordsworth at once continues 'And sure there is a secret Power that reigns | Here . . .' ('Descriptive Sketches' 346–7). Yes indeed, but the secret power is also the unsecret power of Milton. Tennyson's heart-chambering of Hallam is more straightforwardly secret, and is part of the paradox of this poet, a paradox which was caught in a fine sentence of Richard Holt Hutton's: '*In Memoriam* is full of such magnifying-glasses for secret feelings, and doubts, and fears, and hopes, and trusts'.[8]

Self-borrowing and allusions have in common that they will often

---

[8] *Literary Essays* (1888); *Tennyson: The Critical Heritage*, ed. John D. Jump (1967), p. 364.

effect most when what is primary, their subject-matter, is secondarily at one with some impulse which underlies the making of allusions at all. When Tennyson's self-borrowings about time confront the challenge of time with their own nature, time is certainly not reduced to being merely part of the allusion's solipsistic workings; the parallelism is genuine, and it is respectful both of what is inside the poem and of what is outside all poems. Self-borrowing was for Tennyson a way of qualifying his own past without disowning it, and so it is a pleasant coincidence that the lines from 'Edwin Morris' that Churton Collins tactlessly or slyly chose for the title-page of his *Illustrations of Tennyson*, unctuously putting them into the present tense—

> And well his words became him: was he not
> A full-celled honeycomb of eloquence
> Stored from all flowers?

—are lines (the second and third) which Tennyson had borrowed from an earlier poem of his and was here being critical of. Yet those words did become him, words now placed dramatically as a criticism of the gifted but self-gratifying poet Edwin Morris. Stored the lines had been, and now their eloquence was stored from those early flowers of Tennyson's own.

With self-borrowing as with the more usual and less private kind of allusion, what matters is that both the new and the old should be independently yet interdependently respected. Tennyson does not envy or patronize his past self, and he embodies a similar vital propriety when he avails himself of the words of others. As in the section of *In Memoriam* about leaving the family home at Somersby:

> We go, but ere we go from home,
> As down the garden-walks I move,
> Two spirits of a diverse love
> Contend for loving masterdom.
> (CII 5–8)

Tennyson commented: 'First, the love of the native place; second, this enhanced by the memory of A.H.H.' Yet the lines are enhanced by a further memory, of those poems so often remembered in *In Memoriam*: Shakespeare's Sonnets with their evocation in Sonnet 144 of 'two loves' and 'two spirits'. So the two spirits of Tennyson's stanza are not only—though they are primarily—the family love and the Hallam love, but the two spirits of Tennyson and of Shakespeare. Without any of the parricidal melodrama of the anxiety of influence, Tennyson and Shakespeare here benignly contend for loving masterdom.

> These two have striven half the day,
>   And each prefers his separate claim,
>   Poor rivals in a losing game,
> That will not yield each other way.
>
> (CII 17–20)

Rivals, but not—even while still contending—foes; just as Tennyson is necessarily in some sense here the rival of Shelley but is his grateful friend and not his foe; for Tennyson is here having to prefer *his* separate claim with the help of Shelley's words from *Queen Mab*: 'mutual foes, forever play | A losing game into each other's hands'. Tennyson's is no losing game, but a victory (over rivalry and envy, not over Shelley). And so into the last stanza:

> I turn to go: my feet are set
>   To leave the pleasant fields and farms;
>   They mix in one another's arms
> To one pure image of regret.

The love of his family and the love of Hallam become one—even as Shakespeare, and then Shelley, and now Milton ('the pleasant Villages and Farmes'), mix in the hands of Tennyson to become one pure image. It is a pure image of the living, loving relationship—even after acknowledging rivalry and 'loving masterdom'—which is the art of allusion. And 'mix' is exactly the kind of word which should alert us to the creative relationship between these poems present and past.

Such allusions may animate the reader even while they soothe the writer. To the loneliness of the poet or of the man, they offer company, the company of dear dead poets, and they draw comfort while acknowledging despair—'Two loves I have of comfort and dispaire, | Which like two spirits do sugiest me still . . .' (Shakespeare, Sonnet 144).

All comfort will sometimes strike a chill, if only because it is privy to the need to be comforted. Yet Tennyson warmed even to cold comfort:

> Cold comfort unto thee and me
>   But yet a comfort, proving still
> There lives a power to shape our ends
> Rough-hew them as we will!
>
> ('I loving Freedom' 53–6)

Not the 'divinity' called up by Shakespeare, but the power of Shakespeare. It is a power which helps us to shape not only our ends but our means, our words. So it is natural to find elsewhere both of the words 'comfort' and 'power' again in the immediate vicinity of literary allusion in Tennyson. ('For so great a poet', said Humphry House, 'for a man as intelligent as he was, he seems to have lacked to quite an extra-ordinary degree a genuine internal conviction of the value of what he was doing.'[9]) In a very early poem, 'The Coach of Death', 'comfort' and 'power' come together again, and again with the support of another poet's words.

> But some have hearts that in them burn
> With power and promise high,
> To draw strange comfort from the earth,
> Strange beauties from the sky.
>
> (29–32)

For Tennyson is sensing his own power and promise high, while draw-ing strange comfort not from the earth but from the strange beauties of *The Ancient Mariner*:

> This heart within me burns.
>
> I pass, like night, from land to land;
> I have strange power of speech.
>
> (585–7)

We have powers of speech as a community, here in the present, only because we form a community with the past. All language holds communion with the dead, those dead who have no memorial except the language which they maintained, and those other dead who left the memorials of literature.

> How pure at heart and sound in head,
> With what divine affections bold
> Should be the man whose thought would hold
> An hour's communion with the dead.
>
> (*In Memoriam*, XCIV 1–4)

'Communion with the dead', as a phrase, is part of the heritage of the language; it was also the language of the man honoured in *In Memoriam* who had written of

---

[9] *All in Due Time* (1955), p. 125.

> Spirits that but seem
> To hold communion with the dead.

So, in his poem of 'divine affections', Tennyson holds communion with the dead Hallam. Perhaps, too, by a complementary public allusiveness, with an earlier writer; for 'hold | An hour's communion with the dead' suggests some communication with 'O that it were possible we might | But hold some two days' conference with the dead' (*The Duchess of Malfi*), especially if we then sense a further union, a deeper communion, of those words and the great cry in *Maud*:

> O that 'twere possible
> After long grief and pain
> To find the arms of my true love
> Round me once again!
>
> (ii 141–4)

—where the vista of long grief and pain becomes even longer in that it resumes 'Western winde, when wilt thou blow . . .', the age-old human grief and pain returning once again, before circling back to Webster once more, with:

> Ah Christ, that it were possible
> For one short hour to see
> The souls we loved, that they might tell us
> What and where they be.

See them, we shall never, and yet they are indeed able to tell us something. We hold communion with the dead. 'The dead are not dead but alive' ('Vastness' 36).

> Behold a man raised up by Christ!
> The rest remaineth unrevealed;
> He told it not; or something sealed
> The lips of that Evangelist.
>
> (XXXI 13–16)

Once again, something is truly told. Tennyson's lips are not sealed, and that is because his words are raised up by an earlier poet whose lips were not sealed, Alexander Pope:

> rest ever unreveal'd
> Nor pass these lips in holy silence seal'd.
> (*Eloisa to Abelard*)

Tennyson's power to speak of such holy silence makes this not the whole truth, then, that 'The rest remaineth unrevealed'. A truth and an admission remain revealed.

> But thou and I have shaken hands,
> Till growing winters lay me low;
> My paths are in the fields I know,
> And thine in undiscovered lands.
>
> (XL 29–32)

Yet not simply undiscovered, since this truth was one which Tennyson could know because it had been discovered by a traveller who did return: Shelley. 'To seek strange truths in undiscovered lands'. It is not only Hallam and Tennyson, but Tennyson and Shelley who shake hands, meeting and parting, *ave atque vale*.

The word 'influence' itself can focus the relation between the 'strange power of speech' and the heartening example of those who have previously exercised the power. When Tennyson uses the word while in the adjacent lines under the influence of Milton, it is with a dark sense of how little the power of speech is to be relied on. In 'Armageddon', his earliest poem (preceded only by a translation from Claudian and by an unfinished play), he thanks the power of Prophecy.

> I stood upon the mountain which o'erlooks
> The valley of destruction and I saw
> Things strange, surpassing wonder; but to give
> Utterance to things inutterable, to paint
> In dignity of language suitable
> The majesty of what I then beheld,
> Were past the power of man. No fabled Muse
> Could breathe into my soul such influence
> Of her seraphic nature, as to express
> Deeds inexpressible by loftiest rhyme.
>
> (i 14–23)

The 'inutterable' is uttered, in part at least, and this is because Milton comes to breathe influence into Tennyson's soul: 'to express | Deeds inexpressible by loftiest rhyme' has been made less impossible because nearby are Milton's 'Distance inexpressible' and his 'lofty rhyme'. Milton, like his Lycidas, knew to build the lofty rhyme—knew it, and could teach it.

Later in 'Armageddon' (104–7), 'Witchcraft's abominations' can be imagined as 'Obscene, inutterable phantasies' with the help of Milton's imagining of the monsters of Hell as 'Abominable, inutterable', an utterance to which Tennyson in his old age could still owe some of his power to speak, through the mouth of 'Lucretius' (157–8): 'And twisted shapes of lust, unspeakable, | Abominable'.

One of the few occasions when Tennyson does what he was very reluctant to do (and Wordsworth and Byron, for very different reasons, delighted in doing), quote a phrase within quotation marks in a poem, comes when the unutterable is uttered with the acknowledged support of Milton in 'Perdidi Diem':

> My soul is but the eternal mystic lamp,
> Lighting that charnel damp,
> Wounding with dreadful rays that solid gloom,
> And shadowing forth the unutterable tomb,
> Making a 'darkness visible'
> Of that which without thee we had not felt
> As darkness, dark ourselves and loving night . . .
>   (9–15)

Tennyson wrote this poem when he was about 20, and it is one of the earliest of his telling shudders at 'the unutterable tomb'. 'When I was about twenty, I used to feel moods of misery unutterable! I remember once in London the realization coming over me, of the *whole* of its inhabitants lying horizontal a hundred years hence.'[10]

The point is not so much that Tennyson has recourse to words of the *in——able* or *un——able* form, as that he often has recourse to the words of previous poets when engaged with the *in——able* or *un—— able*. 'Toiling in immeasurable sand' ('Will' 16) measures itself against, alongside, Shelley's 'Those deserts of immeasurable sand' (*Queen Mab*); as does 'Forward, backward, backward, forward, in the immeasurable sea' ('Locksley Hall Sixty Years After' 193), backward-forward measuring itself against Shelley's 'the immeasurable sea' (*Daemon of the World*), with Tennyson then continuing: 'Swayed by vaster ebbs and flows than can be known to you or me'. Yet the couplet is swayed by something known to Shelley, just as those 'undiscovered lands' were partly, thanks to Shelley's *Alastor*, 'in the fields I know'.

Not that such allusions, even when they are quiet to the point of reticence or privacy, can save those moments when something is askew or

---

[10] Christopher Ricks, *Tennyson* (1972, rev. 1989), p. 61.

factitious. Thus, although Tennyson may sincerely say of Hallam 'I doubt not what thou wouldst have been' (CXIII 8), he cannot truly imagine that career of Hallam's; Tennyson assumes the voice of Milton: 'A *potent voice* of Parliament', but what had been potent in *Paradise Lost* is here impotent. The truth of Tennyson's poetry is often in inverse proportion to its assurance (T. S. Eliot said of *In Memoriam*: 'Its faith is a poor thing, but its doubt is a very intense experience'),[11] which is why there is a narrowness in the line 'Drunk in the largeness of the utterance' (*The Lover's Tale*, i 462), actually compounded by Tennyson's recalling Keats's utterance, here the nemesis of allusion:

> Some mourning words, which in our feeble tongue
> Would come in these like accents (O how frail
> To that large utterance of the early Gods!)
>
> ('Hyperion')

Tennyson, against the grain of his temperament, sought to turn Keats's sense both of frailty and of largeness, into a single confident impulse. To my ear, one of the few strikingly successful uses in Tennyson of such confident allusion (where finding utterance is itself alluded to) is a satirical one, the insinuating portraiture of 'A Character' (13–18):

> He spake of virtue: not the gods
> More purely, when they wish to charm
> Pallas and Juno sitting by:
> And with a sweeping of the arm,
> And a lack-lustre dead-blue eye,
> Devolved his rounded periods.

The last line of the stanza gets its conclusive mordancy, its rounding-off the rhetorical falsity, from the way in which Horace's *verba devolvit* had devolved to James Thomson: 'Devolving through the maze of eloquence | A roll of periods' ('Autumn'), which in its turn devolved to Tennyson, with Thomson's 'A roll of periods' authoritatively rounded into 'Devolved his rounded periods'. The line is full in its evocation of the finest empty verbalism, and this fullness is partly the cooperative presence of Thomson. It is the opposite of the emptiness of allusion in 'Eleänore' (44–8).

---

[11] *Selected Essays* (1932, 1951 edn.), p. 336.

> How may full-sailed verse express,
> How may measured words adore
> The full-flowing harmony
> Of thy swan-like stateliness,
> Eleänore?

This breezily has Shakespeare's wind in its sails, not full (the repetition of 'full-' within two lines empties it) but empty of inspiration. Shakespeare's lines in Sonnet 86 earned the right (which they then effortlessly waived) to congratulate themselves on how they met the challenge of a rival poet: 'Was it the proud full saile of his great verse . . .'; Tennyson does not rise comparably to the challenge of Shakespeare.

His allusions rise when they speak, not of a fullness reasserted, but of an emptiness encouragingly peopled from the past, an emptiness defied by a poetic solidarity. In early Tennyson, such an allusion might gain the support of its own nature (allusion filling a hollowness) with the support of, among others, Milton. As in 'Ode: O Bosky Brook':

> In midnight full of sound,
> Or in close pastures soft as dewy sleep,
> Or in the hollow deep
> Of woods, whose counterchanged embroidery . . .
>   (55–8)

Compare *Paradise Lost*:

> Abject and lost lay these, covering the Flood,
> Under amazement of their hideous change.
> He call'd so loud, that all the hollow Deep
> Of Hell resounded.
>   (i 312–15)

It is the opposite of a hideous change which has now been counter-changed, and the hollow deep does resound, full of sound. More deeply, in *In Memoriam*, 'hollow'—which has one kind of appropriateness to allusion (which can fill the hollow)—joins 'echo', which has another (an allusion being itself a kind of echo, as Pope appreciated in echoing Dryden's 'echoes').[12] Here Tennyson couches his phantom Nature and her music in the accents of Spenser:

> 'And all the phantom, Nature, stands—
> With all the music in her tone,

---

[12] See pp. 9-10 above.

A hollow echo of my own,—
A hollow form with empty hands.'
(III 9–12)

'From out waste places comes a cry', 'A hollow echo of my own': the cry becomes Tennyson's own, but it comes from a place which is not waste: Spenser's 'The hollow Echo of my carefull cryes' (*The Shepherd's Calendar: August*). A substantial continuity stands against the phantom of the hollow and the empty.

Similarly, the last line of section VII, 'On the bald street breaks the blank day', is informed with something other than blankness, since the poem by Wordsworth ('Ode: Intimations of Immortality') which had just proffered Tennyson the wise innocent assistance of the words 'like a guilty thing' (themselves owed by Wordsworth to *Hamlet*) also furnished Tennyson with the word 'blank' as a shield against misgivings: 'Blank misgivings of a Creature . . .'. With quite a different tone but with the same propriety of self-reference in allusion (proper because the allusion's being in some way about allusion is secondary to the line's sheer descriptive felicity), Tennyson sees Lucretius' vision of the atom-streams of the universe, 'Ruining along the illimitable inane' (40), his words supported by the awe-filled precariousness which Shelley had given to the unusual noun: 'Pinnacled dim in the intense inane' (*Prometheus Unbound*, III iv 20).

The very workings of an allusion may reflect that which they explicitly and primarily work upon:[13] 'And on the liquid mirror glowed | The clear perfection of her face' ('Mariana in the South' 31–2). The glow is not just in the strong delicacy with which 'perfection' replaced yet does not expunge the expected reflection ('And on the liquid mirror glowed | The clear reflection of her face'?), but also in the way in which, by its reflection from Shelley and his 'liquid mirror' (not his alone, of course), the words reflect their own two-in-one meaning and nature. The poignancy is of a loneliness contemplated in ghostly company, and company is for Tennyson—as with 'They mix in one another's arms | To one pure image of regret'—one pure image of the art of allusion.

So a characteristic Tennysonian allusion is drawn to the words 'with me', where the company called for includes a summoned spirit. 'The tide of time flowed back with me' ('Recollections of the Arabian Nights'

---

[13] See p. 9 above.

13) is in the company of Arthur Hallam and his 'the tide of time'. 'Bathe with me in the fiery flood' ('Life of the Life' 9) defiantly delights in the company of the spirit of Shakespeare: 'And the delighted spirit | To bath in fierie floods' (*Measure for Measure*). 'Ah, bear me with thee, smoothly borne' ('Move eastward' 19) has the company not only of the 'happy earth', but also of the poet who had so happily imagined it: the earth, advancing from the west, 'beares thee soft with the smooth Air along' (*Paradise Lost*). *In Memoriam* cries out not to be divided from Hallam: 'Oh, wast thou with me, dearest, then', and it moves to the hope that in death they are not divided:

> If thou wert with me, and the grave
>   Divide us not, be with me now,
>   And enter in at breast and brow,
> Till all my blood, a fuller wave,
>
> Be quickened with a livelier breath . . .
>   (CXXII 9–13)

If we ask what it is which enters and quickens the lines into a fuller wave, part of the answer is the intimate companionship of Hallam's own words in 'To One Early Loved': 'Tho' innumerable waves divide us now'. There is a turn akin to that in 'with me', in the fearful opening of section L:

> Be near me when my light is low,
>   When the blood creeps, and the nerves prick
>   And tingle; and the heart is sick,
> And all the wheels of Being slow.

Tennyson gains the courage to contemplate these fears because 'Be near me' is so magnificently unspecific an address; it speaks to God, and to Hallam, but also—since it avails itself of his words—to the supporting predecessor Shelley: 'My blood is running up and down my veins; | A fearful pleasure makes it prick and tingle: | I feel a giddy sickness of strange awe' (*The Cenci*); and 'urge | The restless wheels of being on their way' (*Queen Mab*).

In the face of lonely suffering and anxiety, these allusions embody the comfort of company: 'Be near me . . .'. Comfort is warm once again. 'Alone and warming his five wits | The white owl in the belfry sits' ('Song—The Owl' 6–7)—not alone, because of the blessed company of Shakespeare: 'Bless thy five wits! Tom's-cold' (*King Lear*).

Knowledge is itself company and solidarity; and Tennyson's knowing, from Shakespeare's Sonnet 78, the phrase 'heavy ignorance', is one of the things shared by the lines in 'The Vision of Sin' travestying the brotherhood of man and the brotherhood of poets:

> 'Drink to Fortune, drink to Chance,
> While we keep a little breath!
> Drink to heavy Ignorance!
> Hob-and-nob with brother Death!'
>
> (191–4)

Tennyson is lightly toasting a brother poet whose words are not dead, this being the proper counterpart to improper hob-nobbing 'with brother Death' or with Shakespeare.

'The poet as heir':[14] what then is central as inheritance for Tennyson? Only a small part is played by what for Byron and his poems had a central importance: the literal inheritance of wealth. Some part, though, for there is in Tennyson a sufficient memory of his father's disinheritance. Here Tennyson's debt to Young's *Night Thoughts* is very different from Wordsworth's, and is—in these lines from what may be Tennyson's earliest original composition (*The Devil and the Lady*, I i 62–4)—exactly a matter of debt:

> Nor would I borrow of that usurer
> Procrastination, whose vast interest
> Is almost higher than his principal.

Tennyson borrows, from Young's *Night Thoughts*, 'Procrastination is the Thief of Time'. But as a borrower, not as a thief—that is, not as a plagiarist. ('Why, you might as well suspect the Rothschilds of picking pockets.')

The metaphor which would see allusion itself as an interest which accrues, this catches something beautifully anti-mercenary in *In Memoriam*:

> But who shall so forecast the years
> And find in loss a gain to match?
> Or reach a hand through time to catch
> The far-off interest of tears?
>
> (I 5–8)

---

[14] See p. 9 above.

For it is not a forecast, but a retrospect, which reaches a hand through time to catch the far-off interest of Shakespeare's tears.

> How many a holy and obsequious teare
> Hath deare religious love stolne from mine eye,
> As interest of the dead.
>
> (Sonnet 31)
>
>   do not take away
> My sorrowes interest, let no mourner say
> He weepes for her.
>
> (*The Rape of Lucrece*)
>
> The liquid drops of Teares that you have shed,
> Shall come again, transformd to Orient Pearle,
> Advantaging their Loan, with interest.
>
> (*Richard III*)

Shakespeare's words come again, transformed, and advantaging their loan with interest, as 'The far-off interest of tears'.

The unworldly grief there in Tennyson's debt to Shakespeare has its satirical complement in another debt to Shakespeare, explicitly contrasting poetry and money, where Tennyson borrows from that usurer Shylock (who says of money 'I make it breed'):

> Here, by this brook, we parted; I to the East
> And he for Italy—too late—too late:
> One whom the strong sons of the world despise;
> For lucky rhymes to him were scrip and share,
> And mellow metres more than cent for cent;
> Nor could he understand how money breeds,
> Thought it a dead thing; yet himself could make
> The thing that is not as the thing that is.
>
> ('The Brook' 1–8)

One of the best collectors of Tennyson's borrowing is a man called Loane.[15] That there is something wrong with the critical sense of that earlier collector, Churton Collins, comes out in the lavish moneyed inappositeness of his metaphors for Tennyson's allusions:

We live amid wealth as prodigally piled up as the massive and myriad treasure-trove of Spenser's 'rich strond', and it is now almost impossible for a poet to strike out a thought, or to coin a phrase, which shall be purely original.

---

[15] G. G. Loane, *Echoes in Tennyson* (1928).

As Virgil has, on a very large scale, drawn on the literary wealth of Greece and of his native land, so Tennyson has, on a corresponding scale, drawn not on that wealth merely, but on the wealth which has been accumulating since.[16]

For it was exactly such metaphors which proved bankrupt when Tennyson tried to expend them on Virgil: 'All the chosen coin of fancy flashing out from many a golden phrase' ('To Virgil' 4). Accumulated wealth crushes such tenderness as we hear in the far off interest of tears. It is growth, not accumulation, which allusion must trust in. Happy growth, though, is not often trusted by Tennyson, and it was imprudent of him to appropriate Marvell's 'vegetable love' for 'The Talking Oak':

> 'I, rooted here among the groves
> But languidly adjust
> My vapid vegetable loves
> With anthers and with dust.'
>
> (181–4)

The words 'languidly adjust' and 'vapid' are all too applicable to Tennyson's lines themselves. Nothing grows, especially nothing more charming than Marvell's original lines.

Growth may be thought of as digestive, and allusion has its likeness to eating and drinking. Again Tennyson seems to me much less successful when being happy at such a thought than when distressed by it. Most of his best allusions embody a contrariety between a malign force and a benign solidarity. If Tennyson's 'Drunk in the largeness of the utterance' is not supported but felled by Keats's 'O how frail | To that large utterance of the early Gods!', 'Drunk' does nothing to help; it merely suggests that Keats is on tap. Whereas Pope was able to 'draw light'[17] most exquisitely and sardonically from Milton's 'draw Light', Tennyson's affirmative line in 'Perdidi Diem' (78) is too flatly parallel to—and in competition with (insufficiently rotated from)—Milton's line in the same passage from *Paradise Lost* ('And drink the liquid Light'): 'The latest energies of light they drink' is not alive with singular energy.

But Tennyson does digest such allusions when the poem speaks of the wrong kind of feeding while the allusion embodies the right kind. The wrong kind, say, because unreflecting, ignorant, and so less than

[16] *Illustrations of Tennyson* (1891), pp. vii, 23.
[17] See p. 10 above.

fully human: 'a savage race, | That hoard, and sleep, and feed, and know not me' ('Ulysses' 4–5).

> What is a man
> If his chiefe good and market of his time
> Be but to sleepe and feede, a beast, no more:
> Sure he that made us with such large discourse
> Looking before and after, gave us not
> That capabilitie and god-like reason
> To fust in us unusd.
>
> (*Hamlet*)

Tennyson, looking before and after, uses Shakespeare's words as part of a large discourse; the words are not hoarded, or slumbered on, but they are honourably fed upon, in contrast to the honourless daily round of which they speak. Once again the word 'know' is a quiet signal.

Or, to stay with the conjunction of sleeping and feeding, there is the sinister non-human predatoriness, deep below consciousness, of 'The Kraken' (12), 'Battening upon huge seaworms in his sleep'. Shelley had netted 'The dull weed some sea-worm battens on' (*Prometheus Unbound*); for his imagination, not dull at all, had fed—not battened— on *Hamlet*: 'duller shouldst thou be than the fat weede | That rots it selfe in ease, on Lethe Wharfe'. ('Fat' fattened into Shelley's 'battens'.) In 'The Kraken', Tennyson feeds—not battens—upon Shelley, swelling 'sea-worms' into 'huge seaworms' within this enormous enlargement by which the monstrous batteners become the even more monstrously battened-upon: from 'The dull weed some sea-worm battens on', to 'Battening upon huge seaworms in his sleep'. 'In his sleep', with its lethal calm and its own digestiveness, is a stroke of grim genius. It was left to T. S. Eliot to tame the Kraken—as he believed the Church of England to tame Christianity—down into 'The Hippopotamus':

> The hippopotamus's day
> Is passed in sleep; at night he hunts;
> God works in a mysterious way—
> The Church can sleep and feed at once.

The numb comedy is not in the spirit of Tennyson, but the way with the allusion somewhat is, particularly in its use within a retrograde evolution or reversion (from the battener to the battened-upon; from the awe-inspiring Kraken to the outdone hippopotamus). So perhaps Tennyson would forgive Eliot; and forgive Robert Lowell, for what, as

an heir of Tennyson, he did in 'Ford Madox Ford' with 'I the heir of all
the ages, in the foremost files of time' ('Locksley Hall' 178):

>   The sun
> is pernod-yellow and it gilds the heirs
> of all the ages there on Washington
> and Stuyvesant, your Lilliputian squares,
> where writing turned your pockets inside out.

Ford's pockets are not the only things that have been turned inside out,
with the great vista of human history transformed into something
moneyed, of the surface, and Lilliputian. Tennyson would not need to
forgive Geoffrey Hill for his smouldering re-creation of the last line of
In Memoriam ('To which the whole creation moves') as 'music's creation
of the moveless dance, | the decreation to which all must move'.[18]

It was in the terms of health and disease that Arthur Hallam (whose
words Tennyson was approaching there, the words 'The Love | Toward
which all being solemnly doth move') characterized the progress or
regress of poetry, in his essay 'On Some of the Characteristics of Modern
Poetry, and on the Lyrical Poems of Alfred Tennyson' (*Englishman's
Magazine*, August 1831). Englishmen had once 'imbibed' knowledge and
power; but 'since that day we have undergone a period of degradation'
and even 'the French contagion'; we are no longer 'untainted'. 'Hence the
melancholy which so evidently characterizes the spirit of modern poetry;
hence that return of the mind upon itself and the habit of seeking relief
in idiosyncrasies rather than community of interest'.

Yet allusion may resist such melancholy; allusion is the return of
mind upon something other than itself, and is an honourable seeking of
relief in community of interest. Many of Tennyson's allusions pit against
disease or degradation or failure their own act of health-giving inheritance and continuity—in *The Princess*, for instance:

>   let the wild
> Lean-headed Eagles yelp alone, and leave
> The monstrous ledges there to slope, and spill
> Their thousand wreaths of dangling water-smoke,
> That like a broken purpose waste in air:
> So waste not thou;
>
>   (vii 195–200)

---

[18] 'Lachrimae: Pavana Dolorosa', *Tenebrae* (1978).

Nothing was left to waste purposelessly in air; something was preserved from John Armstrong's *The Art of Preserving Health* (a book in the Tennysons' library): 'The virgin stream | In boiling wastes its finer soul in air'. In a later Tennyson poem, 'Lucretius' (22), 'those tender cells', ravaged by poison, are likewise cells inherited from Armstrong's *Art of Preserving Health*: 'This caustick venom would perhaps corrode | Those tender cells that draw the vital air.'

Armstrong's poem of 1744 was hardly well-known to Victorian England, and Tennyson's debt to him may have been a private arrangement, an intimate support. But when we hear that 'The woods decay, the woods decay and fall' ('Tithonus' 1), we are to hold against this vision of decay one of Tennyson's favourite passages from Wordsworth, the undecaying vision of paradox: 'The immeasurable height | Of woods decaying, never to be decayed' (*The Prelude*).[19] Yet the consolation is itself paradoxical, since Tithonus envies the woods which decay and fall, and is anguished at the thought that he is decaying, never to be decayed. Once again it is in the spirit of Tennyson's own allusions that William Empson, in 'Missing Dates', should have imagined a dark redesigning of Tennyson's line, yet with allusion's endurance standing against the waste: 'The waste remains, the waste remains and kills'.

One thing that must remain, a central inheritance, is heredity, both the common heredity of man and the particular heredity of men. The poet who thinks of himself ruefully as 'Fame's millionth heir-apparent'[20] has an intuitive sense of a relation between an art of allusion (itself an inheritance such as may be a heredity) and those preoccupations with which such art is continuous. Whether human heredity or family heredity is to be praised—or, more usually, blamed—is often near the heart of a Tennyson poem, as it is near the heart of the Shakespearean tragedy that most often supported Tennyson, *Hamlet*. While still in his early teens, he knew that the Devil can cite *Hamlet* to his purpose.

> I must be violent, fierce,
> And put that ugly disposition on
> Which is my portion by inheritance
> From my great grandsire Lucifer.
> (*The Devil and the Lady*, I v 190–3)

---

[19] vi 624–5; Wordsworth's lines had been published in 1845, before Tennyson's revision (1859) of his early poem, 'Tithon' (1833), which began: 'Ay me! ay me! the woods decay and fall'.

[20] 'Wherefore, in these dark ages of the Press' 4.

What had been bitterly 'antic' ('To put an Anticke disposition on') is good-humouredly ugly.

But take Tennyson's description of *Maud*: 'This poem of *Maud or the Madness* is a little *Hamlet*, the history of a morbid, poetic soul, under the blighting influence of a recklessly speculative age. He is the heir of madness . . .'. 'Morbid, poetic': it is an equivocal comma. The morbidity is personal and historical (and age-old, too), and the influence of the age is 'recklessly speculative' both as calling everything in doubt and as mammonist. 'Did he fling himself down? who knows? for a vast speculation had failed' (*Maud*, i 9). The narrator is 'the heir of madness', and is under the blighting influence of the age; Tennyson creates this highly allusive poem by being the heir of sanity, under the fostering influence of previous ages. 'I the heir of all the ages, in the foremost files of time': those are words which Churton Collins bent upon Tennyson's allusions, mangling them: 'In his own noble words, we moderns are "the heirs of all the ages"'.

The heir of madness: the poetic practice which seeks to be the heir of sanity is a form of therapy, and it has a direct parallel in the way in which Arthur Hallam called upon literary allusion as an act of therapeutic love towards Tennyson: 'Fare thee well. I hope you do fare well, and make head against "despondency and madness"'. If Tennyson did make head against them, it would be because of standing alongside, not only Hallam's imaginative love, but Wordsworth's: 'We Poets in our youth begin in gladness; | But thereof comes in the end despondency and madness'. Resolution and Interdependence, or, 'We Poets'. Hallam had alluded in a similar spirit, but to a different poet, when he brought to bear upon Tennyson's fear of blindness Milton's sense of what might be involved in saying 'We Poets': 'Surely', wrote Hallam to Tennyson, 'you owe it to us all not to let yourself carelessly fall into the misery of blindness. It is a hard and sad thing to barter the "universal light" even for the power of "Tiresias and Phineus prophets old"'. Hallam then continued at once, with an unforced sense of the supreme daily *writing*: 'Write to me yourself on this subject and speak openly and fully'.[21]

> . . . nor somtimes forget
> Those other two equal'd with me in Fate,
> So were I equal'd with them in renown,

[21] Ricks, *Tennyson*, p. 61.

> Blind *Thamyris* and blind *Maeonides*,
> And *Tiresias* and *Phineus* prophets old.
>> (*Paradise Lost*, iii 32–6)

Insanity will speak insanely of heredity:

> And fair without, faithful within,
> Maud to him is nothing akin:
> Some peculiar mystic grace
> Made her only the child of her mother,
> And heaped the whole inherited sin
> On the huge scapegoat of the race,
> All, all upon the brother.
>> (*Maud*, i 483–6)

The inherited sin is both original sin and family malaise, and this in an age when the human race is starting to plead diminished responsibility ('But if sin be sin, not inherited fate, as many will say . . .', 'The Wreck' 85). 'This heir of the liar' (*Maud*, i 761): the words suggest that mendacity is in the blood. 'Our sons inherit us' ('The Lotos-Eaters' 118)—they do not simply inherit *from* us. Tennyson, in conversation, gave this as an instance of the real test of a man: 'Can he battle against his own bad inherited instincts, or brave public opinion in the cause of truth?'[22] And the public opinion might be one which told lies about the human or the family inheritance.

Tennyson asks how to confront sorrow:

> And shall I take a thing so blind,
> Embrace her as my natural good;
> Or crush her, like a vice of blood,
> Upon the threshold of the mind?
>> (*In Memoriam*, III 13–16)

But the poet is not crushed (as in a vice) by a vice of blood; rather he embraces the inherited virtues of Shakespeare ('I do confesse the vices of my blood', *Othello*) and of Shelley (in *Queen Mab*):

> Let priest-led slaves cease to proclaim that man
> Inherits vice and misery, when Force
> And Falsehood hang even o'er the cradled babe,
> Stifling with rudest grasp all natural good.
> Ah! to the stranger-soul, when first it peeps

[22] *Memoir*, i 318.

From its new tenement, and looks abroad
For happiness and sympathy, how stern
And desolate a tract is this wide world!
How withered all the buds of natural good!
No shade, no shelter from the sweeping storms
Of pitiless power! On its wretched frame,
Poisoned, perchance, by the disease and woe
Heaped on the wretched parent whence it sprung
By morals, law, and custom . . .

Tennyson would not have concurred with the religious or political insistences here, but his words show that he did look abroad, here in Shelley,
for sympathy, and found some shelter.

'Proclaim that man | Inherits vice and misery': if man does, it may be
with the help of the devil. What had been a diabolical lineage for
Milton:

And when Night
Darkens the Streets, then wander forth the Sons
Of *Belial*, flown with insolence and wine
(*Paradise Lost*, i 500–2)

—was preserved by Dryden, with a true poetic lineage, as a collusive
political family: 'During his Office, Treason was no Crime. | The Sons of
Belial had a glorious Time.'[23] Dryden here is acknowledging Milton,
without 'insolence', as his poetic father. What Tennyson preserved, as his
portion of the inheritance, was exactly the wounding insolence; not
explicitly the allusive lineage of 'sons of Belial' but its accompanying
zeugma which transforms the sons into this brother who scorns the
brotherhood of man (but who cannot destroy the brotherhood of poets):

What if that dandy-despot, he,
That jewelled mass of millinery,
That oiled and curled Assyrian Bull
Smelling of musk and of insolence,
Her brother . . .
(*Maud*, i 231–5)

It is blighting influence which Tennyson calls upon fostering influence to help him realize in his art. The fear that the world will become
worse (even worse) than it is—this is politics and geology each seen

---

[23] *Absalom and Achitophel* 597–8.

under the other's aspect. Hallam might have helped to resist political destruction, but he could hardly have staved off all disaster, and the imagination of *In Memoriam* goes out most to what it fears:

> I doubt not what thou wouldst have been:
> A life in civic action warm,
>   A soul on highest mission sent,
>   A potent voice of Parliament,
> A pillar steadfast in the storm,
>
> Should licensed boldness gather force,
>   Becoming, when the time has birth,
>   A lever to uplift the earth
> And roll it in another course,
>
> With thousand shocks that come and go,
>   With agonies, with energies,
>   With overthrowings, and with cries,
> And undulations to and fro.
>
> (CXIII 8–20)

Yet within this vision of catastrophe something is steadfast; it is the acknowledgement of that which does not come and go, in the line 'With thousand shocks that come and go'. For Tennyson's alteration, in 1855, of 'many shocks' to 'thousand shocks' calls up *Hamlet*: 'The thousand Naturall shockes | That Flesh is heyre to'. Tennyson is heir to Hamlet's and to Shakespeare's strength, rather as the line to the yew-tree, 'Sick for thy stubborn hardihood' (II, 14), achieves its own hardihood by availing itself of the stubborn hardihood which Walter Scott had achieved within those two words.[24] 'With thousand shocks that come and go': because of what flesh is heir to, the line embodies a hope which disdains the cynical songs within 'The Ancient Sage':

> The poet whom his Age would quote
>   As heir of endless fame—
> He knows not even the book he wrote,
>   Not even his own name.
>
> (146–9)

Every man is an heir, and Tennyson tried to take his own advice, in his capacity as the Ancient Sage: 'Cleave ever to the sunnier side of doubt' (68). Another poem written in old age, 'By an Evolutionist'

---

[24] *Lord of the Isles*, VI xxiii.

(13–14), strives to be grateful to old age for its evolutionary subjugation of the brute and the beast within man.

> If my body come from brutes, though somewhat finer than their
>   own,
> I am heir, and this my kingdom. Shall the royal voice be mute?
>
> (13–14)

But the evolutionary heredity of man might be vitiated by the heredity of a particular man. Tennyson has an epigram, 'Darwin's Gemmule', on Darwin's hypothesis that a gemmule was thrown off from each cell, and transmitted from parents to offspring, thus being responsible for physical inheritance.

> Curse you, you wandering gemmule,
>   And nail you fast in Hell!
> You gave me gout and bandy legs,
>   You beast, you wanted a cell!
> Gout, and gravel, and evil days—
>   (Theology speaks, shaking her head)
> But there is One who knows your ways!

Tennyson found intolerable both the prospect that man might improve beyond recognition and so be superseded, and the prospect that man might degenerate and so be superseded. T. S. Eliot's truthful joke about Whitman and Tennyson encompasses more than just the politics of Tennyson: 'Both were conservative, rather than reactionary or revolutionary; that is to say, they believed explicitly in progress, and believed implicitly that progress consists in things remaining much as they are'.[25]

'Contemplate all this work of Time': what helped Tennyson to contemplate (in *In Memoriam*) both the ascent and the descent of man was his being descended from (and ascending from) previous poets. Geology and evolution rolled on, 'Till at the last arose the man': and, thirteen lines later, the concept of arising rises again:

> Arise and fly
> The reeling Faun, the sensual feast;
> Move upward, working out the beast,
> And let the ape and tiger die.
>
> (CXVIII 25–8)

---

[25] *The Nation and Athenaeum*, 18 December 1926.

This moves upward from Shakespeare's 'sensuall feast' (Sonnet 141), by
an evolution which is paradoxical and mysterious: it does not arise and
fly the words 'sensual feast'; it is not 'working out' Shakespeare; it does
not claim to be Shakespeare's superior, with Shakespeare merely 'The
herald of a higher race'; and so it is fortified against both an intolerable
superseding and an intolerable unadvancingness, fortified by its
creation of an evolution which is a type of true continuity, neither rising
above nor sinking back upon.

'And let the ape and tiger die': but not let die such words themselves.
'. . . I might perhaps leave something so written to after-times as they
should not willingly let it die'. Milton's hopes are any poet's, and
perhaps Edward FitzGerald remembered them when he expressed his
hopes for Tennyson, doing so with a comically convoluted allusion to
Shakespeare and to the whirligigs of the time machine: 'But with all his
faults, he will publish such a volume as has not been published since the
time of Keats: and which, once published, will never be suffered to die.
This is my prophecy: for I live before Posterity.'[26] 'This prophecie
Merlin shall make, for I live before his time' (*King Lear*).

It was the prophecy of sinking which most haunted Tennyson, and
it fused the geological, the evolutionary, and the social:

> A land of old upheaven from the abyss
> By fire, to sink into the abyss again
> ('The Passing of Arthur' 82–3)

—even as the achievement of King Arthur is sinking into the abyss
again. The vision of 'then back into the beast again' made Tennyson
grateful for all the sounding words which are not just watchwords:

> Is there evil but on earth? or pain in every peopled sphere?
> Well be grateful for the sounding watchword, 'Evolution' here,
>
> Evolution ever climbing after some ideal good,
> And Reversion ever dragging Evolution in the mud.
> ('Locksley Hall Sixty Years After' 197–200)

It is not just the word 'reversion' there, but the opening 'Is there . . .',
which makes me hear in Tennyson's lines a reversion to Pope's sounding
words: 'Is there no bright reversion in the sky, | For those who greatly
think, or bravely die?'[27] What had been bright and in the sky may be

---

[26] 17 March 1842; FitzGerald, *Letters* (ed. A. M. Terhune and A. B. Terhune, 1980), i 315.
[27] 'Elegy to the Memory of an Unfortunate Lady' 9–10. See p. 128 above.

dark and 'in the mud'. Yet the evil reversion has its sense of what a bright reversion might be, grateful to Pope (the word 'grateful' perhaps precipitated by Pope's 'greatly'). Tennyson's lines are a dark counterpart to Byron's bright reversion to Pope, Byron tacitly making an exception for Pope within an 'Elegy to the Memory of a Fortunate Gentleman':

> He that reserves his laurels for posterity
> (Who does not often claim the bright reversion?)
> Has generally no great crop to spare it, he
> Being only injured by his own assertion . . .
> (*Don Juan*, Dedication, stanza 9)

For Tennyson, the answer to the question 'Is there no bright reversion in the sky?' is not merely 'No'. Worse, there is a dark reversion in the sky. For it is the sky which brings home the nature of earth, our earth doomed to an extinction manifest in the long vistas of geological and astronomical time and space. 'Man is as mortal as men': and poetry and nature and the very earth itself are all as mortal as man.

Everyone who has read Tennyson knows how urgently and variously this sense of our dying earth pressed upon him. Humphry House seized as especially salient the late poem 'Parnassus' (16) in which there tower above the twin peaks of Parnassus two dark unignorable forms: 'These are Astronomy and Geology, terrible Muses!' The sight is worlds away from the Augustan confidence of Denham: ''Twas this the Ancients meant, Nature and Skill | Are the two tops of their Parnassus Hill' ('On Mr John Fletcher's Works').

In affectionate company, Tennyson could contemplate without terror 'The man in Space and Time'; the company of Horace and of a young girl lend equanimity, for instance, to Tennyson's tender dealings with geology and astronomy in the Epilogue to 'The Charge of the Heavy Brigade at Balaclava'. But though the terrible Muses did not always strike terror into Tennyson, they often struck sadness:

> brought to understand
> A sad astrology, the boundless plan
> That makes you tyrants in your iron skies,
> Innumerable, pitiless, passionless eyes,
> Cold fires, yet with power to burn and brand
> His nothingness into man.
> (*Maud*, i 633–8)

'Iron skies' is itself an extraordinary compacting of the terrible Muses of astronomy and geology. Perhaps his greatest contempt was for those who affected to be moved by this thought of 'nothingness', and the most cutting poem he ever wrote shows how early it was so ('A Character', 1830).

> With a half-glance upon the sky
> At night he said, 'The wanderings
> Of this most intricate Universe
> Teach me the nothingness of things.'
> Yet could not all creation pierce
> Beyond the bottom of his eye.
>
> (1–6)

Tennyson's earliest verses (apart from schoolboy translations of Horace), his 'Translation of Claudian's "Rape of Proserpine"', begin: 'The gloomy chariot of the God of night, | And the wan stars that sickened at the sight . . .'. Yet Claudian's words had not meant quite that; rather, 'the stars darkened by the shadow of his infernal chariot' (Loeb translation).[28] 'Wan' and 'sickened' are Tennyson's, or rather they are Milton's ('The blasted Starrs lookt wan') and Pope's ('The sick'ning stars fade off th' ethereal plain'). Tennyson aligns himself with Milton's vision of the hideous infection of the universe by Sin and Death, and with Pope's vision of the hideous extinction of the universe by universal darkness. The central impulse, even in these earliest lines of Tennyson, is less the imagining of 'the wan stars that sickened at the sight', than our sickening wanly at the sight of the stars. What saves Tennyson from being sickened into silence is the supporting presence of poets who have not faded off the ethereal plain.

This may seem too early, for Tennyson personally and for the age. But these Victorian pangs were eighteenth-century pangs, and the young Tennyson was aware of those poets who had tried to override their fears. When young, he imitated them, misguidedly, and he achieved their hollow hopefulness. So William Mason described the earth's extinction:

> The time will come, when Destiny and Death,
> Thron'd in a burning car, the thund'ring wheels
> Arm'd with gigantic scythes of adamant,
> Shall scour this field of life, and in their rear

---

[28] *Inferni raptoris equis adflataque curru | sidera Taenario caligantesque profundae | Iunonis thalamos . . .*

The fiend Oblivion: kingdoms, empires, worlds
Melt in the general blaze:
                    (*Caractacus*, 1759, pp. 26–7)

at which point Mason hey-presto'd the feats of fame:

> when, lo, from high
> Andraste darting, catches from the wreck
> The role of fame, claps her ascending plumes,
> And stamps on orient stars each patriot name,
> Round her eternal dome.

In 'Time: An Ode', Tennyson explicitly acknowledged a debt to Mason, but it was a bad debt, because it helped the young Tennyson to arrive at spirited vacancies, moving from what was felt:

> On, on they go along the boundless skies,
>   All human grandeur fades away
> Before their flashing, fiery, hollow eyes;
>   Beneath the terrible control
>   Of those vast armèd orbs, which roll
> Oblivion on the creatures of a day.
>   (51–6)

—lines which honourably anticipate the words 'boundless', 'skies', 'hollow', 'eyes' and even 'fires' ('fiery' here) within the 'sad astrology' in *Maud*—moving immediately from this which was felt to what was not.

> Those splendid monuments alone he spares,
>   Which, to her deathless votaries,
> Bright Fame, with glowing hand, uprears
>   Amid the waste of countless years.
> 'Live ye!' to these he crieth; 'live!'
> 'To ye eternity I give—'

—and so for a further nine lines which four more times cry 'Live'. Or there is Erasmus Darwin:

> Roll on, YE STARS! exult in youthful prime,
> Mark with bright curves the printless steps of Time;
> Near and more near your beamy cars approach,
> And lessening orbs on lessening orbs encroach;—
> Flowers of the sky! ye too to age must yield,
> Frail as your silken sisters of the field!
> Star after star from Heaven's high arch shall rush,

Suns sink on suns, and systems systems crush,
Headlong, extinct, to one dark centre fall,
And Death and Night and Chaos mingle all!
—Till o'er the wreck, emerging from the storm,
Immortal NATURE lifts her changeful form,
Mounts from her funeral pyre on wings of flame,
And soars and shines, another and the same.[29]

These are lines which imagined themselves to be an answer, half a century later, to the end of *The Dunciad*, an answer set apparently to culminate in *The Dunciad's* final rhyme ('Thy hand, great Anarch! lets the curtain fall; | And Universal Darkness buries all'): 'Headlong, extinct, to one dark centre fall, | And Death and Night and Chaos mingle all!' Yet not culminating there, because Darwin snatches from 'the wreck' the reassuring figure of Immortal Nature. This too is a reassurance which sought the support of allusion; for the last line, 'And soars and shines, another and the same', attempts (itself both another and the same, a type of the allusion) to do for Pope—'All as the vest, appear'd the wearer's frame, | Old in new state, another yet the same'[30]—what Pope had done for Dryden: 'His Son, or one of his Illustrious Name, | How like the former, and almost the same'.[31]

But Tennyson did not believe that Nature was Immortal. Not even the 'What if . . .' of a poet incomparably greater than Mason or Erasmus Darwin could convince Tennyson. Wordsworth's 'Vernal Ode' was 'composed to place in view the immortality of succession where immortality is denied, as far as we know, to the individual creature':

What if those bright fires
Shine subject to decay,
Sons haply of extinguished sires,
Themselves to lose their light, or pass away
Like clouds before the wind,
Be thanks poured out to Him whose hand bestows,
Nightly, on human kind
That vision of endurance and repose.

(40–7)

Tennyson too believed in God, but not because in showing us the stars

---

[29] *The Economy of Vegetation*, IV (1792).
[30] *The Dunciad* A, iii 31–2. See pp. 41–2 above.
[31] Dryden, *Aeneis*, vi 1194–5.

He bestowed a vision of endurance and repose; rather because He offered, against the desolating vision of the stars, a vision of endurance and repose. God's love would effect what human love must hope to find, 'The countercharm of space and hollow sky' (*Maud*, i 641). When the stars are merry in Tennyson, within this same imagining in *Maud* of the sad astrology which is modern astronomy, it is because he is attended by an unmodern poet, Spenser: 'All night therefore attend your merry play':[32] '—And you fair stars that crown a happy day | Go in and out as if at merry play . . .'. When Tennyson himself writes an epithalamion, and there is a 'happy earth', this is because the love here and now is matched by a poetic companionship undaunted by astronomy. 'Ah, bear me with thee, smoothly borne' is a line borne along by the happy earth in *Paradise Lost*, which 'beares thee soft with the smooth Air along'. Or, still within an epithalamion, there is Tennyson's loving companionship with the poet Thomson, from whom Tennyson here inherited the right kind of gloom; the moon is to rise:

> And touch with shade the bridal doors,
>   With tender gloom the roof, the wall;
>   And breaking let the splendour fall
> To spangle all the happy shores
>
> By which they rest, and ocean sounds,
>   And, star and system rolling past,
>   A soul shall draw from out the vast
> And strike his being into bounds . . .
>   (*In Memoriam*, Epilogue 117–24)

The terrors of vastness ('Swallowed in Vastness, lost in Silence, drowned in the deeps of a meaningless Past', 'Vastness' 34), of star and system, are happily mollified into 'tender gloom'. The question of whether we should call *allusion* such a use of the words of a previous poet is less important than the enduring comfort which Tennyson found here, a solidarity with the unterrible muse of Thomson against the terrible Muses. Even 'Parnassus' is supported less by its final intervention from a divine outer space—'let the golden Iliad vanish, Homer here is Homer there'—than by a smaller muse than Homer's who furnished for Tennyson something which had at least not vanished yet. Tennyson's hope at first, 'Lightning may shrivel the laurel of Caesar, but mine

---

[32] 'Epithalamion'. I am grateful to Dorothy Mermin for this parallel.

would not wither', and his succeeding despair, 'Poet, that evergreen laurel is blasted by more than lightning!', are given the courage to contemplate the possibilities by their tribute to Marvell's laurels, unblasted in 'An Horatian Ode': 'And *Caesars* head at last | Did through his Laurels blast'. At last, perhaps, for the poet too; but not as yet. Which is not a refutation of astronomy and geology, but is a paradoxical inspiration in the face of them. Wordsworth had high hopes of

> Art divine,
> That both creates and fixes, in despite
> Of Death and Time, the marvels it hath wrought.
> ('Lines Suggested by a Portrait' 76–8)

But Tennyson placed his modest hopes in the Marvells that had wrought it.

Geological catastrophe (more specifically, the geological theory of catastrophism), death, and Tennyson's love for Hallam come together in an early sonnet which Humphry House picked out as showing that 'the intensity of affection for Hallam, even in his lifetime, was linked to the terrors of speculation':[33]

> 'Twere joy, not fear, claspt hand-in-hand with thee,
> To wait for death—mute—careless of all ills,
> Apart upon a mountain, though the surge
> Of some new deluge from a thousand hills
> Flung leagues of roaring foam into the gorge
> Below us, as far on as eye could see.
> ('If I were loved, as I desire to be' 9–14)

What the ear hears, not drowned by the roaring foam, is that Tennyson's words—'some new deluge'—are clasped hand-in-hand with Marvell's: 'And Earth some new Convulsion tear', in another poem on 'two perfect Loves', 'The Definition of Love'.

The earth's convulsions are alive, too, in the 'Ode on the Death of the Duke of Wellington', in lines created from Tennyson's continuity with both his own poetry and that of another.

> For though the Giant Ages heave the hill
> And break the shore, and evermore
> Make and break, and work their will . . .
> (259–61)

---

[33] *All in Due Time*, p. 134.

For it is not just that in these lines Tennyson was working his will, making and breaking his own earlier lines from a draft of 'The Palace of Art':

> Yet saw she Earth laid open. Furthermore
> How the strong Ages had their will,
> A range of Giants breaking down the shore
> And heaving up the hill.

If Tennyson can endure the sight of the hills as living heaving hills, it is by turning Wordsworth to a different purpose:

> Or caught amid a whirl of desert sands—
> An Army now, and now a living hill
> That a brief while heaves with convulsive throes—
> Then all is still.

But then Wordsworth himself had not been relying entirely, in this poem 'To Enterprise', on his own enterprise. Note (1822): ' "Awhile the living hill | Heaved with convulsive throes, and all was still". Dr Darwin describing the destruction of the army of Cambyses'.

The 'Ode on the Death of the Duke of Wellington' has tragic courage. 'The Golden Year' has comic courage.

> 'Ah, though the times, when some new thought can bud,
> Are but as poets' seasons when they flower,
> Yet oceans daily gaining on the land,
> Have ebb and flow conditioning their march,
> And slow and sure comes up the golden year.   (27–31)

Yet poets' seasons may still flower long after the poets, and conditioning the march of Tennyson's lines is an old thought which newly buds: Shakespeare's, 'the hungry Ocean gaine | Advantage on the Kingdome of the shoare' (Sonnet 64). The poets' seasons do at least lessen the terror of the aeons of astronomy and geology.

> 'We sleep and wake and sleep, but all things move;
> The Sun flies forward to his brother Sun;
> The dark Earth follows wheeled in her ellipse;
> And human beings returning on themselves
> Move onward, leading up the golden year.

Even the darkest sounds may be lightened by these human things returning on themselves.

> But I should turn mine ears and hear
> The moanings of the homeless sea,
> The sound of streams that swift or slow
> Draw down Æonian hills, and sow
> The dust of continents to be.
>
> (*In Memoriam*, XXXV 8–12)

For 'the homeless sea' is not a friendless thought, since Shelley gave those words his habitation and his name.

> The hills are shadows, and they flow
> From form to form, and nothing stands;
> They melt like mist, the solid lands,
> Like clouds they shape themselves and go.
>
> (*In Memoriam*, CXXIII 5–8)

Nothing stands? Some words of Wordsworth stand, and help to shape the line 'Like clouds they shape themselves and go': 'A thousand, thousand rings of light | That shape themselves and disappear'.[34]

Tennyson believed that only the divine miracle of personal immortality would make it conceivable that there could be such things as

> jewels five-words-long
> That on the stretched forefinger of all Time
> Sparkle for ever . . .
>
> (*The Princess*, ii 355–7)

Geological time, which made jewels, then made them valueless, ephemeral. Yet he was enabled to write, exquisitely and courageously, about such faith and such fears, not only by his religious belief but also by his taking up an inheritance, a various poetic inheritance with which he confronted our human inheritance: our inheriting the earth, and its being a dying earth.

The last poem which he finished, 'The Dreamer', tells us that ' "The meek shall inherit the earth" was a Scripture that rang through his head'. To the willing Voice of the Earth, whirling in space and time, with its 'iron Truth' and its 'Age of gold', the dreamer replies with the lyrical fervour of hope. The mighty J. Paul Getty was doubtless within his rights to say that 'The meek shall inherit the earth, but not its mineral rights', yet Tennyson sang of the fact that mineral rights are only as enduring as minerals themselves.

---

[34] 'The White Doe of Rylston' 969–70.

II

In the Company of Allusion

Plagiarism

When the President—the previous President—of the British Academy invited me to give this lecture, I took up the terms in which he had written, and proposed the subject of plagiarism: 'It relates to "scholarly debate"; it has "general public interest"; and I even like the dark thought that it's something "the Academy exists to promote" . . .'. Judge then of my pleasure when, in his Presidential Address for 1997, the President announced that the lecture would be 'on "Plagiarism", not a subject which the Academy exists to promote, but one in which we all have an interest'.[1]

'SIR,—I am concerned to see your able correspondent W. H. throwing away his valuable time on so threadbare a topic as Plagiarism': Thomas De Quincey, or probably he,[2] in 1827. 'Of plagiarism, little new can be written': Hillel Schwartz, *The Culture of the Copy* (1996).[3]

The news this very day (10 February 1998) in *The Times* is of a student's going to the High Court

to try to force Cambridge University to award him a degree after he was accused of cheating. Kamran Beg is believed to be the first student to challenge the university in court over allegations that he plagiarised part of an essay in his postgraduate finance degree at Trinity College. Mr Beg's solicitor denied his client acted dishonestly and said he had inadvertently omitted attributions or footnotes to passages he had quoted.

Plagiarism is perennial. And annual. 1997 saw the publication here of Neal Bowers's pained book, *Words for the Taking*, the words of which were taken up in many a long review. Subtitled 'The hunt for a plagiarist', it told how some of Bowers's published poems were re-published by another, a pathological tinkerer who had many a name and a squalid criminal record. To Bowers may be added other continuing attentions.

---

[1] I am grateful to the friends who commented on a draft: Kenneth Haynes, Marcia Karp, Michael Prince, Lisa Rodensky, and Christopher Wilkins.
[2] To the Editor of the *Saturday Evening Post*, 3 November 1827; *New Essays by De Quincey* (1966), ed. Stuart M. Tave, p. 181.
[3] Hillel Schwartz, *The Culture of the Copy* (1996), p. 311.

In almost every issue, *Private Eye* takes pleasure in exposing plagiarisms, and not only as the regular feature 'Just Fancy That!' The *Sunday Telegraph* of 3 August 1997 carried a column by Jenny McCartney on the romance novelist Janet Dailey, her plagiarism and psychological problems. A very recent film, *Good Will Hunting*, currently triumphant in the cinemas of Boston Massachusetts (where the film is set), shows in an early scene the hero securing a woman's tender notice by accusing his rival of being about to plagiarize, and the closing words of the film are the retort of rueful friendship, 'He stole my line.'

So much is plagiarism in the air that when the *New Yorker* (22 December 1997) printed a cartoon about it (by Joseph Farris), I saw or imagined the cartoon's own doubleness: in a bookstore where there can be seen a section headed HISTORY, a man browses in the section headed PLAGIARISM. Books that are plagiarisms, I take it; but those shelves could as well consist by now of books on PLAGIARISM.

I choose this subject because it combines the enduring and the current, with a further twist: I shall argue that this dishonesty is too often exculpated by dishonesties, by evasive banter, and by slippery history.

Definition, first. The *Oxford English Dictionary* rules:

plagiarism The wrongful appropriation, or purloining, and publication as one's own, of the ideas, or the expression of the ideas (literary, artistic, musical, mechanical, etc.) of another.

Notice 'wrongful', as constitutive within the definition, and add, constitutive too, that—as Peter Shaw has put it (into italics)—'Throughout history the act of using the work of another *with an intent to deceive* has been branded as plagiarism.'[4]

Marcel Lafollette, in *Stealing into Print: Fraud, Plagiarism, and Misconduct in Scientific Publishing* (1992), has said of plagiarism that 'Its definition is simple'.[5] If he is, as I believe, right, why does Peter Shaw grant—too concessively—that 'There will always remain certain gray areas resistant to definition'? Because it is easy, even for someone as morally alert as Shaw, to let one thing slide into another. That the supporting evidence for the accusation of plagiarism may on occasion be elusive, insufficient, or uncertain is not the same as thinking that the

---

[4] 'Plagiary', *The American Scholar* (Summer 1982), p. 327.
[5] Marcel C. Lafollette, *Stealing into Print: Fraud, Plagiarism, and Misconduct in Scientific Publishing* (1992), p. 49.

definition of plagiarism is uncertain. The grey areas may remain resistant to adjudication without being resistant to definition. It may be perfectly clear what constitutes plagiarism ('using the work of another *with an intent to deceive*') without its being clear that what faces us is truly a case of this. In his lasting book of 1928, *Literary Ethics*, H. M. Paull admits what we should all admit on occasion, 'the difficulty of deciding what is plagiarism and what is legitimate borrowing',[6] but the difficulty of deciding is not the same as the difficulty of defining. That it may in some cases be very hard to make this accusation—like many another accusation—stick, does not entail there being about the accusation anything loose.

Far from there being, as it suits some people to maintain, insuperable problems of definition, there aren't even any superable problems. The morality of the matter, which asks of us that we be against deceit and dishonesty, is clear, and is clearly defined. Those of us who believe, as to plagiarism, that nothing is more important than *not making excuses* should be more than usually careful not to permit the easy excusing that slides in with the misguided concession that the world has never been able to decide what it means by plagiarism.

One of the most adroit of the exculpators, Professor James Kincaid, wrote of plagiarism in the *New Yorker* in 1997 (20 January): 'As for defining it, we leave that to the officials—in this example, Northwestern University.' Quizzing Northwestern's sentence on the responsibilities of 'a conscientious writer', Kincaid asked: 'But how do I distinguish what I have "learned from others" from what I am "personally contributing"? If I subtract everything I have learned from others (including Mother?), what is left?'[7] These are good questions—essential questions for anyone whose profession is teaching—but only if they are genuinely questions, only if jesting Kincaid were to stay for an answer. For him, though, they are rhetorical questions, inviting abdication. Distinctions the conscientious making of which is crucial are guyed as naive nullities.

Kincaid on occasion has recourse to putting the word *original* within quotation marks, 'original', though not exactly quoting it. He does the same with 'plagiarism'. This is the usual intimation that a particular concept is a coercion by power, acquiesced in by naivety. The

6 H. M. Paull, *Literary Ethics* (1928), p. 126.
7 *New Yorker*, 20 Jan. 1997, pp. 93–7.

hermeneutics of suspicion avails itself of this punctuation of suspicion. Some of us at least, it implies, are aware that this concept—like every other concept—is implicatedly problematic; aware, too, that it is more-over not problematic at all, being nothing more than a construction, as they say, imposed by the powers that be or that were.

Not plagiarism, then (something that people mistakenly suppose they understand); rather, 'plagiarism'. But the prophylaxis of quotation marks has itself come under suspicion lately, so the new thing is to announce that one both may be and may not be availing oneself of the nicety.

I do not put the word 'plagiarism' in quotation marks most of the time, but perhaps those quotation marks should be imagined. . . . I have been interested, then, in cultural distinctions between legitimate and illegitimate forms of appropriation. For this reason, I may have used the term 'plagiarism' to describe a wider range of transgressive appropriations than perhaps the word ordinarily signifies.[8]

Laura J. Rosenthal, in *Playwrights and Plagiarists in Early Modern England: Gender, Authorship, Literary Property* (1996). But what may perhaps be more widely transgressive is assuredly narrower in one way: in that it eschews moral considerations. For what could be less morally open to scrutiny than the transgressive? Professor Rosenthal tells us that her purpose is 'to question differences between plagiarism, imitation, adaptation, repetition, and originality'. But rhetorical questioning leads to the required answer: that there is no difference between these things other than that power uses the opprobrious term, plagiarism, when the work emanates from those whom power dislikes. Appropriation of appropriations, saith the Preacher, appropriation of appropriations, all is appropriation.

The objection to such arguments is not that they are strongly polit-ical but that they are weakly, wizenedly, political. Professor Rosenthal's book is itself animated by a political fervour that is clearly and duly moral, but her undertaking then requires her to write as if a political reading—in her case, a reading à la Foucault—had to extirpate from a discussion of plagiarism all moral considerations. What would have to be in moral terms a matter of honesty or dishonesty (plagiarism being dishonest) is replaced—not complemented—by a matter of power,

---

[8] Laura J. Rosenthal, *Playwrights and Plagiarists in Early Modern England: Gender, Authorship, Literary Property* (1996), p. 10.

necessity, the tyrant's plea. The 'cultural distinctions between legitimate and illegitimate forms of appropriation' become a matter of nothing but 'the cultural location of the text and the position of the author',[9] instead of being among several aspects each of them germane. Rosenthal is convincing on particular injustices and prejudices, but her setting does an injustice to politics, in that the room it leaves for conscience is in the animating of the inquiry, not within the inquiry proper.

The consequence of an investigative determination that 'denaturalizes the distinction between imitation and plagiarism'[10] is that the prefix de- becomes a virus, working to demean and to degrade moral thought. That no moral position is natural does not of itself entail that moral positions are nothing but the insistences of power. Moral agreements, though not natural, may be valuable, indispensable, worthy of the respect that they have earned. That plagiarism may valuably be seen under the aspect of politics, and that politics may in turn be valuably seen under the aspect of power at the time, need not and should not issue in the denial that plagiarism asks to be seen too under the aspect of ethics. The extirpation of ethical or moral considerations by such political history is a sad loss, to political history among other needful things.

Plagiarism is a dishonesty. This can be swept to one side, leaving not the dishonest but the culturally conditioned and exclusively power-ruled illegitimate. Or it can be swept to the other side, leaving not the dishonest but—assimilating plagiarism now to copyright—the illegal.

It is natural to move to infringement of copyright when thinking of plagiarism, but crucial that one should be aware of moving. For as Paul Goldstein says in *Copyright's Highway* (1994): 'Plagiarism, which many people commonly think has to do with copyright, is not in fact a legal doctrine.'[11] In a review-article on Goldstein's book and two others (*Times Literary Supplement*, 4 July 1997), James Boyle, a professor of law, pondered 'Problems of defining the limits of copyright in the age of the Internet—and of pop-music parody'. His thoughts on intellectual property are germane to plagiarism, since intellectual property may be seen not only under a legal aspect but under a moral one. Boyle observes that 'there is considerably more dispute about the desirability, role and extent of intellectual property—even among defenders of the free

[9] *Playwrights and Plagiarists in Early Modern England*, p. 13.
[10] Ibid.
[11] Paul Goldstein, *Copyright's Highway* (1994), p. 12.

market—than there was about the desirability of private property in general', and he concludes with the justified asseveration that 'intellectual-property law has become the boundary line, or perhaps the hinge, between art and commerce, between "free speech" and economic monopoly, between public culture and private property'.

The subtlety and tenacity of Boyle's thinking discredit James Kincaid's condescension to the law, setting it right; some of us, Kincaid is confident, have learned from recent literary theory the complexities of intellectual property: 'Still, the law lumbers on as if nothing more complicated than cattle rustling were involved.'[12]

Far from lumbering, intellectual-property law is limber, well aware of the complications. But, to moral considerations the law must always offer a handshake at arm's length. For although the law is a moral matter, being distinguishable from but not distinct from justice, the law acknowledges that there is a moral world elsewhere. A pity, then, that the legal-eyed Alexander Lindey, in *Plagiarism and Originality* (1952), on occasion grants too much to the legal. 'Since any discussion of plagiarism is, from a realistic standpoint, meaningless without reference to the legal consequences, I've devoted quite a bit of space to court cases.'[13] Granted, legal consequences have a remarkable realism, reality even, but it is misleading to speak as if opprobrium or disapproval, such as should be incurred by plagiarism, are from a realistic standpoint meaningless. Again, Lindey writes, truly, that 'Plagiarism and infringement are not the same thing, though they overlap', but he goes on at once to infringe the moral sphere: 'Plagiarism covers a wider field; infringement involves more serious consequences.'[14] It would be wrong to acquiesce in this implication that the legal is of its nature more serious than the moral. That gambling debts may be legally irrecoverable but are honour-bound was and is a social reality of entire seriousness. The consequences of dishonourable behaviour have been, and fortunately still sometimes are, no less serious than legal proceedings.

Lindey's momentary lapse has its literary counterpart, when Donald Davie writes that 'the hymn-writer did not have copyright in his work as other authors did; and so plagiarism is a concept that does not apply'.[15] But plagiarism is distinguishable from infringement of copy-

---

[12] Kincaid, *New Yorker*, 20 Jan. 1997, p. 97.
[13] Alexander Lindey, *Plagiarism and Originality* (1952), p. xiii.
[14] *Plagiarism and Originality*, p. 2.
[15] *The Eighteenth-Century Hymn in England* (1993), p. 18.

right, and if it were *tout court* the case—which I doubt—that plagiarism is a concept that does not apply to hymns, this would have to be a consequence of something other than the hymn-writer's not owning copyright. The same slide can be seen, not this time in a lawyer or a critic but in a literary theorist. In *Hot Property: The Stakes and Claims of Literary Originality* (1994), Françoise Meltzer sometimes lets her attention slip. 'A good example of how originality and, therefore, plagiarism are governed more by the character of the community than by immutable notions of right and wrong is to be seen in the U.S. Copyright form'.[16] The legal rights and wrongs may be manifest in the copyright form, but there are other rights and wrongs. So it is a pity that in her firm account of the accusation of plagiarism levelled at Paul Celan, plagiarism from Yvan Goll, Meltzer should assimilate the moral question of plagiarism to the legal question of copyright.

So was the widow Goll right about the most notorious of her charges? That is, did the phrase 'black milk' belong to her husband? The answer, of course, must be no. First, for a simple reason: even the American copyright form states that one cannot protect 'titles, names and short phrases'. It is impossible to claim the invention of so few words.[17]

This is muddled, muddied. That no one can legally protect short phrases is perfectly compatible with someone's justifiably claiming to have created a short phrase, and this is in turn compatible with someone else's being guilty of plagiarizing a short phrase. 'Black milk'— 'schwarze Milch'—may be insufficiently remarkable as a short phrase for the charge of plagiarism to be substantiable, but there are equally short phrases which it would be worse than imprudent for me, say, to accommodate in a poem of mine without acknowlegement or allusion. T. S. Eliot offers many: 'maculate giraffe', 'sapient sutlers', 'beneficent spider', 'forgetful snow'. One could grant that none of these could be copyright while at the same time believing that the appearance of them outside Eliot might form the prima-facie basis of a plagiarism charge.

To the exculpations of plagiarism that rest upon a limiting of the necessary judgement to legal judgment (breach of copyright then being

---

[16] Françoise Meltzer, *Hot Property: The Stakes and Claims of Literary Originality* (1994), p. 73.

[17] *Hot Property*, p. 74. Meltzer goes on: 'Moreover, Goll's poem was published in New York in 1942, at a time (as Felstiner points out) when Celan was in a Rumanian labor camp and "hardly likely to have seen it".'

the only breach that we need ponder), there have been added the exculpations that seek to call, as a witness for the defence, history. Simply:
plagiarism is a recent construction in need of demystifying. For a
reminder that the construction industry is booming, see *The
Construction of Authorship* (1994), in a very up-to-date series called
'Post-Contemporary Interventions'.[18]

This recency claim has at once to deal with an unwelcome witness
for the prosecution. Call Marcus Valerius Martialis. Martial's testimony
is perfectly clear, is not at all recent, and is notarized in seven poems
about plagiarism. Added to which, there is the further inconvenience,
for the revisionist historian of plagiarism, that it is to Martial that we
owe the very application to literary deception of the word *plagiarius*, the
abductor of the child or slave of another.

> Th'art out, vile Plagiary, that dost think
> A Poet may be made at th'rate of Ink,
> And cheap-priz'd Paper; none e'er purchas'd yet
> Six or ten Penniworth of Fame or Wit:
> Get Verse unpublish'd, new-stamp'd Fancies look,
> Which th'only Father of the Virgin Book
> Knows, and keeps seal'd in his close Desk within,
> Not slubber'd yet by any ruffer Chin;
> A Book, once known, ne'r quits the Author; If
> Any lies yet unpolish'd, any stiff,
> Wanting it's Bosses, and it's Cover, do
> Get that; I've such and can be secret too.
>   He that repeats stoln Verse, and for Fame looks,
>   Must purchase Silence too as well as Books.[19]

The half-dozen other epigrams by Martial take an equally though
differently sardonic tack in their contemptuous rebuking of the dishonesty of the plagiarist.

Since copyright is in hock to the cash-nexus and is a relatively recent
invention, it would suit a certain political slant if plagiarism were a
recent invention too. But what about Martial? He may get reluctantly
acknowledged, but will then find himself labelled a distinctly unusual
case. Revisionism knows that there is some wresting to be done, some
wrestling, the Newest Laocoon. Thomas Mallon, in *Stolen Words* (1989),

---

[18] Martha Woodmansee and Peter Jaszi (eds.), *The Construction of Authorship* (1994).

[19] Epigrams i. 66; this translation by William Cartwright was published 1651.

his study—in detail—of some central plagiarism cases, noticed that 'scholars will tie themselves up in knots exonerating Coleridge. In one book Thomas McFarland sees his thefts as being not plagiarism but "a mode of composition—composition by mosaic organization".'[20] But then the older historians of plagiarism were sometimes off guard. H. M. Paull, for instance, after substantiating the stigma of plagiarism in classical times and thereafter, slips into misrepresenting the history that he himself tells. 'All this shows that such practices now needed an apology'; 'But perhaps the best proof that direct plagiarism was becoming discredited . . .':[21] yet Paull had shown that such practices had always needed an apology, that plagiarism had always been discredited. What, then, moved him to put such a gloss upon the history he had given? His progressivism. For Paull was committed, as his closing pages announce, to the conviction that 'on the whole there has been a distinct progress towards an unattainable ideal: unattainable whilst human nature remains unchanged. Forgery, piracy, and plagiarism, the three most considerable literary crimes, have sensibly diminished.'[22] The closing words of his book are 'contribute to the advancement of the race'. Paull's liberal progressivism is the fitting converse, obverse, of the prelapsarian revisionism which claims that, until the invention of the author, *circa* some time like the seventeenth century, there was no such thing as plagiarism and the deploring of it. In pious times, ere Authors did begin, before to plagiarize was made a sin . . .

Exculpations, then, have long been at work. Harold Ogden White, *Plagiarism and Imitation During the English Renaissance: A Study in Critical Distinctions* (1935), opened with a fervid denunciation of 'modern critics' for imposing the concept of plagiarism upon the past;[23] but despite his insistence that 'Englishmen from 1500–1625' were 'without any feeling analogous to the modern attitude toward plagiarism', his book is full of indictments of plagiarism, from classical and Renaissance times, that are entirely at one with what he deplores as the modern attitude towards plagiarism.[24] How does White effect this? By the simple expedient of substituting for the word plagiarism the word piracy.

---

[20] Thomas Mallon, *Stolen Words* (1989), pp. 32–3.   [21] *Literary Ethics*, p. 110.
[22] Ibid., 332.
[23] Harold Ogden White, in *Plagiarism and Imitation During the English Renaissance: A Study in Critical Distinctions* (1935), p. 202.
[24] See also Schwartz, *The Culture of the Copy*, p. 311.

When the poetaster Bathyllus piratically claimed the authorship of an anony-mously issued poem of Virgil's—so runs the apocryphal anecdote—Virgil retorted: 'I made the verses, another has stolen the honour.' But Martial's protest at the piracies of which he had been the victim is probably the most famous in all literature, because in it he first used the word *plagiarius*, literally 'kidnaper', for a literary thief.[25]

White quotes Florio on fellow-writers: 'What doe they but translate? perhaps, usurpe? at least, collect? if with acknowledgment, it is well; if by stealth, it is too bad.'[26] Is this not the deploring of plagiarism? As so often, a distinction kicked out of the door comes back in through the window. Call all plagiarisms piracy and you have rendered plagiarism non-existent. White certainly shows that imitation was greatly valued in classical times and in the Renaissance, but he does not show that there was no distinction then between imitation and plagiarism, no disap-probation of plagiarism, for he himself reports such disapprobation of unacknowledged, secret, or furtive borrowings. For Donne, White says, and substantiates, 'borrowed matter is to be thankfully acknowledged, not ungratefully purloined by stealth'.[27]

Thomas Mallon acknowledges, as everyone must, that something happened in the seventeenth century, but is it true that 'our basic sense of plagiarism came to be born'—*born*, that exactly—'in the seventeenth century'?[28] Printing had changed something, yes—but 'it was printing, of course, that changed everything'?[29] Everything? Not the nub dishon-esty, the claiming credit for a poem someone else has written.

In *Crimes of Writing* (1991), a book that oddly does no more than mention plagiarism, Susan Stewart has a passing comment: 'plagiarism of course arises as a problem at the same time that other issues of writ-ing's authenticity come to the fore'.[30] But 'problem' there has to cover a lot of ground; it is not the case that condemnation of plagiarism arose as late as the new commodification would like to believe. We are assured by Stewart that in medieval times there was no such thing as plagiarism (reprehensible), and yet the assurance, from Giles Constable, does waver rather: 'the term plagiarism should indeed probably'—indeed probably—'be dropped in reference to the Middle Ages, since it expresses a concept of literary individualism and property that is

---

[25]   *Plagiarism and Imitation During the English Renaissance*, pp. 15–16.
[26]   Ibid., 168–9.   [27]   Ibid., 128.
[28]   *Stolen Words*, p. xii.   [29]   Ibid., 4.
[30]   *Crimes of Writing* (1991) , p. 24.

distinctly modern'.[31] And Martial, was he distinctly modern? He lacked a distinctly modern concept of literary property, no doubt, but he certainly had—and named—the concept of plagiarism.

As with other prelapsarian history, as with any telling of the Fall itself, the moment is elusive, contested, often gets pushed further back. Brean Hammond, in *Professional Imaginative Writing in England, 1670–1740* (1997), makes a good case for dating the 'originality' debate earlier than usual, retrieving it from the eighteenth century: 'there is, I would contend, an earlier cultural formation, that of dramatic writing in the 1670s and 1680s, wherein the problematic nature of borrowing from earlier works was already under heated negotiation'.[32] But why stop there, when it comes to negotiating the problematic nature of borrowing? Best, moreover, for Hammond to tread carefully on this 'original composition' ground, since there have been heavy investments in the eighteenth-century allocation. So Hammond prudently claims less than he might and should: 'In this period therefore, earlier than is sometimes supposed . . . there was the *beginning* of an *attempt* to define "originality" in writing and the *ur-conception* of proprietary authorship' (italics supplied).[33]

Stephen Orgel makes a similar move in his influential article on 'The Renaissance Artist as Plagiarist'. He claims that the charge of plagiarism did not appear significantly until after the Renaissance. One may grant a premiss of his, as to 'different ages', without granting the elisions and assimilations that accompany it. Was Inigo Jones a plagiarist?

Jones's practice may legitimately raise certain questions about the validity, function, philosophic implications of imitation; but such questions will also be profoundly time-bound. Different ages give very different answers to the basic question of what, exactly, it is that art imitates: for example, nature, or other art, or the action of the mind. Modern critics grow uncomfortable when it proves to be imitating other art too closely.[34]

---

[31] Ibid., 30, quoting Constable.

[32] Brean Hammond, *Professional Imaginative Writing in England, 1670–1740* (1997), p. 83.

[33] Ibid., 21, my italics. This 'ur-conception' is later joined by 'prehistory', convenient to the historian, and by 'gestation': 'there is a prehistory to the conception of originality, at least in English culture, that suggests a longer gestation period than either [Martha] Woodmansee or [Mark] Rose allow' (p. 43).

[34] Stephen Orgel, 'The Renaissance Artist as Plagiarist', *ELH: A Journal of English Literary History*, 48 (1981), 479.

Yes, such questions will be time-bound. But what exactly is Orgel's dissent from modern critics here? 'Imitating other art too closely' might be a matter of the servile, the inability to add anything at all—but then on this the modern critic would be at one with the ancient and the Renaissance critic. Or 'imitating other art too closely' ought to apply, given that Orgel's context is plagiarism ('The Renaissance Artist as Plagiarist'), to plagiarism. But here too the modern critic is not shown by Orgel to be at odds with the ancient and the Renaissance critic. Such modern critics as equate even very close imitation with plagiarism are unthinking, yes; but that the accusation of plagiarism is often foolishly and ignorantly levelled has no bearing on whether it can be, and could be back then, responsibly and justly levelled. There was, Orgel concedes, 'a long history of discomfort with Jonsonian borrowing';[35] nevertheless, if Jonson's borrowings were scarcely ever deplored as plagiarism (it was Jonson who did the deploring, launching in *The Poetaster* the missile 'plagiary' in English: 'Why? the ditt' is all borrowed; 'tis Horace's: hang him plagiary'), this need not be because the concept of plagiarism was scarcely present to people's minds but because the distinction between the furtively dishonest (plagiarism) and the openly honourable (imitation) existed and was well understood, with Jonson then judged to be practising not the unhappy former but the happy latter.

But Orgel needs a more dramatic history, a moment to identify, cultural history being one long identification parade. 'By the time Dryden was writing *Of Dramatic Poesy*, however, Jonson's borrowings required a defense': 'He invades authors like a monarch, and what would be theft in other poets, is only victory in him.' Orgel says of Dryden's aphorism: 'This was written only forty-five years after [Inigo] Jones's praise of Jonsonian "translation", and thirty years after Jonson's death. In that short time translation, imitation, borrowing, have become "learned plagiary", "robbery", "theft".'[36]

Now it may well be that the elapsing of the half-century brought about an exacerbation that ministered to ill-judgement in accusations of plagiarism; that it often became an easy, unjust, and uncomprehending charge. But this is not the same as maintaining that what had earlier been understood as translation and imitation, without reference even to the possibility of the accusation of plagiarism, was succeeded by a world in which the honourable terms 'have become' replaced by opprobious

---

terms understood as posited of just the same practices, now without reference even to the possibility of praiseworthy translation and imitation. It is, to me, impossible to credit Orgel's insistence that 'The question of the morality of literary imitation, then, starts to appear significantly in England only after the Renaissance, and on the whole in reaction to it.'[37] Many of Orgel's most telling instances tell a story that is not the one he retails. Thomas Browne sees in plagiarism a great human failing, 'the age-old desire "to plume themselves with others' feathers"'. Orgel remarks: 'It is a vice, as Browne continually laments, that has always been with us: plagiarism is the Original Sin of literature.'[38]

It is when, à propos of plagiarism, Orgel turns to allusion that the gaps in the argument yawn. 'We might want to argue that there is a vast difference between adopting the role of a classic poet and copying his words, but is there? The adoption of roles by Renaissance poets involved a good deal of direct imitation and allusion.'[39] Well, we might admit that there is not a *vast* difference between adopting a role and (without acknowledgement, since Orgel is discussing plagiarism) copying out words, while still believing that there is a crucial difference. And is not allusion incompatible with plagiarism? 'So, to stay for the moment with simple cases, how would a Renaissance audience have responded to blatant plagiarism? Sometimes, obviously, simply as an allusion: a great deal of Renaissance art offered its patrons precisely the pleasures of recognition.'[40] Hearing 'Come my Celia', did the Renaissance reader 'condemn Jonson for plagiarizing Catullus? or did he, on the contrary, admire a particularly witty adaptation of the art of the past to the designs of the present?'

The latter, for sure. But this is because the Renaissance audience well understood that what it was responding to here, what 'Renaissance art offered' here, was *not* 'blatant plagiarism', was not plagiarism. Allusion, plainly; and the defence that the poet is alluding is one that, should it be made good, must exculpate the poet. That the defence is sometimes unconvincing is a different story. Thomas Mallon is right, I should judge, not to accept the defence of Laurence Sterne that maintains that those moments of his are never plagiarisms but always allusions. But allusion has to be the contrary (Orgel's 'on the contrary') of plagiarism, since allusion is posited upon our calling the earlier work into play,

---

[37] Ibid., 484.   [38] Ibid., 483.   [39] Ibid., 479.   [40] Ibid., 480.

whereas the one thing that plagiarism hopes is that the earlier work will not enter our heads. T. S. Eliot said, in an interview in August 1961:

In one of my early poems ['Cousin Nancy'] I used, without quotation marks, the line 'the army of unalterable law . . .' from a poem by George Meredith, and this critic accused me of having shamelessly plagiarised, pinched, pilfered that line. Whereas, of course, the whole point was that the reader should recognise where it came from and contrast it with the spirit and meaning of my own poem.[41]

The fame of Meredith's line, and the conclusive placing of it by both poets, leave me in no doubt that Eliot tells the truth here; but even those who suppose him being wise after the unfortunate event would grant that, if credited, allusion is a defence that must stanch the accusation of plagiarism. And one reason why plagiarism in, for instance, scientific research is importantly different is that it is not at all clear there what it would mean to claim that one was not plagiarizing but alluding to (as against, say, referring to) earlier work.

That such-and-such wording, being an allusion, is not plagiarism, would not have to mean that there could not be any infringement of copyright. Paul Goldstein begins *Copyright's Highway* with the copyright conflict in 1990 when the rap group 2 Live Crew issued their derisive parody of the Roy Orbison/William Dees hit, 'Oh, Pretty Woman'. Parody, being allusive, cannot be plagiaristic, but it may still violate someone's rights—among them, copyright. The lawyer, though, needs to be sensitive to the judgments germane to literary allusion. Alexander Lindey, whose book on *Plagiarism and Originality* I value, ends up on one occasion agreeing amiably to overlook (as an authorial inadvertence) a moment that, contrariwise, solicits the reader's advertence:

A reviewer of Evelyn Waugh's *Scott-King's Modern Europe* praised the following excerpt as a 'burst of stylish writing':

He was older, it might have been written, than the rocks on which he sat; older, anyway, than his stall in chapel; he had died many times had Scott-King, had dived deep, had trafficked for strange webs with Eastern merchants. And all this had been but the sound of lyres and flutes to him.

'Stylish, indeed!' cried a reader with a long memory. The passage, he said, was obviously a paraphrase of the celebrated description of La Gioconda in the chapter on Leonardo in Walter Pater's *The Renaissance*:

---

[41] *Yorkshire Post; The Bed Post* (1962), Kenneth Young (ed.), pp. 43–4.

She is older than the rocks among which she sits . . . she has been dead
many times, and learned the secrets of the grave; and has been a diver in
deep seas . . . and trafficked for strange webs with Eastern merchants . . .
and all this has been to her but as the sound of lyres and flutes.

John K. Hutchens, the book critic who published this intelligence, did not
take it too seriously. It was the sort of thing, he felt, that could have happened
to anybody. He was right.[42]

Oh no he wasn't right. Nor is Mr Lindey. Waugh was not covertly
plagiarizing, but this is because he was overtly alluding. Not waiving
but waving.

An honest misunderstanding, this, on Lindey's part. It is the insufficient honesty with which the particular dishonesty that is plagiarism is
so often treated that is the increasingly sad business. Samuel Johnson
wrote of plagiarism as 'one of the most reproachful, though, perhaps,
not the most atrocious of literary crimes'.[43] The reproach has to be for
dishonesty, and yet how remarkably unreproached plagiarism usually
goes.

The dishonesty is furthermore a point of dishonour. For honour is
doubly at issue: the plagiarist hopes to gain honour from a dishonourable practice. 'His honour rooted in dishonour stood'. Peter Shaw,
in his essay 'Plagiary', showed how kid-gloved the handling or fingering
of plagiarism often is; he limned the psychology or psychopathology of
plagiarism, including the embarrassment that so often overcomes those
who find themselves faced by its two-facedness. His plea for responsible
reproof strikes me as compelling, but it has not slowed down the manufacture of excuses. The usual dealings with this double-dealing are less
than ever honest.

Yet then this, too, has a long history. William Walsh opened his entry
on plagiarism, in his *Handy-Book of Literary Curiosities* (1909), with a
question inviting the answer No: 'Is plagiarism a crime?' He duly
arrived at the conclusion from which he had started: 'On the whole, as
between the plagiarist and his accuser, we prefer the plagiarist. We have
more sympathy for the man in the pillory than for the rabble that pelt
him.' Even the case of Neal Bowers (that notable recent victim of one
David Jones) incited in reviewers a need to dissociate themselves from
his moral urgings. Mark Ford, in the *London Review of Books* (21 August
1997), expressed sympathy with Bowers in some ways (his plight

---

[42] *Plagiarism and Originality*, p. 51.   [43] *The Adventurer*, No. 95, 2 October 1753.

'considerably intensified by the difficulties he experienced trying to persuade others to take these thefts as seriously as he did'), and yet Ford is moved to mock Bowers ('Bowers assumes the mantle of heroic vigilante defending the integrity of poetry against potentially overwhelming forces of evil'), and proffers an insufficiently vigilant argument: 'It's hard to be as appalled by Jones's poetic kleptomania as Bowers insists one ought to be. This is perhaps partly because the two poems stolen from the 1992 issue of *Poetry* are not in themselves mind-blowingly original.' But a judgement on how appalled we should be by the conduct of the plagiarist (and Jones's continuing behaviour was diversely appalling) need not be commensurate with the degree of originality in the poems dishonestly laid claim to. The calculated indecorum of Ford's phrase 'not in themselves mind-blowingly original' gives vent to something, something that is not the same as finding Bowers's book tonally imperfect. Again, one might concur with James Campbell, in his review of Bowers (*Times Literary Supplement*, 28 February 1997), as to failures of tone in Bowers's wounded account ('a sanctimoniousness about his way of telling' the story, Campbell finds) while still judging it unjust of Campbell to deprecate the fact that 'Bowers frowns at colleagues who dare to smile when they hear about it'. As well Bowers might, I should have said. But then this too is continuous with the long history of casting as priggish those who, with a straight face, deplore plagiarism. For one of the touching moments in Bowers's book tells of how he too used to reach for evasive levity, giving his students what he called his 'thou-shalt-not-steal-spiel', 'mocking myself', staging 'my wise guy presentation'.

If I now refer to the demoralizing of plagiarism, I refer to such discussion of it as evacuates morals as well as morale. One form of this might be politics as impervious to individual conscience, with plagiarism 'a cultural category defining the borders between texts and policing the accumulation of cultural capital'.[44] (Policing, in the mode, being a much scarier thing than theft.) Another form might be the genial throwing up of hands, as when a discussion of plagiarism glides from cake-recipes to cooked books and then to not living by bread alone:

To an equally folk-anonymous tradition [as a recipe] belonged Dr. Martin Luther King, Jr., who in his Boston University thesis quietly integrated a few

---

[44] Laura J. Rosenthal, *Playwrights and Plagiarists in Early Modern England*, p. 3.

lines from theologian Paul Tillich and fifty sentences from another's thesis even as he would smoothly merge the rhetoric of evangelical preachers to emerge with his own voice in Montgomery.[45]

Even as? There is a lot of smooth merging going on there. As who should say, *Relax.* '—sure they are unsure. When a young historian, shown to have plagiarized his first book, becomes a Program Officer at the National Endowment for the Humanities, is a high school girl to blame for reworking a magazine piece on who was to blame for Pearl Harbor?'[46] Yes, she may well be. How many wrongs exactly *does* it take to make a right?

The essay that I take as most thoroughly colluding with the greatest number of wrongs is one from which I quoted earlier, that by James Kincaid in the *New Yorker* (20 January 1997). His title was 'Purloined Letters' (once more unto this breach), and his subtitle was 'Are we too quick to denounce plagiarism?' (No, this question does not expect the answer No.) Reviewing Neal Bowers's book, Kincaid speaks roundly ('no doubt about it') and then proceeds to get round it. To follow the moves, one needs an extended quotation.

Summer/Compton/Jones [Bowers's plagiarist] is a cheat, no doubt about it; and now and then we run across other cases of plagiarism that shut before they are open. For instance, one of my own students turned in a paper on 'Great Expectations' which was an exact copy of Dorothy Van Ghent's essay—an essay so celebrated that I recognized it right off and, at the first opportunity, raised the issue with my student. 'Shit!' she said. 'I paid seventy-five dollars for that.' It did seem a cruel turn of the screw to have term-paper companies selling plagiarized essays for students to plagiarize; but ethics are ethics, I told my student.

I could speak loftily on the subject because the ethical issues in her case were so clear-cut. They aren't always.[47]

The exculpatory bonhomie is unremittingly at play and at work. There is the reassuring assurance than Van Ghent's essay was so celebrated that Kincaid really isn't seeking any credit for recognizing it right off. There is the unmisgiving little thrill of ' "Shit!' she said' (Tina Brown's *New Yorker* wouldn't be printing a stuffed shirt)—Kincaid is a robust man

---

[45] Schwartz, *The Culture of the Copy*, p. 313.
[46] *The Culture of the Copy*, p. 314. Another shady business is the use by politicians of ghost-writers; as for 'the most famous political plagiarist of our time', Senator Joseph Biden, see Thomas Mallon's acute pages (*Stolen Words*, pp. 127–30).
[47] Kincaid, *New Yorker*, 20 Jan. 1997, p. 94.

from a robust university where the women students are robust and no professor would take amiss their being so. There is the syntactical *plaisanterie* of 'but ethics are ethics, I told my student'. And then, at the move into the next paragraph, there is the endearingly disparaging adverb 'loftily', disparaging oneself in the nicest possible way and making it clear that, even in the most clear-cut case, to take a moral tone would be a lapse: 'I could speak loftily on the subject because . . .'. Not that we have been given the chance to hear Kincaid speak loftily on the subject; rather, 'ethics are ethics' came across, as it was meant to, as calculatedly mock-pompous. A low move, 'loftily'.

I find this repellent, and not only professionally (professorially), in its combination of failure of nerve with nerve. 'The ethical issues in her case were so clear-cut': and was there any clear-cut dealing with the ethical issues? Nothing is said of what the exposure of her dishonesty meant to and for the forthright swearer; anyway, she deserves a jokey sympathy ($75? 'It did seem a cruel turn of the screw . . .'). But then it is clear just where Kincaid's sympathies are. Apparently all those who are not naive are now aware that building an accusation of plagiarism is akin to 'building legal castles on what literary theory warns is the quicksand of language'. 'But, no doubt because there's so much uncertainty around, fervent denunciations of plagiarists are popular: out-and-out plagiarists are criminals who safeguard the idea of originality they threaten, giving us conscience-clearing villains to hiss. They copy; we don't.' Fervent denunciations of plagiarists are popular? Not in the higher intellectual world, they aren't; there, every conceivable excuse, and many inconceivable ones, will be made for them. True, plagiarists are not criminals (or very seldom are)—they are dishonest, dishonourable, and sometimes sick, people. Kincaid, relishing the problematics of it all, ducks and weaves: 'Even educators may be learning how not just to punish but to employ plagiarism'—really? . . . and then at once the dodge: 'how not just to punish but to employ plagiarism, or something very like it'. Ah. 'Copying or imitating, they say, is vital to gaining initial entry into a discourse.' Not even the arrival of our comfy old friend 'discourse' quite sets my mind at rest. Need no attempt be made to distinguish the dishonesty that is plagiarism from responsible kinds of copying or imitating? 'What all of this suggests is that we might try to entertain the idea that plagiarism, and even originality, are relative concepts.' True, anciently true, in one way. Even Edward Young, who is usually blamed these days for having, in his *Conjectures on Original Composition* (1759), set the world on a grievously wrong course, declared himself 'content with what all must allow, that some Compositions are more so [original] than others'.[48] But not true, Kincaid's point, in so far as it insinuates that disapprobation need not constitute any part of the malpractice that has for centuries been called plagiarism. Kincaid has his thumb in the sliding scales. 'Plagiarism is best understood not as a sharply defined operation, like beheading, but as a whole range of activities, more like cooking, which varies from deliberate poisoning to the school cafeteria to mother's own.'[49] Maybe so, but whether 'sharply' defined or not, plagiarism is, and has always been, defined pejoratively. Amoral jocularity about dishonesty is, in my judgement, immoral. Kincaid tells us not to 'get ourselves in a tizzy'. This demotic moment is the successor to 'but ethics are ethics, I told my student', and it serves the same end as that mock-pomposity: the evacuation of responsibility and of honesty. Demoralization.

In an essay that has been widely cited, 'Two Extravagant Teachings', Neil Hertz subjected to scrutiny and to mockery the Cornell University pamphlet on plagiarism. He wrote of its 'ill-assured moral exhortation',[50] its symptomatic rhetoric. Some of his criticisms strike home—yes, there are lapses of tone, and even gouts of feeling within the admonishments that lend themselves to Hertz's Freudian detections. Even perhaps to his aligning a teacher's anxiety about the young's plagiarism with parental anxiety about the young's masturbation. But there is something wrong with the way in which a concern with the plaintiff's, the teacher's, psyche leaves no room at all for concern with the defendant's, plagiarist's, conduct. It is the teachers alone who are to be morally judged. What, asks Professor Hertz, of the authorities' motivation?

We might attribute it to justifiable moral indignation, the righteous contempt of the honest for the dishonest, but that wouldn't quite account for either the intensity of this rhetoric or its peculiar figuration—or for the strong fascination that student plagiarism generally seems to hold for academics.[51]

The phrasing is prejudicial: 'indignation' contaminated by 'righteous', and 'righteous' contaminated by the likelihood of self-righteousness,

[48] Edward Young, *Conjectures on Original Composition* (1759), p. 7.
[49] Kincaid, *New Yorker*, 20 Jan. 1997, p. 97.
[50] Neil Hertz, *The End of the Line* (1985), p. 144.
[51] Ibid., 149.

with 'fascination' contaminated by prurience. Not, as must be supposed at least sometimes to be the case, a principled dislike of dishonesty, and the exercise of an essential professional responsibility when it comes to judging (often with lifelong consequences) a student's writing.

About any such matter, yes, there can be impurity of motive in the moral insistence; but shouldn't educators in the American world of Hertz (and of me), where the selling of term-papers is big business and is a threat to education, be against plagiarism? Not if Hertz's line of talk were to be followed (whatever his own practice as a teacher), for he moves on to deprecate the 'uneasiness' in teachers 'that produces the ritual condemnation of student plagiarists when they are unlucky enough to be caught'. 'Ritual condemnation': this minimizes or even extirpates moral responsibility, as does 'unlucky', and as does the ensuing reference to 'such a scapegoating'. Scapegoats are, by definition, innocent, they bear the burden of imputed unjust guilt; a dishonest student, or colleague, or novelist, is something else. But Hertz's exculpatory term 'scapegoating' has caught on, and is put to use, with due acknowledgement, by a later critic when for his own reasons he needs to put in a good word for Pecksniff, Pecksniff who stole Martin Chuzzlewit's architectural plans.[52] All is forgiven. But not to those who make scapegoats of plagiarists.

And the future? More of the same, I fear; and in the immediate future, next month to be precise, there will be a new book by Robert Scholes, *The Rise and Fall of English* (1998). He, too, knows, in the matter of plagiarism, that it is the plaintiff, not the defendant, who is the real enemy:

In the academy the introduction to intertextuality received by most students takes the form of a stern warning against plagiarism. In a culture organized around property, patents, and copyrights, plagiarism has become a sin, occasionally a crime. In other cultures, or in certain contexts within our own, this sin does not exist.[53]

Not a sin, agreed, and not a crime, but that might be thought to leave

---

[52] Gerhard Joseph, 'Charles Dickens, International Copyright, and the Discretionary Silence of Martin Chuzzlewit', in *The Construction of Authorship*, ed. Woodmansee and Jaszi, p. 268.
[53] Robert Scholes, *The Rise and Fall of English* (1998), to be published 9 March 1998, pp. 98–9.

plenty of room for plagiarism to be (and not just to have 'become', in what passes here for history and for anthropology) morally wrong, and for exculpations of it to be morally wrong too. 'A stern warning against plagiarism': how relaxedly we accede to the assurance that education should be made of less stern stuff.

In her weighing of plagiarism, 'The Wasp Credited with the Honeycomb' (*Theophrastus Such*), George Eliot first granted imaginatively the ways in which it is true that creation is re-creation, true that we are all indeed in debt to the world that went before and the world that is around, and then went on indeflectibly:

I protest against the use of these majestic conceptions to do the dirty work of unscrupulosity and justify the non-payment of debts which cannot be defined or enforced by the law.

Surely the acknowledgement of a mental debt which will not be immediately detected, and may never be asserted, is a case in which the traditional susceptibility to 'debts of honour' would be suitably transferred.

I think it an honour to teach at a university which has returned, in the courts, to the costly fight against term-paper fraud that it began twenty-five years ago, when a victory was duly secured; on 19 October 1997,

Boston University filed suit in U.S. District Court against eight online companies that sell term papers to students in Massachusetts. The University charges that accepting orders and distributing fraudulent term papers by phone, wire, and mail are acts of wire and mail fraud and violate the Massachusetts law prohibiting such sales and other laws.

But let me end by proposing one stubborn consideration that has, ever since Martial, ministered to these dishonourable exculpations. This is simply but crucially that Martial's inspired figure of speech, *plagiarius*, the thief, has itself had a distortive effect. For it must be conceded, not as bespeaking leniency for the crime of theft but as distinguishing one form of theft from most others, that it is importantly not the case that what the plagiarist does exactly is steal your poem. William Walsh in his *Handy-Book of Literary Curiosities* (1909): 'For although we are pleased to say, in our metaphorical language, that a plagiarist shines in stolen plumes, not a plume is really lost by the fowl who originally grew them.'

The *New Yorker* illustration to Kincaid's article showed a rectangle of print (some lines from the article itself), at pocket height, that had been cut away from a man's clothes and is clutched by the pickpocket, no longer the rightful owner's. But the illustration inadvertently brought home that the invocation of the pickpocket (by Coleridge, by Poe, by many others), or of the thief, both is and is not apt. And in being in some respects unapt, it then ministers to special pleading. For it is scarcely ever the case that the rightful owner actually loses possession of, or credit for, his or her creation. Martin Amis did not wrongfully lose credit for his novel; Jacob Epstein wrongfully gained credit for 'his'.

True, every now and then there will be a case which really does constitute theft, and is contrastively helpful for that very reason: a work claimed by X, published by X, not ever credited to its rightful author. Anne Fadiman, in her essay on Bowers's book in *Civilization* (February/March 1997), tells the touching story of how her mother's work was taken by John Hersey: 'The only time she ever saw her dispatches in print was inside a cover that said BY JOHN HERSEY'. But this is best judged to be piracy. Fadiman says: 'after your words— unlike your VCR—are stolen, you still own them. Or do you?' No, her mother didn't, never had been allowed to. But Glyn Jones still possessed, and still possessed credit for, the passage of prose of which Hugh MacDiarmid possessed himself for his poem 'Perfect'. Neal Bowers tells how a bronze cast that carried a poem of his called 'Art Thief' (mourning the theft of a work of sculpture from the site) was itself then stolen. Stolen. But the plagiarizing of a poem is not characteristically its being lost to its originator.

What then, if anything, is stolen? We often say 'the credit', but even here there is almost always something misleading, the definite article. The plagiarist does not take the credit, he takes credit, credit to which he is not entitled. This is often despicable and always reprehensible, but it cannot be reprehended in quite the terms in which theft ordinarily is. To concede this is not to concede anything else, and is not to make any excuse for the wrongful, rather to make clear what the wrong is.

There is no chance of our ever giving up the vivid figure of speech which thought in terms of theft, but we should be aware that the very terms in which we speak (we are all guilty . . .—how delicious) play a part in contributing to the disingenuous discourse through which plagiarism steals.

The Pursuit of Metaphor

Being in a quandary, I shall be turning to study the quandary that the study of metaphor continues to be in.

My own quandary is immeasurably less important (except to me) but not less real. When this collection of essays (*What's Happened to the Humanities?*) was being bruited, I found myself saying at an explorers' meeting that instead of everybody's talking, yet once more, about 'the state of the humanities' and the changes and chances of late, those of us who resist the claims of certain recent developments—as not truly or not sufficiently developments at all—would do better to get on with such work as we believe in.

For to argue that current literary theory's claims are inordinate may be held to be—losingly therefore—engaging in current literary theory. And to argue that literary theory's claims deserve less attention than they have courted or extorted is, losingly again, to lavish yet more attention upon what (some of us believe) has been quite sufficiently garlanded with attentions already. So (I mooted at this meeting), instead of spending time arguing in favour of doing something other than such recencies as the Other, it would be wise for others simply to do otherwise. The alternative, not the Alterity. This, in the hope that one might strengthen the things that remain. End of my contribution to the meeting.

But not the end of the contribution question. For, alert in genial appropriation, the begetter of *What's Happened to the Humanities?* (Alvin Kernan) promptly wrote asking me to write along—or between—these very lines. 'It is probably ironic, as you more than anyone else will instantly realize, to ask you to participate in a volume that in many ways is doing just exactly what you say we should not do.' Well, such ironic contradictories are often an entertaining sideshow in this life, whether with Sideshow Bob in *The Simpsons*, who goes on television to extirpate television, or with R. S. Thomas, who wrote from his Welsh fastness poems in English about how systemically and systematically corrupt English is. But there remains the particular contradictory quandary. How can one engage in arguing that one would do better not to engage in such arguments? And how, on the other hand, could it be deemed proper to submit here a piece of work genuinely and entirely other than the present set-up—an essay on, say, the young T. S. Eliot's fascination with Jules Laforgue, as evidenced in certain Eliot manuscripts. I have decided to consider metaphor, or rather the pursuit of metaphor. This because of an instructive intractability such as forever balks pursuit. Balking philosophy, it balks theory—and not just theory's recent manifestations. If this assertion can be made good, if it can be shown how demonstrably not at all far any thinking can reasonably get, the further final question will be this: what might we learn from our being so balked? Sweet are the ruses of adversity.

One of the most signal changes in the humanities (more so than in the arts themselves) has been the expanded wholesale trade in philosophizing. Some philosophers have argued that most of what has subsequently been retailed lacks the cogent probity of philosophy, being quasi- and even pseudo-philosophical. It may be ill-judged of people in literary studies to jump in to adjudicate between, say, Searle and Derrida (or between Searle and Rorty); we tend to plump. But the large matter is not that of the particular philosophical deficiencies of much recent theorizing (hygienic though the demonstration of these can duly prove), but that of the endemic and valuable resistance, not hostility, that literary studies (no less than literature) have always needed, of their nature, to put up to the fellow-humanities philosophy and history: history, with its claim that the establishing of facts is its province, and (more pressingly of late) philosophy, with its claim that the pursuit of truth is its province.

For those of us to whom Samuel Johnson is the greatest of English critics, his greatness will not be distinct from his sustained and rational opposition to philosophy and to theory. 'The task of criticism' was, for Johnson, 'to establish principles',[1] and he everywhere made clear that his refusal to elaborate and concatenate the needed concepts beyond a certain point (a point reached early) was not a refusal to continue to think, but a decision to think thereafter about the application of the principles rather than to elaborate principle into theory.[2]

[1] *Rambler* 92 (2 February 1751).
[2] I have written about this in 'Literary Principles as Against Theory', collected in *Essays in Appreciation* (1996).

This particular critical tradition (which is plainly not the only one) continues from Johnson to Leavis, to Empson and Winters and Trilling, and to Davie and Kenner. Philosopher-theorists none. 'I do not think', says Leavis, but only en route to 'that much profit': 'But here it may seem that the question of definition comes up again. What is metaphor? What is imagery? I do not think that much profit is likely to come of trying to answer these questions directly, in general terms.'[3] Such staunch criticism is manifestly not of theoretical or philosophical bent. For thinking that much profit is likely to come of trying to answer these questions ('What is metaphor?') directly, in general terms, must constitute a great part of theoretical criticism.

Resistance these days to theory's empire (an empire zealously inquisitorial about every form of empire but its own) may take many forms. Sometimes the resistance may seek to show the intellectual deficiencies of a particular argument, the non sequiturs, the untruths, and especially the straw men (a growth industry, this last—but then you can't as easily make brickbats without straw men). Sometimes the resistance may argue more experientially, more practically—may, for instance, put the case for proportions, priorities, or fair shares. Time, energy, attention: these are limited resources, and if any opportunity at all is to be found for reading some actual narratives, narratology may have to relinquish some of its demands. These are working considerations, competing claims; they will continue to be argued, as they always have been, with some light and much heat, with some good will and much ill will; but they need not constitute, on either side, an immitigable philosophical disagreement. They permit, fortunately, of concessions and compromises.

Many disagreements are of this last kind. Some are more disagreeable, in that they have to do, not with the strength of claims but with their falsity or falsehood: the claims, say, from publicists of theory that everyone theorizes whether nilly or willy, or that everyone should feel obliged to theorize explicitly and elaboratedly.

There remains, though, an obligation, hard to meet and yet dishonourable to waive, incumbent on those of us who elect principles not theories. The obligation is to set fairly before oneself the least compromising form of the question emanating from the opposition. Why, or when, is it proper to desist from further elaborating of the argument,

[3] *Education and the University* (1943), p. 78.

from further philosophizing? How, in reply to this, would one make the case that pursuit of the theoretical elaborations may be intrinsically misguided, and therefore, though onerous, idle?

Not that such an onus rests only upon those who set store by Horatio's admonition: "Twere to consider too curiously to consider so.' For if it is incumbent on the likes of me to give an instance of, and a succinct argument about, the futility of boundless pursuit, of too curious a considering, it is no less incumbent on the other side, the philosophizers, that they too give arguments, only this time arguments as to why it could never be right to desist from pursuit, or even arguments as to when it just might be right. The philosopher's or theorist's recourse to the accusatory terms 'underdescribed' and 'under-argued' may legitimately be met by an interrogative retort as to whether there is such a thing as overdescription or over-argument to which their enterprise must sometimes be damagingly open.

But from my side: on what grounds might one reasonably abstain from further pursuit and conceptualizing? What would save this from being just a defection, a laziness or cowardice? I take metaphor as a case study in such intractabilities as might give us not only pause but remission. And I take up the pursuit of metaphor for several reasons. First, that it is genuinely, not factitiously, of great philosophical interest. Second, that it has been increasingly attended to, by both philosophers and theorists, during the last half century. And third, that it is agreeably free from some of the dust and heat lately stirred and stoked by other contentions or contests. The pursuit of metaphor—though like everything else it can be invaluably or unvaluably considered under the aspect of politics—has not been party to the harsh political polemics that have been incited by 'the canon'. So it may permit of a larger air, of more light than heat.

As summary justice: no one has ever been able to arrive at satisfactory terms for the constituents, the elements, of a metaphor. If I am right in saying this (and I shall try to make it good), then the pursuit of metaphor—in the abstract, that is to say theoretically or philosophically— is immediately blocked. The constitutive terms, the antitheses, with which we have to make do, will not do. They are indispensable, inadequate, misleading, and unimprovable. Extraordinary efforts have been made; all have failed. The rudiments are immediately the impassable impediments.

Shelley insisted that 'Language is vitally metaphorical; that is, it marks the before unapprehended relations of things.' The definition of *metaphor* in *The Princeton Encyclopedia of Poetry and Poetics* opens: 'A condensed verbal relation.'[4] Whatever else a metaphor may be, it is a relation; on this the ponderings of metaphor concur, whether giving salience to comparison, to similarity, to substitution, or to interaction. But what then are we to make of one immediate token of the immitigable oddities: our engrained, natural, but misleading and entangling habit of using such phrases as 'a metaphor for the times' or 'the metaphor of the rose'?

Since a metaphor is a relation, how can it be right to say, as we all do all the time, 'metaphor *for*'? You would not say, in any such context, 'relation for', and, to use a more fitting way of putting it, 'relation of' or 'relation between', might immediately press you to ponder the constituents—the relation *of* this *to* that, *between* x *and* y. Plainly we know what we mean when we say 'a metaphor for', but what do we mean by it, and what might such a usage tell us about those root quandaries that (I believe) are definitional and more?

On the day on which I type this paragraph (12 December 1995), the *Boston Globe* describes the appalling killing of two children: 'But here you had a metaphor for the times: Two people, a mother and father, walking through a dying city with dead babies in a cloth sack.' The sentence is telling. What it supposes of society is clear. What— less urgently, less searingly, but in another context crucially—it supposes of metaphor is another matter.

Take the same idiom in the cooler setting of the *Times Literary Supplement* (March 24 1995), Bernard Crick in defence of Robert Altman's film *Prêt-à-Porter*: a hostile reviewer 'suggests that "it has been consumed by its subject." But what is its subject—surely not fashion? Surely fashion is only a metaphor for a truly Swiftian satire of the world.' Anyone who uses 'surely' twice in four words ought surely to be resisted, but what matters more is 'only a metaphor for'. There is the propensity for depreciation in 'only' there, with metaphor dwindling into being the member of the entourage who is paid off, dismissed.

Charles Lamb, in 1821, was wary of the Scot: 'You must speak upon

---

[4] ed. Alex Preminger (1965), entry by George Whalley. See also *The New Princeton Encyclopedia of Poetry and Poetics*, ed. by Alex Preminger and T. V. F. Brogan (1993), in which the new entry for *metaphor*, by Wallace Martin, is no less admirably thorough, lucid, and fair-minded.

the square with him. He stops a metaphor like a suspected person in an enemy's country. "A healthy book!" . . . "did I catch rightly what you said?" [5] There is a long history of hostility to metaphor, with Bishop Sprat fiercely blessing the troops in 1667.

One way to underrate and misapprehend metaphor is to slight the literal that goes to the making of it, and the other is to slight that which is not literal. To slight either is to slight the relation itself. Added to which, the concept of the literal is itself stubbornly resistant to clarification, both within and without the relation that is metaphor.

I once asked a friend what would be wrong with my describing the tie I was wearing, one decorated with poisonous frogs, as a metaphor for my enemies within the university 'community'. Sharing my dislike of those particular people, he gratifyingly answered 'Nothing'. Gratifyingly, and yet precariously. I pounced—for the *tie* is not the metaphor; the metaphor is the relation between the tie and those people. When we say 'metaphor for', we are diverting the word 'metaphor' to mean the constituent or the element of the metaphor that is not—not what exactly? . . . And here we fall back upon 'literal'.

Daily impatience, all busyness, chafes at the dual nature of the transfer that metaphor, this recommender of patience, asks us to appreciate. The same goes for our speaking casually, as we do and will continue to do (for reasons that may prove worth attention), of 'the metaphor *of* such-and-such': such as the metaphor of the rose, when what we ought to be identifying as the metaphor is the relation of the rose to, say, human beauty; or the metaphor of the journey, when the metaphor is rather the relation of the journey to, say, ageing. Like 'metaphor for', 'metaphor of' is a phrase designed to veil (and so might help us by directing attention to) inexpugnable difficulties, for the phrase contributes to misimpressions, and works against the realization that what is of the essence is a relation. Metaphor is not only far from simple-minded, it is not single-minded. It is often myriad-minded.

Metaphor asks us not only to balance but to value balancing. There is the danger of imbalance in a notable essay by Fiona Macintosh on the Victorian and Edwardian stage-ban on *Oedipus Rex*:

It may seem incredible to us that Sophocles' tragedy can be reduced to a play about incest *tout court*. But it is important to remember that our readings of

---

[5] 'Imperfect Sympathies', *The London Magazine* (August 1821). There is the life of metaphor in the move from 'healthy' to 'catch'.

the play are essentially post-Romantic and post-Nietzschean, if not also part-psychological and part-anthropological, whereas Redford [Examiner of Plays, 1909] and his colleagues are subjecting Sophocles' play to a reading where incest in its most literal sense is the stumbling block. For us, the incest of Oedipus and Jocasta has been raised to an image of cosmic disorder, a metaphor of the multilayered self, or a schema of the threat to boundaries on which civilization depends. For the late nineteenth and early twentieth-century reader, however, the indelicacy of the subject matter obtrudes.[6]

Thoroughly aware of the old-time danger of reducing *Oedipus Rex* 'to a play about incest *tout court*', this does not beware of the danger attendant upon 'our readings of the play': 'For us, the incest of Oedipus and Jocasta has been raised to an image of cosmic disorder, a metaphor of the multi-layered self.' Here the phrase 'a metaphor of' too much sets 'the subject matter' aside. It was unbalanced of the previous age, fearful of 'incest in its most literal sense', to wince away ('the indelicacy of the subject matter obtrudes'). But is our age any more respectful of 'the subject matter' when we exercise our own way of not having the subject-matter obtrude: by lowering it (while claiming to have 'raised' it) to its *least* literal sense or rather to the not-literal-at-all, 'a metaphor of the multilayered self'?

'A metaphor of'? 'A metaphor for'? Or, another member of the same family, 'as metaphor'? This last has been elevated to the modishly titular, thanks to Susan Sontag, *Illness as Metaphor*.[7] The observation, which then constitutes the ineradicable frustration, is obvious: that it is natural to the language to use the word 'metaphor' not only for the whole but for one of its parts. This, which is not the same as metonymy, is so effortless as seldom to be attended to, but pressure does not have to be effortful.

Reflect upon the oddity of this ordinary usage by which we speak of one aspect or part of metaphor as the metaphor or as metaphorical. From a recent *Times Literary Supplement* again, a review of Terry Eagleton's *Heathcliff and the Great Hunger*: the first chapter 'argues that Heathcliff, who is picked up from the streets of Liverpool by Earnshaw senior, is, whether metaphorically or literally, an Irish victim of the

---

[6] 'Under the Blue Pencil: Greek Tragedy and the British Censor', *Dialogos* 2 (1995), 61–2.

[7] *Illness as Metaphor* (1978). Recent goings with this flow: Hermann Haken, *The Machine as Metaphor and Tool* (1993); A. J. Soyland, *Psychology as Metaphor* (1994); Leonardo Sciascia, *Sicily as Metaphor* (1994); Martin Friedman *et al.*, *Visions of America: Landscape as Metaphor in the Late Twentieth Century* (1994); Kojin Karatani, *Architecture as Metaphor* (1995); and Elaine Marks, *Marrano as Metaphor* (1996).

famine.' Set aside (as a particular case) the convenient airiness of 'whether metaphorically or literally', its handsomely relieving the political argument of so many unwelcome responsibilities; what might induce a more generalized concern is this practice of the language itself, in so speaking—unmisgivingly, it must seem—of something within metaphor as the metaphor or as metaphorical.

Yet the practice is neither recent nor perverse,[8] while at the same time it embodies a central thwarting of elaborated understanding, an imperviousness to philosophical elucidation.

The twentieth-century poet who enjoyed the best philosophical training, and who made the best use, not only in his criticism but in his poetry, of imperviousness to philosophical elucidation, wrote in 1918:

The healthy metaphor adds to the strength of the language; it makes available some of that physical source of energy upon which the life of language depends. '. . . in her strong toil of grace' is a complicated metaphor which has this effect; and as in most good metaphor, you can hardly say where the metaphorical and the literal meet.[9]

But the complications of metaphor extend even beyond T. S. Eliot's case of 'a complicated metaphor' in Shakespeare; not only is there the difficulty of saying where the metaphorical and the literal meet,[10] there is the difficulty—or rather the recognition of an intractability that passes beyond difficulty into impossibility—that is alive in our using the terms 'metaphorical' (or 'the metaphor') and 'literal' for the opposing constituents of a metaphor. Strong toil, strong toils, indeed.

That you can hardly say where the metaphorical and the literal meet— that even a great poet and great critic such as Eliot can hardly say—this is plenty, this is more than enough. But it is not, in itself, enough to make the case of metaphor unusual in perplexity. As John Searle has observed, arguing against deconstruction and about literary theory,

it is not necessarily an objection to a conceptual analysis, or to a distinction, that there are no rigorous or precise boundaries to the concept analyzed or the

---

[8] See Johnson's *Dictionary*: 'metaphorical: Not literal; not according to the primitive meaning of the word; figurative. "The words which were do continue; the only difference is, that whereas before they had a literal, they now have a metaphorical use". Hooker'.

[9] T. S. Eliot, *The Egoist* 5 (October 1918), 114. Quoting *Antony and Cleopatra*, V. ii.

[10] Simon Blackburn gives pride of place to this problem, in the entry for *metaphor* in his *Oxford Dictionary of Philosophy* (1994): 'Philosophical problems include deciding how the border between literal and metaphorical meaning is to be drawn'.

distinction being drawn. It is not necessarily an objection even to theoretical concepts that they admit of application *more or less*. This is something of a cliché in analytic philosophy: most concepts and distinctions are rough at the edges and do not have sharp boundaries. The distinctions between fat and thin, rich and poor, democracy and authoritarianism, for example, do not have sharp boundaries. More important for our present discussion, the distinctions between literal and metaphorical, serious and nonserious, fiction and nonfiction and, yes, even true and false, admit of degrees and all apply *more or less*. It is, in short, generally accepted that many, perhaps most, concepts do not have sharp boundaries, and since 1953 we have begun to develop theories to explain why they *cannot*.[11]

My own allegiances, as is evident, are with Searle, but there remains the oddity, unremarked in his list, of a particular one of those indispensable distinctions such as are not susceptible of strict boundaries. For, offering, first of all, three wide cases and then four of a kind 'more important to our present discussion', Searle sees no need to acknowledge the crucial difference between the first of the latter four and any others of his seven instances: 'the distinctions between literal and metaphorical'. Yet there is a crucial distinction to be made between this first one and all the others: that it is only in the case of the distinction between literal and metaphorical that there obtains the irksome quirk, with its power to balk, that 'metaphorical', like 'metaphor', is not only one of the antithetical terms up for distinction but also the term for the whole within which the distinction is to be made. No such thing is true of the distinctions between fat and thin, rich and poor, democracy and authoritarianism, or those between serious and nonserious, fiction and nonfiction, and, yes, even true and false.

Sometimes in such cogitations a warning may be seen to stand in for an authentic wariness. Take Robert J. Fogelin, in *Figuratively Speaking*:

At various places I have fallen in with others by speaking about the metaphorical or figurative meaning of some expression. There is really nothing wrong with speaking in this way except that it might suggest that an expression can have two distinct meanings, a literal meaning and a metaphorical (or figurative) meaning, and that, in turn, might suggest a commitment to a meaning-shift theory of metaphors of the kind I reject.[12]

---

[11] 'Literary Theory and its Discontents', *New Literary History* 25 (1994), 638.
[12] (1988), p. 95.

But this makes it sound as though falling in with others is a camaraderie (better than falling out with others, eh?), whereas the fact is that no more than the rest of us can Fogelin conceive of not having to fall back upon speaking of 'the metaphorical or figurative' within our understanding of what is within metaphor. 'There is really nothing wrong with speaking in this way'—and then, a touch wistfully still—'except that it might suggest . . .'. No, the case is harsher. What is askew is not just the possible suggestion that the 'literal' and the 'metaphorical (or figurative)' are 'two distinct meanings', but the ubiquitous use of the terms 'literal' and 'metaphorical' at all. Fogelin placates: 'There is really nothing wrong with speaking in this way except . . .'. (The theorists of metaphor have frequent recourse to 'really', sometimes deepened to '*really*'; they ought to be so good as to pay the word a handsome bonus, given how much work they ask of it.) I should not want to retort to Fogelin that there is really something wrong. Rather, that there is really something recalcitrant at the core, such as 'might suggest' that the enterprising pursuit is doomed.

Fogelin has his admonitions: 'Now that does not mean that satires are metaphors, although speaking that way can have a specious ring of profundity. It is easy to understand the temptation to let one member of a family of concepts become the representative of all the rest.'[13] But he does not confront the trickier case, which is not a temptation but a tradition, and which is not that of letting one member of a family of concepts become the representative of all the rest ('metaphor' too lavishly invoked), but that of unrepiningly letting one of the opposing terms within an antithesis also be the term for that which the antithesis comprises.

I. A. Richards asks, in all but innocence, 'when a man has a wooden leg, is it a metaphoric or a literal leg?'[14] It is not the least of the stumbling-blocks that the concept of the literal is itself so perplexing, such a knotting of the handily indispensable and the hand-wringingly unclarifiable. Despite all the wrestling that there has been with the word and the concept of the literal, there has been nothing of an outcome. True, there is many a word or concept by which philosophy continues to be thwarted, but it certainly contributes to the misty mystery of metaphor

---

[13] *Figuratively Speaking*, p. 98.
[14] *The Philosophy of Rhetoric* (1936), p. 118.

that what might have been thought to be the more sturdy of the two terms within it, the 'literal', when approached dissolves into the air.[15]

The Cambridge Dictionary of Philosophy (1995) enters with a definition of *metaphor* as 'a figure of speech (or a trope) in which a word or phrase that literally denotes one thing is used to denote another, thereby implicitly comparing the two things'. The dictionary duly exits with a paragraph about the rejection for the past two centuries of both of the 'traditional themes' in the understanding of metaphor (decorations? elliptical similes?), only, in closing, to fade away into the forest dim: 'And though no consensus has yet emerged on how and what metaphors contribute to meaning, nor how we recognize what they contribute, near-consensus has emerged on the thesis that they do not work as elliptical similes.' Adieu. Either that or a submission to the *Journal of Negative Results*.

Other theorists 'simply assume a commonsense recognition', in a manner that may be creditable but does lessen the layman's awe at philosophical credentials:

We should be cautious about using the term *literal*. Not only is it difficult in many instances to determine what is and what is not literal, but there are theorists who deny the distinction between literal and metaphorical language. At this stage of the study, I shall simply assume a commonsense recognition that there are times when we speak literally and at other times figuratively and that many of us recognise a figurative expression. I shall return to this issue later.[16]

But what does it mean to say that we should be cautious about using the term 'literal' and then feel so free to use it? The warning seems nothing more than small-print against the literally litigious. For, returning to this issue later, we enter a section boldly entitled '**Interaction in Metaphorical and Literal Expression**: Literal and Metaphorical Interaction', and are then assured that 'The problem of distinguishing literal from figurative expressions was broached in the Introduction.' Broaching is acknowledged to be philosophically insufficient, but the

---

[15] See Owen Barfield, 'The Meaning of the Word "Literal" ', in *Metaphor and Symbol*, ed. L. C. Knights and Basil Cottle (1960). Barfield, most courteous of turners of tables, argues that words sometimes held to be based on a transfer from the literal to the metaphorical can be interpreted rather as extended from the metaphorical to the literal. It might be added that the two terms are not equipollent anyway, in that 'literal' does not have a noun which stands as 'metaphorical' does to 'metaphor', *literalness* and *literality* being out of the way, and the noun 'a literal' being something other.

[16] Carl R. Hausman, *Metaphor and Art: Interactionism and Reference in the Verbal and Nonverbal Arts* (1989), p. 3.

next page arrives at no more of an advance than this: 'Let it be conceded that although a hard and fast distinction between literal and metaphorical expressions is not always obvious, there are contrasts evident when a fresh metaphor stands out from the midst of otherwise conventionally used literal discourse.'[17] In any case, there remains, undisentangled by Hausman, the even more snagged matter of 'metaphorical' and 'figurative' there *within* metaphors and figures of speech.

These tangles do much to explain, though little to justify, another turn within what Monroe C. Beardsley once dubbed 'The Metaphorical Twist', namely the use of 'literally' to mean 'metaphorically'. *Private Eye* has long had its eyes and ears open for what, in a metaphor of which one member is the sports commentator David Coleman, it calls 'Coleman-balls'. 'And Greg Lemond has literally come back from the dead to lead the Tour de France.' 'When those stalls open, the horses are literally going to explode.' The grammarians sort it out:

It would seem that the speaker wishes to emphasize the extraordinary nature of what he is describing—"Believe it or not!"—, as well as to draw attention to the hyperbolic language used to describe it. The insertion of *literally* seems often to acknowledge that people tend to use the expression concerned (*somersault, earth shaking*) as merely figurative or exaggeratedly colourful whereas in the present instance the word is to be taken in its literal meaning.[18]

Perhaps. But notice the revenge taken by 'literally', back from the dead: 'merely figurative'. And if 'the figure' and 'the metaphor' can elsewhere be allowed to usurp not only the *galère* but one of the two elements comprising it, why shouldn't the other element 'literally' put in its usurpatious counterclaim?

In defining 'metaphorical', Dr Johnson could not escape 'literal': 'not literal', following this at once with 'not according to the primitive meaning of the word'. But in defining 'metaphor', he tried to do without 'literally': 'The application of a word to an use to which, in its original import, it cannot be put: as, he *bridles* his anger.' But 'original', like 'primitive', is no less dubious, albeit differently so, than 'literal'. For the origins of words, as to the 'literal' and its other (or the 'metaphorical' and its other), are chicken and egg. (Which came first? In the beginning was the word.)

---

[17] *Metaphor and Art*, pp. 52–3.
[18] *A Comprehensive Grammar of the English Language*, ed. Randolph Quirk, Sidney Greenbaum, Geoffrey Leech, and Jan Svartvik (1985), p. 619.

It is all such a mire that a will-o'-the-wisp is only to be expected: how about just calling one of the terms the 'nonmetaphorical' and the other the 'nonliteral'? This is easily effected. But ineffectual. For although such a presto may relieve the prestidigitators, this feint does not bring to lucid order the complication by which there is within the 'nonliteral' something that is then to be differentiated as 'nonliteral'.

The twentieth century's most inaugurative contribution to the understanding of metaphor was made by I. A. Richards in *The Philosophy of Rhetoric* (1936), and it is high time that I acknowledged it; and then, as a contribution to the higher ingratitude, I'll set a bourne how far it's to be believed.

It is greatly to Richards's credit that, introducing his 'two technical terms' ('tenor' and 'vehicle'), he so lucidly identified the crux:

One of the oddest of the many odd things about the whole topic is that we have no agreed distinguishing terms for these two halves of a metaphor—in spite of the immense convenience, almost the necessity, of such terms if we are to make any analyses without confusion. For the whole task is to compare the different relations which, in different cases, these two members of a metaphor hold to one another, and we are confused at the start if we do not know which of the two we are talking about. At present we have only some clumsy descriptive phrases with which to separate them. 'The original idea' and 'the borrowed one'; 'what is really being said or thought of' and 'what it is compared to'; 'the underlying idea' and 'the imagined nature'; 'the principal subject' and 'what it resembles' or, still more confusing, simply 'the meaning' and 'the metaphor' or 'the idea' and 'its image.'

How confusing these ideas must be is easily seen, and experience with the analysis of metaphors fully confirms the worst expectations. We need the word 'metaphor' for the whole double unit, and to use it sometimes for one of the two components in separation from the other is as injudicious as that other trick by which we use 'the meaning' here sometimes for the work that the whole double unit does and sometimes for the other component—the tenor, as I am calling it—the underlying idea or principal subject which the vehicle or figure means.[19]

This stands in need of being quizzed: 'almost the necessity'—why only 'almost'? And what about the use of 'figure' at the end there, to mean one constituent of the figure, in just the way that Richards reprehends with 'metaphor'—and, on the next page, reprehends with 'figure' itself

[19] Ibid., pp. 96–7.

and with 'image'? But Richards's page does stand, and with an unmistakable centrality.

The most successful attempt to identify the constituents of a metaphor has undoubtedly been this of Richards's, with his 'tenor' and 'vehicle'. But the success is that of having become adopted, not that of having escaped the fire as well as the frying pan.[20] For just as the trouble with the analogous subdivision of 'sign' into 'signifier' and 'signified' is that what is signified by the sign is rather the relation of the 'signifier' to the 'signified', and just as the trouble with McLuhan's analogous subdivision into 'medium' and 'message' is that the message is rather the relation of the 'medium' to the 'message', so, upon reflection, the tenor of a metaphor has to be understood as the relation of the 'tenor' to the 'vehicle'. In escaping one particular form taken by the problem of the head term's also being one of the constituents ('metaphor' and 'metaphorical' within metaphor), Richards did not escape the encompassing problem itself.

Nor did he escape putting his thumb on the scale. For even as it becomes too easy to speak of the *merely* metaphorical or the *merely* literal, so it becomes too easy to think less well of a 'vehicle'. All a vehicle does, after all, is deliver, not affect or effect. There is not a due evenhandedness about Richards's very handy terms. 'Tenor' claims too much, since, fully grasped, the tenor of a metaphor is not its 'tenor' but the relation of that to its 'vehicle'; and 'vehicle' is granted too little, has arrived to be dismissed. Which is not at all what Richards's 'interaction' theory of metaphor believes or wants. But then, as often happens, one's terms defy one's arguments.

Richards—this was his most engaging and endearing quality—never lacked hope. His hopes for the clarification of metaphor keep returning to what he trusts will prove to have been the needless confusions of 'traditional' thinking about metaphor. The salvific insights 'have not yet been taken account of'; we need a better theory 'than is yet available'; 'the time was not ripe', and 'I am not sure that it is yet ripe'. Yet me no yets.

T. S. Eliot was right to praise Richards, with circumspection and circumscription:

---

[20] Fogelin, *Figuratively Speaking*, p. 107, on Bessie Smith. 'He was the first to boil my cabbage': 'Here the subject of the sustained metaphor (what I. A. Richards calls the *tenor*) is sexual intercourse, and the object of comparison (Richards's *vehicle*) is cooking'. By great good fortune (onomastication), Fogelin was in a position to add a footnote: 'I owe this example to my colleague, W. W. Cook'.

Mr. Richards' importance—and I have suggested that he is indeed important—is not in his solutions but in his perception of problems. There is a certain discrepancy between the size of his problems and the size of his solutions. That is natural: when one perceives a great problem, one is the size of one's vision; but when one supplies a solution, one is the size of one's training.[21]

Richards saw clearly the oddity by which the crucial terms are used both for the whole and for a part: 'All these words, *meaning, expression, metaphor, comparison, subject, figure, image*, behave so, and when we recognize this we need look no further for a part, at least, of the explanation of the backward state of the study.'[22] But his next sentences falter somewhat: 'Why rhetoricians have not long ago remedied this defect of language for their purpose, would perhaps be a profitable matter for reflection. I do not know a satisfactory answer.' One satisfactory answer to this question, and to Richards's musing, might be that the defect is irremediable, and is one that salutarily sets a limit to the philosophizing drive.

Is philosophizing the proper way of thinking about 'the metaphor proper'? The term is used by *The Oxford Companion to the English Language* (1992): 'Commentators, however, are not usually precise about where the metaphor proper resides: it is sometimes defined as the vehicle alone, sometimes as the combination of tenor and vehicle, and sometimes as tenor, vehicle, and ground together.'[23] Richards's 'ground' never took off. The 'tenor' succeeded in ringing out, and the 'vehicle' in getting moving. But.[24]

It is not that I think I can do any better; rather, that no one can do any better, for reasons that might excite a healthy respect for metaphor's supple obduracy and might discourage philosophy's unsupple such.

And similar objections can immediately be made to the other terminological candidates. For instance, Max Black asks that a metaphor be understood as having two distinct 'subjects', the 'primary' subject and

---

[21] 'Literature, Science, and Dogma', a review of Richards's *Science and Poetry*; *The Dial* 82 (1927), 239–43.

[22] *The Philosophy of Rhetoric*, p. 97.

[23] ed. Tom McArthur (1992), p. 653.

[24] A further but: when Derrida, or his translator F. C. T. Moore, writes respectfully of 'the distinction proposed by I. A. Richards between the metaphorical vehicle and metaphorical tenor', it should be remarked that Richards did not append 'metaphorical' to either term, and with good reason since 'metaphorical' is so often invoked to distinguish the vehicle from the tenor. Jacques Derrida, 'White Mythology', *New Literary History* 6 (1974), 27 n.

the 'secondary' one (formerly in Black's account they had been the 'principal' and 'subsidiary' 'subjects'); he asks too that 'the word used nonliterally' be the 'focus', and the literal be the 'frame'.[25] The terminology may have its uses, but it raises more questions than it settles, not least the tendency of its own metaphors ('focus' and 'frame') and the way in which Black's well-motivated change from 'principal' and 'subsidiary' into 'primary' and 'secondary' fails to abolish the inappropriate intrusion of a set order of importance.

Carl Hausman says, 'I shall call the primary unit the *nucleus*'; he speaks proliferatingly of the 'subjects or anchoring terms of metaphors', of 'what is spoken about, the anchoring nucleus', of 'the subject term' and 'the anchoring subject'. These are not terms that will ever adhere, let alone anchor. As an effort at 'the differentiation of the elements that comprise a metaphor', this too may be valiant, but it lacks the better part of valour.[26]

Monroe C. Beardsley's 'subject' and 'modifier'; Allan Paivio's and Andrew Ortony's 'topic' and 'vehicle' (for 'the similarity metaphor'); George A. Miller's 'referent' and 'relatum' (with its needed note, then, that Tversky [1977] 'calls the referent the "subject" and the relatum the "referent" '); J. D. Sapir's 'continuous term' and 'discontinuous term': *ubi sunt*? Well, all are in *Metaphor and Thought*, edited by Andrew Ortony (1979); but none thrives, or ought to.

What then remains? The imaginative skill by which metaphors are created, especially within great literature. The imaginative skill by which metaphors are apprehended, especially within great criticism. The imaginative skill by which metaphors are made to generalize themselves, especially within great formulations of principle. ('Make the facts generalize themselves': T. S. Eliot's great navigation, working its way between the rock of 'Make the facts into a generalization' and the whirlpool of 'Let the facts generalize themselves.') This last way of thinking, by courtesy not of theories but of principles, is an indispensable alternative to the elaborated and concatenated thinking, and one of its great exponents is Lichtenberg. 'Most of the expressions we use are metaphorical: they contain the philosophy of our ancestors.' 'We do not think metaphors are anything very important, but I think a good

---

[25] 'More about Metaphor', in *Metaphor and Thought*, ed. Andrew Ortony (1979), p. 28.
[26] *Metaphor and Art*, pp. 67, 70–1, 78.

metaphor is something even the police should keep an eye on.' 'The metaphor is much more subtle than its inventor, and so are many things.'[27]

But the phenomenon of metaphors' intractability can itself be drawn upon. We might compare its not being possible to come up with satisfactory terms for the components or constitution of metaphor with other cases, such as the enduring and valuable unsatisfactoriness of our terms of the numinous or for the sexual, or our inability even to say satisfactorily what *kind* of distinction is the prose/poetry distinction, and our inability to find a satisfactory term for what, within a long poem, may unsatisfactorily have to be called a stanza, when it is no such thing, or a verse paragraph, likewise. In all these cases it may be reasonable to wonder whether the matter itself, in refusing to abide our question let alone answer it, is not telling us something. Issuing perhaps a courteous refusal, a chastening answer to our craving for answers and for labels. Knowing to know no more. Bearing witness, yet once more, to the positive truth of Keats's Negative Capability, where it was because several things dovetailed in his mind that he was able to see reason's dovetailing, in imaginative matters, as a lesser capability:

I had not a dispute but a disquisition with Dilke, on various subjects; several things dovetailed in my mind, & at once it struck me, what quality went to form a Man of Achievement especially in Literature & which Shakespeare posessed so enormously—I mean *Negative Capability*, that is when man is capable of being in uncertainties, Mysteries, doubts, without any irritable reaching after fact & reason.[28]

To my mind, therefore, Carl Hausman's words in *Metaphor and Art* are inadvertently misleading in that they narrow the forms that dissent from any such enterprise as his might take:

What is the point of trying to understand a phenomenon that has long been so elusive? Why should writers devote so much effort to the topic? The answer may seem obvious to those who already have been drawn into a study of it. And the need to raise the question may seem pointless to those who have simply appreciated the power of metaphor or who have only wanted to create and use metaphors for poetic or other purposes. But to all who reflect on what fascinates

---

[27] Notebook D: 87, Notebook E: 91, Notebook F: 41. George Lichtenberg, *Aphorisms*, tr. R. J. Hollingdale (1990), pp. 63, 79, 87.
[28] To George and Tom Keats, 21, 27(?) December 1817; *The Letters of John Keats*, ed. Hyder Edward Rollins (1958), i 193.

them, the question is important to consider because even if in its general outlines the answer is obvious, what may not be so obvious is the extent to which both the question and its answers differ depending on the professional perspective.[29]

But someone might decline to pursue 'a phenomenon that has long been so elusive' not just because of being one of 'those who have simply appreciated the power of metaphor or who have only wanted to create and use metaphors for poetic or other purposes'. ('*Only* wanted to create'?) Neither of Hausman's categories would have room for a profoundly imaginative literary critic ('*simply* appreciated'?) or for a thinker whose thought chose to exercise itself not in theory but in principle—or would have room, *a fortiori*, for a great poet such as Wallace Stevens. 'But to all who reflect on what fascinates them': on reflection, this excludes from the reflective everyone other than philosophers, pursuers who are tempted to set no limits to elaborated pursuit, as against a fully realized local attention, not extending but rather in its wholeness wholly attending to the particulars of rapture.

A substantial change of scale is a change of enterprise. The best book on metaphor is the brisk one by Terence Hawkes, *Metaphor* (1972), the 102 pages of which necessarily mount to no more—but no less—than a canter round the field, not a pursuit of the blatant beast of metaphor. Added to which, Hawkes had the wit to furnish for each chapter an epigraph from the most deeply apt of modern poets, Wallace Stevens.

For it is Stevens whose art most comprehends the demarcations of philosophical pursuit. The poem 'The Motive for Metaphor' depends upon its giving a turn to the locution 'a metaphor for'. 'Metaphors of a Magnifico' are not metaphors for a magnifico. 'Thinking of a Relation between the Images of Metaphors' begins its realization of relation by putting before us a simple dual impossibility, that of either including the musical sense of 'bass' (the sound of the word, so sounded, being so different from the silent fish for whom it angles) or of excluding it:

> The wood-doves are singing along the Perkiomen.
> The bass lie deep, still afraid of the Indians.

Nothing will permit of our hearing a bass voice; nothing will permit, given 'singing' and 'deep', of our not straining our ears for that sound too. For the next couplet is this:

> In the one ear of the fisherman, who is all
> One ear, the wood-doves are singing a single song.

It is Stevens who sees from many angles the configuration of these intractables, the opposite and the conceptual oppositions:

> Two things of opposite natures seem to depend
> On one another, as a man depends
> On a woman, day on night, the imagined
>
> On the real. This is the origin of change.
> Winter and spring, cold copulars, embrace
> And forth the particulars of rapture come.
>
> ('Notes towards a Supreme Fiction:
> It Must Change' IV)

The word 'man' may include woman; the word 'day' may include night; as with the word 'metaphor', the term for the whole is also a term for a part. What then, after 'man/woman' and 'day/night', of Stevens's 'imagined/real'? A calmly colossal two-legged enjambment, which 'depends' not only *on* but from, from a line-ending that then proves to be a triplet-ending.

> as a man depends
> On a woman, day on night, the imagined
>
> On the real.

Does imagination 'embrace' reality, or is there a turn, with reality embracing imagination? Why is not the imagined, like the imagination, as much a part of reality, albeit differently so, as anything else? Independence of mind imagines interdependences.

We cannot imagine doing without the opposition of the imagined and the real, and yet we cannot imagine finding it altogether fitting either. We cannot imagine doing without the opposition of literature and life, even while we fully grant not just the legitimacy but the necessity of T. S. Eliot's objection to the opposition or antinomy:

It is the function of a literary review to maintain the autonomy and disinterestedness of literature, and at the same time to exhibit the relations of literature—not to 'life,' as something contrasted to literature, but to all the other activities which, together with literature, are the components of life.[30]

---

[30] *The Criterion* i (July 1923), 421.

All such intractabilities preclude pursuit. A burden, they yet are so good as to rid us of other burdens. A warning against any hubris of the antiphilosophical (different from the right not to accede to philosophy's sway), they also constitute a warning against philosophical hubris, even of the kind that chooses to speak modestly. 'What is your aim in philosophy?—To show the fly the way out of the fly-bottle.'[31] But it is not possible to show the fly the way off the flypaper.

The pursuit of metaphor, then, is offered here as a case (forming part of the case for the committing of energies elsewhere) in which declining the pursuit is not abdication. A reasonable conclusion here might be the words with which Jonathan Culler once concluded the issue of metaphor and the issue of *New Literary History* 'On Metaphor', a gathering that had included Derrida, Ricoeur, and Todorov. Culler's position is not mine (since I continue to believe in 'the notion of metaphor' and to judge it fruitful—it is only the theorizing of metaphor about which I am happily despondent), but he does lend his authority to scepticism about the pursuit of metaphor:

> To say that the notion of metaphor should be scrapped, that it is a positive hindrance to our understanding of reading because it conceals the complexities of interpretation, is an ungenerous conclusion to an issue on metaphor; but the best essays here presented point this way. They explore the paradoxes and impossibilities of the notion (sometimes by illustrating its triviality), or else escape from it to the general problems of interpretation.[32]

Escape? 'What mad pursuit? What struggle to escape?' In concurring, and with a conspicuous theorist to boot, that someone may reasonably refuse to join the pursuit, that the pursuit might even be called off, I should not have to maintain that the pursuit is mad, only that any such refusal is sane.

---

[31] Wittgenstein, *Philosophical Investigations*, tr. G. E. M. Anscombe (1958), i 309.
[32] *New Literary History* 6 (Autumn 1974), 229.

Loneliness and Poetry

Old age
Singles them out as though by first-light,

As though a still-life, preserving some
Portion of the soul's feast, went with me
Everywhere, to be hung in strange rooms,

Loneliness being what it is.
(Geoffrey Hill, 'Soliloquies: Old Poet with Distant Admirers')

Set aside, at once, the loneliness of the writer, about which Geoffrey
Hill is compassionate and dispassionate. Ample, rather too ample, testimony of this has been heard, often from authors not without self-serving self-pity. This has its comic side, as Henry James perfectly well knew
when he plumped this cushion into orotund rotundity.

About the profession of letters in general, the desire to do the best one could
with one's pen . . . he [Henry James] made one remark which I [Logan Pearsall
Smith] have never forgotten. 'My young friend,' he said, 'and if I call you
young—you are so disgustingly, and, if I may be allowed to say so, so nauseat-
ingly young—there is one thing that, if you really intend to follow the course
you indicate, I cannot too emphatically insist on. There is one word—let me
impress upon you—which you must inscribe upon your banner, and that,' he
added after an impressive pause, 'that word is *Loneliness.*'[1]

How deliciously 'My young friend' and 'inscribe upon your banner'
contrive to banter the climactic solemnity of 'that word is *Loneliness.*'
Loneliness in italics and with a capital *L*, or so Logan Pearsall Smith says
on the page, though he could not have assuredly heard James *say* the
word in italics and with a capital.

No, this essay will attend to poetry, to half-a-dozen particular poems
and to how it is that they realize loneliness. More: how it is that, at their
best, such poems are alive to—because of—an acknowledgement not
only of the opportunities but of the limits, and the perils of this particular artistic and human enterprise.

---

[1] Simon Nowell-Smith, *The Legend of the Master* (1947), p. 154.

In a review of Paul de Man's *Aesthetic Ideology*, the political philosopher Alan Ryan wrote about generalization and art. What Ryan said of theory may be applied to philosophy:

> The generalizing urge of theory is at odds with one of the obvious purposes of art, which is to make us listen to *this* set of sounds, or *these* lines of verse. . . .[2]

But verse can be perverse, so let me open with a poem on loneliness of which one especial point is that there is no possibility that it may 'make us listen to *this* set of sounds, or *these* lines of verse'. For the following poem by e. e. cummings is there to be seen but not heard, to be apprehended but (crucially) not to be listened to:

l(a

le
af
fa

ll

s)
one
l

iness

Within loneliness, a leaf falls. Loneliness enfolds a leaf which had once unfolded and now falls.[3]

cummings's poem is unutterable, just as his lower-case *l* for loneliness (unlike Henry James's capitalizing, perhaps, on it) and his *e.* and *e.* and *c.* are unutterable, unvoiceable. The poem strikes some as unutterably silly, unspeakably trivial. But then it is bent upon evoking something that eludes what can be uttered or spoken.

Under one aspect, loneliness has the widespread reach of the most abstract of concepts. Under another aspect, loneliness has the inwardness of the most individually felt life. One immediate challenge for any artistic realization of loneliness comes from the fact that, whatever else art may or may not be, art always constitutes company. Not all

---

[2] *New York Times Book Review*, 10 November 1996.
[3] The opening poem of *95 poems* (1958). Jim McCue has drawn my attention to Christina G. Rossetti's lines: 'Of all the sad sights in the world | The downfall of an Autumn leaf | Is grievous and suggesteth grief'; this, in a poem ('Yet a Little While') for which one great grief is solitude.

company, it is true, is comfortingly companionable, and there is a good company that is not feel-good company. Further, it is the case that the performing arts, when we may share an occasion, stand differently to company. But all the same, how can art at once offer company (as it must) and hope to evoke such wanhope as is loneliness?

A true poem of loneliness will evince an understanding that there is at least a tension between a poem and loneliness. If a poem cannot but be company (and so may be too easily, too built-in, an assuaging of loneliness), at least it can incorporate an understanding of the limits of the sympathetic imagination; it can offer, even while it makes real its sympathy with loneliness, its admission of an imperfection, something forever falling short of the entire. Something, for instance, that cannot quite be said. Quite. Or cannot quite be heard.

How a poem succeeds here will have to include success in the due admission of inevitable failure; how, in Beckett's phrase, to fail better. An analogy might be the success of the sculptor whose work seeks to capture birds in flight—seeks both to convey this and at the same time honestly to acknowledge the uncapturability of such a thing in the art that is sculpture, and to make this a part of the pleasure in the art. A double success, as doubly an admitting.

cummings's poem (no title, no first line or even first word that I, that you or I, can utter) entertains the thought—makes us share the entertaining of the thought—of that which cannot be uttered or realized in utterance. Throughout, the poem teases us out of thought, playing heard melodies against those unheard. The opening line (but then all the line-endings here are beyond voicing)

l(a

has no space between its first letter and its opening mark of parenthesis (a *lunula*, 'little moon', to adopt Erasmus's term); there is no way of uttering this no-space, though it is perfectly describable and perfectly apprehensible by the eye. (And the same goes for all those spaces that ensue.) The third and fourth lines give us the swaying of a chiasmus, the rhetorical figure or ordering (in a rhyme scheme, for instance) which is usually evoked as *ab ba* but here is *af fa*:

af
fa

A happy coincidence, merely, that the words 'le*af f*alls' contain this chiasmus—a coincidence which is then made to play a part in the tilt and countertilt of a falling leaf. But then the curlings of the central punctuation of the poem, the lunulae ( ), are themselves a leaf-like falling / curling / tilting. The movement ( ) invites—as does the describing of a spiral staircase—our hand language. We cannot hear a leaf fall, let alone a leaf falling. But there are sounds to be entertained here even if they cannot be entered or cannot enter us as sounds. Take

fa

It is music, though soundless, for it is a variant of *fah*, the note of a scale, indeed the fourth note of a scale in a movable doh system, with

fa

coming fourth in cummings's poem. (Coming fourth/coming forth: such a homonym should remind us that the eye may discriminate what the ear will assimilate—and vice versa.) And the faint note of 'fa' may co-operate with the alliteration of 'loneliness' and 'leaf', however little we are allowed to sound the words, for 'loneliness' does manifestly, albeit inaudibly, wrap itself around 'a leaf falls'.

There is, as cummings lineates and delineates things, only one unit here that constitutes a word: the word *one*. One is one and all alone, and evermore shall be so. In this poem, *one* is alone and tinged with loneliness. And yet here too cummings has contrived to ensure that there will not be the pat fit which would too much claim an entire assuaging. For the sound of the letters *o n e* within the word from which those letters fall here, 'loneliness', is not the sound of 'one'. And we must own as much.

And how does this leaf, this leaf from cummings's book, come to rest? Upon what does it, in the end, ground itself? No full stop. Part of a word which completes the word and which lies extended (the longest of cummings's units) on the leaf of the page:

iness

A suffix of suffering. If we were to ask where to go from there, what is loneliness?, one answer might be something complete and yet an incompleteness *in esse*, in essence. And given that for cummings I is i, 'iness' may be standing there, standing alone, the first person, the last person.

There are no pronouns in cummings's poem. (Except perhaps for the single word which both is and is not a pronoun in English, 'one', and which in cummings's poem both is and is not—for it is three letters plucked from '*lone*liness'—the word 'one'.) Nothing human, even, except the consciousness that transmits the poem and those consciousnesses that receive it. This, and the human claim to be alone lonely, touched with the perilous human pride in the claim.

And yet, contradictorily, there is, too, something of the pathetic fallacy, the feeling that nature cannot but be imagined as touched by the tears of things. It is the pathetic fallacy, often noble, which—as Ruskin knew—threatens to sentimentalize Romantic and post-Romantic depictings.

There is, to my ear, too plangent, too pleasurable, a repetition when Ben Shahn writes: 'I think of a de Chirico figure, lonely in a lonely street haunted by shadows; its loneliness speaks to all human loneliness.'[4] Better Chekhov, alert to the sheer separation of the medium of a visual art from that medium which can give a title to a picture, the alienation of the one from the other: 'A field with a distant view, one tiny birch tree. The inscription under the picture: loneliness.'[5] Best of all, there is Beckett on the paintings of Jack Yeats:

> What I feel he gets so well, dispassionately, not tragically like Watteau, is the heterogeneity of nature and the human denizens, the unalterable alienness of the two phenomena, the two solitudes, or the solitude and the loneliness, the loneliness in solitude, the impassable immensity between the solitude that cannot quicken to loneliness and the loneliness that cannot lapse into solitude.
>
> I find something terrifying for example in the way Yeats puts down a man's head and a woman's head side by side, or face to face, the awful acceptance of two entities that will never mingle. And do you remember the picture of a man sitting under a fuchsia hedge, reading, with his back turned to the sea and the thunder clouds?[6]

'Two entities that will never mingle': disclaiming all those Victorian claims to blend. And 'a man sitting under a fuchsia hedge, reading, with his back turned', for reading (we read the picture and yet don't read it as we read words) is a way of confronting loneliness, but is also a way of turning one's back on it; at once a way of accepting loneliness (a lonely activity, reading, unlike attending a concert—or a talk) and of escaping or at least eluding loneliness.

[4] *The Shape of Content* (1957), p. 47.
[5] *Notebook*, tr. S. S. Koteliansky and Leonard Woolf (1921), p. 82.
[6] Quoted in James Knowlson, *Damned to Fame: The Life of Samuel Beckett* (1996), pp. 247–8.

Loneliness may be located existentially, but within literature it must first of all be located linguistically. Lichtenberg caught hold of the fact that thinking for ourselves gains from our not thinking by ourselves, for a language is itself already a community of thought:

> If we think much for ourselves we discover that much wisdom has been gathered into language. It is not very probable that we ourselves carry it all in, but much wisdom does in fact reside there, as it does in proverbs.[7]

What wisdom might reside in the English language's locating of loneliness? There is much that is lonely about the word itself:

1. That there are no synonyms for 'lonely' (or 'loneliness')—and this without needing to get into vexed questions about synonymy. A thesaurus will give you many a synonym for 'sad'; for 'lonely' it gives you 'solitary' and 'alone', both of which fall far short of being its synonym. 'Lonesome', even, has a different texture.

2. That dictionary definitions are often immediately inadequate, in that they almost all resort to these synonyms that are no synonyms since they have none of the emotional colouring, none of the plea, that 'lonely' owns.

3. That there are no proverbs about 'lonely' and 'loneliness'; likewise no catch-phrases; and no similes or metaphors. (I know, I know, 'I wandered lonely as a cloud . . .'.—I shall return to Wordsworth, but just think, quick as a flash and happy as a sand-boy, of the language's richness elsewhere when it comes to 'X as a Y.')[8]

4. That the only rhyme for 'lonely' is 'only', in one another's arms and perhaps pockets. Compounding the lonely. Bob Dylan sings this so that it finds its direction home: 'You've gone to the finest school all right, Miss Lonely | But you know you only used to get juiced in it' ('Like a Rolling Stone'). Elsewhere, Dylan calls up a rhyme of a sort, one that refuses to own itself a rhyme:

> Sign on the window says "Lonely,"
> Sign on the door said "No Company Allowed,"

---

[7] *Aphorisms*, tr. R. J. Hollingdale (1990), p. 130; Notebook J. No. 72.

[8] I owe to William Logan the suggestion that unsuccessful attempts at a simile make for loneliness; he has given me, from Frank Wilstach's *A Dictionary of Similes* (1916): 'Lonely as a deserted ship', Anon; 'Lonely as a ghost', Anon; 'Lonely as a trance', Hartley Coleridge; 'Lonely as a crow in a strange country', Joseph Conrad; 'As lonely as the sun', Sir Francis Doyle; 'Lonely as the Arctic Sea', Hamlin Garland; 'Lonely in her gloom as a pale Angel of the Grove', Thomas Moore; and 'Lonely as a catamount', Sam Slick. None of these is a draw.

Sign on the street says "Y' Don't Own Me,"
Sign on the porch says "Three's A Crowd,"
Sign on the porch says "Three's A Crowd."

No company allowed? Company is the thing.

5. That there is no verb; you can isolate someone but not lonely them in any shape or form.

6. That, rather as there is no opposite of 'disappointment' (one has to beat about phrasally), there is no single straightforward opposite of loneliness—opposite in the sense of *not* being lonely; moreover, there is no opposite in the other sense (a line crossed), in the sense of being the opposite of loneliness as foolhardiness is the opposite of courage.

7. That the language's attempts at making 'lonely' and 'loneliness' less alone, less lonely, have all come to nothing; think of the ill-fated, and ill-advised, attempts to infiltrate into the language the following: *lonedom* (1612, nonce-word); *loneful* (1565, 1844, Scots); *lonelihood* (1830 Scott); and *loneness* (1591).

8. That the King James translation of the Bible does not have 'lonely' or any cognate form. (Alone, yes, and solitary and solitarily.)

The formation 'lonely' is itself suggestive, since it is both a contraction and an expansion. The contraction derives from the fact that it is 'lone' which gave us 'lonely', and 'lone' is aphetic *alone*. Something is missing, then, from 'lone' (and so from 'lonely'), but then something is added to 'lone' to give us 'lonely'—the suffix giving an effective and affective expansion. The contraction answers to something about the lonely (cut off); the expansion answers to something else about it (the swell of feeling, the reaching out for the further shore of sympathy).

But as always, what the dictionary brings home is not only some enduring human agreement but a particular historical salience. A historical salience, and a national one. For the French cannot say 'lonely', any more than they can say 'blush'. They can evoke loneliness and blushing, but the language has no word that is manifestly the word for either. *Rougir* does not distinguish blushing from flushing, and *seul* does not distinguish being lonely from being alone. There are then things about loneliness that can be seen and shown just because the language does not (or does) have a word for it.

For, though there must always have been loneliness in our modern English sense, there was not always the word—and when there is not a word, the thing itself can never be quite the same. For to be able to name it, and to name it summarily, is to be at once a beneficiary and a victim of the verbal and the nominal.

Loneliness is in crucial respects a Romantic phenomenon. In Dr Johnson's day, and in his dictionary, *loneliness* is 'solitude; want of company; disposition to avoid company', and *lonely* is 'solitary; addicted to solitude'. These are not wide of the modern mark, but they are importantly not quite it either. What the *Oxford English Dictionary* brings home is that the strong emotional colouring of the words, and no less markedly of their cousin 'lonesome', is a later development—is a Romantic development.

lonely: 1. Of persons, etc., their actions, condition, etc: Having no companionship or society; unaccompanied, solitary, lone. 1607, *Coriolanus* I go alone, Like to a lonely Dragon. 2. *poet.* Of things: Isolated, standing apart; = lone. 1632 Milton, in some high lonely Towr. 3. Of localities: Unfrequented by men; desolate. Milton, 1629, *Nat. Ode* The lonely mountains o're. 4a. Dejected because of want of company or society; sad at the thought that one is alone; having a feeling of solitariness. 1811 Byron, Though pleasure fires the maddening soul, The heart—the heart is lonely still!

So, whatever the intimations in those instances before 1811, it is with Byron that the great dictionary first identifies confidently our sense of what the language has come to mean by 'lonely'. And the same goes for *loneliness*:

1. Want of society or company; the condition of being alone or solitary; solitariness, loneness. 1586, Sidney. 2. Uninhabited or unfrequented condition of character (of a place); desolateness. 1746–47. 3. The feeling of being alone; the sense of solitude; dejection arising from want of companionship or society. 1814 Wordsworth, *Excursion*: He grew up From year to year in loneliness of soul. 4b. *poet.* Imparting a feeling of loneliness; dreary. Shelley, 1813: Wakening a lonely echo.

As Kierkegaard observed in 1837:

There is so much talk of variety being a necessary part of the romantic, but I could almost say the opposite: the absolute loneliness, where not a breath of wind stirs, where no distant baying of hounds can be heard—and yet the trees incline to one another and repeat their childhood memories about when the nymphs lived in them, and imagination then gorges itself in supreme enjoyment. And what else is romanticism?[9]

---

[9] *Papers and Journals*, tr. Alastair Hannay (1996), p. 110.

With Romanticism came new opportunities, new opportunities for self-scrutiny and self-worth but also for self-deception and self-pity. 'Lonely' had much to offer, much that is true and much that is not; feeling, and human illusions of feeling. Take, for instance, the ancient and enduring question as to when, or with what constitution, being alone was not that sad thing loneliness but that positive thing—what, exactly? We don't have a word for a solitude that is to be highly valued, though the word 'solitude' is perfectly compatible with high store.[10] Like Nietzsche, Kierkegaard wrote in praise of solitude:

> It is an awful satire and epigram on the temporalism of the modern age that nowadays the only thing people can think of using solitude for is punishment, gaol. How different, then, our present from that time when, however secular temporalism was, people nevertheless believed in the solitude of the cloister, and solitude was revered as the highest, as the category of the eternal; how different now that it is abhorred as an abomination and used only for the punishment of criminals. Alas, what a change![11]

T. S. Eliot was styptic in 1933 about I. A. Richards, who was Romantic in the sense in which T. E. Hulme deplored Romanticism as 'spilt religion'. Richards's incredulity about the religious made him—so Eliot believed—credulous about the religiose.

> What he [Richards] proposes ... is nothing less than a regimen of Spiritual Exercises.
>
> I. *Man's loneliness (the isolation of the human situation)*
> Loneliness is known as a frequent attitude in romantic poetry, and in the form of 'lonesomeness' (as I need not remind American readers) is a frequent attitude in contemporary lyrics known as 'the blues.' But in what sense is Man in general isolated, and from what? What *is* the 'human situation'? I can understand the isolation of the human situation as Plato's Diotima expounds it, or in the Christian sense of the separation of Man from God; but not an isolation which is not a separation from anything in particular.[12]

Attempts to discriminate in the abstract the opposing valuations of being alone have proved ineffectual, unconvincing. When Arland Ussher in 1957 offered Beckett an abstract antithesis, Beckett was not moved to embrace it exactly:

---

[10] See Wesley J. Wildman, 'In Praise of Loneliness', *Loneliness*, ed. Leroy S. Rouner (1998), in which the present essay first appeared.
[11] *Papers and Journals*, p. 258.
[12] *The Use of Poetry and the Use of Criticism* (1933), p. 132.

Arland Ussher suggested in a letter to Beckett that he thought one of the main problems of life was how to 'convert loneliness (the worst of conditions) into aloneness (which is the best)'. Beckett replied: 'What you say about loneliness and aloneness is very good (and true for some). From the former I suffered much as a boy, but not much in the last 30 years, bending over me in my old dying-bed where I found me early and the last words unending.'[13]

'Aloneness' was not going to catch on, especially not as an approbatory term. We can see in Beckett's great predecessor Wordsworth how unremittingly vigilance was called for and called upon. It is the lesser Wordsworth, the complaisant one, who gives the world such lines of easy antithesis as this:

> To the deep quiet and majestic thoughts
> Of loneliness succeeded empty noise
> And superficial pastimes;
>   (*The Prelude*, 1805, iii 210–12)

It is the great Wordsworth who, in 'I wandered lonely as a cloud', acknowledges, incarnates, an antithesis much less gratifying or easy.

> I wandered lonely as a cloud
> That floats on high o'er vales and hills,
> When all at once I saw a crowd,
> A host, of golden daffodils;
> Beside the lake, beneath the trees,
> Fluttering and dancing in the breeze.
>
> Continuous as the stars that shine
> And twinkle on the milky way,
> They stretched in never-ending line
> Along the margin of a bay:
> Ten thousand saw I at a glance,
> Tossing their heads in sprightly dance.
>
> The waves beside them danced; but they
> Out-did the sparkling waves in glee:
> A poet could not but be gay,
> In such a jocund company:
> I gazed—and gazed—but little thought
> What wealth the show to me had brought:
>
> For oft, when on my couch I lie
> In vacant or in pensive mood,

---

[13] Knowlson, *Damned to Fame*, p. 396.

> They flash upon that inward eye
> Which is the bliss of solitude;
> And then my heart with pleasure fills,
> And dances with the daffodils.

'Lonely as a cloud | That floats on high': so familiar is the simile as to make its sheer oddity invisible, so high has it come to float. *Is* a cloud lonely, with any of the emotional colouring with which the poet imbues himself? (Or is this the earlier, less pleading, sense of 'lonely', responsibly offered?) Wordsworth is not even moved to remark that the cloud is the only one in the sky.[14] What happens to this thought of loneliness, this likening? It is floated. And in due course there floats in the word whose company the word 'lonely' always seeks: 'company'.

> A poet could not but be gay
> In such a jocund company:

'A poet could not but be gay'—and a reader? For this catches at once the glory and the peril of poems of loneliness. A poem, even when it is not 'jocund', cannot but be company; and knowing this to be so is what a poem must realistically, honestly, temper. The company of a poem, like the company of that company of daffodils, cannot but come, but it does come to pass. It palliates, which is a great deal and is much less than one would wish. It mitigates, to use a word of which Wordsworth elsewhere avails himself delicately and temperately, imagining the light of a distant taper by night, when the sky

> affords no company
> To mitigate and cheer its loneliness.[15]

And yet, even in subsequent moods that are not gay, the memory of the daffodils, like and yet unlike the revisited memory of the poem for us, will offer still some mitigation of loneliness, some pleasure that distinguishes sad loneliness from that state which may or may not be sad, solitude:

> For oft, when on my couch I lie
> In vacant or in pensive mood,

---

[14] Contrast the unmistakable clarity of 'She dwelt among the untrodden ways':

> —Fair as a star, when only one
> Is shining in the sky.

[15] 'Even as a dragon's eye that feels the stress' 7–8.

> They flash upon that inward eye
> Which is the bliss of solitude;
> And then my heart with pleasure fills,
> And dances with the daffodils.

'That inward eye': this summoning to be the outward eye, the eye of flesh (the unforgettable phrase of the Book of Job), the eye without which one could not read this very poem. 'Which is the bliss of solitude': how feelingly this sees that solitude may be welcomed (the bliss of solitude as the bliss that is solitude) even while it acknowledges—for 'of' is so adept—that 'the bliss of solitude' may rather mean the bliss that is the blissful part of solitude. As we may speak of 'the rewards of the academic life', acknowledging that there are those other things.

It is the very wording alone which can protect the loneliness / solitude distinction against being inert or complacent. In her poem 'Crusoe in England', Elizabeth Bishop calls up a figure who might be forgiven for being sceptical about the bliss of solitude:

> The books
> I'd read were full of blanks;
> the poems—well, I tried
> reciting to my iris-beds,
> "They flash upon that inward eye,
> which is the bliss. . .". The bliss of what?
> One of the first things that I did
> when I got back was look it up.

How sardonically this replaces the wild daffodils with 'my iris-beds', with the iris making a strange oeillade at Wordsworth's 'inward eye'. But then the allusion does itself act as company, even as memorized poems have brought company and comfort to prisoners. For Crusoe had been in an open prison. Post-Wordsworthian (with affectionate anachronism), Bishop's is a Crusoe who feels tenderly towards self-pity:

> I often gave way to self-pity.
> "Do I deserve this? I suppose I must.
> I wouldn't be here otherwise. Was there
> a moment when I actually chose this?
> I don't remember, but there could have been."
> What's wrong about self-pity, anyway?
> With my legs dangling down familiarly
> over a crater's edge, I told myself

"Pity should begin at home." So the more
pity I felt, the more I felt at home.

Wordsworth escaped self-pity, and the sentimentalizing of the distinction between loneliness and solitude, with the small crucial prophylaxis of the equivocation alive in the words 'the bliss of solitude'. Emily Dickinson sought more directly to characterize 'another Loneliness' (a haunting collocation, with 'Loneliness' aching for 'another'), 'another Loneliness' than the sorrowful one, but she too needed a prophylaxis against overconfidence or complacency:[16]

> There is another Loneliness
> That many die without –
> Not want of friend occasions it
> Or circumstance of Lot
>
> But nature, sometimes, sometimes thought
> And whoso it befall
> Is richer than could be revealed
> By mortal numeral –

This poem, with its 'Loneliness' and 'befall' (and its abstention from pronouns) may have sown the seeds of e. e. cummings's poem. Like cummings, Dickinson effects—though by different means—that salutary thing which is the refusal to permit of any confidently entire voicing. (Can loneliness be voiced?) There is the famously unutterable in Dickinson's punctuation, including that final mark—

> By mortal numeral –

and in Dickinson's capitalization (you cannot *say* a capital letter): Loneliness and Lot, the only two capitalizings here, alliterating too, signal to one another, each stationed at a line ending. But it is not part of the lot of Loneliness, unlike that of Lot itself, that it should be granted the company of rhyme. Tennyson's friend Arthur Hallam wrote exquisitely that 'Rhyme has been said to contain in itself a constant appeal to Memory and Hope' ('The Influence of Italian upon English Literature', 1831). And, one might add, to company. Then there is the double possibility as to the sounding, the rhythm and sense, of the simple line

> But nature, sometimes, sometimes thought

---

[16] *The Poems of Emily Dickinson*, ed. R. W. Franklin (1998).

The comma after 'nature' has the effect of declining the certainty that here is a perfectly balanced chiasmus ('ab ba': think again of e. e. cummings and his 'af fa'), for though the line can perfectly well be syntactically a chiasmus, and should probably be heard as a tiny modulation of

> But nature sometimes, sometimes thought

the punctuation, the comma after 'nature', cannot but hold open the possibility of 'sometimes' doubly bent upon thought, which would then not be found so simply equipollent with nature:

> But nature, [—] sometimes, sometimes thought

It is these withholdings, even when so much is positively granted, that protect such a poem of loneliness against its being—in that fine phrase of Frank Kermode's—'too consolatory to console'. That there is something in a particular poem that cannot be sounded: this may certainly serve many an end, but one such end is a caveat about the limits of realization, a warning against our sentimental wish for entire comfort and company. One of Emily Dickinson's truest poems on loneliness has 'sound' in its first line, punning deeply: 'The Loneliness One dare not sound.' ('Loneliness One': a collection like and unlike 'another Loneliness'.) It is a happy coincidence that the dictionary says of homonym: 'Applied to words having the same *sound* [my italics] but differing in meaning.' As the stanza moves, 'sound' will prove to be stationed so that it might have rhymed with 'plumbing', with which it is linked by sense but not by sound or rhyme:

> The Loneliness One dare not sound –
> And would as soon surmise
> As in it's Grave go plumbing
> To ascertain the size –
>
> The Loneliness whose worst alarm
> Is lest itself should see –
> And perish from before itself
> For just a scrutiny –
>
> The Horror not to be surveyed –
> But skirted in the Dark –
> With Consciousness suspended –
> And Being under Lock –
>
> I fear me this – is Loneliness –
> The Maker of the soul

It's Caverns and it's Corridors
Illuminate – or seal –

Needless to say, there is much here that, seizing upon loneliness, is yet
not a matter of what cannot be sounded. There is the single simple shift
of pronoun, from the stoical impersonality of the opening line, 'One':
'The Loneliness One dare not sound' to the all-too-personal note of the
last stanza: 'I fear me this—is Loneliness', where the pronoun 'I' is then
compounded by 'me', so that the faintly archaic phrase 'I fear me' ('I am
afraid that . . .') becomes further darkened by a transitive: 'I fear me'.
That is one dark truth about loneliness, that it may emanate from or
cause a fear of oneself, or rather of what has to be admitted to be 'me'.

The Loneliness whose worst alarm
Is lest itself should see –
And perish from before itself
For just a scrutiny –

The lines anticipate Beckett's *Film*, which realizes a terror in the face of
George Berkeley's insistence that *esse est percipi* ('to be is to be seen'); at
the end of the film, Buster Keaton is confronted in the mirror by the
eye that has all along pursued him: his own eye, his own face, only to
'perish from before itself | For just a scrutiny'.

Throughout Dickinson's poem there are—there had to be—effects
which do have to be sounded. Here no word alliterates with
'Loneliness', or rather 'Loneliness' alliterates (it comes three times) only
with itself. There's Loneliness for you. The rhyme 'surmise / size' is one
that sardonically downsizes 'surmise' to 'size'; and what the sequence '*as
soon surmise*' has in common with the rhyming sequence '*as*certain the
size' is that each of them summons up a fearful *assize*. But against these
audible effects there are set those which cannot be made audible though
the eye can register them with confidence: Dickinson's outré capitaliza-
tions and her dash, including again that final mark which seals in part
and in part breaks off:

Illuminate – or seal –

One of Dickinson's illuminations of loneliness takes the form of an
acknowledgement that loneliness may itself be hugged for company,
perversely consolatory:

It might be lonelier
Without the Loneliness –

Another illumination issues from the attempt to imagine to the limit:

> I tried to think a lonelier Thing
> Than any I had seen –
> Some Polar Expiation – An Omen in the Bone
> Of Death's tremendous nearness –
>
> I probed Retrieveless things
> My Duplicate – to borrow –
> A Haggard comfort springs
>
> From the belief that Somewhere –
> Within the Clutch of Thought –
> There dwells one other Creature
> Of Heavenly Love – forgot –
>
> I plucked at our Partition –
> As One should pry the Walls –
> Between Himself – and Horror's Twin –
> Within Opposing Cells –
>
> I almost strove to clasp his Hand,
> Such Luxury – it grew –
> That as Myself – could pity Him –
> Perhaps he – pitied me –

An extraordinary apprehension, that a Polar Expedition is a Polar Expiation. The poem has the characteristic Dickinson ineffability of capitalization and punctuation (so attuned, among other things, to a salutary acknowledgement of a falling-short), but the hiding place of the poem's power is elsewhere. Its realizing of loneliness is most pervasively a matter of the pronoun, that part of speech which may so set one person apart from another (with Dickinson's having a single 'our' to open a hope of bringing together an 'us').

The poem begins with 'I' and ends with 'me'. The first person, from first to last? The run ('I . . .' 'I . . .' 'I . . .' 'My . . .' 'I . . .') arrives at 'our' ('I plucked at our Partition'), but the poignancy, the loneliness, of this 'our' rises from the fact that the 'one other Creature' who would go to constitute the possibility of an 'our' has been characterized in the preceding lines as a wisp of hope, not an actuality. And when the pronoun 'One' follows, this too is not another; it is a surrogate 'I' within a simile:

> I plucked at our Partition –
> As One should pry the Walls –

> Between Himself – and Horror's Twin –
> Within Opposing Cells –

So that 'One' is 'I' revisited; even more lonelily, the 'Himself' who follows is again nobody but 'I' revisited:

> I plucked at our Partition –
> As One should pry the Walls –
> Between Himself – and Horror's Twin –

Himself is Myself is Herself. And the desperate closing stanza continues to make grim play with the fact that 'his' and 'Him' and 'he' are nothing other than 'I' and 'Myself' and 'me' seen under a wishful aspect, the aspect of a walled simile or figment. The heartbreak of this last stanza is nowhere more audible than in the rhyme that is craved, the pronoun that is craved and might now, at last, in the nick of time, still put in an appearance. For how is the poem's rhyming consummated? From 'seen/bone', through 'things / springs', 'Thought / forgot', and 'Walls / Cells', to 'grew/me'—not, as it so easily and yet impossibly might have been, 'grew / you'.

I end with two poems, one by the great Victorian poet William Barnes, whom Philip Larkin loved, and one by Larkin.

I choose Barnes's poem partly because it is called, not 'Loneliness' but 'Lonesomeness'—and not 'Lonesomeness' but 'Lwonesomeness.' The word 'lonesome' was already, even then, en route to mawkishness and furry self-fondling ('chiefly in emotional sense', *OED*), but the Dorset dialect in which Barnes mostly wrote is a protection against too easy a lapsing into the feeling of the poem. We are to sympathize, not (the word did not then exist, which was something of a mercy) to empathize, leave alone to 'identify with'.

Lwonesomeness

> As I do zew, wi' nimble hand,
>   In here avore the window's light,
> How still do all the housegear stand
>   Around my lwonesome zight.
> How still do all the housegear stand
> Since Willie now've a-left the land.
>
> The rwose-tree's window-sheädèn bow
>   Do hang in leaf, an' win'-blow'd flow'rs
> Avore my lwonesome eyes do show
>   Theäse bright November hours.

Avore my lwonesome eyes do show
Wi' nwone but I to zee em blow.
The sheädes o'leafy buds, avore
The peänes, do sheäke upon the glass,
An' stir in light upon the vloor,
Where now vew veet do pass.
An' stir in light upon the vloor
Where there's a-stirrèn nothèn mwore.

This win' mid dreve upon the maïn,
My brother's ship, a-plowèn foam,
But not bring mother, cwold, nor raïn,
At her now happy hwome.
But not bring mother, cwold, nor raïn,
Where she is out of pain.

Zoo now that I'm a-mwopèn dumb,
A-keepèn father's house, do you
Come of en wi' your work vrom hwome,
Vor company. Now do.
Come of en wi' your work vrom hwome,
Up here a-while. Do come.

The title speaks of 'Lwonesomeness'; the first stanza has 'my lwonesome zight', and then the second stanza twice has 'my lwonesome eyes'— whereupon, as by an effort of considerate courage, the word is heard no more. The speaker breaks free of pressing the emotional word upon her hearer; oh, the sense of loneliness will be alive throughout, but that is something else and is only human. The poem is not addressed to us (we overhear it), and the person to whom she speaks (we shall never know just who this is—a friend? a relative? a lover perhaps?) is someone upon whom she has, clearly, some claim.

Once again, the pronouns tell a lonely tale. The first stanza: 'I . . .' 'my'. The second stanza: 'my . . .' 'my . . .' 'I . . .'. Poignantly, there are no pronouns in the third, the central stanza, where persons and the absence of persons become reduced to 'vew veet'. The fourth stanza: 'My'—and then, newly, with a fresh sadness, 'her' and 'she' (mother). And then in the last stanza, the tender plea of love and for love, 'Vor company': 'I' into 'you . . .' 'your . . .' 'your . . .'.

Notice—we register it even if we don't consciously observe it—the truncated final line in both the last two stanzas; earlier, the last line has always—like the other lines—had eight syllables; now it is reduced to six: 'Where she is out of pain'; 'Up here a-while. Do come.'

But it is the plea, the hushed but obdurate plea, of those last two words of the poem that consummate its sympathy and ours. The speaker has spoken of herself with rueful truthfulness:

> Zoo now that I'm a-mwopèn dumb,

—and the rhyme, taken up from the penultimate stanza ('foam / hwome'), becomes 'dumb / hwome / hwome' (becoming the repeated line that has sadly graced every stanza). The rhyme—'dumb / hwome / hwome'—catches up the repeated 'Come', an internal rhyme, an inward rhyme. For 'Come' comes, first in a sentence of twenty words, then in one of ten words, and then, finally, in one of two words: 'Do come', where not only does 'come' rhyme, but 'do' is the other rhyme word of this concluding stanza: at the line endings, 'do you', into 'Now do', and at last into 'Do come'.

> Zoo now that I'm a-mwopèn dumb,
> A-keepèn father's house, do you
> Come of en wi' your work vrom hwome,
> Vor company. Now do.
> Come of en wi' your work vrom hwome,
> Up here a-while. Do come.

In conclusion, Philip Larkin, 'Friday Night in the Royal Station Hotel':

> Light spreads darkly downwards from the high
> Clusters of lights over empty chairs
> That face each other, coloured differently.
> Through open doors, the dining-room declares
> A larger loneliness of knives and glass
> And silence laid like carpet. A porter reads
> An unsold evening paper. Hours pass,
> And all the salesmen have gone back to Leeds,
> Leaving full ashtrays in the Conference Room.
>
> In shoeless corridors, the lights burn. How
> Isolated, like a fort, it is—
> The headed paper, made for writing home
> (If home existed) letters of exile: *Now*
> *Night comes on. Waves fold behind villages.*

The intense loneliness here is partly a matter of there being no pronouns (except for the bleak 'it is'). And a matter of those 'corridors', reminiscent of Dickinson's bringing together the 'Loneliness' of the soul and 'its Corridors'. And those 'chairs | That face each other'.

How the sounds co-operate. 'Hours pass': is 'hours' there one syllable or two, how long is the stretch? (Gerard Hopkins resorted to a diacritical mark: 'What hours, O what black hoürs we have spent | This night!') Or listen to Larkin's alliteration: for instance, the story told by the only immediately successive alliterations in the poem: 'darkly downwards . . .' 'larger loneliness . . .' 'laid like . . .' 'Leeds, | Leaving'—where there is assonance too—and finally 'Now | Night'. 'Light' was there at the head of the first line, moving 'downwards'; 'Night', at the head of the last line.

It is the 'larger loneliness' of the alliteration on the letter *l* that permeates the poem; one line, and one line alone, contains no *l*, and this is the line which, introducing the end of the poem, cuts across the syntax with a weary sigh: 'The headed paper, made for writing home'. What is a poem but a headed paper (headed, in this case, 'Friday Night in the Royal Station Hotel') made for writing home, and for bringing home? The line itself is adrift in apposition, with no verb to help it head somewhere:

> In shoeless corridors, the lights burn. How
> Isolated, like a fort, it is—
> The headed paper, made for writing home
> (If home existed) letters of exile: *Now*
> *Night comes on. Waves fold behind villages.*

Unimaginable, such a letter; unsold, the evening paper that a porter reads; but not unimagined, by the poet or by his readers, the poem itself. Still, there within a poem that speaks of silence ('And silence laid like carpet'), there is the unspeakability of the penultimate parentheses '(If home existed)' and of the closing italics with their eerie unheard waves.

About Larkin's great enterprise (in the sense both of his being so enterprising and of what he undertakes), like Barnes's, Dickinson's, Wordsworth's, cummings's diverse enterprises, I am clear in my own mind. The poets have more than a narrowly therapeutic aim, but they would agree with Robert Graves that one at least of the things that poetry can be is a medicine chest stocked against mental disorders (and emotional deprivations), and they would agree with Dr Johnson that the only end of writing is to enable the reader better to enjoy life or better to endure it. As to my own enterprise here, it has been to try to show the ways in which, in the very moment in which a great poem realizes loneliness for us, it acknowledges humanely the limits of the human imagination. A poem can claim so much, yes, and can claim only so much. And the 'close reading' of poems, a lonely activity which can yet be shared, may do something to ameliorate our propensity to evacuate the suffering, not only of others but of ourselves, into abstraction. There are the particulars of rapture and, likewise takingly, those of grief.

A. E. Housman and 'the colour of his hair'

'You know, you and I do not always agree', Jonathan Swift wrote to his friend Charles Ford, 8 September 1711: 'One thing is that I never expect Sincerity from any man; and am no more angry at the Breach of it, than at the colour of his Hair'.

'Oh who is that young sinner with the handcuffs on his wrists?' In 1895, A. E. Housman dealt swingeingly with the imprisonment of Oscar Wilde, whose first trial had been in April and who was sent to Reading Gaol in November. His crime: the giving of homosexual offence. The world's judgement (Housman's poem fiercely urged) is as unjust as taking a man 'to prison for the colour of his hair'.

Why, of all capricious gravamina, did Housman seize upon this? Because, while flamboyantly arbitrary, the colour of one's hair had come to allude to just such a cruel perversion of injustice. Arbitrary though punishment for the colour of one's hair is, there was nothing arbitrary about Housman's choosing it as his indictment. For it had become a type of the arbitrarily unjust, and so—itself by way of being a tradition—it was the more sharply fitted to the case, a case where there converged with it another good old English tradition, the punitive repudiation that is now dubbed homophobia.

To bring into play, footnotable play, the precedents *in re* the colour of one's hair, is not only to see Housman's instance of preposterous crime as at once impertinent and pertinent, but to take the measure of the poem's *saeva indignatio*.

Laurence Housman, who in 1937 (a year after his brother's death) respectfully chose to publish this unreleased poem,[1] was right to see it as a poem of protest against society's laws, but he was limited in seeing the poem as that only. The poem's protest, as often in Housman, is partly against that part of life which is society's doing and wrongdoing,

---

[1] *A.E.H.* (1937), p. 226: Additional Poems XVIII.

but is more largely against all else. Society's laws, yes, but nature's too, and, above all, the laws of 'Whatever brute and blackguard made the world'. This, even a chorus of priests might have to acknowledge:

> Oh wearisome Condition of Humanity!
> Borne under one Law, to another bound:
> Vainely begot, and yet forbidden vanity,
> Created sicke, commanded to be sound:
> What meaneth Nature by these diverse Lawes?
> (Fulke Greville, Chorus Sacerdotum, from *Mustapha*)

What meaneth Society by these perverse laws? 'The laws of God, the laws of man' (*Last Poems* XII): there the sway and the swaying constitute the even-handed scales of Housman's handy-dandy.

> Oh who is that young sinner with the handcuffs on his wrists?
> And what has he been after that they groan and shake their fists?
> And wherefore is he wearing such a conscience-stricken air?
> Oh they're taking him to prison for the colour of his hair.
>
> 'Tis a shame to human nature, such a head of hair as his;
> In the good old time 'twas hanging for the colour that it is;
> Though hanging isn't bad enough and flaying would be fair
> For the nameless and abominable colour of his hair.
>
> Oh a deal of pains he's taken and a pretty price he's paid
> To hide his poll or dye it of a mentionable shade;
> But they've pulled the beggar's hat off for the world to see and stare,
> And they're haling him to justice for the colour of his hair.
>
> Now 'tis oakum for his fingers and the treadmill for his feet
> And the quarry-gang on Portland in the cold and in the heat,
> And between his spells of labour in the time he has to spare
> He can curse the God that made him for the colour of his hair.

It was not until thirty years after Laurence Housman published the poem that there appeared—likewise after its author's death—his essay on his brother's love and friendship, 'A. E. Housman's "De Amicitia" '.[2] (The Latin has all the decent lack of obscurity of a learned language.) Laurence Housman's words, which manifest a tender probity, are well known but they remain unexhausted:

I do not pretend to know how far my brother continued to accept throughout

---

[2] Annotated by John Carter, *Encounter*, xxix 4, October 1967. Laurence Housman had died in 1959.

life, in all circumstances, the denial of what was natural to him, but I do know that he considered the inhibition imposed by society on his fellow-victims both cruel and unjust. That fact is made abundantly plain in the poem which, after considerable hesitation, I decided to publish, even though its literary merit was not high—the one beginning

'Oh who is that young sinner with the handcuffs on his wrists?'

It refers quite evidently to those who inescapably, through no fault of their own, are homosexual—having no more power of choice in the matter than a man has about the colour of his hair, which, as the poem says, he may hide out of sight, or dye to a 'more mentionable shade', but cannot get away from.

Here, then, was a poem expressing contemptuous anger against society's treatment of these unhappy victims of fate, and a sympathy which went so far as to imply no blame. That poem he had left me at liberty to publish: had he objected to publication he would either have so marked it—as he did one or two others for literary reasons—or would have destroyed it. My only reason for hesitation was that its meaning was so obvious, that intelligent readers would be unlikely to refrain (nor did they) from making the true deduction; and my brother had relatives still living to whom this might give pain. I felt nevertheless, that the risk must be taken; it was something of a public duty that I should make known so strong an expression of feeling against social injustice [. . .][3]

This is admirably executed, down to the duly dry touch—what with prison and infringements of liberty—of 'That poem he had left me at liberty to publish . . .'. The brotherly paragraphs are truthful, and yet they are not the whole truth. For Laurence Housman's exclusive emphasis, tripled, upon society ('imposed by society', 'society's treatment of these unhappy victims of fate', 'social injustice'), has the effect of narrowing the poem's perturbation, as though—were society to be so good as to abolish its prohibitive laws—all would be well. Not so.

How small, of all that human hearts endure,
That part which laws or kings can cause or cure.[4]

Samuel Johnson, like A. E. Housman, was a radical conservative, and Johnson's great apophthegm, aware of society's injustices, is aware too of life's condition.

For one reason that 'Oh who is that young sinner . . .' should not be seen only as social protest is its famously being a sombre pendant to two poems which Housman did publish, next year (1896), consecutively

---

[3] *Encounter*, pp. 36–7.
[4] Among the lines supplied by Johnson for Goldsmith's *The Traveller* (429–30).

too: *A Shropshire Lad* XLIV, 'Shot? so quick, so clean an ending?', and XLV, 'If it chance your eye offend you'. Laurence Housman found in his brother's copy of *A Shropshire Lad*, alongside XLIV, the newspaper cutting which has since become famous. Dated August 1895, it quotes a letter by a young Woolwich cadet who had committed suicide, racked by cowardice and despair at his sexual nature while spurred to self-slaughter by 'as yet': 'I thank God that as yet, so far as I know, I have not morally injured, or "offended," as it is called in the Bible, anyone else'. When Housman congratulates this dead young man, it is with no sense, no implication, that the man had been wrong to feel shame at his sexual self.

> Shot? so quick, so clean an ending?
> Oh that was right, lad, that was brave:
> Yours was not an ill for mending,
> 'Twas best to take it to the grave.

Housman these days is liable to find himself harshly judged by the new censoriousness that has replaced the old much worse one; his shade may be told that he was a household traitor to his sexual nature (and others') by lacking pride in being 'gay'. Out, out. But Housman wrote what he meant; the poem praises the young man for doing something not only 'brave' but 'right'; and when it goes on immediately 'Yours was not an ill for mending', there is no reason to suppose that for the poet, in this poem or elsewhere, the ill *was* an ill for mending, being after all not truly an ill at all but only deemed so by a social injustice that the mending of man's laws would rectify. It is not social condemnation only that gives such balanced obduracy to Housman's line 'Souls undone, undoing others', or to the stanza that had set the soul before us:

> Oh soon, and better so than later
> After long disgrace and scorn,
> You shot dead the household traitor,
> The soul that should not have been born.

There are the clean lines of admiration:

> Undishonoured, clear of danger,
> Clean of guilt, pass hence and home.

But the admiration is along lines which invoke honour (a magnificently positive double negative, 'Undishonoured'), an invocation that resists any emancipated or enlightened insistence that there is in homosexuality no dishonour or guilt of which one should yearn to be 'clean'. So too, Housman's ensuing poem, *A Shropshire Lad* XLV, comes to an end in praise of the healthy courage that had brought itself to put an end, not to something which was not really sick at all (merely deemed so, socially, wrongly), but to soul-sickness:

> And if your hand or foot offend you,
> Cut it off, lad, and be whole;
> But play the man, stand up and end you,
> When your sickness is your soul.

The Biblical injunction to be willing to inflict upon oneself the cutting-off of hand or foot is inestimably more grave than to cut one's hair or 'dye it of a mentionable shade'. But 'the colour of his hair' constitutes a tradition, secular and Biblical, that is germane to the conviction that Housman's poem, tragically, should not be restricted to social protest.

It had been, earlier in the nineteenth century, Macaulay who had given new life to an old association of injustice with the capricious indictment of the colour of one's hair.[5] He launched a flight of ferociously precise fancy in his essay on 'Civil Disabilities of the Jews' (*Edinburgh Review*, 1831).

The English Jews are, as far as we can see, precisely what our government has made them. They are precisely what any sect, what any class of men, treated as they have been treated, would have been. If all the red-haired people in Europe had, during centuries, been outraged and oppressed, banished from this place, imprisoned in that, deprived of their money, deprived of their teeth, convicted of the most improbable crimes on the feeblest evidence, dragged at horses' tails, hanged, tortured, burned alive, if, when manners became milder, they had still been subject to debasing restrictions and exposed to vulgar insults, locked up in particular streets in some countries, pelted and ducked by the rabble in others, excluded every where from magistracies and honours, what would be the patriotism of gentlemen with red hair? And if, under such circumstances, a proposition were made for admitting red-haired men to office, how striking a speech might an eloquent admirer of our old institutions deliver against so revolutionary a measure! 'These men,' he might say, 'scarcely consider themselves as Englishmen. They think a red-haired Frenchman or a red-haired German more closely connected with them than a man with brown hair born in their own parish. If a foreign sovereign patronises red hair, they love him better than their own native king . . .'

---

5 Here and elsewhere I am grateful to John Gross.

And so inexorably on, in Macaulay's Swiftian fantasy exposing cruel realities. The Civil Disabilities of the Jews have constituted an incitement to criminal dealings and to the law's injustices. To this intersection (alive in Housman's poem) of hair-colour and the law's injustices, and to an implication of Macaulay's seizing *red* hair, I shall return.

In John Locke's earlier supposition in 1689—more calm, more level, and no less telling—it had been black hair that was postulated, this in relation to religious toleration:

Suppose this business of religion were let alone, and that there were some other distinction made between men and men, upon account of their different complexions, shapes and features, so that those who have black hair, for example, or grey eyes, should not enjoy the same privileges as other citizens; that they should not be permitted either to buy or sell, or live by their callings; that parents should not have the government and education of their own children; that they should either be excluded from the benefit of the laws, or meet with partial judges: can it be doubted but these persons, thus distinguished from others by the colour of their hair and eyes, and united together by one common persecution, would be as dangerous to the magistrate, as any others that had associated themselves merely upon the account of religion?[6]

Here too 'the laws' are crucial; here too there is the yoking, once again scornful, of 'the colour of their hair' with religion, an association which is, I suggest, alluded to in Housman's poem.

But it is the greatest legal historian, and legal thinker, of Victorian England, Sir James Fitzjames Stephen, who furnished the crucial stage by which this yoking of crime and the colour of one's hair, previously pressed into service by Locke and Macaulay, may arrive at Housman and sexual opprobium. Stephen had written on Macaulay, mentioning the argument that 'Jews ought to be allowed to sit in Parliament', in the *Saturday Review* (18 August 1866). He had written expansively there (9 March 1867) on Locke's letters on toleration, and he further referred to these in the preface to the second edition of his *Liberty, Equality, Fraternity* (1874).

Two arguments in Stephen's *Liberty, Equality, Fraternity* converge.

Pondering the age-old intricacy of the relations between morality and the law, Stephen deplored not only Mill's liberalism but his laxity. For Mill, turning a blind eye towards an inconvenient inconsistency,

---

[6] *Epistola de Tolerantia* (1689); *Letters concerning Toleration* I; *Locke and Liberty*, ed. Massimo Salvadori (1960), pp. 138–9.

had seen nothing wrong in continuing to find publicly criminal such conduct as should, by Mill's own arguments, have been a matter for private life only. On the general proposition, Stephen is insistent:

> Other illustrations of the fact that English criminal law does recognize morality are to be found in the fact that a considerable number of acts which need not be specified are treated as crimes merely because they are regarded as grossly immoral.

'Which need not be specified': Stephen's reticence is not a matter of laying his finger against the side of his nose or upon his lips. His modern editor specifies. 'Stephen here refers to what the Victorians generally called "unnatural vice". Sodomy was a capital crime until 1861' (R. J. White).[7]

Stephen proceeded at once to indict Mill for paltering.

> I have already shown in what manner Mr Mill deals with these topics. It is, I venture to think, utterly unsatisfactory. The impression it makes upon me is

---

[7] Archie Burnett, whose Clarendon Press edition of Housman's poems (1997) is of the greatest interest and value, annotates *abominable* in 'the nameless and abominable colour of his hair': 'OED's earliest example (1366) refers to "The abhomynable Synne of Sodomye", and the earliest example of "abomination" 1. (1395) refers to "abhominacioun of bodili sodomie". Also Lev. 18:22 "Thou shalt not lie with mankind, as with womankind: it is abomination" '.

John Sparrow in a letter to the *New Statesman* (1942, xxiii 226) related 'nameless' and 'abominable' to legal statutes against sodomy, and added: 'Another echo of this phraseology (and one with which Housman was himself doubtless familiar) occurs in Chapter XLIV of Book IV of Gibbon's *Decline and Fall of the Roman Empire*: "I touch with reluctance, and dispatch with impatience, a more odious vice, of which modesty *rejects the name*, and nature *abominates* the idea." ' (Archie Burnett notes that Housman, in the preface to his edition of Lucan, alluded to this phrasing from Gibbon.) To these dark glosses there might be added the false etymology which long held sway. Under 'abominable', of which the true etymology is the Latin ab and omen, OED has:

> In med. L. and OFr., and in Eng. from Wyclif to 17th c., regularly spelt *abhominable*, and explained as *ab homine*, quasi 'away from man, inhuman, beastly', a derivation which influenced the use and has permanently affected the meaning of the word. No other spelling occurs in the first folio of Shaks., which has the word 18 times; and in *L.L.L.*, V. i. 27, Holophernes abhors 'the rackers of ortagriphie', who were beginning to write *abominable* for the time-honoured *abhominable*.

(There is a grim irony in 'time-honoured'.) *OED* has a further entry under the false spelling:

> *abhominable, abhomination*, etc., the regular spelling of ABOMINABLE, ABOMINATION, etc., in OFr., and in Eng. from their first use of 17th c., due to an assumed derivation from *ab homine*, 'away from man, inhuman, beastly', which influenced their early use, and has coloured the whole meaning of the words to the present day.

'The present day': this first fascicle of the *OED* was published in 1884. The word 'coloured' catches something for my argument.

that he feels that such acts ought to be punished, and that he is able to reconcile this with his fundamental principles only by subtleties quite unworthy of him. Admit the relation for which I am contending between law and morals, and all becomes perfectly clear. All the acts referred to are unquestionably wicked. Those who do them are ashamed of them. They are all capable of being clearly defined and specifically proved or disproved, and there can be no question at all that legal punishment reduces them to small dimensions, and forces the criminals to carry on their practices with secrecy and precaution. In other words, the object of their suppression is good, and the means adequate.

Yet it is characteristic of Stephen that at this point he should turn away from too eager a prosecution, with a breadth of mind and a genuineness of concession seldom found in a conservative thinker—and far too seldom acknowledged by liberals to be even possible to a conservative thinker:

In practice this is subject to highly important qualifications, of which I will only say here that those who have due regard to the incurable weaknesses of human nature will be very careful how they inflict penalties upon mere vice, or even upon those who make a trade of promoting it, unless special circumstances call for their infliction.

This caveat, which is quite other than a rhetorical move, is a form of 'however'—one that is duly followed by a further 'however', turning the argument back to Stephen's axis of conviction:

It is one thing however to tolerate vice so long as it is inoffensive, and quite another to give it a legal right not only to exist, but to assert itself in the face of the world as an 'experiment in living' as good as another, and entitled to the same protection from law.[8]

Such is Stephen's judicious position on 'grossly immoral' acts and their criminality. It is in the next chapter of *Liberty, Equality, Fraternity* that the colour of one's hair enjoys its day in court:

The rule, 'All thieves shall be imprisoned,' is not observed if A, being a thief, is not imprisoned. In other words, it is not observed if it is not applied equally to every person who falls within the definition of a thief, whatever else he may be. If the rule were, 'All thieves except those who have red hair shall be imprisoned, and they shall not,' the rule would be violated if a red-haired thief were imprisoned as much as if a black-haired thief were not imprisoned. The imprisonment

[8] *Liberty, Equality, Fraternity* (1873, 2nd edn. 1874); ed. R. J. White (1967), p. 154.

of the red-haired thief would be an inequality in the application of the rule; for the equality consists not in the equal treatment of the persons who are the subjects of law, but in the equivalency between the general terms of the law and the description of the particular cases to which it is applied. 'All thieves not being red-haired shall be imprisoned' is equivalent to 'A being a thief with brown hair, B being a thief with black hair, C being a thief with white hair, &c., shall be imprisoned, and Z being a thief with red hair shall not be imprisoned.'

Given the prejudice against red hair, it is good of Stephen to invert his instance so that, for once, red hair would be favoured. What is striking, though, and is the sort of thing that might strike such a fancy as Housman's, is that Stephen moves immediately to a relating of red hair to an imaginable psychopathology:

In this sense equality is no doubt of the very essence of justice, but the question whether the colour of a man's hair shall or shall not affect the punishment of his crimes depends on a different set of considerations. It is imaginable that the colour of the hair might be an unfailing mark of peculiarity of disposition which might require peculiar treatment. Experience alone can inform us whether this is so or not.[9]

There is more than a hint of the sexually aberrant in this odd coupling, with 'the colour of the hair' as possibly 'an unfailing mark of peculiarity of disposition which might require peculiar treatment'. More than a century after Stephen, it has not been many years since the alternative to being taken to prison for this colour of one's hair was the meting out of peculiar treatment to rectify peculiarity of disposition. Aversion therapy against perversion. Oh who is that young patient with the limpness of the wrists?

'For the colour of his hair': what do most readers see? We see red. And this not only because of Macaulay, for Macaulay in his turn had been availing himself, so as to hold anti-Semitism up to ridicule, of the age-old prejudice against red hair. The *OED* cites, under 'red-haired', George Chapman, *Bussy D'Ambois* III. i (1607), 'Worse than the poison of a red-hair'd man'. Swift needed the commonplace opprobium, in *Gulliver's Travels* IV: 'It is observed, that the Red-haired of both Sexes are more libidinous and mischievous than the rest'. Even Stevie Smith has a poem 'From the Italian: *An old superstition*':

---

9 *Liberty, Equality, Fraternity,* p. 186.

A woolly dog,
A red-haired man,
Better dead
Than to have met'em.

Though the colour of the hair is in Housman's poem left unspecified (grossly immoral 'acts which need not be specified'), the reiterated line is calculated to call up an ancient prejudice, prejudice being in any such case the nub.

Take, for instance, the word 'poll': 'To hide his poll or dye it of a mentionable shade'. A poll of hair may be any colour, but is likely to conjure up red, for not only is 'redpoll' many a species of bird, but there had been Peter Pindar in 1787 ('Large red-poll'd, blowzy, hard, two-handed jades'), and there was—by a coincidence, in 1895, the very year of Housman's poem and Wilde's trial—'The celebrated . . . herd of Red-Polled cattle': 'The Duke of York is getting together a large and choice herd of Red-Polls' (*Westminster Gazette*, 29 March 1895).[10] There is an onomastic felicity in its having been, exactly a century later, in 1995, a scholar of the name of Whitehead whose book noted the echo of the phrase 'such a head of hair as yours' from Arthur Conan Doyle's Sherlock Holmes story 'The Red-Headed League' (1891), a story where the person with red hair is indeed innocent of crime.[11]

But if red hair were darkly called up by Housman, there might come with it a further darkness. There is, so far as I know, only one person whose name identifies a colour, and this the colour of hair, and the colour red. (Rufus means red, and so is another story.) *OED*:

Judas-coloured (of the hair or beard) red (from the mediaeval belief that Judas Iscariot had red hair and beard):

c.1594 Kyd: And let their beards be of Judas his own colour.

1695 Motteux: Observations on the Judas-colour of his Beard and hair.

1673 Dryden: There's treachery in that Judas-coloured beard.

1879 Dowden: An ugly specimen of the streaked-carroty or Judas-coloured kind.

Dryden spat this more than once.

---

[10] Notable in the Nineties; the first entry in the *OED* is 1891: 'The Norfolk and Suffolk Red Polled breed stands highest for dairying purposes. The Red Polls are handsome symmetrical animals of medium size'. Further OED citations for the breed are from 1895, 1896, and 1898.

[11] John Whitehead, *Hardy to Larkin: Seven English Poets* (1995), p. 60.

[Now the Assembly to adjourn prepar'd,
When *Bibliopolo* from behind appear'd,
As well describ'd by th' old Satyrick Bard:]
With leering Looks, Bullfac'd, and Freckled fair,
With two left Legs, and Judas-colour'd Hair,
With Frowzy Pores, that taint the ambient Air.

('Lines on Tonson')

But is Judas to be glimpsed in Housman's poem? To the colour of the hair there might be added hanging: 'In the good old time 'twas hanging for the colour that it is'. Yes, 'sodomy was a capital crime until 1861', but there might be Judas's self-infliction too. For to the compound *Judas-coloured* there may be added the compound *Judas-tree*: 'From a popular notion that Judas hanged himself on a tree of this kind' (*OED*).

The Gospel according to Saint Matthew reports that Judas 'repented himself', 'saying, I have sinned' (Housman: 'sinner', 'conscience-stricken air'); Judas 'went and hanged himself' (Housman: 'hanging'); for Judas, there was 'the price of blood', 'the price of him that was valued' (Housman: 'and a pretty price he's paid').

For there is the further compound, *Judas-kiss*. The Gospel according to Saint Matthew: 'Now he that betrayed him gave them a sign, saying, Whomsoever I shall kiss, that same is he: hold him fast. And forthwith he came to Jesus, and said, Hail master; and kissed him'. The Gospel according to Saint Luke: 'But Jesus said unto him, Judas, betrayest thou the Son of man with a kiss?' Moreover, the Judas-kiss lent itself to homosexual solicitation; Wilde was to take up the suggestion of it from within *The Ballad of Reading Gaol*, to furnish the concluding antithesis of the poem:

And all men kill the thing they love,
By all let this be heard,
Some do it with a bitter look,
Some with a flattering word,
The coward does it with a kiss,
The brave man with a sword!

Housman, praising the cadet who had bitten a bullet, contemplated unflinchingly the thought of 'The soul that should not have been born'. Those words probably came to him from Saint Matthew:

but woe unto that man by whom the Son of man is betrayed! it had been good for that man if he had not been born. Then Judas, which betrayed him, answered and said, Master, It is I? He said unto him, Thou hast said.

Macaulay had needed the same verse:

> The same reasoning which is now employed to vindicate the disabilities imposed on our Hebrew countrymen will equally vindicate the kiss of Judas and the judgment of Pilate. 'The Son of man goeth, as it is written of him; but woe to that man by whom the Son of man is betrayed.'

In conclusion something must be said of why it matters whether Judas is to be glimpsed in 'Oh who is that young sinner . . .'. One answer is that Judas widens the focus of the poem's burning glass, not away from the laws of man but beyond them to take in too the laws of God. For Judas has always provoked a great unease about divine justice. Did not God's providence, and Christ's mission, need Judas, and is not some gratitude due to him for being, at the very least, of such service? Bob Dylan and Jorge Luis Borges have this much in common, that both have pondered whether Judas Iscariot had God on his side. Here is the thinking of Nils Runeberg, Borges' Nils Runeberg:

> Skilfully, he begins by pointing out how superfluous was the act of Judas. He observes (as did Robertson) that in order to identify a master who daily preached in the synagogue and who performed miracles before gatherings of thousands, the treachery of an apostle is not necessary. This, nevertheless, occurred. To suppose an error in Scripture is intolerable; no less intolerable is it to admit that there was a single haphazard act in the most precious drama in the history of the world. *Ergo*, the treachery of Judas was not accidental; it was a predestined deed which has its mysterious place in the economy of the Redemption.
>
> Judas, alone among the apostles, intuited the secret divinity and the terrible purpose of Jesus. The Word had lowered Himself to be mortal; Judas, the disciple of the Word, could lower himself to the role of informer (the worst transgression dishonour abides) and welcome the fire which can not be extinguished. ('Three Versions of Judas')[12]

For Judas, 'dishonour abides', unlike for the cadet whom Housman had celebrated as 'Undishonoured'. It is not only society whose injustices cry out. For Housman the great blasphemer, the injustice visited upon a man damned to prison for the colour of his hair might cry out to the fellow-suffering visited upon a man damned for playing his indispensable part in the economy of the Redemption.

---

[12] 1944; *Fictions*, translated by Anthony Kerrigan (1962).

To this cosmic injustice there is no end in sight. Even as I wrote, the current issue of the *London Review of Books* (20 February 1997) contained a reply by William Klassen to Frank Kermode's review of *Judas: Betrayer or Friend of Jesus.*

Despite Professor Kermode's suggestion to the contrary, I approached my mandate to write a life of Judas with the firm conviction that Judas was a traitor and that all the Gospels were unanimous in portraying him as such. In time that conviction had to yield to the evidence.

Judas the traitor (Housman and 'the household traitor'). Of Judas it is written: 'It had been good for that man, if he had not been born'. Housman: 'The soul that should not have been born'. But would Jesus's *raison d'être* have lived had Judas not been born? What does God's plan owe to Judas's felicitous culpability?

'He can curse the God that made him for the colour of his hair'. 'My suggestion', Klassen wrote, 'that Judas was acting as a faithful Jew, carrying out not only God's will as understood by Jesus but also the will of Jesus himself, at least deserves some consideration'. As does the thought that 'Oh who is that young sinner . . .' is not only a Locke-located, a Macaulay-maculate, and a Stephen-steeped poem, but a Judas-coloured one.

Yvor Winters: Allusion and Pseudo-Reference

Thirty years ago, Robert Lowell passed a summary judgement on the critic who had died three years earlier and who had loved to execute summary justice: 'Winters, a Humanist, our Malherbes, maybe wrote the clearest criticism . . . intuitive, authoritative, perverse'.[1]

Yet Winters's judgement on a critic whose memory we honour, Cleanth Brooks, was less clear cut than was Winters's wont. With weird wit, Winters presented himself as 'more hesitant' than Brooks; this, in paraphrasing Sidney's sonnet, 'Highway since you my chiefe *Pernassus* be':

Highway, since I write most often under your influence, I beg you to bear me to my lady; and, since you appear to be doing so, my Muse and I will thank you. May you never suffer infamy, and—as a final proof of my sincerity—may you kiss Stella's feet for hundreds of years. I do not offer this paraphrase as an equivalent of the poem (in this respect I am far more hesitant than that modern master of paraphrase, Mr. Cleanth Brooks); nor do I offer it in levity. The rational framework of a poem should bear inspection, and the framework of this poem is trivial and inconsecutive.[2]

Yet for Winters to dub Brooks 'that modern master of paraphrase' was not a sarcasm but an irony, since Winters genuinely thought Brooks a master here: 'Mr. Cleanth Brooks has given us an excellent paraphrase of this poem [Donne's 'The Canonization'] and has demonstrated beyond doubt the solid rationality of its structure'.[3]

It was the use to which Brooks sometimes put his masterly paraphrases that Winters objected to, and in particular their being enlisted to justify bad writing as valuably imitative of a bad state of affairs.

---

[1] The interview's ellipsis; *the Review* No. 26, Summer 1971, p. 20. I gratefully acknowledge an invitation from Bliss Carnochan and Helen Pinkerton to a conference at Stanford University in 2000, honouring the centenary of Winters's birth, my remarks there forming the basis for the present essay.

[2] *Forms of Discovery* (1967), p. 31.   [3] Ibid., 75.

Mr. Brooks commonly employs the same kind of defense in dealing with passages in other poems which he recognizes as badly written; for example, in dealing with the epitaph in Gray's *Elegy* and with a passage in Wordsworth's *Intimations*. That is, he invokes as a respectable principle what I have called elsewhere the fallacy of imitative form.[4]

On Gray's *Elegy*:

Then follows *The Epitaph*, in three stanzas. Many critics have objected to the obviously bad writing in these lines; Mr. Cleanth Brooks justifies the bad writing by saying that this is what one would expect in a country churchyard. Perhaps one would expect it in a country churchyard, but one does not expect it as the conclusion of a poem which has often been called a great one—it is bad writing in either place.[5]

It is not, however, the intersection of Winters and Brooks as to 'the fallacy of imitative form' that matters here, but the critics' intersection as to allusion, reference, and what Winters called pseudo-reference, reference to the non-existent. Winters mocked Brooks, or at least bantered him, when it came to T. S. Eliot's allusions, to what Winters deemed to be Eliot's compulsive borrowing—for Winters could not bring himself to call it allusion. The borrowings 'are usually employed ironically, but almost always, so far as one can judge, because of some sort of thematic relevance—the relevance is likely to be far-fetched, however, and the exegetes make very amusing reading, Mr. Brooks in particular'.[6]

As to Winters's crisp term 'pseudo-reference', I shall defer bringing it into play until the end, after looking at some allusions within Winters's own poetry and at Winters's criticism.

Here is a poem by Winters.

The Lie

I paved a sky
With days.
I crept beyond the Lie.
This phrase,
Yet more profound,
Grew where
I was not. I
Was there.

---

[4] Ibid., 363–4.   [5] Ibid., 156–7.   [6] Ibid., 321.

In the third line, Winters has a capital L for 'the Lie', crucially, doubly so. First, in that this cannot but call into play the poem that Winters judged 'one of the best' of Sir Walter Raleigh's poems, 'The Lie',[7] which opens:

> Goe soule the bodies guest
> Upon a thankeless arrant,
> Feare not to touch the best
> The truth shall be thy warrant.
> Goe since I needs must die,
> And give the world the lie.

Second, in that an inaudibility (the difference between a lower-case l and an upper-case L) is disconcertingly apt to what it is to lie; something that can be seen cannot be heard here, cannot be truly voiced. Moreover, five of the poem's eight lines can be seen under the aspect of allusion itself and its profound paradoxes, allusion being something that is at once elsewhere and here, elsewhen and now, one's own and yet another's:

> This phrase,
> Yet more profound,
> Grew where
> I was not. I
> Was there.

'Yet more profound': the only unrhyming line. Something is to be plumbed. For my part, I cannot make sense of Winters's 'The Lie' unless I assume that it alludes to Raleigh's 'The Lie'; and then it becomes difficult to make sense of Winters's relation to allusion, for which his criticism can find no room.

His poems, though, find plenty of room for it. Not only do they incorporate allusions, they often have a turn of phrase that directs us to what allusion is, its being an aspect under which the poem's own practice may be seen. Still within the Elizabethan and Jacobean world, consider the relation of these two poems by Winters to a famous turn of phrase in a speech by Polonius in *Hamlet*. Here is the first of 'Two Old-Fashioned Songs', a poem entirely without punctuation—except (a crucial exception) that is in lines and is in stanzas.

---

[7] Ibid., 22: 'a catalog of the corruptions of the world; the subject was one to which Raleigh's mind and temperament made him acutely sensitive, and his personal experience did nothing to diminish the sensitivity'. By one of life's little ironies, it may be untrue that 'The Lie' is by Raleigh; even as we speak, Raleigh's poems are being stripped from him.

Danse Macabre

Who was who and where were they
Scholars all and bound to go
Iambs without heel or toe
Something one would never say
Moving in a certain way

Students with an empty book
Poets neither here nor there
Critics without face or hair
Something had them on the hook
Here was neither king nor rook

This is something some one said
I was wrong and he was right
Indirection in the night
Every second move was dead
Though I came I went instead

It is 'Indirection' that is a direction to us, a pointed and pointing reminder. (With what an odd sound and silence 'Iambs' anticipates *I was, I came, I went*, where there is nevertheless never an *I am*.) And then one notices the other pointers towards allusion—and what may be its indirection—in the poem ('This is something some one said'; 'second move'; 'Though I came I went instead'). Likewise in a poem by Winters that manifestly calls up not only *The Prince* of Machiavelli but the Prince of Denmark:

The Prince

The prince or statesman who would rise to power
Must rise through shallow trickery, and speak
The tongue of knavery, deceive the hour,
Use the corrupt, and still corrupt the weak.

And he who having power would serve the State,
Must now deceive corruption unto good,
By indirection strengthen love with hate,
Must love mankind with craft and hardihood:

Betray the witless unto wisdom, trick
Disaster to good luck, escape the gaze
Of all the pure at heart, each lunatic
Of innocence, who draws you to his daze:

And this frail balance to immortalize,
Stare publicly from death through marble eyes.

Here it is not only 'indirection' that directs us, but 'By indirection'. A frail balance: such may allusion be, yet seeking to immortalize. The poem speaks in the accents of Polonius ('who having power would serve the State') to Reynaldo, setting him to spy upon Laertes:

> See you now;
> Your bait of falshood, takes this Carpe of truth;
> And thus doe we of wisedom and of reach
> With windlesses, and with assaies of Bias,
> By indirections finde directions out:
> So by my former Lecture and advice
> Shall you my Sonne;
>
> (*Hamlet*, II. i)

For allusion may be not only an art of indirection (by which one finds directions out), but a bait that takes truth, and that lands advice.

Advice and wisdom are again called for in a poem by Winters that balances Shakespeare (*Hamlet*, again) and Ben Jonson, in their happy emulation towards immortality, a poem that alludes to Jonson's beloved Shakespeare.

> A Post-Card to the Social Muse
> Who Was Invoked More Formally
> By Various Marxians
> And Others
> In the Pages
> Of the New Republic
> During the Winter
> Of 1932–3
>
> Madam, since you choose
> To call yourself a Muse,
> I will not be too nice
> To give advice.
>
> Passion is hard of speech,
> Wisdom exact of reach;
> Poets have studied verse;
> And wit is terse.
>
> Change or repose is wrought
> By steady arm and thought:
> The fine indignant sprawl
> Confuses all.

> Do not engage with those
> Of small verse and less prose;
> 'Twere better far to play
> At bouts-rimés.

One way of being brief is by compacting one's own words with another's; so Winters's 'wit is terse' makes succinct what in Polonius was long-winded:

> Therefore, since Brevitie is the Soule of Wit,
> And tediousness the limbes and outward flourishes,
> I will be brief.
>
> (*Hamlet*, II. ii)

Polonius's self-praise ('we of wisedom and of reach') supplies Winters with his corrective turn, 'Wisdom exact of reach'; this, as praising wisdom, not praising ourselves as wise ones. Whereupon the poem moves from words bent by Shakespeare to words bent upon Shakespeare. 'Of small verse and less prose': Winters, beckoning towards allusion in '"Twere better far to play', has in his memory Jonson's poem 'To the Memory of My Beloved, the Author Mr William Shakespeare: and what he hath left us' ('he' now becoming not only Shakespeare but Jonson, what he too hath left us):

> And tell, how farre thou didst our *Lily* out-shine,
>   Or sporting *Kid*, or *Marlowes* mighty line.
> And though thou hadst small *Latine*, and lesse *Greeke*,
>   From thence to honour thee, I would not seeke
> For names; but call forth thund'ring *Æschilus*,
>   *Euripides*, and *Sophocles* to vs.

Winters, who listed this poem as 'among the greatest' of Jonson's,[8] must have enjoyed converting into contemptuous dislike of the 'various Marxians' what was in Jonson so beloved, so mighty, an honouring.

When he calls up Raleigh, Shakespeare, or Jonson, Winters brings into play for his poetry such poetry as he respects. But is it illuminating or is it obfuscating for us to bring into play, when we attend to Winters's poetry, his criticism? Donald Davie becomes even more sure that we should do no such thing in the very moment of his advising us:

---

[8] *Forms of Discovery* (1967), p. 64.

It is advisable—I might even say, it is absolutely necessary—to suppress whatever one may know of Winters's criticism, when approaching his poems. That is the only way for those poems to get a fair hearing.[9]

But it would be perverse to define a fair hearing as that which these poems would not receive from their author, judging from his judgements elsewhere. One way forward, though, may be to remind ourselves that poets, by and large, are more generous or magnanimous than critics—and that poems are more so than poets. Winters as critic does not have much time for many poets; as poet, though, he has not only time but place for many poems, including those by poets whom as a critic he 'places' to the point of displacing them. Particularly, of course, poets whom he finds guilty of Romanticism: William Collins, Keats, Tennyson, and Arnold.

Collins is disparaged both in particular (the 'Ode to Evening') and in general: 'We know, of course, that Collins was a melancholiac and doubtless found cause for his favorite emotions in everything'.[10] Winters says nothing of Collins's 'Ode, Written in the beginning of the Year 1746', a poem that honours those who fell in the battle between the English army and the Scottish rebels at Falkirk:

> How sleep the Brave, who sink to Rest,
> By all their Country's Wishes blest!

But it is not that Winters does nothing with this ode. It is by its gratitude, and with gratitude to it, that he is enabled to rise to a patriotic occasion, a stateliness in matters of state, pronouncing what he gathers should be his country's wishes.

On the Death
Of Senator Thomas J. Walsh

> An old man more is gathered to the great.
>   Singly, for conscience' sake he bent his brow:
> He served that mathematic thing, the State,
>   And with the great will be forgotten now.
> The State is voiceless: only, we may write
>   Singly our thanks for service past, and praise
> The man whose purpose and remorseless sight
>   Pursued corruption for its evil ways.

---

[9] Introduction to *The Collected Poems of Yvor Winters* (1978); *Two Ways out of Whitman: American Essays* (ed. Doreen Davie, 2000), p. 34.
[10] *Forms of Discovery*, p. 154.

How sleep the great, the gentle, and the wise!
Agëd and calm, they couch the wrinkled head.
Done with the wisdom that mankind devise,
    Humbly they render back the volume read—
Dwellers amid a peace that few surmise,
    Masters of quiet among all the dead.

It is not only that Winters would never have effected the line 'How sleep the great, the gentle, and the wise!' (the line with which, at last, Winters's poem awakes) had it not been for Collins's 'How sleep the Brave, who sink to Rest'; it is that throughout Winters's poem there is a sense of what it is that the wisdom of the past can mount to, and of how it can be brought home to us by allusion. 'We may write' because of 'our thanks for service past', and because of 'the wisdom that mankind devise'; it is of true alluders that it may be said that 'Humbly they render back the volume read'. 'And with the great will be forgotten now'? Not so. The great are not forgotten, and Winters's calling upon Collins on such an occasion (Collins who, in those words of his poem, 'Returns to deck' Winters's poem) must accord to Collins, in this poem at least, that endurance which Winters the critic denies him. Collins: 'By Forms unseen their Dirge is sung'. By courtesy of Collins's form unseen, your dirge is sung. Collins rests in peace but is not silent, one of those 'Masters of quiet among all the dead'.

The same magnanimity that is often lacking in the criticism may be found elsewhere in the poems. Winters thought ill of Keats:

John Keats offers melancholy for the most part unexplained, melancholy for its own sake, combined with detail which is sensuous as regards intention but which is seldom perceived with real clarity. There is almost no intellect in or behind the poems; the poems are adolescent in every respect. Most readers of our time have encountered Keats when they were young, have been touched by his unfortunate history, and have formed their taste on his poetry at a time when they knew little other poetry for comparison, and their feeling about him is immovable; they cannot imagine that he might be a bad poet.[11]

But when Winters was engaged upon some of his most urgent imagining, it was he who could not imagine that Keats might be a bad poet. Either that, or he was in bad faith in imping his wings with feathers from Keats's viewless wings of poesy. Worse ('For there is an upstart crow, beautified with our feathers', Greene on Shakespeare—well,

---

[11] *Forms of Discovery*, pp. 178–9.

Greene or Nashe or Chettle): the only argument that would protect
Winters against the charge of plagiarism, or of an irresponsible failure
to stop and wonder whence his lines came and what might make them
more than the latest tissue, would be that he, Winters, is alluding—and
therefore not plagiarizing, since the plagiarist wishes you not to know
the source and the alluder wishes you to. T. S. Eliot made clear that this
was the nub when he was accused of plagiarism: 'of course, the whole
point was that the reader should recognise where it came from and
contrast it with the spirit and meaning of my own poem'.[12]
    Here is Winters by courtesy of Keats.

Apollo and Daphne

Deep in the leafy fierceness of the wood,
Sunlight, the cellular and creeping pyre,
Increased more slowly than aetherial fire:
But it increased and touched her where she stood.
The god had seized her, but the powers of good
Struck deep into her veins; with rending flesh
She fled all ways into the grasses' mesh
And burned more quickly than the sunlight could.

And all her heart broke stiff in leafy flame
That neither rose nor fell, but stood aghast;
And she, rooted in Time's slow agony,
Stirred dully, hard-edged laurel, in the past;
And, like a cloud of silence or a name,
The god withdrew into Eternity.

Keats begins *Hyperion: A Fragment*:

Deep in the shady sadness of a vale
Far sunken from the healthy breath of morn,

Winters begins *Apollo and Daphne*:

Deep in the leafy fierceness of the wood,
Sunlight

Much of Winters's poem then proves to be a metamorphosis of Keats's
great opening lines, with their 'fiery', 'cloud on cloud', 'No stir', 'leaf', and
'fell'. Allusion is a form of metaphor, and here a form of metamorphosis.

---

[12] *Yorkshire Post*, August 1961; *The Bed Post* (1962), ed. Kenneth Young, pp. 43–4. See
p. 232 above.

This is fine if Winters's poem is teaming with Keats, but not if it is teeming with Keats. But then 'Apollo and Daphne' is alive to, and with, a sense of the figures of speech that might be called into play to suggest allusion itself: something 'cellular and creeping'; something that 'Increased'—more, 'increased and touched'; one of the 'powers of good' that is 'rooted', and that constitutes a 'hard-edged laurel, in the past'— but not only there.

Sometimes a poem by Winters is the child or foster-child of parents both of whom Winters the critic deplores. One parent may be Keats again, the author of 'Ode to a Nightingale', 'a mediocre poem with a very few good lines and some of the worst lines of the century'.[13] The other parent reveals himself as Tennyson, who in Winters's criticism is subjected to a disdainful paragraph that begins:

Alfred Tennyson deserves the neglect into which he is obviously falling. His talent was a mild one; he gradually perfected his style, in the sense of smoothing the surface, of controlling a particular tone; but the tone is one of imperceptive sweetness.

It ends: 'In general, however, Tennyson has nothing to say, and his style is insipid'.[14] But where would Winters's 'Inscription for a Graveyard' be without Keats and Tennyson? It is from the graveyard of Tennyson that the poem rises, and from the night-world that is half in love with easeful death.

Inscription for a Graveyard

When men are laid away,
Revolving seasons bring
New love, corrupting clay
And hearts dissevering.

Hearts that were once so fast,
Sickened with living blood,
Will rot to change at last.
The dead have hardihood.

Death is Eternity,
And all who come there stay.
For choice, now certainty.
No moment breaks away.

Amid this wilderness,
Dazed in a swarm of hours,—

---

[13] *Forms of Discovery*, p. 179.   [14] Ibid., 181.

> Birds tangled numberless!—
> Archaic Summer towers.
>
> The dead are left alone—
> Theirs the intenser cost.
> You followed to a stone,
> And there the trail was lost.

It is the 'Ode to a Nightingale' that prompts those 'Birds tangled numberless' in 'Summer':

> That thou, light-wingèd Dryad of the trees,
>   In some melodious plot
> Of beechen green, and shadows numberless,
>   Singest of summer in full-throated ease.

And it is Tennyson whose enduring lines of hardihood and blood, set in a graveyard, lend themselves to Winters's not failing, his being 'Sickened' but not 'Sick':

> And gazing on thee, sullen tree,
>   Sick for thy stubborn hardihood,
>   I seem to fail from out my blood
> And grow incorporate into thee.
>
> (*In Memoriam* II)

There is no question but that Winters has both Keats and Tennyson among his sources here, and moreover that the memories are meant to live as allusions is made manifest in those lines of the poem that, as with other such instances, may be understood as alluding to the nature of allusion itself. *The dead have hardihood.* Thanks to them, not all *Will rot to change at last.* For *No moment breaks away.* The *Archaic* still *towers.* *The dead are left alone?*—not so. *You followed, And there the trail was lost?*—not so. The allusions are findings, trouvailles. And they grow incorporate into thee.

T. S. Eliot wrote in 1931:

A poet cannot help being influenced, therefore he should subject himself to as many influences as possible, in order to escape from any one influence. He may have original talent: but originality has also to be cultivated; it takes time to mature, and maturing consists largely of the taking in and digesting various influences.[15]

---

[15] A lecture in Dublin (1936), published in *Southern Review* (Autumn 1985), and then in *T. S. Eliot: Essays from the Southern Review* (ed. James Olney, 1988), as 'Tradition and the Practice of Poetry', p. 13. For the application of this to Wordsworth, see p. 90 above.

Winters is well-advised, then, by his self as poet, to plait one influence with another (Keats *and* Tennyson)—or to plait one poet's poem with another (Tennyson and Tennyson), as went to the weaving of this poem by Winters.

Moonrise

The slow moon draws
The shadows through the leaves.
The change it weaves
Eludes design or pause.

And here we wait
In moon a little space,
And face to face
We know the hour grows late.

We turn from sleep
And hold our breath a while,
As mile on mile
The terror drifts more deep.

So we must part
In ruin utterly—
Reality
Invades the crumbling heart.

We scarce shall weep
For what no change retrieves.
The moon and leaves
Shift here and there toward sleep.

Again there are the tacit acknowledgements of the poem's own practice with sources and allusions: 'The change it weaves', set against 'For what no change retrieves'. These acknowledgements provide some prophylaxis against what might otherwise be too unmisgiving a coinciding of Winters's 'The slow moon draws' (and 'deep', later, at the line-ending) with Tennyson's voicing:

the slow moon climbs: the deep
Moans round with many voices.

('Ulysses')

That Tennyson's is one of the lasting voices, whatever the critic Winters might rule, comes out in this sense that two poems of his have gone to the fashioning of what Ulysses glimpsed, ''Tis not too late to seek a newer world'. For what is it that we are face to face with in Winters's tenderly musing stanza?

> And here we wait
> In moon a little space,
> And face to face
> We know the hour grows late.

Not only Tennyson's Ulysses but his Lady of Shalott (she who 'drifts'), at the very end:

> But Lancelot mused a little space;
> He said, 'She has a lovely face;
> God in his mercy lend her grace,
> The Lady of Shalott.'

Tennyson's 'mused a little space' is sound-changed into 'moon a little space'; and Tennyson's lines lend their grace to Winters's.

There are many moments within Winters's poems that glance towards allusion and its nature, for instance in the paradox of what has to come to an end and yet continues to speak as though there were no ending. He ends a poem 'To My Infant Daughter' with such a turn of mind:

> True art is slow to grow.
> Like a belated friend,
> It comes to let one know
> Of what has had an end.

Not just *know*, but *know of*:

> It comes to let one know
> Of what has had an end.

An end? And yet not so. For this sings as if its song could have no ending, and one of the ways in which songs have no ending—as with 'The Solitary Reaper' itself—is their living on in later songs, one form of this, being allusion. Yet for Winters as critic, allusion is not to be found among the 'Forms of Discovery'. He closes his mind and his ears to this form that metaphor may take.

But before turning to this, and to pseudo-reference, let me adduce the presence of Matthew Arnold in Winters's criticism and poetry, and 'Dover Beach' as the central crucial poem that Winters can live neither with nor without.

Winters explicitly placed Arnold within 'the intellectual, and anti-romantic, tendency of the nineteenth century'[16]—an honourable place to be, since Winters was against Romanticism. He admired Robert Bridges for going beyond while not repudiating Arnold: 'The Affliction of Richard' is 'the experience of the intellectual who has progressed beyond the disillusionment of "Dover Beach", but who has not forgotten his scepticism or its bitterness'.[17] Yet this generalized praise of Arnold is braced against, or by, Winters's disapprobation. Once upon a time, in *Maule's Curse* (1938), Arnold's 'Dover Beach' could be adduced by Winters 'if one is in need of a standard'.[18] In 1946, Winters could at least begin with high praise, while moving at once to a lethal use of the word 'normally':

> Arnold, one of the great poets of the nineteenth century in some four or five short poems and in a few additional passages, is normally one of the worst poets in English; his style is a deadly tissue of clichés and other amateur poeticisms.[19]

Twenty years later, this has hardened even further:

> Matthew Arnold exhibits the worst faults of the period most of the time: he is sentimental to the point of being lachrymose; he offers the worst pseudo-poetic diction imaginable; he is capable, although not invariably guilty, of very crude rhythm. He wrote a few excellent lines, most of them contained in two unsuccessful poems, *Philomela* and *Dover Beach*.
>
> *Dover Beach* offers more, but only a little. The description in the first stanza is one of the finest passages in the century, but the last line of the stanza is an abject cliché. From here on the poem is bad.
>
> > Sophocles long ago
> > Heard it on the Aegean.
>
> This would do, but then 'it brought into his mind' (this phrase is an awkward introduction to a metaphor) 'the turbid ebb and flow of human misery' (a cliché, or so it seems). Then: 'we find also in the sound a thought.' The village poet or orator, the lady who addresses club meetings, usually 'find a thought' in something; the locution is on that level, and no excuses can palliate it. The poem from here on is merely a morass of bad diction, and it ends with a solution so weak as to be an evasion of the problem posed.[20]

---

[16] *The Uncollected Essays and Reviews of Yvor Winters* (ed. Francis Murphy, 1973), p. 273.
[17] Ibid., 274.
[18] *In Defense of Reason* (1947), p. 260.
[19] *Edwin Arlington Robinson* (1946), p. 95.
[20] *Forms of Discovery*, pp. 183–4.

Yet 'Dover Beach' is the poem that haunts so many of Winters's poems, and haunts them as conjured, invoked, by them as a presiding spirit.

The Slow Pacific Swell

Far out of sight forever stands the sea,
Bounding the land with pale tranquillity.
When a small child, I watched it from a hill
At thirty miles or more. The vision still
Lies in the eye, soft blue and far away:
The rain has washed the dust from April day;
Paint-brush and lupine lie against the ground;
The wind above the hill-top has the sound
Of distant water in unbroken sky;
Dark and precise the little steamers ply—
Firm in direction they seem not to stir.
That is illusion. The artificer
Of quiet, distance holds me in a vise
And holds the ocean steady to my eyes.

Once when I rounded Flattery, the sea
Hove its loose weight like sand to tangle me
Upon the washing deck, to crush the hull;
Subsiding, dragged flesh at the bone. The skull
Felt the retreating wash of dreaming hair.
Half drenched in dissolution, I lay bare.
I scarcely pulled myself erect; I came
Back slowly, slowly knew myself the same.
That was the ocean. From the ship we saw
Gray whales for miles: the long sweep of the jaw,
The blunt head plunging clean above the wave.
And one rose in a tent of sea and gave
A darkening shudder; water fell away;
The whale stood shining, and then sank in spray.

A landsman, I. The sea is but a sound.
I would be near it on a sandy mound,
And hear the steady rushing of the deep
While I lay stinging in the sand with sleep.
I have lived inland long. The land is numb.
It stands beneath the feet, and one may come
Walking securely, till the sea extends
Its limber margin, and precision ends.
By night a chaos of commingling power,
The whole Pacific hovers hour by hour.

> The slow Pacific swell stirs on the sand,
> Sleeping to sink away, withdrawing land,
> Heaving and wrinkled in the moon, and blind;
> Or gathers seaward, ebbing out of mind.

From the Aegean to the distant northern sea, and then—after crossing the Atlantic—to the Pacific.

Of course the similarity of setting in 'Dover Beach' and 'The Slow Pacific Swell' (of place and hour) must make likenesses likely, but the overlapping here goes beyond that, does it not?

In the sequence of Winters's poem:

Arnold: 'stand' / Winters: 'stands' (twice)
Arnold and Winters: 'land'
Arnold: 'tranquil' / Winters: 'tranquillity'.
Arnold and Winters: 'sound' (Winters, twice)
Arnold and Winters: 'distant' (plus Winters, 'distance')
Arnold: 'darkling' / Winters: 'dark' and 'darkening'
Arnold and Winters: 'Retreating'
Arnold: 'dreams' / Winters: 'dreaming'
Arnold and Winters: 'sea'
Arnold: 'heard' / Winters: 'hear'
Arnold and Winters: 'night'
Arnold and Winters: 'withdrawing'
Arnold: 'Into his mind the turbid ebb' / Winters: 'ebbing out of mind'
Arnold and Winters: 'the moon'

When 'The Slow Pacific Swell' asserts, 'This is illusion', I want to ask 'And allusion?' The exquisite contrariety in Winters's words 'Firm in direction' (playing firmness against the inclination of 'in direction' to merge into 'indirection') makes me wonder whether the indirection that is allusion is being called into play, especially given Winters's twice elsewhere calling up that moment of Polonius's: 'By indirections finde directions out'. And how odd the sudden place-name 'Flattery' is ('Once when I rounded Flattery'), for all the world as if its other sense could be quite put by; imitation, and particularly such imitation as is allusion, is the sincerest form of flattery. Winters's word 'dissolution' then happens (is it that, only?) to be perfectly apt to the kind of evocation of 'Dover Beach' that I hear in the *sound* (the pun that both of the poets triply sound) of the poem, dissolution (not crystallization, as other kinds of allusion may be), a dissolving, a saturation, in the spirit of the great phrase from Chapman's Homer that so moved Keats: 'The sea had soaked his heart through'.

The unannounced subtitle of 'The Slow Pacific Swell' might be 'An Allusion to Arnold', on Augustan lines. This is not the same as Arnold's being a source only. Contrast Wilfred Owen's 'Strange Meeting', which went to the making of Winters's poem but not to its meaning. Owen (it is a strange meeting) was unexpectedly admired by Winters, who reviewed Blunden's edition of 1931: 'He is a very imperfect poet. But I have lived with his poems for more than ten years, and I venture the opinion that he is a poet of more than ordinary durability and interest'.[21] True, 'Strange Meeting' seemed to Winters 'very even in texture, but, for me, rather evenly vague', yet one line of it seems to have lodged not at all vaguely with him:

> But mocks the steady running of the hour.

> *   *   *

> And hear the steady rushing of the deep

—a line followed later in 'The Slow Pacific Swell' by

> The whole Pacific hovers hour by hour.

Winters's sense of rhythm, by no means unerring, here is entirely alert (assisted by Owen's sense of where to position the word 'hour'), in the hovering effect of the word and its declining to be assuredly either a monosyllable or a dissyllable: 'hovers hour by hour'.

The presence of 'Dover Beach' in 'The Slow Pacific Swell' would be less haunting if the case were unique, but Winters very often has 'Dover Beach' in mind, at heart, in play. 'The Fable' opens:

> Beyond the steady rock the steady sea,
> Its movement more immovable than station,
> Gathers and washes and is gone.

—Arnold's 'Gleams and is gone' (a turn of phrase that has not gone— on the contrary). 'The Fable' speaks, as does 'Dover Beach', of 'peace'; it urges, as does 'Dover Beach', 'listen' (where we may listen to Arnold's injunction too), immediately following this with a glimpse of 'The foam receding down the sand' (Arnold's 'down the vast edges drear').

---

[21] *Uncollected Reviews*, p. 117.

And others too of Winters's poems find it impossible to dismiss 'Dover Beach' from their world. 'On a View of Pasadena from the Hills' owes much to Winters's natural observation of the scene, but it also owes much to his being saturated in 'Dover Beach': Winters's calling up of 'No light', of 'the windows', of the 'dream', and of 'the naked salty shore'. Not that 'Dover Beach' is the only poem alluded to; when Winters writes, 'Those towers are now the hiving place of bees', he has in mind not only a hiding place of his power but a hiving place: the line 'His Helmet now, shall make a hive for Bees', from 'His Golden lockes, Time hath to Silver turn'd' (Sir Henry Lee, formerly attributed to George Peele). And when, again in 'The Fable', Winters exclaims 'Peace to all such, and to all sleeping men!', he is inviting us to hear that he has turned to benign purposes the magnificent pseudo-concession of the 'Epistle to Dr. Arbuthnot' when it turns to, and upon, Addison:

> Peace to all such! but were there one whose fires
> True Genius kindles, and fair Fame inspires . . .

Who would not weep . . .?; but in Winters's reconceiving of Pope's use of this commonplace, 'Peace to all such', there is nothing for such tears.

Allusion is a matter of what we are to hear, and then to listen to. 'The Slow Pacific Swell' admonishes us, 'listen', and this with an echo of the moment in 'Dover Beach': 'Listen! you hear the grating roar . . .'. Not that 'Dover Beach' owns the franchise of this poetic injunction, but it is this poem that has most unforgettably made us listen for it; and Arnold may be heard behind Winters's recurrent invocation of it. 'And listen! where the wind is heard': a moment in 'The Last Visit', a poem that ends with lines that should not be said to speak of allusion but might be understood as intimating allusion too:

> a strange
> Presence will be musing there.
> Ruin has touched familiar air,
> And we depart. Where you should be,
> I sought a final memory.

But no memory is final. Listen to Winters's 'Two Songs of Advent': 'Listen! listen! for I enter now your thought'. Does not 'Dover Beach' enter, with its 'Listen' and its 'Find also in the sound a thought'?

It is one particular abstract noun, though, that turns the presence of 'Dover Beach' into a certainty: the noun, not certainty, but certitude.

'Dover Beach' offers the only unignorable use of the word in our literature:

> for the world, which seems
> To lie before us like a land of dreams,
> So various, so beautiful, so new,
> Hath really neither joy, nor love, nor light,
> Nor certitude, nor peace, nor help for pain;

The word possesses Winters through half a dozen poems:

> Man walks with an unshaken certitude,
> ('The Bare Hills. II: Exodus')

> The final certitude of speech
> ('For the Opening of the William
> Dinsmore Briggs Room')

> Each in the certitude the other gave,
> ('To a Woman on her Defense of her
> Brother Unjustly Convicted of
> Murder')

—this, in the immediate vicinity, as in 'Dover Beach', of love: 'Strong in your love, and by your love made free'.

> Hard in his certitude
> ('The Old Age of Theseus')

> The mind, lost in a word's lost certitude
> ('To Emily Dickinson')

And, conclusively:

> The poet's only bliss
> Is in cold certitude—
> ('On Teaching the Young')

Certitude mattered to Winters as exactly not certainty, or rather, no longer such, no longer *OED* 2. 'Objective certainty.? *Obs.*; b. Fixedness, permanency; invariableness. *Obs.*'

certitude

1. Subjective certainty; the state of being certain or sure of anything; assured conviction of the mind that the facts are so and so; absence of doubt or hesitation; assurance, confidence. (There has been a growing tendency since the time of Hobbes to restrict the word to this sense; which, though not etymologically founded, is practically useful.)

—including 1864 Newman: My argument is . . that certitude was a habit of mind, that certainty was a quality of propositions.

b. A feeling of certainty in a particular case; the opposite of a doubt.

—including 1617 Donne: Delude themselves with imaginary Certitudes of Salvation.

2 c. Sureness of action, execution, or event; unfailing quality.

—the last citation, 1886 Swinburne: trust in the certitude of compensatory justice.

It is of the nature of literary art that certainty is not even to be aspired to; certitude is another matter, and I trust in the certitude of 'Dover Beach' and its being called into play by Winters's poems, whatever as critic he might have preferred to be the case. The question is not that of conscious intention, since those of us who believe in Freudian slips may posit the existence of unconscious intentions, a co-operative unconscious or subconscious.

Winters the critic has no time for allusion and its imaginative dealings with time. He shrinks all allusions to 'borrowings' merely, or to what he disparages as 'quotations' or as 'reminiscences' gathering nothing but wool or dust. Why cannot Winters conceive of, leave alone attend to, allusion? Because he cannot bear modern poetry in general, and Eliot and Pound in particular, and in repudiating them he misguidedly repudiates even the possibility of allusion as a form of discovery.

And what is one to say of the last eight lines of *The Waste Land*, which are composed, as nearly as I can determine with the aid of the notes, of unaltered passages from seven sources? A sequence of such quotations cannot by any stretch of the imagination achieve unity, and its disunity can be justified on no grounds except the Adams-Eliot doctrine of modern art, of which the less said by this time the better. The method is that of a man who is unable to deal with his subject, and resorts to the rough approximation of quotation.[22]

Is Pound, for example, a man who possesses this historical sense, when he writes a formless revery loaded with quotations and literary reminiscences, but having no other discernible relationship to past literature? And is Eliot another such man, when he does almost the same thing with less skill?[23]

the purely derivative poetry of T. S. Eliot . . .—he offers quotations from the best poets, along with a few footnotes and commentaries of his own.[24]

---

[22] *In Defense of Reason*, p. 500.　　[23] Ibid., 481.　　[24] *Uncollected Essays*, p. 228.

Winters reduces allusions to references; he speaks of 'Pound's reading' and then of Pound's 'references to the reading', and of the difficulty of 'running these references down',[25] as if allusion were reference pure and simple. Allusion, like any other way with language, may fail, but to stipulate that an allusion is nothing other or more than a reference is to deny it even the chance to succeed. And allusion, when a success, is a succession.

To call it reference, moreover, is to permit of its contamination by the modernist device that Winters most loathed. His taxonomy of pseudo-reference offers many species, with almost all of them involving something that is invoked but is non-existent:[26] Explicit Reference to a non-existent symbolic value; Implicit Reference to a non-existent symbolic value; Explicit Reference to a non-existent or obscure principle of motivation; and—most central to Winters's campaign of detoxification—

Reference to a non-existent plot. This is most easily illustrated by selections from T. S. Eliot.

Gerontion, at any rate, is the most skillful modern poem in English to employ any large measure of pseudo-reference; the superiority of its pseudo-reference to most of that of Crane and of Yeats probably derives from the fact that it is deliberate, whereas theirs is commonly in a large part unintentional—in *Gerontion* it is mystification instead of confusion, or at least is employed willfully and deliberately as a means of bringing certain recognized, and, for the author, irreducible confusion, under a little control.[27]

As judgement, this strikes me as monstrously unjust, but as description it is sharply attentive; it illuminates what 'Gerontion' is up to, even though it is determined that this shall not amount to anything.

Pseudo-reference, then, in so often invoking something non-existent (such as a non-existent plot), constitutes a travesty of allusion, for how could you call into play the non-existent? And Winters's hostility to pseudo-reference in the work of 'the experimental school in American poetry' moved him, mistakenly, to a hostility towards or an indifference towards allusion. Because he deplores pseudo-reference, and because the great modern master of pseudo-reference, Eliot, is also a master of allusion (allusion moreover being, for Winters, reference merely),

---

[25] *The Function of Criticism* (1957), p. 47.
[26] *In Defense of Reason*, 'The Experimental School in American Poetry: Type IV Pseudo-Reference', p. 40 ff.
[27] *In Defense of Reason*, p. 87.

Winters is led to subjugate allusion in the most extreme way, by pretending that it does not exist.

His book on Edwin Arlington Robinson has as chapter 3 'Literary Influences on Robinson's Style', but there is nothing about allusion in it. *In Defense of Reason* has a teasing moment when it seems that Winters might be about to engage with allusion, in that the paragraph speaks of 'the transition from allusion to allusion',[28] but no, this evaporates, for Winters has this phrase as synonymous with his earlier ones, 'recollection to recollection' and 'references to a number of stories', so any hope that allusion might be recognized, however passingly, slips away.

Perhaps Winters is at his most perverse (to pick up Robert Lowell's word) when he engages with a speech very near the end of Marlowe's *Doctor Faustus*, a soliloquy impelled by a supremely chilling allusion to classical literature.

> O lente, lente currite noctis equi:
> *The starres moove stil, time runs, the clocke will strike,*
> *The divel wil come, and Faustus must be damned.*
> *O Ile leap up to my God: who pulls me downe?*
> *See see where Christs blood streames in the firmament.*
> *One drop would save my soule, half a drop, ah my Christ.*

The slow smooth movement of the Latin line, especially as it appears in the context of the English language and a different meter, accentuates the nervous rapidity, suggesting terror, of the next two lines. The extra syllable in the fourth foot of the fifth line prepares the way for the violent aberration of the sixth: in the sixth line there are six feet instead of five, the fourth of these being inverted, and the fifth, although normally accented, having a rhetorical cesura between the unaccented syllable and the accented, so that the latter part of the line is divided into two rhetorical units of a foot and a half apiece. The rhythm of this line is so curious that it quite eludes description; but that it contributes to the expression of agony and terror I should assert without hesitation. In fact, the main power of this entire passage is derived from its sound.[29]

Winters could not avert his eyes from 'the Latin line', but he did his best to avert his mind from it, judging that nothing whatsoever need be said about where exactly the line was from and what it was doing here. All the lacerating pathos of the contrast between the lover's cry that the

---

[28] *In Defense of Reason*, p. 496.
[29] Ibid., 548–9. Neither Marlowe nor *Doctor Faustus* is in the index to *In Defense of Reason*, because Winters names neither of them here.

horses of the night be stayed so that he might love the longer, and the hell-bent desperation of Faustus's invoking of that cry—all this is neglected, since to pay any attention to it would be to give credit to allusion. Winters as poet gives credit to allusion, and is the richer for giving it; Winters the critic impoverishes his appreciation here by wilfully limiting himself to prosody alone, a passionate analysis but one that is needlessly amputated. Is none of the 'power' worth speaking of, whether 'main' or not, derived from Marlowe's allusion to Ovid's very words?

Winters wrote movingly of what a poet may learn from his predecessors:

The presence of Hardy and Arnold, let us say, in so far as their successful works offer us models and their failures warnings or unfulfilled suggestions, should make it easier to write good poetry; they should not only aid us, by providing standards of sound feeling, to test the soundness of our own poems, but, since their range of experience is very wide, they should aid us, as we are able to enter and share their experience, to grow into regions that we had not previously mastered or perhaps even discovered. The discipline of imitation is thus valuable if it leads to understanding and assimilation.[30]

Yet one form of 'the discipline of imitation' eluded him or seemed to him a delusion: allusion. When he was being the critic, that is; not when he was being the poet. 'The poems and the criticism can be matched up, right enough', Donald Davie believed, 'and the one can be made to validate the other'.[31] Not, I believe, in this respect.

Cleanth Brooks, who was not a poet, and who was—as a critic—not just disadvantaged by this, has a truer appreciation of this particular form of discovery. As when Brooks praises a stanza from Housman's Jubilee poem of 1887, opening *A Shropshire Lad*:

> To skies that knit their heartstrings right,
> To fields that bred them brave,
> The saviours come not home to-night:
> Themselves they could not save.

Brooks values allusion as bonus, not price of admission.

Here the irony achieves a sort of climax, for the last lines echo the passage in the Gospels in which Christ, hanging on the cross, is taunted with the words: 'Others he saved; himself he cannot save.' To apply the words associated with

---

[30] Ibid., 23.   [31] *Two Ways out of Whitman*, p. 34.

the Crucified to the dead soldiers is audacious, but again the words are perfectly applicable, quite simply and literally fitting the case of the absent soldiers. Indeed, a reader who failed to catch the Biblical allusion would not feel that the lines were forced or strained. For soldiers, who must necessarily risk losing their own lives in order to save others, are often to be found in such a plight: Others they saved, 'Themselves they could not save'.[32]

'That modern master of paraphrase, Mr. Cleanth Brooks', is here a master when it comes to appreciating allusion—as Winters did not in his criticism but did in realizing his poems.

[32] 'Alfred Edward Housman', *Anniversary Lectures Under the Auspices of the Gertrude Clarke Whittall Poetry and Literature Fund* (1959); *A. E. Housman: A Collection of Critical Essays* (ed. Christopher Ricks, 1968), p. 75.

David Ferry and the Shades
of the Dead

Nomen est omen. A poet-translator whose name is Ferry might anticipate his being cast as Charon. Not, though, the grim ferryman; rather, his bright brother, the unsung one who sings the dead back to life. In his rendering of Politian's 'Of Violets', he ferries the fifteenth-century poem back from the dead.

Neo-Latin verses (Politian having been a professor at the University of Florence) are sometimes unjustly judged to be written in a deader than dead language. The destination of the present essay is a neo-Latin poem by Samuel Johnson that David Ferry rendered exquisitely as 'The Lesson'; meanwhile, there are things to be remarked on the way there.

> The virtuous shades of the dead come back to play
> Among the grasses the violets intersperse.
>   ('Of Violets')[1]

The shades not only come back to mind, they come back to play. The faint archaism of 'shades' repudiates any factitious proffer of Politian Our Contemporary. For 'shades' quietly insists that the past is over though not done with. The past is to be made present to us, not to be made the present. And 'shades' is itself shadowed, darkened, lest we forget.

> The night is falling; the shades are gathering around;
> The walls of Pluto's shadowy house are closing you in;
>   (Horace, 'To Sestius')

'The virtuous shades of the dead'—the ordering is precise: not such narrow piety as would honour only 'The shades of the virtuous dead', but a different interspersing of the words. Ferry sings anew another of the songs of the dead, Ronsard's imagining the plight of the woman

---

[1] The poems are quoted from *Of No Country I Know: New and Selected Poems and Translations* (1999).

who is spurning him. En route to the final dismaying threat, there is pity for her, off in the future, in the poignancy of movement, hers and Ronsard's and Ferry's:

> When you are very old, at night, by candlelight,
> Sitting up close to the fire, unwinding or winding the
>   thread,
> Marveling you will murmur, telling over the songs of the
>   dead,
> 'Ronsard praised this body before it became this fright.'
>   ('Quand vous serez bien vieille')

It is the last word of the quatrain, 'fright', that is suddenly tight, unexpectedly right. As noun, 'this fright' is anachronistically slangy, the tense arrival of a turn from the future, from Ferry's day, not Ronsard's or even the woman's within her chastened unwinding lifetime. The anachronism is to the point (how frightening now to see that your body will one day become demeanedly 'this fright'); to the point, not as postmodernist time-warp, but as an intimation of immortality even in this glimpse of mortality. In his translations Ferry takes the risk of such anachronism, crucially albeit sparingly; but then in translation, as in other realizations of the poet's art, nothing would be riskier than playing safe.

Take the children playing in Montale's 'La Farandola dei Fanciulli'.

> How far back the ancient past seems now.
> Those kids dancing around and playing,
> By the railroad track, up back of the beach,
> On the gravel and cinders of the railbed,
>
> Weeds suddenly breaking into blossom
> In the heat of the day, a flowering of thirst.
> It's as if being naked and nameless
> Was being sunlight, flower, heat-shimmer.

So ample, this small poem. What makes it so spacious is its sense of time, of different times. 'How far back the ancient past seems now'. *Seems*, for the past, even the ancient past, is so near while yet so far. It is the tone and nationality of the phrase 'Those kids' that make the different times strangely congruous; strangely, because of the datedness, the dateability of such a casualness, but congruous because the whole poem is perfectly audible twentieth- (and twenty-first) century American English. The same goes for the move from 'How far back' to 'up back of the beach'; the colloquial prepositional cluster reaches back to the dignity of an earlier phrasing, but neither use of the word 'back' is allowed to snub the other. And all this is maintained by, or even constituted of, the interplay between the termination in *-ing* that is, as so often in Ferry, participial and more: 'dancing . . . playing . . . breaking . . . flowering . . . being . . . being'.[2]

> It's as if being naked and nameless
> Was being sunlight, flower, heat-shimmer.

Ferry, most meticulous of poets, is characteristically exact here: not 'It's as if A. were X., Y., Z.', but 'It's as if A. was X., Y., Z.'. *It's as if it were* . . .: this is the fancied, the might have been. *It's as if it was* . . .: this, though it is not what was the case exactly, is the past, the used to be, a try at it. Hopkins chose both to begin and to end a knotty poem with a line that knows the difference between 'It was' and 'It were', as well as the difference between both of those and 'It's as if it was'.

> It was a hard thing to undo this knot.
> The rainbow shines, but only in the thought
> Of him that looks. Yet not in that alone,
> For who makes rainbows by invention?
> And many standing round a waterfall
> See one bow each, yet not the same to all,
> But each a hand's breadth further than the next.
> The sun on falling waters writes the text
> Which yet is in the eye or in the thought.
> It was a hard thing to undo this knot.

An allusion shines, but only in the thought of him that looks. Yet not in that alone, for who makes allusions by invention? By invention only, and not by discovery too? The inventiveness of Ferry is complemented by his powers of discovery.

---

[2] Ferry often teases us into thought by relating the participial *-ing* to endings that are no such thing: say, everything, nothing, anything. In Goethe, 'Roman Elegy VIII': 'Thinking' into 'nothing'. In Guillén, 'Unos Caballos': 'grazing', 'growing', 'Morning before the beginning of anything human', 'understanding', 'nothing', and 'grazing' (this last returning to the first such word in the poem). The sonnet from Ronsard proliferates these endings, yet with such tact as to make this not a matter of conscious noticing, rather of what will silently register when, for instance, the last four lines of the fourteen contain no such endings; up till then, 'Sitting . . . unwinding . . . winding . . . Marveling . . . telling . . . dozing . . . spinning . . . hearing . . . things . . . singing . . . nothing . . . Taking'. Ferry's translation of 'Levis Exsurgit Zephirus' is buoyed by this throughout; see p. 325.

There is the simple fidelity with which, in translating Baudelaire's 'Les Aveugles', he accommodates the French poet's allusion to Pascal. Pascal: 'Le silence éternel de ces espaces infinis m'effraie'. Baudelaire: 'le noir illimité, | Ce frère du silence eternel'. It's as if the word 'frère' in the French prompts Ferry to apprehend the brotherhood as not only that of night and silence but, next, that of Baudelaire and Pascal, and then in due course, silently but not unnoticeably, that of Baudelaire and Ferry.

Ferry moves Baudelaire's lines on the eternal silence (Baudelaire, like Pascal, having created something that is far from silent) from being the ninth and the tenth lines of the sonnet to being the inauguration of his poem. 'The Blind People' is his, though not his alone, and to open it as he does is to grant tacitly that the question for any translation or imitation is first of all—though not in the last resort—'What is the difference between the original and this rendering of it?' Ferry's words 'What is the difference . . .?' correspond to an unease in the Baudelaire poem ('je me traine aussi!') although not to its wording, so here too there is a difference.

> What is the difference between the unlimited
> Blackness they walk in this ridiculous
> Fashion through, and the eternal silence?

Something is to be seen here, and so it is elsewhere in the translation when Baudelaire's line, 'Leurs yeux, d'où la divine étincelle est partie', is opened by Ferry to take in a Miltonic vision: 'the divine light gone | Forever from their eyes'. For those last four words (which are five words in 'Lycidas'[3]) offer a heartbreaking vista of a blest afterlife, all the more heartbreaking because nowhere to be discovered in Baudelaire's poem.

> There entertain him all the Saints above,
> In solemn troops, and sweet Societies
> That sing, and singing in their glory move,
> And wipe the tears for ever from his eyes.
>   ('Lycidas' 178–81)

Again there is perfect tact, since the phrase 'Forever from their eyes' is entirely equable and unfussing; and yet the rendering by Ferry does itself sing, and singing in its glory move—move us perhaps to tears. The

---

[3] Ferry: 'Forever'; Milton, 'for ever'. C. S. Calverley has a witty quizzing of the word or words, beginning: 'Forever; 'tis a single word! | Our rude forefathers deemed it two: | Can you imagine so absurd | A view?'

effect of saddened equanimity owes much to the fact that, on this occasion, there is no call for anachronism: Milton's lines, coeval with Pascal, were in existence when Baudelaire wrote. What had been the brotherhood of Pascal and Baudelaire ('Ce frère du silence éternel', from the author of 'mon semblable, mon frère') is now the brotherhood of Milton and Ferry, the society of poets being one of the sweet societies. 'The rainbow shines, but only in the thought | Of him that looks' (Hopkins). 'The Blind People' must move from the sense of *look* that is *perceive* ('my stupid | Questions when I look at them', and 'What are they | Looking up at the sky for . . .?'), to *look* as *appear to the eyes of others*: 'How foolish, | And terrible, they look'. There is all the difference in the world between these two senses of *look*, the one world being sightless and the other not. What is the difference . . .?

Milton puts in something more than an appearance not only within the Baudelaire translation but within that from Politian, 'Of Violets'.

> Too happy violets, which that hand plucked
> That wrenched me, miserable, from myself—
> She held you, violets, to her lips, perhaps;
> Perhaps her lips and breath have breathed on you
> The breath of her whom I love, the changing colors
> Of her breathing, making you blush and pale;
> From the breath of her lips your fragrance is breathed upon
>   you;
> The sovereignty of her fragrance clings to you.

More than one fragrance clings to these lines themselves; or rather, it is not exactly fragrance that is breathed upon the lines by Milton and by Keats, it is something more acrid and sour. For 'Too happy' cannot but bring with it a memory of the heart-ache in 'Ode to a Nightingale':

> 'Tis not through envy of thy happy lot,
>   But being too happy in thine happiness—

and, more darkly yet, 'That wrenched me, miserable, from myself' must be redolent of the dolour of Satan:

> Me miserable! which way shall I flie
> Infinite wrauth, and infinite despaire?
> Which way I flie is Hell; my self am Hell;
>   (*Paradise Lost*, iv 73–5)

The moment in 'Of Violets' is allusion, not as sweet society, but as soured such. And yet not altogether so, since the effect is of Paradise Lost and Regained, even if only in the imagining of a happiness of which the lover has not despaired, he who ends his lamentation by expressing his gratitude to the violets:

> Stay with me now, perpetual in beauty,
> O violets, o quietness of heart,
> For I am in the wretchedness of love,
> Creature of sighs and weeping, because of my lady.

There is a tantalizing question of anachronism if Keats and Milton are felt as transported, translated, to Politian's earlier days. And the same is true if Ferry is believed to have brought within the compass of Hölderlin's 'Mnemosyne' an allusion to Hopkins, for Hölderlin died the year before Hopkins was born. Yet the ending of the first poem within 'Mnemosyne' assuredly does not insist that we recall Hopkins's 'Pied Beauty', given how ordinarily ubiquitous is the closing injunction that the poems share. 'Mnemosyne' dwells beautifully and disconcertingly upon the beautiful, opening so much:

> Flowers, streams, hills, meadows, valleys—
> Everything beautiful praises the Lord,
> In order to find out whether or not He is.

The poem passes to and through more beauty: 'A wedding day is beautiful' (not, though, to be confused with the beauty of a marriage), and then it comes to rest in an injunction that is heartfelt but weary and wary:

> But everything is as it is, one way or another.
> What does it all add up to, after all? Praise Him.

Hopkins, with the most famous such ending in English poetry, closes 'Pied Beauty' with two lines of simple laudation that, after a listing of all those 'dappled things', offer them all up: these,

> He fathers-forth whose beauty is past change:
> Praise him.

But in Hopkins the last two words are a line in itself. In Ferry's Hölderlin, the two lines are one; moreover, the one line, the final line, is extended beyond ten syllables (what does it all add up to?) and is proffered in the knowledge that it could perfectly well have been lineated so as to insist upon its alignment with Hopkins.

What does it all add up to, after all?
Praise Him.

And this, what does it all add up to? An inspired allusiveness, diffus-
ing instead of crystallizing, and inviting us to praise God and
Hölderlin even while, without its inviting us to praise Ferry, it ought
to make clear to us why he is deserving of praise. Something, once
again, has been fathered-forth whose beauty is past change.

The sharpest instance of what may be thought of as thrillingly
anachronistic allusion (with its opportunities and its dangers) is the
flash of and from Robert Lowell within a translation from the
goliardic tradition. The poem is one of Ferry's finest, saying a very
great deal.

> Levis Exsurgit Zephirus
> —Goliardic
>
> The wind stirs lightly as the sun's
> Warmth stirs in the new season's
> Moment when the earth shows everything
> She has, her fragrance on everything.
>
> The spring royally in his excitement
> Scatters the new season's commandment
> Everywhere, and the new leaves open,
> The buds open, and begin to happen.
>
> The winged and the fourfooted creatures
> According to their several natures
> Find or build their nesting places;
> Each unknowingly rejoices.
>
> Held apart from the season's pleasure
> According to my separate nature
> Nevertheless I bless and praise
> The new beginning of the new days,
>
> Seeing it all, hearing it all,
> The leaf opening, the first bird call.

The rhyming is a feat of entire blitheness, of holy mirth. Who
would have thought that these sounds could chime so? For the
conventional—and not usually false—opinion as to the effect of
rhyming a word with itself, such as 'everything' upon 'everything' in
the opening stanza, is that it sets one's teeth on edge; and the same is

usually the case with the off-rhyme of, say, 'creatures' | 'natures'. Had not Shakespeare established this in the opening soliloquy of *Richard III*?[4]

> I, that am curtail'd of this faire Proportion,
> Cheated of Feature by dissembling Nature . . .

But in Ferry's hands, in his handling, these ways of rhyming find them-selves restored to pristine delight. The effect is extraordinary, and there-fore requires us to bear in mind what is ordinarily the case. And this may help us to understand what Ferry is supremely up to when into this evocation of a world of entire delight, a world without woe, he suddenly brings a memory of 'To Speak of Woe That Is in Marriage', the poem by Robert Lowell that is recalling the grimly humorous insistences of the Wife of Bath.

Ferry:

> The spring royally in his excitement
> Scatters the new season's commandment
> Everywhere, and the new leaves open,
> The buds open, and begin to happen.

Lowell:

> 'The hot night makes us keep our bedroom windows open.
> Our magnolia blossoms. Life begins to happen.
> My hopped up husband drops his home disputes,
> and hits the streets to cruise for prostitutes,
> free-lancing out along the razor's edge.
> This screwball might kill his wife, then take the pledge.[']

The audacity of this moment in Lowell is matched only by the audac-ity of invoking it in 'Levis Exsurgit Zephirus'. I ought to say that I used to think that not even Ferry's art could make this act of pacifying Lowell a true part of his, Ferry's, art of pacifying. (Not at all the same as placat-ing or propitiating.) But I have come to find that nothing is truer to Ferry's sense of what it has been given to him to do than this exemplary restoration.

For it is Wordsworth who is Ferry's great example here.[5] Ferry has written about Wordsworth with full love and with no sentimentality.[6]

---

[4] See p. 115.
[5] On Wordsworth and restorative allusion, see p. 93.
[6] *The Limits of Mortality: An Essay on Wordsworth's Major Poems* (1959).

And it is Ferry who, in our time, has most realized Wordsworth's highest of hopes in the face of the darkest of diagnoses:

> For the human mind is capable of excitement without the application of gross and violent stimulants; and he must have a very faint perception of its dignity and beauty who does not know this, and who does not further know that one being is elevated above another in proportion as he possesses this capability. It has therefore appeared to me that to endeavour to produce or enlarge this capability is one of the best services in which, at any period, a Writer can be engaged; but this service, excellent at all times, is especially so at the present day. For a multitude of causes unknown to former times are now acting with a combined force to blunt the discriminating powers of the mind, and unfitting it for all voluntary exertion to reduce it to a state of almost savage torpor.
>
> When I think upon this degrading thirst after outrageous stimulation I am almost ashamed to have spoken of the feeble effort with which I have endeavoured to counteract it; and reflecting upon the magnitude of the general evil, I should be oppressed with no dishonorable malady, had I not a deep impression of certain inherent and indestructible qualities of the human mind, and likewise of certain powers in the great and permanent objects that act upon it which are equally inherent and indestructible.[7]

Of twentieth-century poets, Robert Lowell is the one who found ways of making not just respectable but honourable these 'gross and violent stimulants', this 'thirst after outrageous stimulation'. And the paradox of 'savage torpor' is one that the best of Lowell's writing makes not only real but—in the words that Keats applied to the genius of Wordsworth—'explorative of those dark Passages'.[8] Ferry's genius is the opposite of Lowell's, and—like Wordsworth's—it is explorative and restorative.

One of Ferry's most remarkable feats of translation is his transformation into a poem, 'Johnson on Pope', of a dozen lines from *The Lives of the Poets*. The translation is from haunted prose to haunting poetry, only that and all that. But it is with another Johnsonian poem of Ferry's, 'The Lesson', that I now trust to make good my sense that he makes all these aspirations good.

---

[7] Preface to *Lyrical Ballads* (1800); *Prose Works*, i 128–30.
[8] To J. H. Reynolds, 3 May 1818; *Letters*, i 281.

In Rivum a Mola Stoana Lichfeldiæ diffluentem

Errat adhuc vitreus per prata virentia rivus,
  Quo toties lavi membra tenella puer;
Hic delusa rudi frustrabar brachia motu,
  Dum docuit blanda voce natare pater.
Fecerunt rami latebras, tenebrisque diurnis
  Pendula secretas abdidit arbor aquas.
Nunc veteres duris periêre securibus umbræ,
  Longinquisque oculis nuda lavacra patent.
Lympha tamen cursus agit indefessa perennis,
  Tectaque qua fluxit, nunc et aperta fluit.
Quid ferat externi velox, quid deterat ætas,
  Tu quoque securus res age, Nise, tuas.

The Lesson
—from the Latin of Samuel Johnson

The stream still flows through the meadow grass,
as clear as it was when I used to go in swimming,
not good at it at all, while my father's voice
gently called out through the light of the shadowy glade,
trying to help me learn. The branches hung down low
over those waters made secret by their shadows.
My arms flailed in a childlike helpless way.

And now the sharp blade of the axe of time
has utterly cut away that tangle of shadows.
The naked waters are open to the sky now
and the stream still flows through the meadow grass.

Matthew Arnold, in his unmatched essay 'The Study of Poetry' (1880), formulated a principle precise and passionate: 'The superior character of truth and seriousness, in the matter and substance of the best poetry, is inseparable from the superiority of diction and movement marking its style and manner. The two superiorities are closely related, and are in steadfast proportion one to the other.' (Inseparable, not indistinguishable.) It is the movement of Ferry's poem, of his poems, that is especially of note. His transitions are masterly, but then translation partakes of transition. His rhythms and cadences are at once tentative and firm, always with an entire respect for the integrity of the poem he is translating, manifesting itself anew in the integrity of the poem he creates.

'In Rivum a Mola Stoana Lichfeldiæ diffluentem': the traditional thing is to judge neo-Latin poetry guilty until it is proven innocent. Johnson himself knew that neo-Latin poetry by the English was seldom of the best: 'The pretensions of the English to the reputation of writing Latin founded not so much on the specimens . . . which they have produced, as on the quantity of talent diffused through the country' (from William Windham's *Diary*). But Johnson put in a good word for this exercise of talents, within praise of one of his masters: 'Pope had sought for images and sentiments in a region not known to have been explored by many other of the English writers; he had consulted the modern writers of Latin poetry, a class of authors whom Boileau endeavoured to bring into contempt, and who are too generally neglected' (*The Lives of the English Poets*, 'Pope'). The contempt into which Boileau endeavoured to bring modern Latin poetry, Richard Porson vented. 'For all modern Greek and Latin poetry he had the profoundest contempt. When Herbert published the *Musæ Etonensis*, Porson said, after looking over one of the volumes, "Here is trash, fit only to be put behind the fire" ' (*Porsoniana*, in Samuel Rogers's *Table Talk*).

Latin poems written by speakers of Latin are one thing, a thing for us distant and difficult enough. Latin poems written posthumously, written centuries after Latin became what we call a dead language: these press anew the old question of whether it has been left to us ever truly to appreciate Latin (or Greek) poetry.

Robert Frost was Johnsonianly robust. He insisted not that we have little chance of ever being inward enough with the ancient languages but that we have no chance.

The living part of a poem is the intonation entangled somehow in the syntax idiom and meaning of a sentence. It is only there for those who have heard it previously in conversation. It is not for us in any Greek or Latin poem because our ears have not been filled with the tones of Greek and Roman talk. It is the most volatile and at the same time important part of poetry. It goes and the language becomes a dead language the poetry dead poetry. . . . When men no longer know the intonation on which we string our words they will fall back on what I may call the absolute length of our syllables which is the length we would give them in passages that meant nothing. The psychologist can actually measure this with a what-do-you-call-it. English poetry would then be read as Latin poetry is now read and as of course Latin poetry was never read by Romans.[9]

---

[9] To Sidney Cox, 19 January 1914; *Selected Letters*, ed. Lawrance Thompson (1964), pp. 107–8.

Critics of the classics may be great in proportion as they recognize that there is an irreducible truth in what Frost says.

What then of Latin poetry that was never written by Romans?

A neo-Latin poem is written in a language unheard conversationally. Oratorically, it may be heard, even in our day. I felt a twinge of Oxonian pride a few years ago, during the sesquicentennial celebrations at Boston University, when the Vice-Chancellor of Oxford University was among those in the procession of kindly tributes. 'When you invited us', he intoned to the President of Boston University, 'you said that we might if we wished speak in a language other than English. I assume that you meant Latin.' Whereupon he uttered ceremonial Latin, being then so good as to translate it into English, British English.

There are paradoxes about dead languages in themselves: if truly dead, how can they still be alive in ceremony, as well as alive to those who can still read, with deep delight, great classical literature? There is a further contrariety when someone living in our world, our language, turns to such a language tellingly.

Let me begin 'The Lesson'.

> The stream still flows through the meadow grass,

As soon as we reach a verb, and this is soon, we hear the subdued oxymoron of moment and movement in 'still flows'. This has something of T. S. Eliot's sense of a world—like that of Ferry's translation— of light and shadows.

> daylight
> Investing form with lucid stillness
> Turning shadow into transient beauty
> With slow rotation suggesting permanence
> ('Burnt Norton' III)[10]

'As a Chinese jar still | Moves perpetually in its stillness' ('Burnt Norton' V): Eliot anticipated Ferry as to the simultaneity of mobility and immobility in the word 'still'. 'The stream still flows.' Still waters run deep.

When Ferry first published his poem in *Raritan* (Spring 1986), the first line ran, not 'through the meadow grass', but 'through the

---

[10] Ferry opens his translation of Rilke, 'Herbsttag':

> Now it is the right time, Lord. Summer is over.
> Let the autumn shadows drift upon the sundials,
> And let the wind stray loose over the fields.

meadowgrass'; I take it that the later gentle expatiation of what had been a compound noun ('meadowgrass' consonantally thickened, *wgr*, at its middle), this one word then becoming in revision relaxedly and expansively two words, was effected so as the better to go with the flow. The line now becomes all monosyllables except for the apt expanse of 'meadow'; the trisyllabic 'meadowgrass' had been perhaps a touch coagulated.

The words 'through the meadow grass' flow through the poem, concluding both its first and its last line. But the last line is not in toto the first line, being it in toto and more, given the modest modification of the syntax and rhythm which prefixes the closing line with 'And'. Not, now, 'The stream still flows through the meadow grass,' but 'and the stream still flows through the meadow grass.' This realizes something which both is and is not the same, even as the rhythm and cadence of a stream change from moment to moment, within its enduring flow. The stream has modulated itself; you don't step twice into the same stream of the line.

One flow is that of the stream that is translation; Ferry's stream of consciousness, and not only because of the stream of time, is Johnson's and yet not. 'How like the former, and almost the same' (Dryden, *Aeneis*, vi 1195): Ferry, whose Horace has established him in the line of great translators from the Latin,[11] gives us something at once repeated and other, even as his conclusion gently calls out, through the light of the poem, to its opening. How fittingly, too, the final line—'and the stream still flows through the meadow grass'—takes up not only the opening line, extendedly revisited, but also, from a few lines earlier, the starting anew with 'And': 'And now the sharp blade of the axe of time.'

The internal nature of memory, and the nature at once internal and external of the entirely fluid: these ask on occasion the conjunction of an external rhyme with an internal one. So it is that, at the end of its line, 'the shadowy glade' is later threatened (but is not in the end lopped) by 'the sharp blade of the axe of time'. It is not only the rhyme *glade / blade*, and not only the thick alliteration *shadowy / sharp*, but the syntax 'the [adjective] [noun]', which prompts our readerly memory within this poem devoted to a writer's memory and everyone's memory.

---

[11] D. S. Carne-Ross: 'it is heartening to be able to report that a true Horatian poet is now writing in Cambridge, Massachusetts, David Ferry' (Introduction to *Horace in English*, ed. Carne-Ross and Kenneth Haynes, 1996). Ferry: *The Odes of Horace: A Translation* (1997), and *The Epistles of Horace* (2001).

Over time, the time taken and given by the poem, 'shadowy' is both cut back and expanded to 'shadows': cut back, in that it is axed from three to two syllables; expanded, in that an epithet comes to take on the substantiality that is a noun—and a plural noun at that, and a plural noun repeated. Twice a line ends in shadows: 'over those waters made secret by their shadows', foreshadowing 'has utterly cut away that tangle of shadows'. In the actual landscape, yes, the trees have been cut away; in the landscape of memory, no, for there the shadows of the shadowy glade have all the continuing haunting life of shades. There is a comfort, despite the sense of loss, when a line comes to repose again upon the darkened noun followed with a period:

> over those waters made secret by their shadows.
> . . . . .
> has utterly cut away that tangle of shadows.

Such a memorious shadowing is at one with the way 'way' has come back in this next sentence (not the next line, discreetly), to be heard in 'away': 'a childlike helpless way', 'Has utterly cut away' (as if the word 'away' were a sad contraction of the entire phrase '*a* childlike helpless *way*'). This last effect is then deepened by the double internal rhyme, not just of '*utt*erly *cut*' but of '*utt*erly *cut* away'. There the reduction of the trisyllabic 'utterly' to the monosyllabic 'cut' does itself feel like the cutting of something away.

Johnson himself delighted in such truly sound effects.

> Should Reason guide thee with her brightest Ray,
> And pour on misty Doubt resistless Day;
> (*The Vanity of Human Wishes* 145–6)

The alliterating monosyllables *Doubt* and *Day* may meet as equals, equipollent, but how dextrously the trisyllabic 'res*ist*less Day' triumphs, irresistibly, over the disyllabic 'm*ist*y Doubt'.

The chastened realization of the cutting away owes something to another small crucial change that Ferry made to the poem after periodical publication. In *Raritan*, there was this flowing on:

> The branches hung down low
> Over those waters made secret by their shadows.
> My arms flailed in a childlike helpless way.
> And now the sharp blade of the axe of time
> Has utterly cut away that tangle of shadows.

In *Dwelling Places*, the sequence is open ('open to the sky now'), is cut
and opened up, there upon the page:

> The branches hung down low
> over those waters made secret by their shadows.
> My arms flailed in a childlike helpless way.
>
> And now the sharp blade of the axe of time
> has utterly cut away that tangle of shadows.

The risk of such a cutting enactment, with two successive lines cut from
one another, is that the severance will not so much dramatize as melo-
dramatize the timely utterance of 'And now'. What saves Ferry's lines
from melodrama is not only the chastened sobriety of manner and
movement but the quiet assurance with which 'And now' is duly
succeeded by 'now / and', a chiasmus that operates across a chasm both
of lines traversed and of a line-ending crossed:

> The naked waters are open to the sky now
> and the stream still flows through the meadow grass.

There the first line ends with no insistence on an ending (there is no
end to the natural world and one's memories of it, however much the
Binsey poplars or the *lauriers* may have been cut), and this is achieved
by the successive openness of sound: 'The naked waters are open to the
sky now', with both *sky* and *now* ending open-mouthed, no termination
of sound and then no punctuation at the line-ending, only the naked
space. (Completely, or rather incompletely, different from the sibilants
that close the first and last lines of the poem: 'grass'.) This so evoking
the open is Wordsworthian: there was no end to how much
Wordsworth could strangely utter by stationing *sky* at the line-ending:

> oh! at that time
> While on the perilous ridge I hung alone,
> With what strange utterance did the loud dry wind
> Blow through my ears! The sky seemed not a sky
> Of earth—and with what motion moved the clouds!
>
> (*The Prelude* (1805), i 346–50)

Ferry shares with Wordsworth a gratitude for the ample flexibility of
so modest a word as 'it'.[12]

---

[12] In his translations, Ferry—whose mastery of *it* is the Wordsworthian mastery of *thing*—
does enormous things with this tininess. There is the conclusive calm of the horses in Guillén,

> The stream still flows through the meadow grass,
> as clear as it was when I used to go in swimming,
> not good at it at all,

We are to take the measure of the simple power of 'it'. I can imagine a misguided critic deprecating the recurrence of 'it' there, especially with the change of referent, the first 'it' being the stream and the second swimming. Clumsy in Ferry? Not at all, but attentive to clumsiness and meant to call an honest ungainliness to mind (as, again, often in Wordsworth), and aware of the precariousness of gait which precludes flowing swimmingly through those dental endings: 'no*t* goo*d* a*t* i*t* a*t* all.' The sequence 'at it at' is a challenge to the prejudice in favour of the fluent, the flowing, the overvaluing good Surrey and the undervaluing great Wyatt.

'Not good at it at all.' I am reminded of Ezra Pound's objecting to one of the greatest openings to a poem even of Eliot's:

> Here I am, an old man in a dry month,
> Being read to by a boy, waiting for rain.
>   ('Gerontion')

Pound underlined in the manuscript. '~~Being read to by~~ a ~~boy~~'; he wrote in the margin '? to by'; and he wrote above Eliot's opening words, entries one below the other: 'b—b—b / B d + b b / consonants, / & two prepositions'.[13] Eliot stuck to his heaved cutlass.

As Ferry's poem rounds the bend into the ensuing line—

> not good at it at all, while my father's voice
> gently called out through the light of the shadowy glade,

—the inverted foot, 'gently' but strikingly at the head of the line, is the opposite of how such an inversion of stress is often employed. The accents are not those, say, of Milton, swinging round the corner with a vengeance:

'Unos Caballos': 'The serenity of heaven is realized ‖ In their obliviousness of it, grazing there.' There is the protraction in Goethe, 'Roman Elegy VIII': 'and that all this seemed to go on | For a very long time, the slow time that it took ‖ For you to grow up'. There is the awe of the divine in Hölderlin, 'Mnemosyne': 'He can change any or all of it just as He pleases. | Law is nothing He needs of what we know of it'; 'But everything is as it is, one way or another. | What does it all add up to, after all? Praise Him.' There is deep blankness in Baudelaire, 'Abyss': 'God has written out something on the face of the dark ‖ In a hand absolutely sure of what it is doing'. And there is the sheer gratitude in 'Levis Exsurgit Zephirus', which ends: 'Seeing it all, hearing it all, | The leaf opening, the first bird call.'

13 *Inventions of the March Hare*, p. 351.

> And over them triumphant Death his Dart
> Shook, but delaid to strike, though oft invok'd
> (*Paradise Lost*, xi 488–9)

—but instead the milder accents of gentleness's power. There is a related effect in the gentle calling out of a line that is undulatingly hypermetrical, a line with two further syllables at ease with any elision that we might fluidly practise. Not, say, 'gently called through the light of the shady glade', but 'gently called *out* through the light of the shad*owy* glade'. It would have been so easy to take out the word 'out', to reduce the line to the expected.

The idiom 'not good at it at all' is markedly unJohnsonian, and not only because of anachronism. A crux for the translator must be this: what do you do about translating a poem that could have been written in English had the English-speaking author wished? This is a particular form of translation; it is a very special case, but it must connect with the more usual and more general case, of asking how, say, Baudelaire would have written such-and-such in English. Johnson, after all, could perfectly well have written this poem in English if he had wanted to; it is not only that he wrote so many fine poems in English, but that he even wrote in English about swimming—though he was to change the word 'Swim' to 'Roll':

> Must helpless Man, in Ignorance sedate,
> Swim darkling down the Current of his fate?
> (*The Vanity of Human Wishes* 345–6)

(Was Johnson's 'helpless' here of help to Ferry when it came to his 'helpless'?) The second line of this, the text of 1749, became in 1755: 'Roll darkling down the Torrent of his fate?'—*Swim* having perhaps suggested too great a control over the element when immersion was destructive. Johnson, in his physical strength, enjoyed such control in swimming; he became a powerful audacious swimmer, his father's tender lesson having taken and stayed.

Ferry's translation is radically unJohnsonian, and this as a consequence of the fact that Johnson chose not to write a poem in Johnsonian English—since he chose not to write it in English at all. Ferry does not in any way go for a Johnsonian manner, whether that of Johnson's poetry, or prose on the page or in conversation. 'Not good at it at all' is unmisgivingly distant from any way in which Johnson would have been good at putting it. The odd effect, since Johnson has so

marked a character as a stylist, whether in poetry or prose, is of a kind
of foreignness when the poem is put back (or rather *not* put *back*) into
English. For on this occasion what the translator has to do is make it
sound as if it were in a vernacular that is not Johnson's; Johnson's
eschewal is being respected and honoured.

The process at work is complicated; the lines that issue from the
process are simple and direct.

One way of catching Ferry's success, of letting his success catch the
light, is to compare what others make of Johnson's Latin here. There is
the verse translation by John Wain:

> Here, as a boy, I bathed
> my tender limbs, unskilled, frustrated, while
> [. . .]

The movement has the wrong kind of clumsiness, an alien gawkiness
that makes it feel, with its Latinate deposits, like Johnson on a bad day.
The translation by J. P. Sullivan in David Fleeman's Penguin edition of
Johnson's poems is straight prose: 'wherein as a boy I so often bathed
my tender limbs; here I frustrated my deluded arms with unpractised
movements, while . . .'. But should even the unpractised be quite that
unlimber? The sequence, though true to the words of the original, is
not true to its spirit. And something similar goes for the verbal ineptitude, which cannot be justified by invoking physical ineptitude (the
fallacy of imitative form . . .), when the Yale edition by E. L. McAdam
offers the following: 'where so often as a boy I bathed my young body.
Here I was frustrated by the awkward movement of my arms playing
me false when . . .'.

To Johnson, the Latin language offered the decency of distance and
decorum. Not being his language, it offered a chance of creating a poem
that both was and was not exactly *his*. It provided, as in his great poem
on completing the Dictionary, a *cordon sanitaire* between himself and
the blurting of personal feeling or (the Romantic failing) 'self-expres-
sion'. To speak directly of his father he needed indirection, something
other than his mother tongue. He could be the more personal when he
was not being nakedly so. Leave it to waters to be naked.

To write in Latin was to temper the personally moving with historic
impersonality. Being himself was sometimes to mean being someone
other than the known public man Johnson. He did not publish the poem,
which was written late in life; it appeared three years after his death.

His father had given him these swimming lessons, never to be forgotten either in memory or as skill. At the very end of his life, at the age of 75 in November 1784, Johnson remembered how he had taught himself a lesson, a lesson that involved his father and the element of water. To Mr. Henry White, a young clergyman, with whom he now formed an intimacy, so as to talk to him with great freedom, he mentioned that he could not in general accuse himself of having been an undutiful son. 'Once, indeed, (said he,) I was disobedient; I refused to attend my father to Uttoxeter-market. Pride was the source of that refusal, and the remembrance of it was painful. A few years ago, I desired to atone for this fault: I went to Uttoxeter in very bad weather, and stood for a considerable time bareheaded in the rain, on the spot where my father's stall used to stand. In contrition I stood, and I hope the penance was expiatory.'[14]

It is a moving and justly famous moment in Boswell: Johnson, years on, standing in the rain, its waters absolving him. Bareheaded.

> 'I am a man,
> More sinn'd against, than sinning.'
> 'Alack, bareheaded?'

Johnson, bareheaded in 'very bad weather', knew that he was, in this matter, a man more sinning than sinned against.

The memory of his disobedience to his father may be arched against the memory of his obedience to his father's tender lesson. Ferry catches this happiness of relation in the lovely living sequence 'trying to help me learn':

> when I used to go in swimming,
> not good at it at all, while my father's voice
> gently called out through the light of the shadowy glade,
> trying to help me learn.

The delicacy of this comes from the fact that 'trying to help me' constitutes a unit in itself, a unit of sense: 'trying to help me' *and*—one learns this in the reading, in the flow—'trying to help me learn'. Further, much more evocative than would have been the protracted stiffness of 'trying to help me to learn', where the formal phrasing would have been the opposite of the informal rueful gaucherie of 'not good at it at all'.

When Ferry first published the poem, it had no title, or rather it had

---

[14] *Life of Johnson*, ed. Hill and Powell, iv 372–3.

as a title what would ordinarily look more like a subtitle: 'Adapted from the Latin of Samuel Johnson'. There was a propriety in this, a self-abnegation by the translator that might itself be a lesson to translators. But even better than propriety is grace, and in *Dwelling Places* the poem gained its due title:

> The Lesson
> —*from the Latin of Samuel Johnson*

The poem is, in Ferry's translation, one of the great evocations of what a true lesson is, of what education is, of what it is to educe. Ferry dropped the last two lines of Johnson's poem, where the lesson feels too admonitorily that of a dominie: 'You also, Nisus, heedless of what swift time brings from outside or what it wears away, do what is yours to do.' Perhaps time has worn away our amenability to so moralizing a destination for the poem. Certainly Ferry judged it best to do what is his to do.

'The Lesson', as poem, as translation, at once educational and educative, is a lesson in love.

Acknowledgements

Of the dozen essays, three are now first published (Burns, Wordsworth, and Byron), and one now published in an expanded form (Ferry).

Minor revisions have been made to the published texts:

Dryden and Pope: 'Allusion: the Poet as Heir', *Studies in the Eighteenth Century*, ed. R. F. Brissenden and J. C. Eade (Australian National University Press, Canberra, 1976).

Keats: 'Keats's sources, Keats's allusions', *The Cambridge Companion to Keats*, ed. Susan J. Wolfson (Cambridge University Press, Cambridge, 2001).

Tennyson: 'Tennyson Inheriting the Earth', *Studies in Tennyson*, ed. Hallam Tennyson (Macmillan, London, 1981).

Plagiarism: 'Plagiarism', *Proceedings of the British Academy* 97 (Oxford University Press, Oxford, 1998).

Metaphor: 'The Pursuit of Metaphor', *What's Happened to the Humanities?*, ed. Alvin Kernan (Princeton University Press, Princeton, 1997).

Loneliness: 'Loneliness and Poetry', *Loneliness*, ed. Leroy S. Rouner (University of Notre Dame Press, Notre Dame, 1998).

Housman: 'A. E. Housman and "the colour of his hair" ', *Essays in Criticism* xlvii (Oxford University Press, 1997).

Winters: 'Yvor Winters: Allusion and Pseudo-Reference', Cleanth Brooks Memorial Lecture (Institute of United States Studies, University of London, 2001). A shortened version was published in the *TLS* (22 June 2001), as 'Unacknowledged Legislators'.

Ferry: 'The Lesson', *Under Criticism: Essays for William H. Pritchard*, ed. David Sofield and Herbert F. Tucker (Ohio University Press, Athens, 1998).

The author is grateful to friends for their advice: Anne Ferry, David Ferry, Kenneth Haynes, Marcia Karp, Lisa Rodensky, John Silber, and Harry Thomas; and to the University of Toronto for the invitation to deliver the Alexander Lectures in 1988.

The author and publishers would like to thank the following for permission to reprint copyright material in this work.

Elizabeth Bishop: extracts from 'Crusoe in England' from *The Complete Poems: 1927–1979*. Copyright © 1979, 1983 by Alice Helen Methfessel. Reprinted by permission of Farrar, Straus and Giroux, LLC.

E. E. Cummings: 'l(a' is reprinted from *Complete Poems 1904–1962*, by E. E. Cummings, edited by George J. Firmage, by permission of W. W. Norton & Company. Copyright © 1991 by the Trustees for the E. E. Cummings Trust and George J. Firmage.

T. S. Eliot: prose quotations in the prefatory note reproduced by permission of Valerie Eliot.

David Ferry: 'La Farandola dei Fanciulli' [Montale]; 'Levis Exsurgit Zephirus' [Goliardic]; 'The Lesson' [Johnson]; excerpts from 'Of Violets' [Politian]; 'Quand vous serez' [Ronsard]; 'The Blind People' [Baudelaire]; 'Mnemosyne' [Hölderlin]. From *Of No Country I Know— New and Selected Poems and Translations*, University of Chicago Press, 1999. Reproduced by permission of David Ferry.

Philip Larkin: 'Friday Night in the Royal Station Hotel' from *Collected Poems* by Philip Larkin. Copyright © 1988, 1989 by the Estate of Philip Larkin. Reprinted by permission of Farrar, Straus and Giroux, LLC and Faber & Faber Ltd.

Wallace Stevens: 'The Planet on the Table' from *The Collected Poems of Wallace Stevens*, copyright 1954 by Wallace Stevens and renewed 1982 by Holly Stevens. Used by permission of Alfred A. Knopf, a division of Random House, Inc. and Faber & Faber Ltd.

Yvor Winters: 'The Lie', 'Danse Macabre', 'The Prince', 'A Post-Card to the Social Muse'. From *Collected Poems* by Yvor Winters. Reprinted with permission of Ohio University Press/Swallow Press, Athens, Ohio. 'On the Death of Senator Walsh', 'Apollo and Daphne', 'Inscription for a Graveyard', 'Moonrise', 'The Slow Pacific Swell' from *The Selected Poems of Yvor Winters*, edited by R. L. Barth. Reprinted with permission of Ohio University Press/Swallow Press, Athens, Ohio.

Every effort has been made to clear the necessary permissions. Any omissions will be rectified in future reprints.

Index

3 5282 00702 8015

Lightning Source UK Ltd.
Milton Keynes UK
17 November 2010

163042UK00001B/29/P

9 780199 269150